The
1900s

HEADLINES IN HISTORY

Books in the Headlines in History series:

The 1000s
The 1100s
The 1200s
The 1300s
The 1400s
The 1500s
The 1600s
The 1700s
The 1800s
The 1900s

The 1900s

HEADLINES IN HISTORY

James Miller, *Book Editor*

Bonnie Szumski, *Editorial Director*
Scott Barbour, *Managing Editor*

Greenhaven Press, Inc., San Diego, California

Every effort has been made to trace the owners of copyrighted material. The articles in this volume may have been edited for content, length, and/or reading level. The titles have been changed to enhance the editorial purpose.

Library of Congress Cataloging-in-Publication Data

The 1900s / James Miller, book editor.
    p. cm. — (Headlines in history)
    Includes bibliographical references and index.
    ISBN 0-7377-0545-0 (pbk. : alk. paper)—
ISBN 0-7377-0546-9 (lib. : alk. paper)
    1. History, Modern—20th century. 2. Twentieth century.
I. Miller, James, 1943–   II. Series.

D421 .A123 2001
909.82—dc21

00-064034

Cover photos: (top) Hitler accepting the ovation of the Reichstag, Digital Stock; (bottom, left to right) the fall of the Berlin Wall, © AFP/CORBIS, Mohandas K. Gandhi, Hulton Getty Collection/ Archive Photos; World War I battle scene, © Bettmann/CORBIS
Harry Truman Library, 212
Library of Congress, 40, 93, 117, 124, 184, 273
NASA, 259
National Archives, 64, 77, 140

Copyright © 2001 by Greenhaven Press, Inc.
P.O. Box 289009, San Diego, CA 92198-9009

Printed in the USA

CONTENTS

Chapter 1: The Twentieth Century Begins, 1900–1914

1. A Law of Acceleration

At the dawn of the twentieth century, a brilliant thinker
of the late nineteenth century muses about how historical change is accelerating and considers how poorly
his traditional education has prepared him for it.

2. 1900: The Promise of a New Century

A modern American historian depicts the hopes and
fears of people in the Western world as the twentieth
century opens.

3. Votes for Women

An English historian recalls the controversies surrounding the suffragist movement at the beginning of the twentieth century, when the issue of whether women should
be allowed to vote aroused strong feelings on both sides.

4. Revolution Ravages Mexico

During the decade of 1910–1920, Mexico experienced
the first of the great revolutions and civil wars that
would grip many developing nations during the
twentieth century.

Chapter 2: The Great War, 1914–1918

1. The Coming of World War I

A modern British historian analyzes the blunders of

European statesmen as the Continent stumbles through the crisis that will end in the outbreak of the Great War.

Chapter 3: The Great War's Aftermath, 1919–1930

Chapter 4: The Totalitarian Challenge, 1933–1940

Chapter 5: Asia in Turmoil, 1931–1945

A French historian sympathetically analyzes how the Chinese Communist Party made itself the champion of the peasants' cause during the 1930s and 1940s.

Chapter 6: World War II, 1939–1945

Chapter 8: The Revolt Against Hegemony 1960–1980

ern oil, the shaky integrity of the American presidency, and
the threat of a Soviet-American nuclear confrontation.

Chapter 9: The Century Ends, 1980–2000

C hronological time lines of history are mysteriously fascinating. To learn that within a single century Christopher Columbus sailed to the New World, the Aztec, Maya, and Inca cultures were flourishing, Joan of Arc was burned to death, and the invention of the printing press was radically changing access to written materials allows a reader a different type of view of history: a bird's-eye view of the entire globe and its events. Such a global picture allows for cross-cultural comparisons as well as a valuable overview of chronological history that studying one particular area simply cannot provide.

Taking an expansive look at world history in each century, therefore, can be surprisingly informative. In Headlines in History, Greenhaven Press attempts to imitate this time-line approach using primary and secondary sources that span each century. Each volume gives readers the opportunity to view history as though they were reading the headlines of a global newspaper: Editors of each volume have attempted to glean and include the most important and influential events of the century, as well as quirky trends and cultural oddities. Headlines in History, then, attempts to give readers a glimpse of both the mundane and the earth-shattering. Articles on the French Revolution, for example, are juxtaposed with the then-current fashion concerns of the French nobility. This creates a higher interest level by allowing students a glimpse of people's everyday lives throughout history.

By using both primary and secondary sources, students also have the opportunity to view the historical events both as eyewitnesses have experienced them and as historians have interpreted them. Thus, students can place such historical events in a larger context as well as receive background information on important world events.

Headlines in History allows readers the unique opportunity to learn more about events that may only be mentioned in their history textbooks, or may be ignored entirely. The series presents students with a variety of interesting topics that span cultural, historical, and political arenas. Such a broad span of material will allow students to wander wherever their curiosity will take them.

The Twentieth Century: Patterns of Change

In 1900, when the twentieth century opened, kings and emperors still held control in such major European powers as Germany, Russia, Austria-Hungary, and Turkey. Colonial empires—the largest being the British, French, German, Dutch, Portuguese, Italian, and Japanese—encompassed most of Africa's and Asia's non-white (and non-Japanese) peoples. China, the most important exception, was still an empire (although the ruling family was of non-Chinese origin), but seemed on the verge of either being partitioned among the imperialist powers or dissolving in chaos. Mexico and most other Latin American countries were ruled by small, wealthy cliques, behind (or over) whom stood the imposing power of European and American investors. The United States had joined the ranks of the imperialist powers, having in 1898 defeated Spain, seized the Spanish colonies of the Philippines and Puerto Rico, and turned Cuba into an American satellite. In 1900 British troops were fighting a nasty little war, complete with barbed-wire concentration camps and devastating machine-gun battles, against the two small white-ruled, Dutch-speaking republics in the interior of southern Africa—a war that would soon result in the creation of the Union of South Africa, a thoroughly segregated state that gave its black majority no political rights at all.

In 1900, democratic politics prevailed in the United States (for its white, not its black, citizens); in Great Britain (although the majority of the people of British-ruled Ireland probably hoped for independence, or at least self-government); in Canada, Australia, and New Zealand (in all of which British-appointed governor-generals still wielded significant power, and none of which pursued independent foreign policies); and in France, Italy, and some smaller countries of northern and western Europe. Nowhere, however, could women take part in national politics, and women rarely had the vote even in local affairs. Outside Russia, socialist parties had generally shed their older revolutionary aims (but generally not their revolutionary rhetoric), yet nowhere did they form part of a democratic government, and in most capitalist democracies the word *socialist* still seemed quite disreputable, vaguely eccentric, and slightly menacing. Workers generally worked far more than forty hours a week, rarely enjoyed paid vacations, and outside Germany (which was not a political democracy) had no social security pensions, no health insurance, and no guarantees of even minimal government help should they lose their jobs. Some elements of a consumer society—such as well-advertised standard brands, department stores, and professional sports—were already visible in Europe and North America, but pay was still low by today's standards, and such things as family cars, credit cards, and labor-saving electrical appliances were unimaginable. Outside the United States, Canada, Australia, and New Zealand, old land-owning, titled aristocracies remained prominent in both politics and everyday life, and everywhere the new aristocracy of big money wielded enormous—and largely untaxed—power. Anti-Semitism was a fact of life everywhere, but its ugliest manifestations occurred in France, Austria, Russia, and Romania. In virtually every Western society, white racism was rampant (while the Japanese appropriated similar attitudes to justify their own alleged supremacy in Asia), supported by the authority of the most respected science of the day.

Central and eastern Europe and the Middle East, where the imposing empires of Germany, Austria-Hungary, and Russia, as well as the declining Ottoman (or Turkish) Empire, all held sway, had at best only rudimentary elements of democratic politics. In Germany the kaiser (who was also the king of Prussia) was an important political figure who named the chancellor (the head of the government) and set the political agenda, usually unwisely and always noisily; the elected legislature had some power but could not determine national policy. In Austria-Hungary, rancor between a host of national minorities (Germans, Hungarians, Czechs, Croats, Slovaks, Poles, Romanians, and others) effectively prevented legislatures from accomplishing much, besides engaging in occasional inkpot throwing, and the aging emperor-king who had been ruling since 1848 still made the final decisions. Russia was ruled by an unusually stupid czar, Nicholas II, who had the final say in all matters, unrestrained by any legal political parties, legislature, or constitution. Politics in the small Balkan states (Serbia, Romania, Bulgaria, and Greece) was thoroughly corrupt and often violent. The Ottoman sultan ruled what is now Albania and Kosovo, Macedonia, northern Greece, Turkey,

Syria, Iraq, Jordan, Lebanon, Israel, and most of Saudi Arabia by his authority as caliph—the successor to the prophet Muhammad.

In 1900 European science stood at the apex of its prestige and authority. Germany, with its great universities and laboratories, dominated the scientific world, although Great Britain, France, and Austria-Hungary also maintained important centers of research. By comparison, the United States was an awkward provincial outpost of mainstream intellectual work; Americans who wanted to pursue serious science or scholarship normally went to Germany or England for advanced training.

Only a tiny minority of cutting-edge scientists knew that there was reason to doubt the universal validity of the laws of physics that had been worked out in the late seventeenth century by Sir Isaac Newton—laws that lent rocklike solidity to educated people's understanding of how the physical universe worked. In 1900 Viennese physician Sigmund Freud published a book called *The Interpretation of Dreams,* which questioned the prevailing assumption that all normal people are completely rational in their thinking. But practically no one read Professor Freud's book, and those few who did mostly thought it nonsense, verging on the obscene, for his theory claimed that human lives are unconsciously dominated by sex and repressed childhood traumas. Even more obscure than Freud was a young Swiss (but German-born) patent official named Albert Einstein, who in his spare time wrestled with a wholly new way to understand the physical world.

Thus the world in 1900 seemed to its European and white North American inhabitants rich, rational, and overwhelmingly successful. As the history of the twentieth century unfolded, the wealth of the industrial capitalist world generally increased—on the whole enormously, despite substantial losses caused by numerous sweeping revolutions, two major wars, and one major depression. How rational the behavior of the world's leaders remained is sometimes debatable, but certainly the frank advocates of irrationalism whose voices figured so prominently in twentieth-century society and culture did not, in the end, dominate global policy making.

The twentieth century's promise of material accomplishment was borne out spectacularly, though catastrophe punctuated triumph. The century's dominant trend was an acceleration of all the superlatives: more wealth, more technological mastery, more scientific knowledge, more population, more urbanization, more government, more power, more democracy. Many groups who were oppressed at the century's beginning eventually won a far greater claim on the world's collective conscience and its sense of social justice, even if they did not necessarily control a greater share of the world's wealth: people whose forebears in 1900 were the subjects of colonial empires; members of racial and religious minorities within the world's developed societies; women; working people. There has also been more violence, more vicious hatred (racial, class, religious, and national), and more destruction than any sane person alive in 1900 could have dreamed possible. Millions of innocent lives were snuffed out because of the hatreds of those in (or lusting for) power: the combatants and noncombatants in two world wars and many lesser skirmishes; the casual victims of revolutions and civil wars; the ethnic, racial, and religious minorities subjected to genocide; the cumulative millions who were destroyed in political terror. If human beings probed ever more deeply into the ultimate questions of how the universe works, they also discovered the means for destroying all life on earth. At least once, in the Cuban missile crisis of 1962, the world approached the brink of a nuclear conflagration, and at the century's end fears of chemical or biological warfare threatened to become as pervasive as the mid-century terrors of atomic annihilation. By the 1990s, moreover, there was well-grounded (though not always well understood) wariness about the implications of the information revolution, genetic engineering, and environmental degradation. No one a hundred years before conceived of such opportunities or such perils. Truly, in the twentieth century everything had run to extremes.

In explaining twentieth-century global history, it is important to distinguish between impersonal trends and specific events in which the accidents of personality and judgment played a fateful role. The century's history is rich in examples of both kinds of historical causation, and instances of both are discussed in the selections that make up this book. Accelerating scientific knowledge is a good example of both trends and individual efforts at work. Thus discoveries are made by solitary individuals (Einstein, for example) or close-knit teams (such as Francis Crick and James Watson, the codiscoverers of the structure of DNA), although such breakthroughs would likely have been made by other researchers seeking the answers to widely recognized scientific problems. Certainly, however, the accumulation of know-how must be considered a historical trend that lone individuals seldom bend decisively in one direction or another. Out of myriad possibilities that individual efforts may generate, solutions are adopted that best respond to the economic incentives that impersonal market situations present. The rapid development of electronic computing and telecommunications, especially since the 1970s, is a dramatic and familiar example. So, in the first half of the twentieth century, was the spread of assembly-line mass-production technology, which unleashed an enormous surge of productivity.

Accumulations of political power and the reshaping of political institutions likewise tend to blend individual accomplishment with cumulative trends, especially in relatively "normal" times—in the absence, that is, of great crises. In societies that had a basic commitment to democracy, for example, the expansion of voting rights to previously disfranchised groups, or the enlargement of governmental power to undertake new social responsibilities, owed much to political leaders who took advantage of free institutions to demand greater rights for the interest groups they represented. Familiar examples include the early-twentieth-century demand for women's suffrage and the mid-twentieth-century civil rights movement in the United States. As selections in this book will show, neither the suffragist nor the civil rights campaigner easily prevailed over the legal and social barriers that they combated, and the individual abilities of such leaders as British suffragist Emmaline Pankhurst and American civil rights crusader Martin Luther King Jr. proved crucial. But once achieved, such rights and such governmental responsibilities took on a momentum of their own, and became irreversible.

Invoking the examples of such long-term trends, however, raises the important question of inevitability. Can such events as the coming of World War I or the Bolshevik seizure of power in Russia, the victory of communism in China or the extermination of European Jews by the Nazis, the outbreak of the Cold War or the downfall of communism in the Soviet Union, properly be described as "inevitable"?

Inevitable is a dangerous word for historians, and many refuse to use it at all, for it implies that a certain outcome was bound to happen. Each of the great events just mentioned represents a major *break* in a trend, an interruption of previously "normal" patterns. The examples cited here, which rank among the twentieth century's most dramatic, most fateful, and sometimes most traumatic events, are among the subjects considered in the selections in this book. In most if not all of these events historians can detect the head-on collision of several "normal" trends, and often the transforming impact of key individuals to whom the chaos of the times gives a challenge and an opportunity to redirect events—or, conversely, who fail to rise to the perhaps extraordinary demands of the situation and help bring on catastrophe. Or, again, sheer accident can play a fateful role in bringing on huge events.

The outbreak of World War I is a good example. By 1914 rival blocs of European states were armed to the teeth. Each side nursed grievances against the other, including fears that each was losing ground to its rivals and frustrations at having had to retreat the last time a crisis broke out. Mass-circulation newspapers whipped up hysteria against real and imagined "national foes." In all nations, racist and sexist preoccupations with "national virility" kept the public on edge, conscious that some vague coming crisis would work transforming miracles on the stifling routines of everyday reality. None of the prominent politicians and kings in whose hands crucial decisions rested were particularly shrewd or visionary and all felt under intense pressure to act "decisively." Into this volatile brew suddenly fell a spark, in the form of a political assassination in the Balkans that occurred after so much bungling by both its victim and its perpetrators that it is hard to believe it actually happened. Yet within just over a month—between June 28 and August 1, 1914—this act of gratuitous violence plunged Europe into World War I. The statesmen on whom responsibility rested to carry out rational policies on behalf of their countries made their initial decisions impulsively, without considering all implications. Then, as the crisis snowballed, they tended either to panic or to act automatically, following prearranged contingency plans.

The causes and effects of World War I are worth pondering in some detail, because the conflict cost millions of lives and demolished four empires. Czarist Russia, for example, failed to sustain the effort necessary to wage war successfully, and internal dissent forced the bumbling Czar Nicholas to abdicate in 1917. This in turn set up the circumstances in which the Bolshevik Party, led by an obscure revolutionary called Lenin, seized control of a revolution in which more democratic forces lacked the ruthlessness to retain the power that had fallen into their hands. The Bolsheviks, it now seems clear, were by no means the foreordained revolutionary "saviors" of Russia: Only a leader of Lenin's truly extraordinary drive could have instilled in the rag-tag Bolshevik Party the determination to make a seemingly reckless grab for power in the late fall of 1917.

Likewise, Germany's traumatic defeat in World War I was a significant—if not decisive—part of the explanation for the Nazis' seizure of power in that country in 1933. German nationalists' resentment over their country's defeat certainly helped Hitler and his Nazi Party win the elections that brought them to the brink of power in the winter of 1932–1933, but so did the dreadful suffering of middle-class Germans in the Great Depression. Anti-Semitism was certainly a factor, too, but Germany was by no means the only European country at that time in which Jews were widely disliked. These were all long-term trends now intersecting; yet accidents and uncanny personal factors also helped propel Hitler into power. Like Lenin, Hitler was an extraordinary individual, uniquely combining evil intention with masterful political skill; but what if Corporal Hitler, who was several times wounded and gassed as a soldier on the western front, had been among the millions of World War I dead? What if other politicians, intriguing for power in depression-wracked Berlin, had not misjudged the situation so badly as to think that they could put Hitler in power and make him their puppet?

What of the outbreak of the Cold War, that long drawn-out clash of the Western capitalist democracies with the Soviet Union after these two future adversaries had warily joined hands to destroy

Nazism? Here too was a convergence of opposing long-term trends. On one hand was Russia's historical drive for security on its vulnerable western frontier, across which Hitler's armies had so recently attacked. On the other hand was the Western democratic leaders' conviction that the dangerous entrenchment of Soviet power deep in central Europe threatened continental security. For years, Western historians have debated whether the West bears (or at least shares) major responsibility for the Cold War because its leaders were too inflexible in refusing Soviet dictator Joseph Stalin the security that he craved. With more evidence recently made available from once-closed Soviet sources, it is now becoming apparent that the major determinant of Soviet behavior in the closing months of World War II and the early postwar years was Stalin's own cynicism and paranoia—the same lethal psychological traits that drove him to murder millions of his own citizens in the 1930s. Without Stalin, would the Cold War have taken the form that it did?

The effects of chance and personality are likewise apparent in the circumstances surrounding the reemergence of the world's two most populous nations, China and India, as independent nations between the early 1930s and the late 1940s. It is difficult to imagine two leaders of national regeneration as different as India's Mohandas Gandhi and China's Mao Zedong, yet each left a characteristic stamp on global history. Gandhi's nonviolent strategy for achieving Indian self-government proved to be decisive leverage (though he never considered it a mere means to an end) against British rule. Gandhi succeeded in large measure because democratic Britain could never suppress a political movement that so effectively seized the moral high ground, a lesson that was not lost on Martin Luther King and other American civil rights leaders. Gandhi saw nonviolent civil disobedience as a transforming spiritual movement applicable to all cultures and appropriate for use against even the most ruthless barbarism, such as Nazi Germany. It is questionable whether Gandhi's principles would in fact have restrained Hitler, Stalin, and the Japanese militarists, at least soon enough to prevent these tyrants from wiping out millions of lives. (Characteristically, Hitler thought the British soft-headed fools for not summarily shooting Gandhi.) In contrast, the resistance of China's paramount leader of the era of the Japanese invasion, the Communist revolutionary Mao Zedong, was anything but nonviolent. But Mao's revolutionary romanticism, too, had a long afterlife. In the mid-1960s, when he was an aging leader in danger of being turned into a figurehead by the managerial elite that had taken control of the Chinese People's Republic, Mao returned to the fray by inciting millions of frustrated young urban Chinese to bring the nation to the breaking point in the Great Cultural Revolution, aimed at violently "rejuvenating" the state and the Chinese Communist Party that he himself had founded years before. Like

Gandhi's nonviolent civil disobedience, Mao's Cultural Revolution is impossible to imagine without the impetus of these magnetic personalities.

One of the most dramatic and decisive instances of the influence of personality in world affairs came in 1962, during the Cuban missile crisis. The Soviet decision secretly to introduce nuclear weapons and the means to deliver them into Cuba, and to use this unsettling of the global balance of power to the USSR's advantage, was almost entirely the responsibility of Nikita Khrushchev, the Soviet Union's first durable post-Stalinist leader. When, several months later, the Soviet installations were detected at a stage close to completion by American surveillance aircraft, the necessity for formulating and carrying out the U.S. response to the challenge fell to President John F. Kennedy. During a nerve-wrenching ten-day period in October 1962, the world's fate hung in the balance. Unknown to Kennedy and the other American policy makers, Soviet nuclear warheads were already operational in Cuba, and the Soviet commander there had authority to deploy them if American troops landed. As it became likely that American naval vessels would stop Cuba-bound Soviet ships carrying in more munitions, or that American airstrikes would be ordered against Soviet bases on the island, a rapidly escalating military clash seemed almost unavoidable. The eventual decision to retreat was largely Khrushchev's, after a series of secret, back-channel contacts between unofficial American and Soviet representatives prepared the groundwork for a face-saving resolution. A sharper contrast to the fatal blundering of Europe's senior statesmen into war in the summer of 1914 would be hard to imagine. We may owe the fact that the twentieth century—and with it all human history—did not abruptly end in the autumn of 1962 largely to the personalities of Nikita Khrushchev and John F. Kennedy.

This book offers thirty-three readings on key events in the history of the twentieth-century world. Most of the readings are drawn from authoritative scholarly accounts, although some are journalists' assessments of contemporary events, and one is a great novelist's eyewitness account. Each reading begins with background notes that set the scene, supply context, and identify the writer. The readings are best approached chronologically, but none requires prior knowledge for clear understanding. In approaching each reading, you are encouraged to consider to what extent the circumstances and actions described reveal the decisive role of an individual in history. Conversely, consider the validity of each event as part of an impersonal tide of events. Reflecting on such questions is an essential obligation of every working historian, and of every reader of history.

The Twentieth Century Begins, 1900–1914

PREFACE

In 1900 the dominant mood in the Western world was one of confidence tinged with apprehension. The highly productive economies of most European and North American countries were giving their citizens a rising abundance of material goods. In most of the Western countries male citizens had the vote and played a direct role in running local affairs, and in some Western countries these citizens' votes also determined the direction of national policies. In important ways, people felt in control of their lives, and they were told by national leaders and by the important men (there were few women) of science and industry that the future looked even brighter.

And yet there was reason for uneasiness. People who understood the scientific trends of the day knew that the dizzy pace of discovery was raising as many fundamental questions as it was providing confident answers. National leaders not only sang the praises of their own country's greatness but also warned of the deadly threat that rival nations presented. If life, as the biologists taught, meant the survival of the fittest, surely nations and races (a subject on which there was perpetual discussion in 1900) also competed, and woe betide the losers! National "virility," literally measured by comparing the birth rates of rival states (and thus the relative sizes of the next generation's armies), was hotly debated, and the course of the debate often affected whether male citizens thought women should be entrusted with the vote.

Outside the core of western European nations and those parts of the world heavily settled by European emigrants (the United States, Canada, Australia, and New Zealand), the outlook was far from optimistic. Not always: Japan was proving that non-Western nations could successfully imitate the European model, which combined strong government, technical education, industrialization, nationalism, militarism, and imperialism. In 1904–1905, Japan would prove its coming-of-age by defeating the most backward of the European great powers, Russia, in a war for the control of Korea and southern Manchuria. But elsewhere, the remaining non-European states were having trouble even maintaining their independence. China, caught in the depths of its poverty, overpopulation, and outmoded autocracy, was saved from partition only by the imperialist states' failure to agree among themselves how that ancient empire should be divided up. Yet China was stirring: some of its younger generation were beginning to study the Europeans' ideologies (liberal democracy, nationalism, and socialism), and in the Boxer Rebellion of 1900 the Chinese people themselves expressed their deep revulsion against foreign encroachments. These were only the first signs of what would become a mighty revolutionary tide sweeping China in the next half-century. India, the world's second most populous country, seemed firmly under British rule, but there too men (rarely women) of the elite were studying British ways with an eye to learning how to regain national independence, and in South Africa an expatriate young Indian named Mohandas Gandhi was fusing Western and Indian religious and philosophical ideas into a philosophy of nonviolent protest that would, like the coming Chinese Revolution, have worldwide significance. In Muslim countries (which spanned the globe from North Africa to the East Indies) the Islamic tradition was explored by intellectuals and nationalists in the hope that it would provide guidance in re-creating national communities. In 1900 sub-Saharan Africa had too recently been forced into the European imperialists' colonial systems for its people to have time to react with much more than shock, but even in some colonies the Europeans were starting to build the school systems out of which would emerge future generations of national leaders.

Latin America in 1900 remained politically independent (thanks largely to the converging interests of Great Britain and the United States, which both agreed that this part of the world should not be partitioned into colonies), but economically the region was firmly under the control of North American and European bankers and investors. Most of its people were desperately poor; only tiny oligarchies prospered. Here again, however, slow economic development and internal political conflict were sowing the seeds of future turmoil. In 1911 Mexico became the first Latin American nation to embark on the cycle of revolutionary turmoil; it would not be the last.

A Law of
Acceleration

Henry Adams

Henry Adams (1838–1918) was the great-grandson of one president of the United States, the grandson of another, and the son of a U.S. minister to Great Britain. He was among the greatest American historians of the nineteenth century, and he composed perhaps the finest autobiography ever written in the United States, *The Education of Henry Adams* (originally published in 1918). A sensitive and highly original observer of the American scene, Adams came to think of himself as an "outsider." Born into one of America's most distinguished families, Adams saw American society evolve in directions that he found mystifying and somewhat humiliating. The modern America that had emerged by 1900 offered little opportunity for gentlemen (like Adams) of the old elite unless they were willing to offer their services as captains of industry or to compete for votes as democratic politicians. Neither role was congenial to Adams. He felt himself unprepared by his classical nineteenth-century education to understand modern science and industry (though he tried hard), and his family's concept of how it should render public service did not include grubbing in corrupt electoral politics.

Written in an elegant and ironic style, with the author always referring to himself in the third person, *The Education of Henry Adams* offers a brilliant intellectual account of how a man of the nineteenth century viewed the dawning of the twentieth-century world. In the excerpt that follows, Adams discusses how the pace of historical change—as well as the accumulation of scientific knowledge and of technological know-how—had been accelerating to a dizzy pace during his lifetime. These, he says, are thoughts that occurred to him in 1904.

Excerpted from "A Law of Acceleration," by Henry Adams in *The Education of Henry Adams* (New York: Modern Library, 1918). Copyright © 1918 by the Massachusetts Historical Society.

Images are not arguments, rarely even lead to proof, but the mind craves them, and, of late more than ever, the keenest experimenters find twenty images better than one, especially if contradictory; since the human mind has already learned to deal in contradictions.

The image needed here is that of a new centre, or preponderating mass, artificially introduced on earth in the midst of a system of attractive forces that previously made their own equilibrium, and constantly induced to accelerate its motion till it shall establish a new equilibrium. A dynamic theory would begin by assuming that all history, terrestrial or cosmic, mechanical or intellectual, would be reducible to this formula if we knew the facts.

For convenience, the most familiar image should come first; and this is probably that of the comet, or meteoric streams, like the Leonids and Perseids; a complex of minute mechanical agencies, reacting within and without, and guided by the sum of forces attracting or deflecting it. Nothing forbids one to assume that the man-meteorite might grow, as an acorn does, absorbing light, heat, electricity—or thought; for, in recent times, such transference of energy has become a familiar idea; but the simplest figure, at first, is that of a perfect comet—say that of 1843—which drops from space, in a straight line, at the regular acceleration of speed, directly into the sun, and after wheeling sharply about it, in heat that ought to dissipate any known substance, turns back unharmed, in defiance of law, by the path on which it came. The mind, by analogy, may figure as such a comet, the better because it also defies law.

Motion is the ultimate object of science, and measures of motion are many; but with thought as with matter, the true measure is mass in its astronomic sense—the sum or difference of attractive forces. Science has quite enough trouble in measuring its material motions without volunteering help to the historian, but the historian needs not much help to measure some kinds of social movement; and especially in the nineteenth century, society by common accord agreed in measuring its progress by the coal-output. The ratio of increase in the volume of coal-power may serve as dynamometer.

The coal-output of the world, speaking roughly, doubled every ten years between 1840 and 1900, in the form of utilized power, for the ton of coal yielded three or four times as much power in 1900 as in 1840. Rapid as this rate of acceleration in volume seems, it may be tested in a thousand ways without greatly reducing it. Perhaps the ocean steamer is nearest unity and easiest to measure, for any one might hire, in 1905, for a small sum of money, the use of 30,000 steam-horse-power to cross the ocean, and by halving this figure every ten years, he got back to 234 horse-power for 1835, which was accuracy enough for his purposes. In truth, his chief trouble came not from the ratio in volume of heat, but from the intensity, since he could get no basis for a ratio there. All ages of history have known high intensities, like the iron-furnace, the burning-glass, the blow-pipe; but no society has ever used high intensities on any large scale till now, nor can a mere bystander decide what range of temperature is now in common use. Loosely guessing that science controls habitually the whole range from absolute zero to 3000° Centigrade, one might assume, for convenience, that the ten-year ratio for volume could be used temporarily for intensity; and still there remained a ratio to be guessed for other forces than heat. Since 1800 scores of new forces had been discovered; old forces had been raised to higher powers, as could be measured in the navy-gun; great regions of chemistry had been opened up, and connected with other regions of physics. Within ten years a new universe of force had been revealed in radiation. Complexity had extended itself on immense horizons, and arithmetical ratios were useless for any attempt at accuracy. The force evolved seemed more like explosion than gravitation, and followed closely the curve of steam; but, at all events, the ten-year ratio seemed carefully conservative. Unless the calculator was prepared to be instantly overwhelmed by physical force and mental complexity, he must stop there.

Thus, taking the year 1900 as the starting point for carrying back the series, nothing was easier than to assume a ten-year period of retardation as far back as 1820, but beyond that point the statistician failed, and only the mathematician could help. Laplace would have found it child's-play to fix a ratio of progression in mathematical science between Descartes, Leibnitz, Newton, and himself. Watt could have given in pounds the increase of power between Newcomen's engines and his own. Volta and Benjamin Franklin would have stated their progress as absolute creation of power. Dalton could have measured minutely his advance on Boerhaave. Napoleon I must have had a distant notion of his own numerical relation to Louis XIV. No one in 1789 doubted the progress of force, least of all those who were to lose their heads by it.

Pending agreement between these authorities, theory may assume what it likes—say a fifty, or even a five-and-twenty-year period of reduplication for the eighteenth century, for the period matters little until the acceleration itself is admitted. The subject is even more amusing in the seventeenth than in the eighteenth century, because Galileo and Kepler, Descartes, Huygens, and Isaac Newton took vast pains to fix the laws of acceleration for moving bodies, while Lord Bacon and William Harvey were content with showing experimentally the fact of acceleration in knowledge; but from their combined results a historian might be tempted to maintain a similar rate of movement back to 1600, subject to correction from the historians of mathematics.

The mathematicians might carry their calculations back as far as the fourteenth century when algebra seems to have become for the first time the standard measure of mechanical progress in western Europe; for not only Copernicus and Tycho Brahe, but even artists like Leonardo, Michaelangelo, and Albert Dürer worked by mathematical processes, and their testimony would probably give results more exact than that of Montaigne or Shakespeare; but, to save trouble, one might tentatively carry back the same ratio of acceleration, or retardation, to the year 1400, with the help of Columbus and Gutenberg, so taking a uniform rate during the whole four centuries (1400–1800), and leaving to statisticians the task of correcting it.

Or better, one might, for convenience, use the formula of squares to serve for a law of mind. Any other formula would do as well, either of chemical explosion, or electrolysis, or vegetable growth, or of expansion or contraction in innumerable forms; but this happens to be simple and convenient. Its force increases in the direct ratio of its squares. As the human meteoroid approached the sun or centre of attractive force, the attraction of one century squared itself to give the measure of attraction in the next.

Behind the year 1400, the process certainly went on, but the progress became so slight as to be hardly measurable. What was gained in the east or elsewhere, cannot be known; but forces, called loosely Greek fire and gunpowder, came into use in the west in the thirteenth century, as well as instruments like the compass, the blowpipe, clocks and spectacles, and materials like paper; Arabic notation and algebra were introduced, while metaphysics and theology acted as violent stimulants to mind. An architect might detect a sequence between the Church of St. Peter's at Rome, the Amiens Cathedral, the Duomo at Pisa, San Marco at Venice, Sancta Sofia at Constantinople and the churches at Ravenna. All the historian dares affirm is that a sequence is manifestly there, and he has a right to carry back his ratio, to represent the fact, without assuming its numerical correctness. On the human mind as a moving body, the break in acceleration in the Middle Ages is only apparent; the attraction worked through shifting forms of force, as the sun works by light or heat, electricity, gravitation, or what not, on different organs with different sensibilities, but with invariable law.

The science of prehistoric man has no value except to prove that the law went back into indefinite antiquity. A stone arrowhead is as convincing as a steam-engine. The values were as clear a hundred thousand years ago as now, and extended equally over the whole world. The motion at last became infinitely slight, but cannot be proved to have stopped. The motion of Newton's comet at aphelion may be equally slight. To evolutionists may be left the processes of evolution; to historians the single interest is the law of reaction between force and force—between mind and nature—the law of progress.

The great division of history into phases by Turgot and Comte first affirmed this law in its outlines by asserting the unity of progress, for a mere phase interrupts no growth, and nature shows innumerable such phases. The development of coal-power in the nineteenth century furnished the first means of assigning closer values to the elements; and the appearance of supersensual forces towards 1900 made this calculation a pressing necessity; since the next step became infinitely serious.

A law of acceleration, definite and constant as any law of mechanics, cannot be supposed to relax its energy to suit the convenience of man. No one is likely to suggest a theory that man's convenience had been consulted by Nature at any time, or that Nature has consulted the convenience of any of her creations, except perhaps the *Terebratula.* In every age man has bitterly and justly complained that Nature hurried and hustled him, for inertia almost invariably has ended in tragedy. Resistance is its law, and resistance to superior mass is futile and fatal.

Fifty years ago, science took for granted that the rate of acceleration could not last. The world forgets quickly, but even today the habit remains of founding statistics on the faith that consumption will continue nearly stationary. Two generations, with John Stuart Mill, talked of this stationary period, which was to follow the explosion of new power. All the men who were elderly in the [eighteen] forties died in this faith, and other men grew old nursing the same conviction, and happy in it; while science, for fifty years, permitted, or encouraged, society to think that force would prove to be limited in supply. This mental inertia of science lasted through the eighties before showing signs of breaking up; and nothing short of radium fairly wakened men to the fact, long since evident, that force was inexhaustible. Even then the scientific authorities vehemently resisted.

Nothing so revolutionary had happened since the year 300. Thought had more than once been upset, but never caught and whirled about in the vortex of infinite forces. Power leaped from every atom, and enough of it to supply the stellar universe showed itself running to waste at every pore of matter. Man could no longer hold it off. Forces grasped his wrists and flung him about as though he had hold of a live wire or a runaway automobile; which was very nearly the exact truth for the purposes of an elderly and timid single gentleman in Paris, who never drove down the Champs Élysées without expecting an accident, and commonly witnessing one; or found himself in the neighborhood of an official without calculating the chances of a bomb. So long as the rates of progress held good, these bombs would double in force and number every ten years.

Impossibilities no longer stood in the way. One's life had fattened on impossibilities. Before the boy [Adams] was six years old, he had seen four impossibilities made actual—the ocean-steamer, the railway, the electric telegraph, and the Daguerreotype [an early form of photography]; nor could he ever learn which of the four had most hurried others to come. He had seen the coal-output of the United States grow from nothing to three hundred million tons or more. What was far more serious, he had seen the number of minds, engaged in pursuing force—the truest measure of its attraction—increase from a few scores or hundreds, in 1838, to many thousands in 1905, trained to sharpness never before reached, and armed with instruments amounting to new senses of indefinite power and accuracy, while they chased force into hiding-places where Nature herself had never known it to be, making analyses that contradicted being, and syntheses that endangered the elements. No one could say that the social mind now failed to respond to new force, even when the new force annoyed it horribly. Every day Nature violently revolted, causing so-called accidents with enormous destruction of property and life, while plainly laughing at man, who helplessly groaned and shrieked and shuddered, but never for a single instant could stop. The railways alone approached the carnage of war; automobiles and fire-arms ravaged society, until an earthquake became almost a nervous relaxation. An immense volume of force had detached itself from the unknown universe of energy, while still vaster reservoirs, supposed to be infinite, steadily revealed themselves, attracting mankind with more compulsive course than all the Pontic Seas or Gods or Gold that ever existed, and feeling still less of retiring ebb.

In 1850, science would have smiled at such a romance as this, but, in 1900, as far as history could learn, few men of science thought it a laughing matter. If a perplexed but laborious follower could venture to guess their drift, it seemed in their minds a toss-up between anarchy and order. Unless they should be more honest with themselves in the future than ever they were in the past, they would be more astonished than their followers when they reached the end. If Karl Pearson's [a British economist and statistician] notions of the universe were sound, men like Galileo, Descartes, Leibnitz, and Newton should have stopped the progress of science before 1700, supposing them to have been honest in the religious convictions they expressed. In 1900 they were plainly forced back on faith in a unity unproved and an order they had themselves disproved. They had reduced their universe to a series of relations to themselves. They had reduced themselves to motion in a universe of motions, with an acceleration, in their own case, of vertiginous violence. With the correctness of their science, history had no right to meddle, since their science now lay in a plane where scarcely one or two hundred minds in the world could follow its mathematical processes; but bombs educate vigorously, and even wireless telegraphy or airships might require the reconstruction of society. If any analogy whatever existed between the human mind, on one side, and the laws of motion, on the other, the mind had already entered a field of attraction so violent that it must immediately pass beyond, into new equilibrium, like the Comet of Newton, to suffer dissipation altogether, like meteoroids in the earth's atmosphere. If it behaved like an explosive, it must rapidly recover equilibrium; if it behaved like a vegetable, it must reach its limits of growth; and even if it acted like the earlier creations of energy—the saurians and sharks—it must have nearly reached the limits of its expansion. If science were to go on doubling or quadrupling its complexities every ten years, even mathematics would soon succumb. An average mind had succumbed already in 1850; it could no longer understand the problem in 1900.

Fortunately, a student of history had no responsibility for the problem; he took it as science gave it, and waited only to be taught. With science or with society, he had no quarrel and claimed no share of authority. He had never been able to acquire knowledge, still less to impart it; and if he had, at times, felt serious differences with the American of the nineteenth century, he felt none with the American of the twentieth. For this new creation, born since 1900, a historian asked no longer to be teacher or even friend; he asked only to be a pupil, and promised to be docile, for once, even though trodden under foot; for he could see that the new American—the child of incalculable coal-power, chemical power, electric power, and radiating energy, as well as of new forces yet undetermined—must be a sort of God compared with any former creation of nature. At the rate of progress since 1800, every American who lived into the year 2000 would know how to control unlimited power. He would think in complexities unimaginable to an earlier mind. He would deal with problems altogether beyond the range of earlier society. To him the nineteenth century would stand on the same plane with the fourth—equally childlike—and he would only wonder how both of them, knowing so little, and so weak in force, should have done so much. Perhaps even he might go back, in 1964, to sit with Gibbon on the steps of Ara Cœli.*

Meanwhile he [Adams] was getting education. With that, a teacher who had failed to educate even the generation of 1870, dared not interfere. The new forces would educate. History saw few lessons in the past that would be useful in the future; but one, at least, it did see. The attempt of the American of 1800 to educate the American of 1900 had not often been surpassed for folly; and since 1800 the forces and their complications had increased a thousand times or more. The attempt of the American of 1900 to educate the American of 2000, must be even blinder than that of the Congressman of 1800,

* An allusion to the way in which the great eighteenth-century British historian Edward Gibbon was inspired to write his classic *The Decline and Fall of the Roman Empire* in 1764. Adams here is wondering whether the twentieth century will discover time travel.

except so far as he had learned his ignorance. During a million or two of years, every generation in turn had toiled with endless agony to attain and apply power, all the while betraying the deepest alarm and horror at the power they created. The teacher of 1900, if foolhardy, might stimulate; if foolish, might resist; if intelligent, might balance, as wise and foolish have often tried to do from the beginning; but the forces would continue to educate, and the mind would continue to react. All the teacher could hope was to teach it reaction.

Even there his difficulty was extreme. The most elementary books of science betrayed the inadequacy of old implements of thought. Chapter after chapter closed with phrases such as one never met in older literature: "The cause of this phenomenon is not understood"; "science no longer ventures to explain causes"; "the first step towards a causal explanation still remains to be taken"; "opinions are very much divided"; "in spite of the contradictions involved"; "science gets on only by adopting different theories, sometimes contradictory." Evidently the new American would need to think in contradictions, and instead of Kant's famous four antinomies, the new universe would know no law that could not be proved by its anti-law.

To educate—one's [Adam's] self to begin with—had been the effort of one's life for sixty years; and the difficulties of education had gone on doubling with the coal-output, until the prospect of waiting another ten years, in order to face a seventh doubling of complexities, allured one's imagination but slightly. The law of acceleration was definite, and did not require ten years more study except to show whether it held good. No scheme could be suggested to the new American, and no fault needed to be found, or complaint made; but the next great influx of new forces seemed near at hand, and its style of education promised to be violently coercive. The movement from unity into multiplicity, between 1200 and 1900, was unbroken in sequence, and rapid in acceleration. Prolonged one generation longer, it would require a new social mind. As though thought were common salt in indefinite solution it must enter a new phase subject to new laws. Thus far, since five or ten thousand years, the mind had successfully reacted, and nothing yet proved that it would fail to react—but it would need to jump.

1900: The Promise of a New Century

Barbara W. Tuchman

The arrival of the year 1900, like the recent turn of the millennium, excited great popular interest. In 1900, people's thoughts focused mainly on the prospect of more progress. But in the background, notes historian Barbara W. Tuchman, were already signs of several trends that should have made Westerners—and especially Europeans—uneasy. Social unrest and resentment at imperialist domination was sweeping through China. A bloody war in South Africa was demonstrating both the lethal power of modern weaponry and the difficulty that modern armies could have in overcoming determined guerrilla resistance. Psychologist Sigmund Freud and physicist Max Planck were publishing scientific findings that called into question all that modern people thought they knew about the unconscious and the physical structure of the universe. Germany and Great Britain were escalating their arms race, and strutting Kaiser Wilhelm II was demanding a "place in the sun" for his German Reich. Harbingers of what would be the twentieth century's immense economic and scientific advances, and of its horrifying violence, were both in plain view—though very few at the time could grasp their meaning.

The Twentieth was already unmistakably modern, which is to say it was absorbed in pursuit of the material with maximum vigor and diminished self-assurance; it had forgotten decadence and acquired doubt. Mechanical energy and material goods were redoubling and dominant, but whether beneficent had somehow become a question. Progress, the great certainty of the Nineteenth, no longer appeared so sure.

Excerpted from *The Proud Tower: A Portrait of the World Before the War, 1890–1914,* by Barbara Tuchman (New York: Macmillan, 1962). Copyright © 1966 by Barbara Tuchman, renewed 1994 by Dr. Lester Tuchman. Reprinted with permission from Russell & Volkening as agents for the author.

People felt awe at the turn of the century, as if the hand of God were turning a page in human fate. Cannons were fired at midnight in Berlin to mark the moment and one listener heard the sound "with a kind of shiver: one knew all that the Nineteenth Century had carried away; one did not know what the Twentieth would bring."

To begin with, it brought violence. The new century was born brawling, in the Boxer Rebellion, in the Philippines, in South Africa, although the brawls were still on the periphery. In 1900 France was restless and so filled with frustrated rage that *Punch* [the leading British humor magazine] predicted her first act on the day after the International Exposition closed would be to declare war on England, "for they have been held in for so long it will be necessary to do something desperate at once." In 1900 the Kaiser exhorted German troops embarking on the punitive expedition to Pekin [Beijing] to emulate Huns in ruthlessness. In the course of the Boxer Rebellion he experienced the inconvenience of too much zeal in the munitions business. Learning that a German gunboat had suffered seventeen hits in a duel with Chinese forts equipped with the latest Krupp cannon, he sent Fritz Krupp an angry telegram: "This is no time when I am sending my soldiers to battle against the yellow beasts to try to make money out of so serious a situation."

Money and bigness governed. [U.S. financier J.P.] Morgan in 1900 bought out Carnegie to form with Rockefeller and a hundred other firms the corporate colossus, U.S. Steel, the world's first billion-dollar holding company. King Leopold of Belgium, the Morgan of Europe, a builder too big for his country, created a money-making empire out of the Congo while British and Americans, busy killing Boers and Filipinos, loudly deplored his methods. Three hundred men, it was said, "all acquainted with each other, controlled the economic destiny of the Continent."

In 1900 Oscar Wilde, a bloated ruin at forty-four, died in Paris, and Nietzsche, aged fifty-five and mad, died at Weimar. "Then in 1900," wrote W.B. Yeats, "everybody got down off his stilts; henceforth no one went mad; nobody committed suicide; nobody joined the Catholic Church or if they did I have forgotten. Victorianism had been defeated." Some welcomed, some regretted the defeat but the fact was clear. As if to mark the event, the Queen herself incredibly was no more.

The year 1900 conveyed a sense of forces and energy running away with the world. [American historian] Henry Adams felt moved to evolve a "Law of Acceleration" in history. He felt as if he could never drive down the Champs Elysées without expecting an accident or stand near an official without expecting a bomb. "So long as the rate of progress held good, these bombs would double in force and number every ten years. . . . Power leaped from every atom. . . . Man could no longer hold it off. Forces grasped his wrists and flung him about as though he had hold of a live wire or a runaway automobile."

Adams' choice of simile was apt, for the automobile was one of the century's two most potent factors of future social change; the other was man's unconscious. Although unrecognized in potential, it too was formulated in 1900, in a book, *The Interpretation of Dreams*, by a Viennese doctor, Sigmund Freud. Although the book attracted little attention and it took eight years to sell out the edition of six hundred copies, its appearance was the signal that Victorianism indeed was dead.

The International Exposition of 1900 covering 277 acres in the heart of Paris displayed the new century's energies to fifty million visitors from April to November. If they could not for this Exposition equal the Eiffel Tower of the last, the French built with the same *élan* a new miracle of engineering and beauty in the Pont Alexandre III, whose low graceful arch spanned the Seine in a single leap. It was considered "peerless in all the world" and the two new permanent exhibition buildings on the right bank, the Grand and Petit Palais, were unanimously acknowledged to be "suitable and grand." Not so the Porte Monumentale, or main gate, in the place de la Concorde, built of what appeared to one observer to be lath, plaster, broken glass, putty, old lace curtains and glue. At its top, instead of a traditional goddess of Progress or Enlightenment, a plaster Parisienne in evening gown welcomed the world with open arms. Although considered gay and chic by some, the gate was generally deplored as the epitome of the new vulgarity of the new century. Multicolored electric lights played on towering electrically powered fountains at night; the new Metro was opened in time; a track for automobile testing and racing was built at the Expo annex at Vincennes. Of all the wonders the public's favorite was the *trottoir roulant,* a double moving sidewalk circling the grounds, one half of which moved twice as fast as the other. In the temporary buildings, the architects, striving for sensation, had achieved what seemed exciting originality to some and "a debauch of stucco" to others. Industrial exhibits in the Palaces of Machinery, Electricity, Civil Engineering and Transportation, Mining and Metallurgy, Chemical Industries and Textiles, displayed all the extraordinary advances of the past decade.

Of the national pavilions the most popular was the Russian, an exotic Byzantine palace with a Trans-Siberian Railway exhibit in which the visitor could sit in a sumptuous railway carriage and enjoy a moving panorama of the scenery. The Viennese was a fantasy of *Art Nouveau* with fretwork balconies in the form of curling vines and the sinuous lines of the new style curving through ceramics and furniture. The United States had the greatest number of exhibits but Germany's show was the most imposing, clearly superior in quality and arrangement. It affirmed an intense will to surpass every other exhibitor. Germany's dynamos were the largest, the spire of her pavilion the tallest, its searchlight the brightest, its restaurant the most expensive. The Kaiser himself, it was rumored, had commanded the finest china and silver, the most delicate glassware, the most luxurious service, so that one felt in the presence, as one visitor said, of a real style "William the Second."

In all the Exposition the two largest single exhibits were Schneider-Creusot's long-range cannon and Vickers-Maxim's collection of ferocious, quick-firing machine guns. Beholders gazed at them with solemn thoughts. An English correspondent in particular was moved to philosophize on the real meaning of the Exposition for the new era it introduced. Schneider's great gun seemed to him to hold the world collected in Paris under its threat and to mark the passage of war from a realm of sport to a realm of science in which the making of weapons absorbed the ingenuity of mankind. If a lull ever came, he wrote, the arts of peace might revive, "but meanwhile the Paris Exhibition has taught us that the triumph of the modern world is purely mechanical."

The triumphs continued. In 1900 Max Planck broke the chains of classical Newtonian physics to formulate the quantum theory of energy. In Switzerland in 1905 Albert Einstein obtained his doctorate at the University of Zurich with a dissertation on a new theory of relativity. In 1901 wireless telegraphy spanned the Atlantic and Daimler supplanted the horseless carriage with a vehicle distinctly a motorcar. In 1903 a motorized dirigible flying machine flew at Kitty Hawk. But no epoch is all of a piece. To some the almost daily new miracles accomplished by science and mechanics still carried, not a threat as to Henry Adams, but a promise of progress in social justice. "It seemed merely a matter of decades," thought Stefan Zweig, a young intellectual of Vienna, "before the last vestiges of evil and violence would finally be conquered."

In 1900 the German Naval Law precipitated the abandonment of isolation by England. Providing for nineteen new battleships and twenty-three cruisers in the next twenty years, it made explicit Germany's challenge to British supremacy at sea, the fulcrum of Britain's existence. It convinced Britain that she needed friends. In 1901 the Hay-Pauncefote Treaty put a bottom under good relations with the United States. In 1902 the isolation of self-sufficient strength, once so splendid and confident, was ended forever by a formal alliance with Japan. In 1903 the new King of England, Edward VII, prepared the ground for reconciliation with France by a visit of ceremony to Paris carried out with tact and aplomb. In 1904 the new policy culminated in an Anglo-French Entente, disposing of old quarrels, establishing a new friendship and fundamentally defining the balance of Europe.

Votes for Women

George Dangerfield

In 1910, women did not possess the vote at the national level anywhere in the world (although they could vote in certain American states and in Finland, a semiautonomous Russian province). Suffragists' demand for the vote, which had been part of the political debate in many countries since the mid-1800s, challenged basic male assumptions about proper gender roles. Nowhere did the controversy become more raucous than in England. Historian George Dangerfield's classic book *The Strange Death of Liberal England* entertainingly dissects the stormy political battles that rocked the comfortable British world between 1900 and the outbreak of World War I—battles over self-determination for Ireland, over the power of the House of Lords to block legislation demanded by the House of Commons, and over whether women should get the right to vote. Suffragists such as Mrs. Emmaline Pankhurst and her daughters showed how "unladylike" they could be in forcing the Liberal Party's prime minister, Herbert Asquith, to face the issue of women's rights head-on. The political violence that the suffragists precipitated in 1910 was another foreshadowing of the new century's coming turmoil.

Despite the uproars that Dangerfield describes, not until 1918 would British women finally secure the right to vote. Nevertheless, the prewar suffragist campaign in Britain (and in the United States as well) marked the opening of one of the most important global trends in the twentieth century: the struggle of women to achieve full equality.

The first characteristic scene in the Woman's Rebellion does not open until November of 1910. Mrs. Pankhurst, now the acknowledged leader of the militant suffrage movement, had agreed that, with a new king [George V] on the throne, it would be more seemly for the women to declare an armistice. But she was also determined that the W.S.P.U. [Women's Social and Political Union] should be more downright in its methods; for experience had taught her that nothing short of a profound and prolonged shock would ever persuade Mr. Asquith's Government to give women the Vote.

The Government—uneasily aware that Mrs. Pankhurst's was one of those causes which Liberalism ought to uphold—had tried to rid itself of responsibility by declaring that women's suffrage was not a party measure.[That is, the Liberal government announced that party members in Parliament could vote as they chose, and would not be bound by party discipline.] But when a highly controversial question is removed from party politics, the chances are that it will never get anywhere; and Mrs. Pankhurst, with her former knowledge of the vagaries and procrastinations of municipal politics, had a shrewd suspicion that Mr. Asquith, that consummate parliamentarian, never *intended* women's suffrage to get anywhere.

As early as February, 1910, the Government had shown some disposition to yield, and, for at least a short while, Mrs. Pankhurst thought that Mr. Asquith might—just *might,* she had no reason to suppose more—have come over to her way of thinking. The W.S.P.U., if it had any political affiliations, was a Labor movement, but a number of Liberal women were known to be in sympathy with it, and a wise Prime Minister would not want to offend them. As his part in the truce, Mr. Asquith professed himself ready to smile upon what was known as the Conciliation Bill, which would enfranchise about a million women: to be specific, women owners of business premises paying £10 a year rental and upwards, and women householders; and when the Bill came up for its first reading on July 12, it was passed by 299 to 189.

But that, in effect, was as far as the Bill ever got. Now Mrs. Pankhurst was to have all her suspicions justified; now, moving with some finesse but not too delicately, the Ministerial hand played havoc with all her aspirations. The question at issue seemed to be a very simple one: should the Bill go to a Grand Committee of the House, or to a Committee of the whole House; in the first event, a special Committee would deal with it promptly and separately while the Commons transacted their usual business; in the second, special facilities from the Government would be needed to bring it safely through the Committee stage. The second reading was secured after an interesting debate, in which Mr. F.E. Smith [a prominent member of Parliament] appeared as the women's most obdurate opponent; but when a second division was taken, as to which Committee should see the Bill on to its third reading, Mr. Asquith let it be known that he wished all franchise bills to go to a Committee of the whole

House; and a number of the Bill's sincerest supporters agreeing with him (whether from carelessness or loyalty), to a Committee of the whole House the Bill went, by a vote of 320 to 175.

The Bill had been exiled into a very wilderness; and Mr. Asquith's was the hand which had sent it there. For a day or two, Mrs. Pankhurst did not comprehend the enormity of what had been done to her; but at last she realized that the Bill would never reach its third reading unless the Cabinet agreed to give it facilities. And then she realized, too, that facilities would never be given. The treachery of the Government, the stupidity of her own supporters in the Commons—how could these things be borne? For a while she did nothing; the truce should be kept; she could be patient. But when Parliament re-assembled in November, and if nothing were done—then they should see what it was to thwart her!

But November found Mr. Asquith in the midst of his battle with the [House of] Lords, with an election not a month away; and everything pointed to the melancholy truth that he had not the slightest thought of doing anything for the women. It had been foolish, really, to expect anything of him; his wife, who had supported him loyally all the way to Number 10, Downing Street [the prime minister's official residence in London], was naturally an ardent anti-suffragette. And so the W.S.P.U., not bothering to wait for the inevitable, matured its plans, and on November 18, when Parliament re-opened, it was ready for Mr. Asquith.

Friday, November 18, has gone down into Suffragette History as "Black Friday." That afternoon, while Mr. Asquith was telling the Commons that he had advised the Crown to order a dissolution, and that government business (in which no mention was made of women's suffrage) would take precedence at all the few sittings which were left—small bands of women began moving from the W.S.P.U. headquarters at Caxton Hall. They carried little purple bannerettes, bearing such legends as "Asquith Has Vetoed the Bill," "Where There's a Bill, There's a Way," "Women's Will Beats Asquith's Won't"; and they were headed, one and all, towards Parliament Square.

In Parliament Square, the police were assembled in great numbers. They had their instructions. Women were not to be arrested, except for extreme provocation, but they *were* to be kept away from the Houses of Parliament. In these simple tactics may be discerned the ingenious mind of Mr. [Winston] Churchill, who then presided at the Home Office [the British equivalent of the U.S. Department of Justice] and who had been, at one time, loud in his support of the suffragettes. His voice had sensibly diminished in the last year, until the W.S.P.U. was inclined to reckon him among the more subtle of its enemies; and certainly no enemy could have devised a more unspeakable ordeal than was implicit in the instructions of Mr. Churchill to the police.

As the women advanced into Parliament Square, the police pushed them back: gently at first, and with laughter. But the skirted warriors were not so easily repulsed; their method was simply to push, with gloved hands, against the constabulary chest; and push they did, returning to the fray over and over again. The laughter of the crowd, and it was large, took on a coarser note; the police grew flushed and angry. Women should not behave in this unnatural way; and ladies (surely most of their tormentors were ladies) . . . it was inconceivable that *they* should so far forget themselves. Suddenly the atmosphere changed; and Jason and his argonauts could not have warded off the Harpies with more rage and despair than did those policemen in Parliament Square.

Bannerettes were torn and trampled; women were struck with fists and knees, knocked down, dragged up, hurled from hand to hand, and sent reeling back, bruised and bleeding, into the arms of the crowd. They were no longer demonstrators; they were monsters, their presence was unendurable. They were pummeled and they were pinched, their thumbs were forced back, their arms twisted, their breasts gripped, their faces rubbed against the pailings: and this went on for nearly six hours.

The crowd, with instinctive sympathy for a loser, grew more in favor of the women as the dreary and indecent conflict dragged on, hour after hour; though, to be sure, only one onlooker seems to have dared to interfere with the police. But there was a certain number of tough characters who did not choose to let this opportunity slip, and some suffragettes were dragged away and miserably ill-treated; indeed, one woman is said to have died, a year later, as the result of having been indecently assaulted in a side street. The battle ended at last by lamplight. The Square was cleared. By the wall of the House of Lords, a number of anxious women kneeled around Miss Ada Wright, who had been knocked down a dozen times in succession, and was in a very bad way. A few torn bannerettes, a trampled hat or two, some fragments of clothing, remained on the field of battle until next morning— singular trophies of the Government's victory.

But was it a victory? Mrs. Pankhurst, who had been admitted to the House of Commons in the afternoon, stayed for a while in the Prime Minister's room; but Mr. Asquith did not appear. He had left the House. On Lord Castlereagh's moving an amendment, however, that the Conciliation Bill should be considered as part of the Government's business, he came hurrying back to his seat to ask that the amendment should not be pressed. But the temper of the House was against him. Member after member arose to beg him to receive the women's deputation, and put an end to the disgraceful scenes which were going on outside; and at last they dragged from him a promise that he would make a statement next Tuesday. As for Mrs. Pankhurst, waiting miserably by the Strangers' Entrance, he made no attempt to see her.

In this he made his usual mistake; as he underestimated Sir Edward Carson and the Orangemen [the Ulster Unionist Party], so also he underestimated Mrs. Pankhurst and the W.S.P.U. He was very clement: the police had, in the end and in spite of Mr. Churchill's strategy, arrested 115 women and 4 men, and almost all of these were released. He was also very evasive. His Tuesday statement promised that the Government would provide facilities for the Bill "in the next Parliament"; but the Bill must be framed on a democratic basis and admit of free amendment. Perhaps he thought that the women could be deceived for ever; that they would not see that "the next Parliament" by no means implied the next *Session,* nor realize how little chance a women's suffrage Bill "on a democratic basis" had of passing through both Houses without drastic and destructive amendments. But

A member of the W.S.P.U. is arrested by London police for participating in a suffrage demonstration.

if he thought so, he was grievously mistaken: eager eyes searched every phrase of his illusory statement; it was pronounced unsatisfactory; and once again the W.S.P.U. prepared for action.

On the next morning, Mrs. Pankhurst led a deputation to Downing Street; a deputation or an army—the words were soon to be synonymous. The police were caught unawares, and only a thin line of them, hastily summoned, barred the street's entrance. The Inspector attempted to parley: "Push forward," shouted Sylvia Pankhurst, standing on the roof of her taxi, and "Shove along, girls," said Mrs. Haverfield—a lady who had done rescue-work among disabled horses in the South African War, and who habitually wore a hunting stock and a small black riding hat. The ladies pushed forward, the police gave way, and Downing Street suddenly blossomed with tense faces and purple bannerettes.

At this precise moment, some malign fate prompted Mr. Asquith to leave his house, and he was with difficulty rescued by the police—now reënforced by a mounted detachment—and hustled into a taxi, through the departing window of which an enraged female thrust her fist. Mr. Augustine Birrell also chose this moment to wander into the scene; but he was not so fortunate. Leaping in natural alarm for a taxi, he fell heavily and sprained his ankle.

When the street was cleared at last and with difficulty, for Mrs. Pankhurst and her following put up a spirited fight, who should make *his* appearance but the Home Secretary! Only one suffragette remained, leaning in utter exhaustion against a wall. Mr. Churchill, as usual, was unable to resist the dramatic gesture. He beckoned a policeman. "Drive that woman away," he said; though he knew her perfectly well to be a Mrs. Cobden-Sanderson, his hostess on several occasions, and an intimate friend of his wife's family. The story went around London and made a bad impression: and a few days later, when the Home Secretary was traveling by rail from London to Bradford, a young man named Franklin very nearly got into his compartment with a horse-whip, and received six weeks' imprisonment for his pains.

The total number of arrests, from "Black Friday" onwards, was now 280. Seventy-five women were actually convicted, among them Mrs. Haverfield—whose offense was leading police horses out of their ranks in the course of what had come to be known as the "Battle of Downing Street."

And then peace descended again. The Liberals had been returned to power, the battle with the Lords had reached its final stage, and Mr. Asquith appeared to be in a receptive mood. It was freely rumored that when the Conciliation Bill, now re-drafted to exclude the £10 occupiers' clause, was introduced once more on May 5, 1911, the Government would do nothing to block its passage. On Census Night—April 2—a large number of women refused to stay at home to receive the census officials, and spent their time in the streets or in one of the four all-night entertainments which the Suffrage Societies had got up for them; but apart from this mild remonstrance the suffragettes were quiet. On May 5, the Bill passed its First Reading by 255 to 88.

Revolution
Ravages Mexico

Michael C. Meyer, William L. Sherman, and Susan M. Deeds

In 1910, after the death of its longtime dictator Porfirio Díaz, Mexico plunged into a decade of revolutionary violence. Presidents came and went, often by coup d'état followed by assassination. Guerrilla bands and peasant armies (such as those of Pancho Villa and Emiliano Zapata) fought tenaciously in both the northern and southern parts of the country. The United States intervened several times, but succeeded only in antagonizing most of the Mexican people.

The cost of this upheaval was enormous, and was little noticed by the outside world, preoccupied as it was by World War I (1914–1918). As historians Michael C. Meyer, William L. Sherman, and Susan M. Deeds explain in their book *The Course of Mexican History*, ordinary Mexican people suffered horribly, and for most there was very little corresponding gain in material prosperity or human dignity. The civil wars in Mexico foreshadowed similar horrors that would occur throughout the Third World during the twentieth century.

T he rapid changes in the presidential chair, the heated debates [of politicians] and the redounding phrases of the Constitution of 1917 surely had little immediate meaning to the Mexican masses. It was the violence of that first revolutionary decade which most dominated their lives and left Mexico a country without charm or gaiety. For every prominent death—Francisco Madero, José María Pino Suárez, Pascual Orozco, Emiliano Zapata, or Venustiano Carranza— a hundred thousand nameless Mexicans also died. By any standard the loss of life was tremendous. Although accurate statistics were not recorded, moderate estimates calculate that between 1.5 and 2 million lost their lives in those terrible ten years. In a country with a population of roughly 15 million in 1910, few families did not directly feel the pain as one in every eight Mexicans was killed. Even Mexico's high birthrate could not offset the carnage of war. The census takers in 1920 counted almost a million fewer Mexicans than they had found only a decade before.

Some of the marching armies were equipped with small medical teams, and Pancho Villa even fitted out a medical train on which battlefield operations could be performed. But medical care was generally so primitive that within a week after a major engagement deaths of wounded often doubled or tripled losses sustained immediately on the battlefield. And in more cases than one likes to recount captured enemy prisoners, both federals and rebels, were executed rather than cared for and fed. Civilian deaths rose into the hundreds of thousands as a result of indiscriminate artillery bombardments and, in some cases, the macabre policy of placing noncombatants before firing squads in pursuit of some imperfectly conceived political or military goal.

It is axiomatic that war elicits not only the worst in man but often psychotic behavior in otherwise normal human beings. While Mexican history does not have names such as Andersonville [a Confederate POW camp during the Civil War], Dachau, Auschwitz, or My Lai to connote atrocity, the cumulative stress of exhaustion and constant exposure to death did produce its psychiatric casualties during the first decade of the Revolution and, on occasion, led to behavior that can only be termed sadistic. The inhumanity visited upon civilians by soldiers became legendary in the folklore of the Revolution. One could pass off stories of mutilated prisoners hanged from trees or telephone posts as exaggerations had not scores of eager photographers captured hundreds of horrifying scenes for posterity. Bodies with hands or legs or genitals cut off were a grotesque caricature of a movement originally motivated by the highest ideals.

Fratricidal horrors so outrageous and so cataclysmic exacted burning resentment and fear in the civilian population. An approaching unit invariably meant trouble for poor, rural Mexicans. The best that could be hoped for was a small band demanding a meal. But often the demands were more outrageous as the war could not lend itself to decency or compassion. In northern Mexico tens of thousands of rural Mexicans joined their middle class and wealthy counterparts in seeking the security of the United States. On a single day in October 1913 some eight thousand refugees crossed the border from Piedras Negras, Coahuila, to Eagle Pass, Texas. While the vast majority left the country with the idea of returning once the situation stabilized, most remained in the United States. But in central and southern Mexico there was virtually no place to run, and the civilian population had no choice but to keep their heads low and resign themselves to the worst. The documentary evidence from the period suggests forcefully that the excesses of war cannot be attributed simply to one side or another. Both federals and rebels were guilty. An excellent community study of a village in Morelos corroborates the contemporary sources. Informants who had lived through the revolutionary period declared that both sides posed an equal threat in this war without scruple.

Fear in the rural areas was challenged only by frustration. Two months spent clearing a field and planting crops under a burning sun could be wiped out in five minutes as an army of five hundred horsemen galloped through the carefully tilled rows of corn and beans. Then they might stop at the one-room hut and confiscate the one milch cow and four turkeys that held out some promise for a slightly less redundant diet in the six months to follow.

There is precious little published evidence upon which to assess the impact of the early Revolution on life in rural Mexico. But the findings of Professor Luis González, in his perceptive and beautifully written account of the Michoacán village of San José de Gracia (population about 1,200 in 1910) are probably not atypical. By 1913, when violence engulfed the region for the first time,

> Don Gregorio Pulido had given up taking local products to Mexico City, for bands of revolutionaries made the roads unsafe for travel. The San José area began to return to the old practice of consuming its own products. Trade declined. Padre Juan's goal of increasing prosperity receded in the distance. From 1913 on, increased poverty was the rule. . . . Everything in San José shifted into reverse. The revolution did no favors for the town or the surrounding *rancherías*. . . . Parties of rebels often came to visit their friends in San José, either to rescue the girls from virginity, or to feast happily on the delicious local cheeses and meats, or to add the fine horses of the region to their own. . . . They summoned all the rich residents and told them how much money in gold coin each was to contribute to the cause. In view of the rifles, no one protested.

The "armies" the peones of rural Mexico saw and feared did not look much like armies. Standard uniforms were unheard of among the rebels, and weapons consisted of whatever could be found or appropriated. Sometimes makeshift insignias identified rank but gave slight clue as to group affiliation. Anonymity served rebel commanders well as it left them unconcerned with the niceties of accountability, but it caused problems for the rural *pacífico* [noncombatant] wanting to respond correctly to the question, "Are you a Huertista, a Villista or a Carrancista?"

For Mexican women the Revolution often had a degrading personal meaning. With husbands, fathers, and sons serving somewhere in the ranks, they were subjected to the terror and indignity of wanton assault. But many did not mope or simply stay home to become the target of rape. Freeing themselves from the eternal task of grinding corn, thousands joined the Revolution and served the rebel armies in the capacity of spies and arms smugglers. So active were the women in smuggling ammunition across the border in Ciudad Juárez that the United States Customs Bureau was forced to employ teams of female agents to search the undergarments of suspicious, heavy-looking ladies returning from shopping sprees in El Paso.

Perhaps the most noteworthy role assumed by women was that of *soldadera*. The soldaderas were more than camp followers. They provided feminine companionship, to be sure, but because neither the federal army nor the rebel armies provided commissary service, they foraged for food, cooked, washed, and, in the absence of more competent medical service, nursed the wounded and buried the dead. Both sides were dependent upon them, and in 1912 a federal battalion actually threatened mutiny when the secretary of war ordered that the women could not be taken along on a certain maneuver. The order was rescinded. Not infrequently, the soldaderas actually served in the ranks, sometimes with a baby slung in a *rebozo* or a young child clinging to their skirts. Women holding officer ranks were not uncommon in the rebel armies.

The soldadera endured the hardships of the campaign without special consideration. While the men were generally mounted, the women most often walked, carrying bedding, pots and pans, food, firearms, ammunition, and children. Often the men would gallop on ahead, engage the enemy in battle, and then rest. By the time the women caught up, they were ready to move again, and the soldadera would simply trudge on. Losing her special "Juan" in battle, she would wait an appropriately decent period and then take on another, to prepare his favorite meal and share his bed. Not a few gave birth in makeshift military camps, and some even on the field of battle.

The hard life of the soldadera was a relative thing. A fascinating oral history of a Yaqui woman from Sonora who was deported to Yucatán, cut her hands raw on the henequen plants, and saw her babies die from lack of adequate care, reveals that she was thrilled to become a soldadera. She later recalled that "her personal misery decreased by impressive leaps and bounds. . . . At no point during the next several years did she view her life as anything but a tremendous improvement after Yucatán."

While, with the protection of anonymity, men could treat women as virtual slaves, public displays were more often marked by the type of chivalric indulgence so long identified with the Hispanic tradition. One traveler to Mexico City in 1918 was especially amused by the sign he found posted in the streetcar:

GENTLEMEN: When you see a lady standing on her feet you will not find
it possible to remain sitting with tranquility. Your education will forbid
you to do so.

GENERAL MANAGER OF THE RAILWAYS

In an oblique and unintended sort of way the Revolution contributed to the emancipation of the Mexican woman. As the shortage of adult males in the cities contracted the labor supply, women
began to make some inroads into the business world. At first their
contributions consisted of the simplest type of work in the stores,
but once escaped from the confines of the house they would not be
persuaded easily to return. In Yucatán, at least, a concerted policy
of women's liberation was initiated by Governor Salvador Alvarado.
A farsighted revolutionary, Alvarado declared: "I have always believed that if we do not elevate the role of women we will find it impossible to build a country." Not only did he lower the age of majority of women from age thirty-one to twenty-one, but he actively
began placing women in open positions in state government. In 1916
he sponsored a Congreso Femenino in Mérida, Yucatán. Four major
themes were discussed: the social means to be employed to remove
the yoke of tradition; the role of primary education in women's liberation; the arts and occupations the state should support to prepare
the women for a fuller life; and the social functions women should
employ to contribute toward a better society.

The Revolution, to be sure, had different meanings to different
Mexicans during those years of greatest violence. But a most recurrent theme is the fear of the leva, the institution that snatched away
the male population for service in the military. . . .

Edith O'Shaughnessy, the wife of the United States chargé in
Mexico City, described the leva in her memoirs.

> I was startled as I watched the faces of some conscripts marching to the
> station today. On so many was impressed something desperate and de-
> spairing. They have a fear of . . . eternal separation from their loved ones.
> They often have to be tied in the transport wagons. There is no system
> about conscription here—the press gang takes any likely looking per-
> son. Fathers of families, only sons of widows, as well as the unattached,
> are enrolled, besides women to cook and grind in the powder mills.

Among those who suffered most were foreign residents of Mexico. Because the Revolution was in part a reaction against Diaz's
coddling of foreign interests, not a few revolutionaries took out their
wrath on the foreign community. Cast in the role of exploiters, foreign oilmen and miners were forced to pay not only taxes to the government but tribute to various groups of rebels and bribes to local
bandits. But other frugal and industrious foreigners, without the
slightest claim to exploitation, suffered worse. After a battle for con-

trol of Torreón in 1911 over two hundred peaceful Chinese residents
were murdered simply because they were Chinese. A few years later
Spanish citizens in Torreón were expelled from the country and their
property confiscated by Pancho Villa. Colonies of United States
Mormons in Chihuahua and Sonora were terrorized to such an extent that they finally packed up those belongings they could carry
and left their adopted home.

City dwellers, too, were subject to the ravishments of war. Almost
all of the larger cities in the country hosted battles at some time between 1910 and 1920, and some witnessed three or four major engagements and were turned into debris before the decade ran its
course. The sight of burning buildings, the sound of wailing ambu-
lances, and the nausea of mass burials brought home in tangible
terms the most immediate meaning of the Revolution. Starvation
reached major proportions in Mexico City, Guadalajara, and Puebla.

The construction boom of the Porfiriato [late nineteenth-century
Mexico] ended shortly after the outbreak of hostilities. While a few
unfinished public projects were completed, for the most part those
workmen who could be spared from the ranks were kept busy clearing debris, repairing damaged structures, knocking down gutted
buildings, and trying to put the railroad lines back in operation.

The early Revolution took a terrible toll in education. Hundreds
of schools were destroyed and hundreds of others abandoned. In the
Federal District alone the number of primary schools in operation
declined from 332 in 1910 to 270 ten years later. The story repeated
itself in city after city, town after town. Total primary school attendance in the country declined from 880,000 to 740,000 in the same
ten-year period.

The Great War, 1914–1918

PREFACE

World War I (or the Great War, as it was often known before World War II) was the pivotal event in twentieth-century European and global history.

Although there had been local wars and wars between various great powers during the nineteenth century, not since 1815 had there been a general war between *all* of the major powers on the Continent. Nor had Europe seen a successful revolution in a major country since the French Revolution of 1789. Despite the rise of national states in Germany and Italy, and despite the retreat of the Ottoman Empire from almost all of the Balkan Peninsula, nineteenth-century European history had been an era in which peace and stability were more "normal" than war and upheaval. The truly revolutionary changes that had occurred in the course of the nineteenth century had been the spread of industrialization across Europe, the rise of a modern class system of economic and social relationships, the general trend toward democratic self-government, and the tremendous extension of European (and American) power around the globe. None of these changes had involved major wars or sweeping political revolutions; change, however rapid, had been more evolutionary than abrupt.

In 1914 that evolutionary pattern changed radically. A conflict in the Balkans spiraled out of control after it was mishandled by several of the great powers whose interests were directly at stake. Within weeks all but one of the Continental great powers was at war, and within a year the final holdout (Italy) was also in the fray. Throughout Europe, enthusiastic crowds greeted the outbreak of war as a cleansing stroke that would result in a quick settling of scores with rival nations and would be gloriously over within weeks or months. But the war turned into a stalemate. The modern weapons that each side deployed ensured that the bloodshed was ghastly without either side being able to win a decisive victory.

In 1917 the weakest of the great powers, Russia, collapsed, its government and its society unable to bear the strain. So thorough was the breakdown of Russia's civil society that no significant political group from before the revolution was able to take control of the state. Power fell to the most ruthless and daring leader of all—the radical leftist Vladimir Ilich Lenin, whose tiny Bolshevik Party had exerted almost no influence in Russia before the czar's downfall (an event for which the Bolsheviks could claim absolutely no credit). Lenin and the faction-ridden Bolsheviks whom he browbeat into taking action succeeded only because of the extreme desperation of Russia's ordinary people—hungry workers in the capital city of Petrograd (later Leningrad and now, again, St. Petersburg), soldiers who knew that further resistance to the German invaders was useless, and peasants determined to seize land for themselves. And the Bolsheviks held power because they—or rather Lenin—alone had the ruthlessness to give in to Germany's extortionate peace terms in order to stop the fighting on the eastern front and then to clamp upon seething, civil war–torn Russia a terroristic dictatorship.

World War I had fateful results for twentieth-century history. Defeated and humiliated Germans nursed their grievances for more than a decade but eventually turned to a leader who promised to reverse the war's outcome and to restore a greater German empire: Adolf Hitler, who himself had been an obscure enlisted man during the Great War. The Soviet Russian regime of Lenin and his successor, Joseph Stalin, would clearly never have emerged without Russia having suffered so grievously in the Great War. The Western Allies, who imposed the Treaty of Versailles, would almost certainly never have prevailed on the battlefield had not the United States intervened in the conflict in 1917; yet having contributed crucially to the war's outcome, the American public became disillusioned with Europe's quarrels and assumed no responsibility for enforcing the war's outcome. Nothing in the wartime experience convinced Europeans that their continent must substitute national reconciliation and open markets for the prewar closed economies and hostile alliances. Many historians consider the Second World War of 1939–1945 simply a renewal of the Great War after a troubled, twenty-year truce.

The Coming of
World War I

Martin Gilbert

Repeated international crises punctuated the years after 1900, as the rival blocs of Europe's most powerful nations (Germany and Austria-Hungary; France, Russia, and Great Britain) maneuvered for advantage and built up their military and naval might. But always one side or the other backed down without pressing matters to the point at which the great powers felt driven to go to war with each other.

On June 28, 1914, the heir to the Austro-Hungarian throne, Archduke Franz Ferdinand, was assassinated by a Serbian terrorist in Sarajevo, the capital of the Austro-Hungarian province of Bosnia-Herzegovina. The assassination plot had been amateurish, and the conspirators (a band of students, indirectly egged on by a faction in the Serbian military) had almost failed. Many in the Austro-Hungarian government were secretly relieved that the irascible and unpredictable Franz Ferdinand would not succeed to the crown. But the Austro-Hungarian authorities feared that Serbian nationalism threatened the multinational empire's stability, and they decided to use the assassination as an excuse to crush their small, upstart southern neighbor. Even though a secret government investigation showed no evidence implicating Serbian officials in the plot, the Austro-Hungarian foreign office prepared a stiff ultimatum to Belgrade—so stiff that it was sure to be rejected. The aged Austro-Hungarian ruler, Franz Joseph, was persuaded to accept this course of action, even though it was known that Russia, Serbia's ally, would not likely fail to respond to this challenge. Unwisely, Germany gave Austria-Hungary a "blank check," authorizing its ally to deal with Serbia as it saw fit.

British historian Martin Gilbert explains how, between July 23 and August 1, 1914, this crisis rapidly escalated into a full-scale war be-

Excerpted from *A History of the Twentieth Century*, vol. 1, by Martin Gilbert. Copyright © 1997 by Martin Gilbert. Reprinted with permission in the U.S. from HarperCollins Publishers, Inc. and in Canada from Stoddart Publishing Co., Limited, Toronto.

tween Europe's two great power blocs—a titanic struggle that many believe opened the way for so many of the disasters that would rack global history for the rest of the twentieth century.

![horizontal divider bar]

Franz Josef had accepted the terms of the ultimatum three days after the Austrian Council of Ministers had approved it. The terms, as delivered in Belgrade on the evening of July 23, were wide-ranging. Linking the Belgrade government with the assassination—something that the secret report had specifically denied—the ultimatum consisted of a total of fifteen demands. The Serbian government must commit itself to condemnation of anti-Austrian propaganda. There must be a joint Austro-Serbian commission to investigate the Archduke's murder. There must be a Serbian army order condemning the Serbian military involvement with the murders. There must also be a firm Serbian promise of no further Serbian intrigue in Bosnia. Serbia would also have to give an undertaking to punish anyone who circulated anti-Austrian propaganda, either in schools or in the various nationalist societies. In addition, Austrian officials would participate in the judicial process, and in the process of punishment, of those connected with the plot.

Whether one sovereign State could accept such stern demands from another was much debated. [British foreign secretary] Edward Grey, one of the arbiters of the Liberal conscience, went so far as to call it 'the most formidable document that was ever addressed from one State to another'. In strictest secrecy the Russian government agreed to the mobilization of thirteen army corps to be used 'eventually' against Austria-Hungary, should Austria declare war on Serbia. In a public announcement the Russian government declared that Russia 'cannot remain indifferent' to the Austro-Serbian crisis. There was a new-found scepticism among British diplomats that, if the war widened beyond the Balkans, Britain would be able to stay clear of it. 'We shall be lucky,' one British diplomat wrote to his wife two hours before the Austrian ultimatum was due to expire, 'if we get out of this without the long-dreaded European war, a general bust-up in fact'.

Anticipating a Serbian rejection of the ultimatum, Franz Josef ordered partial mobilization of the Austro-Hungarian forces, to start three days later; even partial mobilization was a process that, given the size of the Habsburg empire and the complexity of its war machinery, would take sixteen days to complete.

Serbia also mobilized, at three o'clock on the afternoon of July 25; but the Serbian government understood that even if Russia were in due course to enter the war against Austria-Hungary, Serbia's ability to resist an onslaught across her exposed eastern frontier, or even across the Danube against the capital, was limited. She therefore replied to the ultimatum in conciliatory tone. Everything demanded of her was agreed; the only qualification regarded the Austrian demand—certainly the most controversial of all—that Austrian officials would participate in the judicial process, and in the process of punishment, of those connected with the assassination. This demand, the Serbians asked, should be submitted to the International Tribunal at The Hague. If the tribunal accepted its legality, then Serbia would agree to it.

In Austria-Hungary it was assumed that it was only a matter of days before war with Serbia. 'For the first time in thirty years,' Sigmund Freud wrote in a letter to a friend, 'I feel myself to be an Austrian and feel like giving this not very hopeful Empire another chance. Morale is excellent everywhere. Also the liberating effect of courageous action, and the secure prop of Germany, contribute a great deal to this.'

It was the Russian Tsar [Nicholas II] who took the initiative in trying to turn the Serbian reply into the basis of a reduction of tension and a withdrawal from the brink of conflict. The Tsar's proposal, made on July 27, was that negotiations should begin on the basis of the Serbian reply. The Austrian government rejected this proposal; they wanted full compliance to their ultimatum, without even that one condition, or they would go to war.

In every European capital the diplomatic manoeuvres were followed from day to day, and with a constantly changing focus. In Paris, on July 27, [writer] André Gide noted in his journal 'a certain easing of the strain this morning. People are relieved and at the same time disappointed to hear that Serbia is giving in'. But on the following day, while at Dieppe, he recorded that the hotel buses were 'loaded with the trunks of departing guests. Everyone expects the worst'.

The British government, like the Tsar, sought some way whereby talking rather than fighting would follow the Austrian ultimatum and the Serbian reply. What concerned Britain was the spread of the conflict beyond the Balkans, and the drawing in of Russia's ally France, exposing Britain to the need to support—or to abandon—France in its hour of need. The lack of any binding alliance with France meant that the British parliament might have the power, or the Cabinet the will, to insist upon neutrality in the case of a German attack on France. But public opinion in Britain could easily be roused by any German action against France to demand an active British response. To avert such a development, and the possible drawing in of Britain to a continental war, the British government proposed that day a four-Power conference of Britain, France, Italy and Germany, 'for the purpose of discovering an issue which would prevent complications'.

The Kaiser, fired up by the thought of a swift defeat of Russia, and oblivious to what might happen to his own country, to his rule and his dynasty if there were to be such 'complications'—and with them a two-front war—refused to accept the British call for a conference. A reply was returned from Berlin to London that such a conference was 'not practicable'. Even the British understood at last that despite their lack of treaty entanglements they too might be drawn in to the conflict. On the day of the German rejection of a conference, the British War Office instructed a senior general to take immediate measures to guard what were characterized as 'all vulnerable points' in southern Britain. Armed guards were also put on ammunitions dumps and oil storage depots throughout Britain.

In Berlin, the German government, whose pledge of support for Austria had been the crucial factor in the initial Austrian resolve to issue an ultimatum, now pressed the Austrians to strike at Serbia before any wider complications ensued. 'We are urgently advised to act at once and face the world with a *fait accompli*,' the Austrian ambassador in Berlin informed his masters in Vienna by telegram on July 28. When the Austrians pointed out to the Germans that it would be another two weeks before the Austrian mobilization was completed, and before an attack on Serbia could begin in optimum military conditions, the Germans pressed Austria not to wait so long. The mood in Berlin was clear and bellicose, but not untinged with panic; Austria must crush Serbia before the Russians could respond, and before Germany herself could be drawn in—as a result, not of her national interest, but of her alliance with Austria.

The mood in Vienna was for war with Serbia, so much so that on July 28 the British ambassador in Vienna, a diplomat of wide experience, informed London that 'postponement or prevention of war with Serbia would undoubtedly be a great disappointment in this country, which has gone wild with joy at the prospect of war'. The war envisaged by the Austrians, and causing the joy, was perceived as a swift and victorious one, more like a colonial expedition (Austria-Hungary having no colonies) than a struggle between equals; Serbia was a small, vexatious State with pretensions of grandeur that must be 'taught a lesson' once and for all, and if Serbian territory along the Austrian southern border were to be annexed as a result, so much the better.

There remained the question of how the Austrians would respond to the Serbian reply to their ultimatum. The first Austrian instinct was to withdraw their ambassador to Serbia, Baron Giesl, from Belgrade, as a sign of their extreme displeasure. For their part, the Serbs, fearing an immediate Austrian attack across the Danube on

Belgrade, withdrew their government to the southern city of Nis and their General Staff to the town of Kragujevac, seventy miles south of Belgrade. In a train approaching Budapest, Hungarian detectives arrested the Serbian Chief-of-Staff, General Putnik, who was on his way by train back to Serbia, and was being subjected to hostile demonstrations at the stations through which he passed.

Putnik had been taking the waters at a Bohemian spa [in Austria-Hungary], for the sake of his health, which was not good. After his arrest in the train he was held in Budapest under double guard with fixed bayonets. At Franz Josef's insistence, however, he was released, and escorted to the frontier with a considerable show of respect due to a military leader of a neighbouring State, and the victor of two Balkan Wars (an asthmatic, he was said to have gone through the Turkish campaign in his carpet slippers).

General Putnik's detention in Budapest, and his return to Serbia, caused a stir in the European press, and first consternation and then relief in Serbia; but the question that came to dominate all political and newspaper speculation was the Serbian reply to Austria. Did such an essentially conciliatory reply really provide a cause for war? Suddenly even the Kaiser had his doubts, which he expressed in private, and in his own colourful prose, on the morning of July 28, when finally he read the full text of the Serbian reply (of three days earlier). Reading it side by side with the full text of the Austrian ultimatum, he could see no reason why Austria should embark on a full-scale war. 'A great moral victory for Vienna,' he wrote in the margin of his copy of the Serbian reply, 'but with it every reason for war is removed and Giesl ought to remain quietly in Belgrade. On the strength of this we should never have ordered mobilization.'

Having blown hot for so many days, the Kaiser suddenly blew cold. A full-scale Austrian invasion of Serbia was not needed; all that was necessary, he wrote, was that 'as a visible *satisfaction d'honneur* for Austria, the Austrian army should temporarily occupy Belgrade as a pledge'. Then negotiations could begin to end the brief military conflict. 'I am convinced,' the Kaiser wrote to von Jagow [an official in the German foreign office], 'that on the whole the wishes of the Danube monarchy [Austria-Hungary] have been acceded to. The few reservations that Serbia makes in regard to individual points can in my opinion be well cleared up by negotiations. But it contains the announcement *orbi et urbi* [to the whole world] of a capitulation of the most humiliating kind, and with it every reason for war is removed.'

It was too late for such conciliatory counsel. At noon that day, scarcely an hour after the Kaiser penned these un-bellicose words, Austria declared war on Serbia, confident of German support if the war widened. The declaration of war was sent by [Austro-Hungarian]

Count Berchtold, not, as would have been usual, to the Serbian Foreign Ministry at Belgrade, but to the Serbian General Staff at Kragujevac, informing the Serbians that, as from the time of the despatch of the telegram from Vienna, 11.10 in the morning on July 28, the Royal Government of Serbia not having replied in a satisfactory manner to the Note which was sent to them on July 23, the Imperial and Royal Government finds itself obliged to provide for the safeguarding of its rights and interests, and for this purpose to have recourse to force of arms. Austria-Hungary therefore regards herself from this moment as in a state of war with Serbia.'

This telegram reached the Serbian General Staff one hour and forty minutes later. Although Serbian mobilization was not yet complete, strenuous efforts had been made to provide a military force that could defend Belgrade from any sudden attack. There were those who, watching the first moments of the Austro-Serbian war from afar, believed that had the Austrians launched an attack on Belgrade at once, they could have captured the city with a single battalion. But even in those opening hours, as many as 20,000 Serb soldiers and volunteers were being mustered outside the city, and on the day of the Austrian declaration of war a force of 10,000 men and 24 cannon was within marching distance of the capital. The Austrians hesitated to strike, and by their hesitation lost a chance to make a spectacular conquest, though whether they could have held Belgrade with the forces then available to them, once the Serb defence force had arrived, was an open question. It was not one which the Austrian General Staff wished to put to the test.

Serbia, weakened as she was by the bloodletting of the two Balkan wars, and short as she was of war material which was still in the process of being manufactured, mostly abroad, had the incentive of the defence of their native soil, and of the capital, as a spur to tenacious action. The Austrians, recognizing this, decided to strike instead across the River Drina, which had served for more than fifty miles as the border between Austrian-annexed Bosnia-Herzegovina and Serbia. It was the land across the Drina that Austria hoped to annex from Serbia, thus enlarging her Bosnian province.

An ambitious plan had been devised in Vienna, whereby, avoiding any attack on Belgrade, the Austrian army would cross the Drina and advance into the centre of Serbia, seizing the two principal towns of the region, Valievo and Kragujevac, and cutting Belgrade off from the south of the country. Austria, for all its talk of war, and its ultimatum, was not ready to launch this attack at the time of the declaration of war on July 28. It was to be more than a week before any forward military move could be attempted. This gave the Serbs invaluable time to prepare their defences and their strategy. Meanwhile, the Powers were no longer content to watch and warn; following the Austrian declaration of war, each Power had begun to contemplate military action of its own.

The Austrian declaration of war, leading as it did to no military advance and no battles on the ground, and to no immediate loss of Serb territory, did not necessarily call for the rushing forward of new combatants. Russia and Germany, despite their continuing preparations, were not inexorably bound to come to blows, and were far from ready to do so. In what way would the war widen? Winston Churchill [then First Lord of the Admiralty], on whom the responsibility for Britain's naval war would rest, wrote to his wife on learning of the Austrian declaration of war on Serbia: 'I wondered whether those stupid Kings and Emperors could not assemble together and revivify kingship by saving the nations from hell but we all drift on in a kind of dull cataleptic trance. As if it was somebody else's operation.'

Following up this late-night thought, on the morning of July 29 Churchill proposed in the British Cabinet that a conference should be convened of all the European sovereigns, who should 'be brought together for the sake of peace'. It was a central fact of European life that the Kaiser and the Tsar, and King George V and the Tsar, and the Kaiser and King George V, were kinsmen; and that their family links were those of social and personal friendship. Surely families would not go to war with each other, however much their public opinions might be roused to nationalistic fervour?

On July 29, the day after the Austrian declaration of war on Serbia, and the day of Churchill's suggestion for a conference of European royalty, the Kaiser's brother, Prince Henry of Prussia, who was at that moment enjoying the pleasures of yachting in British waters, called on his cousin King George V at Buckingham Palace. The King told him, so the Prince reported to his brother in Berlin, 'We shall all try to keep out of this, and shall remain neutral.' When Admiral Tirpitz [head of the German navy] told the Kaiser that he doubted that Britain would in fact remain neutral, the Kaiser, basing himself on his brother's report, told the admiral: 'I have the word of a King, and that is good enough for me.' But even if George V had given his word, which seems unlikely (he certainly had no constitutional right to do so), that would only serve to liberate Germany to attack France without any British reaction. It would not prevent the entry of Germany into a European war, only limit the repercussions of German entry.

The attraction to the Kaiser of a war limited in this way made a Franco-German conflict all the more likely. No longer fearing a British intervention, Germany could contemplate defeating France first, and then turning on Russia. This had been the basis of General von Schlieffen's plan a decade earlier. [Schlieffen had prepared Germany's military plan to be followed if a war broke out.] The war would be widened in the expectation of then containing, and winning, it. But in widening the war by drawing in France, the conflict would in reality be on the verge of an even greater extension. British neutrality, so confidently presumed by the Kaiser, and so keenly hoped for by a majority in the Cabinet room in London, was not the outcome which British public opinion and street fervour, worked up by the mass-circulation newspapers, seemed to favour. There was also a wild card: the German military plan for the swift defeat of France depended upon a rapid movement of German forces through Belgium.

The route through Belgium had been chosen by General von Schlieffen to create the greatest surprise for France, and to by-pass the line of French fortresses defending the eastern approaches. Belgium was unlikely to put up a prolonged fight against the overwhelmingly strong forces of Germany; but her neutrality was protected by a treaty dating back more than sixty years [to 1839]. One of the signatories of that all-but-forgotten treaty was Britain. In striking at France across Belgian soil, the Kaiser had to convince himself that Britain would not honour a Treaty to which she had affixed her seal.

Any true, or only partial, understanding of the realities even of a limited war was eclipsed in the European public mind by the growing fervour of the mass of the population, themselves drawn from every segment of each society, from working men whose traditional ideology was antiwar, to shopkeepers and professional men and women whose sons would be among the first to be sent to the war fronts. When, during July 29, the German Crown Prince arrived at his palace in Berlin by car, a British diplomat who happened to witness the scene reported to London: 'The crowd cheered wildly. There was an indescribable feeling of excitement in the air. It was evident that some great event was about to happen'.

That 'great event' was imminent. During July 29 the Austrian naval flotilla on the Danube opened fire on Belgrade. The Tsar panicked. 'To try to avoid such a calamity as a European war,' he telegraphed (in English) to the Kaiser, 'I beg you in the name of our old friendship to do what you can to stop your allies from going too far.' But those allies, Austria-Hungary, were not to be restrained, even if the Kaiser felt able to try to restrain them. His reply—'I am exerting my utmost influence to induce the Austrians to arrive at a satisfactory understanding with you'—showed how far he was out of touch with the warlike mood in Austria to which, less than three weeks earlier, he had himself contributed so much; and ignored, too, the warlike mood in Berlin, to which he had also been a principal contributor.

The Tsar was doing his utmost to keep Russia out of the war. That same day, July 29, he suggested to the Kaiser that the whole 'Austro-

Serbian' problem, towards which both Germany and Russia had contributed their exacerbatory efforts, should be handed over to the International Court at The Hague—the very body which Serbia had
sought to enlist as the arbiter of its sole disputed item in the Austrian
ultimatum. The Kaiser was also casting about for means of keeping
out of the war, now that Austrian guns had opened fire on the Serbian capital. His idea, which he communicated late that evening to
the Tsar, was that Russia should 'remain a spectator of the Austro-
Serbian conflict', thereby sparing Europe 'the most horrible war she
has ever witnessed'.

A note of stark realism had entered into the correspondence between the two imperial rulers at the very moment when their respective countries were about to hurl themselves at each other's
throats. The Tsar, to prove his pacific intentions, cancelled Russia's
order for general mobilization. But the German General Staff refused
a surprise suggestion by the Kaiser that Germany respond in similar
vein. War Offices with their plans and hierarchies of command, not
palaces with their volatile sovereigns, were in command of the situation in St Petersburg and Berlin. The Tsar was quickly prevailed
upon to augment the mobilization measures that he had just reduced,
for fear, his advisers insisted, that unless he did so, and brought yet
more Russians under arms, the Polish provinces of the Russian Empire would be at risk of a German annexation. [Before World War I,
there was no independent Poland, and Germany and Russia shared
a common border running through what is now central Poland.]

'Monarchy and privilege and pride will have it out before they die
—at what a cost!' the American ambassador in London, Walter H.
Page, wrote to President Wilson on July 29. 'If they do have a general war they will set back the march of progress in Europe as to set
the day forward for American leadership. Men here see that clearly.
Even in this kingdom every ship is ready, every crew on duty, and
every officer of the Admiralty office in London sleeps with a telephone by his bed which he expects to ring, and the telegraph men are
at their instruments every minute.'

Page added: 'It's the Slav and the German. Each wants his day, and
neither has got beyond the stage of tooth and claw.' Page's wife had just
spoken to Prince Henry of Prussia 'who wishes to fight'— Page informed Wilson—'who talks like a medieval man, and so loves the blood
of his enemies that, if he can first kill enough of them, he is willing to
be whipped. He went home [to Germany] last night.'

One last struggle took place in Berlin between those who felt the
situation could still be restricted to an Austro-Serbian war, and those
who anticipated, and did not shrink from, a much wider conflict. On
the morning of July 31, [German chancellor] Bethmann-Hollweg,
once peace-loving, next bellicose, and then peace-loving (or war-

fearing) again, telegraphed to Count Berchtold in Vienna, pressing the Austrians not to mobilize against Russia. That same morning, however, the Chief of the German General Staff, General von Moltke, in a message to his opposite number in Vienna, advised the Austrians to mobilize against Russia at once. 'Who rules in Berlin, Moltke or Bethmann?' was Berchtold's wry question. The answer was that von Moltke ruled in Berlin. In vain did the German industrialist Walther Rathenau write in the *Berliner Tageblatt* that day: 'The government has left us in no doubt of the fact that Germany is intent on remaining loyal to her old ally. Without the protection of this loyalty, Austria could not have ventured on the step she has taken. Such a question as the participation of Austrian officials in investigating the Serbian plot is no reason for an international war.'

Two years later, Rathenau recalled the mood of July 31 in Berlin. 'Rejoicing in July sunshine,' he wrote, 'the prosperous and happy populace of Berlin responded to the summons of war. Brightly clad, with flashing eyes, the living and those consecrated to death felt themselves to be at the zenith of vital power and political existence. . . . I could not share in the pride of the sacrifice of power. Nevertheless, this delirious exaltation seemed to me a dance of death, the overture to a doom which I had foreseen would be dark and dreadful.'

That day, confident of active German military support, Austria mobilized. The German government then made the first of its moves in direct support of Austria, sending an ultimatum to Russia to 'cease every war measure against us and Austria-Hungary' within twelve hours. Russia rejected this ultimatum.

The Kaiser and his General Staff prepared to go to war against Russia. One obstacle remained, the ten-year-old alliance between France and Russia. Germany therefore asked France to state categorically that she would remain neutral in the event of a war between Germany and Russia. But France declined to abandon her alliance with Russia, or to give Germany a free hand in marching eastward. Within hours, the orders went out to more than four million Frenchmen to make their way to their barracks.

In Paris, the socialist leader and parliamentarian Jean Jaurès had called repeatedly for the solidarity of all European socialists against war. On July 31 he was assassinated by a French nationalist fanatic. Fanaticism was becoming usual. In Munich that day, among a crowd clamouring for war, and for the chance to serve in the German army, Adolf Hitler was photographed gesticulating, hat in hand. In Paris, the crowds cheered as the cavalrymen rode by, and enthusiastic cries of 'To Berlin!' rent the air.

In the Trenches
of World War I

Erich Maria Remarque

Most Europeans expected that the war that broke out in August 1914 would be short and glorious—that their country would overwhelm its enemies before Christmas. Hundreds of thousands of young men enthusiastically volunteered.

What they found was a "sausage grinder" war that, in northern France and later in northern Italy, bogged down in a horrible slaughter between armies dug into trenches and pounding each other with heavy artillery, machine guns, and poison gas. (In eastern Europe there was also a terrible bloodletting, but the German, Austro-Hungarian, and Russian armies were somewhat more mobile.) Before it all ended, approximately 10 million combatants would die.

Erich Maria Remarque survived the war to become an outspoken pacifist. In 1928 he published a novel based on what he had seen. Translated into English as *All Quiet on the Western Front,* it tells the story of a young German volunteer of 1914 who stays alive until October 1918, just weeks before the end. It has always been considered one of the greatest war novels of all time, and its graphic description of trench warfare is an important historical document in its own right.

Attack, counter-attack, charge, repulse—these are words, but what things they signify! We have lost a good many men, mostly recruits. Reinforcements have again been sent up to our sector. They are one of the new regiments, composed almost entirely of young fellows just called up. They have had hardly any training, and are sent into the field with only a theoretical knowledge. They do know what a hand-grenade is, it is true, but they have very little idea of cover, and what is most important of all, have no eye for it. A fold in the ground has to be quite eighteen inches high before they can see it.

Although we need reinforcement, the recruits give us almost more trouble than they are worth. They are helpless in this grim fighting area, they fall like flies. Modern trench-warfare demands knowledge and experience; a man must have a feeling for the contours of the ground, an ear for the sound and character of the shells, must be able to decide beforehand where they will drop, how they will burst, and how to shelter from them.

The young recruits of course know none of these things. They get killed simply because they hardly can tell shrapnel from high-explosive, they are mown down because they are listening anxiously to the roar of the big coal-boxes falling in the rear, and miss the light, piping whistle of the low spreading daisy-cutters. They flock together like sheep instead of scattering, and even the wounded are shot down like hares by the airmen.

Their pale turnip faces, their pitiful clenched hands, the fine courage of these poor devils, the desperate charges and attacks made by the poor brave wretches, who are so terrified that they dare not cry out loudly, but with battered chests, with torn bellies, arms and legs only whimper softly for their mothers and cease as soon as one looks at them.

Their sharp, downy, dead faces have the awful expressionlessness of dead children.

It brings a lump into the throat to see how they go over, and run and fall. A man would like to spank them, they are so stupid, and to take them by the arm and lead them away from here where they have no business to be. They wear grey coats and trousers and boots, but for most of them the uniform is far too big, it hangs on their limbs, their shoulders are too narrow, their bodies too slight; no uniform was ever made to these childish measurements.

Between five and ten recruits fall to every old hand.

A surprise gas-attack carries off a lot of them. They have not yet learned what to do. We found one dug-out full of them, with blue heads and black lips. Some of them in a shell-hole took their masks off too soon; they did not know that the gas lies longest in the hollows; when they saw others on top without masks they pulled theirs off too and swallowed enough to scorch their lungs. Their condition is hopeless, they choke to death with haemorrhages and suffocation.

In one part of the trench I suddenly run into Himmelstoss. We dive into the same dug-out. Breathless we are all lying one beside the other waiting for the charge.

When we run out again, although I am very excited, I suddenly think: "Where's Himmelstoss?" Quickly I jump back into the dug-out and find him with a small scratch lying in a corner pretending to be wounded. His face looks sullen. He is in a panic; he is new to it too. But it makes me mad that the young recruits should be out there and he here.

"Get out!" I spit.

He does not stir, his lips quiver, his moustache twitches.

"Out!" I repeat.

He draws up his legs, crouches back against the wall, and shows his teeth like a cur.

I seize him by the arm and try to pull him up. He barks.

This is too much for me. I grab him by the neck and shake him like a sack, his head jerks from side to side.

"You lump, will you get out—you hound, you skunk, sneak out of it, would you?" His eye becomes glassy, I knock his head against the wall—"You cow"—I kick him in the ribs—"You swine"—I push him toward the door and shove him out head first.

Another wave of our attack has just come up. A lieutenant is with them. He sees us and yells: "Forward, forward, join in, follow." And the word of command does what all my banging could not. Himmelstoss hears the order, looks round him as if awakened, and follows on.

I come after and watch him go over. Once more he is the smart Himmelstoss of the parade-ground, he has even outstripped the lieutenant and is far ahead.

Bombardment, barrage, curtain-fire, mines, gas, tanks, machine-guns, hand-grenades—words, words, but they hold the horror of the world.

Our faces are encrusted, our thoughts are devastated, we are weary to death; when the attack comes we shall have to strike many of the men with our fists to waken them and make them come with us—our eyes are burnt, our hands are torn, our knees bleed, our elbows are raw.

How long has it been? Weeks—months—years? Only days. We see time pass in the colourless faces of the dying, we cram food into us, we run, we throw, we shoot, we kill, we lie about, we are feeble and spent, and nothing supports us but the knowledge that there are still feebler, still more spent, still more helpless ones there who, with staring eyes, look upon us as gods that escape death many times.

In the few hours of rest we teach them. "There, see that waggle-top? That's a mortar coming. Keep down, it will go clean over. But if it comes this way, then run for it. You can run from a mortar."

We sharpen their ears to the malicious, hardly audible buzz of the smaller shells that are not easily distinguished. They must pick them out from the general din by their insect-like hum—we explain to them that these are far more dangerous than the big ones that can be heard long beforehand.

We show them how to take cover from aircraft, how to simulate a dead man when one is overrun in an attack, how to time hand-grenades so that they explode half a second before hitting the ground; we teach them to fling themselves into holes as quick as lightning be-

Young men who volunteered for service during WW I were unprepared for the horrors of trench warfare.

fore the shells with instantaneous fuses; we show them how to clean up a trench with a handful of bombs; we explain the difference between the fuse-length of the enemy bombs and our own; we put them wise to the sound of gas shells;—show them all the tricks that can save them from death.

They listen, they are docile —but when it begins again, in their excitement they do everything wrong.

Haie Westhus drags off with a great wound in his back through which the lung pulses at every breath. I can only press his hand; "It's all up, Paul," he groans and he bites his arm because of the pain.

We see men living with their skulls blown open; we see soldiers run with their two feet cut off, they stagger on their splintered stumps into the next shell-hole; a lance-corporal crawls a mile and a half on his hands dragging his smashed knee after him; another goes to the dressing station and over his clasped hands bulge his intestines; we see men without mouths, without jaws, without faces; we find one man who has held the artery of his arm in his teeth for two hours in order not to bleed to death. The sun goes down, night comes, the shells whine, life is at an end.

Still the little piece of convulsed earth in which we lie is held. We have yielded no more than a few hundred yards of it as a prize to the enemy. But on every yard there lies a dead man.

We have just been relieved. The wheels roll beneath us, we stand dully, and when the call "Mind—wire" comes, we bend our knees. It was summer when we came up, the trees were still green, now it is autumn and the night is grey and wet. The lorries stop, we climb out—a confused heap, a remnant of many names. On either side stand people, dark, calling out the numbers of the brigades, the battalions. And at each call a little group separates itself off, a small handful of dirty, pallid soldiers, a dreadfully small handful, and a dreadfully small remnant.

Now someone is calling the number of our company, it is, yes, the Company Commander, he has come through, then; his arm is in a sling. We go over to him and I recognize Kat and Albert, we stand together, lean against each other, and look at one another.

And we hear the number of our company called again and again. He will call a long time, they do not hear him in the hospitals and shell-holes.

Once again: "Second Company, this way!" And then more softly: "Nobody else, Second Company?"

He is silent, and then huskily he says: "Is that all?" He gives the order: "Number!"

The morning is grey, it was still summer when we came up, and we were one hundred and fifty strong. Now we freeze, it is autumn, the leaves rustle, the voices flutter out wearily: "One—two—three — four——" and cease at thirty-two. And there is a long silence before the voice asks: "Anyone else?"—and waits and then says softly: "In squads——" and then breaks off and is only able to finish: "Second Company——" with difficulty: "Second Company—march easy!"

A line, a short line trudges off into the morning.

Thirty-two men.

The Bolsheviks Take Power

Robert V. Daniels

The Bolshevik Revolution of 1917 was a direct consequence of World War I. Before the war the Bolsheviks were a minority faction of the Russian Social Democratic Party. Their leader, Vladimir Ilich Lenin (1870-1924), a revolutionary living in exile in Switzerland, was scarcely known outside the contentious ranks of the Russian Marxists. World War I gave him the opportunity he would never have had in peacetime. The czarist government could not sustain the war effort, and by March 1917 (February 1917 by Russia's prerevolutionary calendar) Russia was plainly losing the war. Food riots in Petrograd (as the capital, St. Petersburg, had been renamed) led to the czar's overthrow and the proclamation of a democratic republic, which tried to keep the war going.

At this point the Germans conceived the clever strategy of allowing Lenin to travel back to Russia in a sealed train, in the hopes that his radical revolutionary agitation would fatally disrupt Russia's war effort. The scheme succeeded even beyond the Germans' expectations. Russia's vast armies of peasant conscripts had no desire to keep fighting, especially because in their native villages other peasants were spontaneously seizing landlords' estates. Russia's major cities were controlled not so much by the democratic Provisional Government as by councils (the Russian word for council is *soviet*) of factory workers and soldiers and sailors. The Bolsheviks controlled neither the peasant movement nor the urban soviets, but under Lenin's incessant prodding they did everything possible to whip up peasants', workers', and soldiers' demands for "land, bread, peace." The Provisional Government's political ineptitude and its determination to stand loyally by its Western allies cost it popular support, despite the fact that it had scheduled democratic elections for a national Congress of Soviets.

In November 1917—by the old Russian calendar, it was still October—the Bolsheviks organized a swift uprising in Petrograd that toppled the Provisional Government, led by Alexander Kerensky. Ostensibly, Lenin, his chief associate Leon Trotsky, and the Bolshevik Party had acted in the name of the Petrograd Soviet. Actually, they had seized power for themselves and would hold it until the collapse of the Soviet Union in 1989–1991.

Was the uprising of "Red October" the result of a carefully thought-out plan, or of its ruthless Marxist logic? Or was it the product of luck, its enemy's blunders, and the implacable will of Lenin, prevailing over the hesitations of his fellow Bolsheviks (including an obscure Georgian known as Joseph Stalin)? American historian Robert V. Daniels, a life-long student of Russian history, discusses the myth and reality of the Bolshevik seizure of power in this excerpt from his book *Red October.*

The October Revolution did shake the world. In the eyes of its followers and its enemies alike, it announced the final battle between the international proletariat and the worldwide system of capitalism, the fulfillment of Marx's prophecy. The October Revolution promised a new dawn in human history, a new era of liberation and equality. Its spirit and its doctrine became a new faith for millions of people all over the world, who looked to Moscow as the new Jerusalem. . . .

It is only natural that an event that has aroused such commitments and antagonisms should be viewed by both its heirs and its enemies alike as the result of deep historical forces or a long-laid master scheme. Since the days of the October uprising itself, it has been difficult for either side to take stock of the extraordinary series of accidents and missteps that accompanied the Bolshevik Revolution and allowed it to succeed. One thing that both victors and vanquished were agreed on, before the smoke had hardly cleared from the Palace Square, was the myth that the insurrection was timed and executed according to a deliberate Bolshevik plan.

The official Communist history of the revolution has held rigidly to an orthodox Marxist interpretation of the event: it was an uprising of thousands upon thousands of workers and peasants, the inevitable consequence of the international class struggle of proletariat against bourgeoisie, brought to a head first in Russia because it was "the weakest link in the chain of capitalism." At the same time it is asserted, though the contradiction is patent, that the revolution could not have succeeded without the ever-present genius leadership of

Lenin. This attempt to have it both ways has been ingrained in Communist thinking ever since Lenin himself campaigned in the name of Marx for the "art of insurrection."

Anti-Communist interpretations, however they may deplore the October Revolution, are almost as heavily inclined to view it as the inescapable outcome of overwhelming circumstances or of long and diabolical planning. The impasse of the war was to blame, or Russia's inexperience in democracy, or the feverish laws of revolution. If not these factors, it was Lenin's genius and trickery in propaganda, or the party organization as his trusty and invincible instrument. Of course, all of these considerations played a part, but when they are weighed against the day by day record of the revolution, it is hard to argue that any combination of them made Bolshevik power inevitable or even likely.

The stark truth about the Bolshevik Revolution is that it succeeded against incredible odds in defiance of any rational calculation that could have been made in the fall of 1917. The shrewdest politicians of every political coloration knew that while the Bolsheviks were an undeniable force in Petrograd and Moscow, they had against them the overwhelming majority of the peasants, the army in the field, and the trained personnel without which no government could function. Everyone from the right-wing military to the Zinoviev-Kamenev Bolsheviks judged a military dictatorship to be the most likely alternative if peaceful evolution failed. [Zinoviev and Kamenev were important Bolshevik leaders who opposed attempting a coup.] They all thought—whether they hoped or feared—that a Bolshevik attempt to seize power would only hasten or assure the rightist alternative.

Lenin's revolution, as Zinoviev and Kamenev pointed out, was a wild gamble, with little chance that the Bolsheviks' ill-prepared followers could prevail against all the military force that the government seemed to have, and even less chance that they could keep power even if they managed to seize it temporarily. To Lenin, however, it was a gamble that entailed little risk, because he sensed that in no other way and at no other time would he have any chance at all of coming to power. This is why he demanded so vehemently that the Bolshevik Party seize the moment and hurl all the force it could against the Provisional Government. Certainly the Bolshevik Party had a better overall chance for survival and a future political role if it waited and compromised, as Zinoviev and Kamenev wished. But this would not yield the only kind of political power—exclusive power—that Lenin valued. He was bent on baptizing the revolution in blood, to drive off the fainthearted and compel all who subscribed to the overturn to accept and depend on his own unconditional leadership.

To this extent there is some truth in the contentions, both Soviet and non-Soviet, that Lenin's leadership was decisive. By psychological pressure on his Bolshevik lieutenants and his manipulation of the fear of counterrevolution, he set the stage for the one-party seizure of power. But the facts of the record show that in the crucial days before October 24th Lenin was not making his leadership effective. The party, unable to face up directly to his browbeating was tacitly violating his instructions and waiting for a multi-party and semi-constitutional revolution by the Congress of Soviets. Lenin had failed to seize the moment, failed to avert the trend to a compromise coalition regime of the soviets, failed to nail down the base for his personal dictatorship—until the government struck on the morning of the 24th of October.

Kerensky's ill-conceived countermove was the decisive accident. Galvanizing all the fears that the revolutionaries had acquired in July and August about a rightist *putsch* [coup], it brought out their utmost—though still clumsy—effort to defend themselves and hold the ground for the coming Congress of Soviets. The Bolsheviks could not calculate when they called the Red Guards to the bridges and sent commissars to the communications centers, that the forces of the government would apathetically collapse. With undreamed-of ease, and no intention before the fact, they had the city in the palms of their hands, ready to close their grip when their leader reappeared from the underground and able to offer him the Russian capital in expiation of their late faintheartedness.

The role of Trotsky in all this is very peculiar. A year after the revolution Stalin wrote, "All the work of the practical organization of the insurrection proceeded under the immediate direction of the chairman of the Petrograd Soviet, Comrade Trotsky. It can be said with assurance that for the quick shift of the garrison to the side of the soviet and the bold insurrectionary work of the MRC [Military Revolutionary Committee, headed by Trotsky] the party is indebted firstly and mainly to Comrade Trotsky." This passage was naturally suppressed during Stalin's heyday, but after the de-Stalinization of 1956 Soviet historians resurrected it—as proof of another of Stalin's errors, overestimating Trotsky! In fact they are right, though the whole party shared Stalin's accolade at the time: Trotsky in October was at the height of his career as the flaming revolutionary tribune, yet he shied away from the outright insurrection that Lenin demanded. Trotsky exemplified the feelings of the main body of the Bolshevik leadership, eager for power yet afraid either to take a military initiative or to face Lenin's wrath. Trotsky talked revolution but waited for the Congress—until the moment of Lenin's return to Smolny [the building where the Bolsheviks had their headquarters]. Then, like most of the party leadership, he persuaded himself that he had been carrying out Lenin's instructions all along; any statement he had made about waiting for the Congress became, in retrospect, a political lie "to cover up the game." But in truth there was far more lying about the October Revolution after the event than before.

How important was the matter of waiting for the Congress of Soviets? What difference would it have made if Kerensky had not precipitated the fighting and the Congress had assembled peacefully to vote itself into power? Lenin, for one, believed it made a vast difference, and his view is underscored from the opposite direction by the conduct of the Mensheviks and Right SRs after the uprising. [The Mensheviks and SRs were moderate leftist parties.] They were bitter and intransigent and unwilling to enter a meaningful coalition where they might have balanced the Bolsheviks. The Bolsheviks— a majority of them, at least—were emboldened by the smell of gunpowder, and ready to fight to the end to preserve the conquests of their impromptu uprising. The same was true of the Left SRs, reluctant though they had been for violence. Many moderates, on the other hand, were so enraged that they were prepared to join hands with the Ultra-Right, if need be, to oust the Bolshevik usurpers. If the Congress had met without insurrection—a large "if"—Russia would have remained for the time being on the course of peaceful political compromise; with prior insurrection a fact, Russia was headed on the path to civil war and dictatorship.

The October Revolution gave the impetus to the whole subsequent development of the Soviet Russian regime and the worldwide Communist movement. If the revolution had not occurred as it did, the basic political cleavage of Bolsheviks and anti-Bolsheviks would not have been so sharp, and it is difficult to imagine what other events might have established a similar opportunity for one-party Bolshevik rule. Given the fact of the party's forcible seizure of power, civil violence and a militarized dictatorship of revolutionary extremism followed with remorseless logic.

This is not to say that every subsequent development in Soviet Russia was entirely predetermined by the violent revolution of October. A host of other circumstances and political events helped shape the Communist regime from this time on—the Civil War, the death of Lenin, the challenge of industrialization, the threat of foreign enemies, and above all the rise to power of Joseph Stalin, who accomplished a new "revolution from above" more far-reaching than the Revolution of 1917. It was in this epoch, the 1930's, that the most enduring fundamentals of the present Soviet system, economically, socially and intellectually, were laid down, in the course of events that were as much a counterrevolution against 1917 as an extension of it. . . .

Was the October Revolution necessary, not in the sense of historical inevitability, but as a required step to achieve the revolutionaries' program? An affirmative answer to this question is the first principle of Leninism. For the moderate socialists, who shared the theoretical program, the answer was an equally emphatic no. The question itself involves a problematical assumption: did the revolutionary seizure of power in fact achieve the Bolshevik program at all? Actions do not always produce the results intended, and this is particularly true of political violence. What actually happened to the Bolshevik promises of 1917, "All Power to the Soviets," the magic triad "Bread, Land, and Peace," the ideal of "workers' control" and abolition of bureaucracy, self-determination for the peoples of Russia, the doctrine of the dictatorship of the proletariat and international civil war against capitalism? Every one of these points was decreed into law by the Second Congress of Soviets, and together they constituted the program by which the Bolsheviks justified their resistance to a coalition government and their establishment of a one-party dictatorship. But it was not many years before most of the program had been violated by its authors or their heirs.

"All Power to the Soviets" appeared to be a reality on the 26th of October, 1917, but it was mostly power to the Bolsheviks in those soviets. The procedures of parliamentary responsibility—of the cabinet to the Central Executive Committee and of the latter to the Congress of Soviets and the electorate—lasted scarcely six months. By July, 1918, all the parties but the Communists were outlawed, and the locus of decision-making, both centrally and locally, shifted from the soviets to the organization of the Communist Party. Through single-slate elections and Communist Party discipline the whole system of soviets and executive committees was reduced to an administrative and propaganda auxiliary of the party. . . .

The promise of workers' control of industry, the highest hope of the Bolsheviks' favored constituents, fell by the wayside even sooner than the soviets. Lenin was quick to decide (if he ever had any real illusions on this score) that industry could not be run by untrained committees, and he had no intention of dispensing with the bureaucratic and coercive apparatus of government. Deprived of power in the soviets and in the factories, the Russian proletariat (save for its members who climbed up into the party bureaucracy) found that the triumph of the dictatorship in its name was a very hollow victory.

Peace and the international civil war were intimately linked in Lenin's mind: he waged peace not for its own sake but because he thought the issue would rouse the masses against their governments throughout Europe. When he found himself in power, thanks to the peace issue as much as anything, he had to choose: peace with Germany and the postponement of international revolution or "revolutionary war" by a country in chaos with no army that would fight. Over the agonized cries of many of his most ardent followers, Lenin unhesitatingly chose the former, and concluded the Treaty of Brest-Litovsk with Germany in March, 1918. The priorities were set for good: ever since, international revolution has been subordinated, as an occasional and expendable instrument, to the great-power interests of the Soviet Union.

Self-determination for Russia's national minorities became a quick reality in some cases—Finland, practically independent already and recognized as such by the Soviet government in December, 1917; and Poland and the Baltic provinces, lost under the terms of Brest-Litovsk. Elsewhere—in Belorussia [now Belarus], the Ukraine, the Caucasus—the Communists did not tolerate the dismemberment of the Russian Empire. After the Civil War, in the theoretically federal system of the Soviet Union, they restored the authority of the Russian center.

Bread and land were interdependent by nature, and impossible to deliver simultaneously. Bread symbolized the dislocation and underdevelopment of the whole Russian economy, while the immediate gratification of the peasants' land hunger meant worse shortages in the food delivered to the cities. Russian agriculture was a problem that would tax even the wisest government; it [was] always . . . the Soviet regime's greatest difficulty. The first Communist solution was to give the peasant the land, but take the bread from him—the "requisitions" of the War Communism period. The NEP ["New Economic Policy"] of 1921–28 left the peasant the land and the free commercial disposal of his bread, while the urban economy barely inched back to the level of tsarism. Stalin found this arrangement a major barrier to the political and economic power that he desired, and forcibly imposed on the whole Russian peasantry the system of collectivized agriculture. The land, as the peasant understood possession of it, was gone as absolutely as it had been under serfdom.

This chronicle of disappointment in the aftermath of revolution is not peculiar to Russia. The high hopes of revolution are always more than offset by the institutionalized violence that revolution begets, and by the subtle return of the hated but deep-seated characteristics of a nation's past. The distinctive thing about the Russian Revolution, compared with the other great revolutions of modern history, was the seizure and consolidation of power by the radical extremists, instead of a counterrevolutionary military or fascistic take-over. It was this unique success of the Left that was responsible for the special appeal of revolutionary Russia as the idealized model both for social renovation in the West and for national regeneration in the East.

The Bolsheviks had a singular role both in Russian and world history, a role they would never have played without the sheer force of Lenin's personality—his determination to seize power no matter what and his unrelenting pressure on the party he had created to make it prepare to seize and hold power in defiance of the historical odds. Lenin could have disappeared from the scene at any one of a number of critical points: he could have been kept out of Russia by a more cautious German policy in April, 1917; he could have been caught crossing the border into Finland in August; he could have been recognized and arrested by the cadet patrol on the night of October 24. There was only one Lenin, and had any one of these contingencies gone the other way, his followers could not have found a substitute.

Nor would they have cared to. Lenin was always ahead of his party, pushing it always into bolder, more violent, more irreversible action than it cared to contemplate. There was an inertia, a mixture of democratic scruple and skin-saving timidity, that caused the party to lag behind whenever Lenin was not physically confronting his lieutenants to commit them to action. (The moderate socialist parties had the same qualities in greater measure and no Lenin to offset them.) In October the crucial test between the party's inertia and Lenin's drive for power was the question of an insurrection *before* the Congress of Soviets. Had it not occurred, dividing the socialist parties over the issue of violent change, the whole subsequent development of Russian politics could have been different. Here enters the greatest and most ironic contingency of all—Kerensky's desperate decision to attempt what looked like a counter-coup, but instead brought out the Bolsheviks' full forces in a panicky defense, and turned the city of Petrograd into an armed camp surrounding the Winter Palace. By this odd stroke of luck Lenin won what he had been unable to get from his party—a commitment of the revolution to violence that made dictatorship of one sort or another the only alternative.

The spirit of combat embodied in the October Revolution soon permeated most of Russian life; it was heavily reinforced by the grueling experience of the Russian Civil War from 1918 to 1920. All of the noble utopianism that animated Russian society in 1917 soon came to grief between the relentless millstones of grim reality and the Communist determination to hold power at any cost. The manner of the revolution eventually destroyed its spirit.

The drift of Soviet Communism away from the inspiration of the revolution did not, however, prevent it from clinging to the revolutionary story as one of its principal sources of legitimacy. The revolution became . . . in official Soviet history "a revolution opening a new era in human history." The history of the revolution became an official myth, that had to prove and justify certain things—the inevitability of Communist Party rule in Russia; the genius of Lenin without whom the inevitable would never have come about; the iniquity of all Lenin's opponents, Bolshevik as well as non-Bolshevik; the retrospective treacherousness of Lenin's supporters, who later ran afoul of Stalin; the vacillation of Stalin,whose successors could not forego the temptations of rewriting history in turn.

The ironic thing is that none of this revolutionary legend is necessary for the recognition of the substantial achievements of the Soviet regime. These achievements, above all the industrialization of the country and the development of the military potential of a superpower, have little to do with the program of the October Revolution. They were inherent in the resources, human and material, that Russia would have offered to any post-revolutionary government. Little of the actual Soviet future was clear in the minds of the people who made the revolution, only to be devoured by the power they had created. They had forgotten the warning of their number-two prophet, Friedrich Engels [Karl Marx's chief collaborator], written forty-two years before: "People who boasted that they had made a revolution have always seen the next day that they had no idea what they were doing, that the revolution *made* did not in the least resemble the one they would have liked to make."

Wilson's Fourteen Points

Woodrow Wilson

U.S. president Woodrow Wilson went before Congress in January 1918 to declare publicly the principles on which he believed the Allies should make peace with Germany and the other Central Powers, ending the Great War. These Fourteen Points, as they immediately became known, appear here. Why is this presidential statement of war aims such an important document in modern history? To answer this question, we need to understand the context in which Wilson was speaking.

Both the Allies and the Central Powers hoped to make vital territorial gains at the other's expense in the event of victory, and each side wanted to make the other pay the war's horrendous monetary cost. The Allies had negotiated secret treaties among themselves envisioning extensive annexations, including dividing up Germany's entire colonial empire. German leaders dreamed of creating what they called *Mitteleuropa* (Middle Europe), a huge block of German-dominated territory that would enable them to dominate the continent, and they also wanted to add to their colonial empire overseas. Wilson, an American liberal, distrusted power politics, and he hoped that Europeans' age-old national hatreds could be slaked to produce a more peace-loving world. Thus he hoped that the peace settlement would reflect principles of justice and self-determination, not revenge and aggrandizement.

The Bolshevik's seizure of power in Russia in November 1917 (by the Western calendar) also gave impetus to Wilson's public pronouncement of war aims. As soon as they took power, the Bolsheviks published the texts of the secret treaties that czarist Russia had signed with the Western allies—treaties that made it clear that the Allies were not simply waging

Excerpted from Woodrow Wilson's *Fourteen Points,* as presented to Congress in January 1918, Washington, D.C.

a defensive war from which they did not expect to make gains in the event of victory. Disclosure of these secret treaties sent shock waves through Western public opinion—exactly what Lenin had hoped to produce by publishing these documents. Was all the bloodshed and expense really necessary (many ordinary people asked) in order to redraw the maps and acquire new colonies? War-weariness began to spread rapidly in France, Italy, and Great Britain; there were signs that French troops might mutiny. And as yet there were no significant numbers of American troops in Europe ready to join the fight. Perhaps the Allied war effort might collapse before American help could become effective.

Wilson's Fourteen Points, therefore, represented a major effort by the American president to redefine the Allied cause in the Great War—to make it a crusade for justice, self-determination, and a democratic, peace-loving future. To a remarkable extent, the Fourteen Points served that purpose. When, in the fall of 1918, after American forces were arriving in sufficient numbers to turn the military tide, the German government asked for an armistice on the basis of the Fourteen Points, which it assumed meant just, generous terms. Yet the Treaty of Versailles that Germany was forced to sign in June 1919 hardly represented a peace of mutual reconciliation. In the light of these realities, the American public in particular turned away from interest in European affairs, deeply disillusioned with power politics.

In a larger sense, however, Wilson's Fourteen Points enunciated the concerns that would dominate American international policy throughout the twentieth century, and still do at the dawn of the twenty-first century. The fourteenth point, for example, calls for a world league to keep the peace and do justice around the globe: This was the genesis not only of the post–World War I League of Nations, but also of the post–World War II United Nations. His appeals for freedom of the seas, mutual disarmament, openly negotiated international treaties (instead of agreements full of secret clauses), freer trade, and human rights have been foundation stones of America's foreign policy ever since World War I. So, too, has been the belief that territorial conflicts between foreign nations are best resolved by ensuring national self-determination, defined as the majority wishes along with legally guaranteeing the minority's human rights. Such principles, however, are no easier to achieve today than they were when Woodrow Wilson negotiated the Treaty of Versailles: witness such difficult contemporary problems as achieving peace and self-determination in Northern Ireland, former Yugoslavia, and Kashmir.

I. Open covenants of peace, openly arrived at, after which there shall be no private international understandings of any kind, but diplomacy shall proceed always frankly and in the public view.

President Wilson's Fourteen Points *listed many diplomatic concerns that still motivate U.S. foreign policy today.*

II. Absolute freedom of navigation upon the seas, outside territorial waters, alike in peace and in war, except as the seas may be closed in whole or in part by international action [of the League of Nations] for the enforcement of international covenants.

III. The removal, so far as possible, of all economic barriers, and the establishment of an equality of trade conditions among all the nations consenting to the peace, and associating themselves [by forming a League of Nations] for its maintenance.

IV. Adequate guarantees given and taken that national armaments will be reduced to the lowest point consistent with domestic safety.

V. A free, open-minded, and absolutely impartial adjustment of all colonial claims, based upon a strict observance of the principle that, in determining all such questions of sovereignty, the interests of the populations concerned must have equal weight with the equitable claims of the Government whose title is to be determined.

VI. The evacuation of all Russian territory, and such a settlement of all questions affecting Russia as will secure the best and freest cooperation of the other nations of the world in obtaining for her an unhampered and unembarrassed opportunity for the independent determination of her own political development and national policy, and assure her of a sincere welcome into the society of free nations, under institutions of her own choosing; and, more than a welcome, assistance also of every kind. . . .

VII. Belgium, the whole world will agree, must be evacuated and restored, without any attempt to limit the sovereignty which she enjoys in common with all other free nations. No other single act will serve as this will serve to restore confidence among the nations in the laws which they have themselves set and determined for the government of their relations with one another. Without this healing act the whole structure and validity of international law is forever impaired.

VIII. All French territory should be freed and the invaded portions restored, and the wrong done to France by Prussia in 1871 in the matter of Alsace-Lorraine, which has unsettled the peace of the world for nearly fifty years, should be righted, in order that peace may once more be made secure in the interest of all.

IX. A readjustment of the frontiers of Italy should be effected along clearly recognizable lines of nationality.

X. The peoples of Austria-Hungary, whose place among the nations we wish to see safeguarded and assured, should be accorded the freest opportunity of autonomous development.

XI. Rumania, Serbia, and Montenegro should be evacuated; occupied territories restored; Serbia accorded free and secure access to the sea; and the relations of the several Balkan states to one another determined by friendly counsel along historically established lines of allegiance and nationality; and international guarantees of the political and economic independence and territorial integrity of the several Balkan states should be entered into.

XII. The Turkish portions of the present Ottoman Empire should be assured a secure sovereignty, but the other nationalities which are now under Turkish rule should be assured an undoubted security of life and an absolutely unmolested opportunity of autonomous development, and the Dardanelles [the straits connecting the Black Sea and the Mediterranean] should be permanently opened as a free passage to the ships and commerce of all nations under international guarantees.

XIII. An independent Polish state should be erected which should include the territories inhabited by indisputably Polish populations, which should be assured a free and secure access to the sea, and whose political and economic independence and territorial integrity should be guaranteed by international covenant.

XIV. A general association of nations must be formed under specific covenants for the purpose of affording mutual guarantees of political independence and territorial integrity to great and small states alike.

In regard to these essential rectifications of wrong and assertions of right, we feel ourselves to be intimate partners of all the governments and peoples associated together against the Imperialists. We cannot be separated in interest or divided in purpose. We stand together until the end.

Chapter

3

The Great War's Aftermath, 1919–1930

PREFACE

With the restoration of peace after the Great War, the Western world struggled to get back to what U.S. president Warren Harding (1921–1923)—garbling his words—called "normalcy." But instead of a return to what people of the time nostalgically remembered as prewar stability, the 1920s proved to be a decade of intense cultural and social conflict throughout the Western world. A postwar economic surge, the arrival of what we would now call a consumer-oriented economy, and a bitter clash between modern and traditional ways of life permeated society in most of the industrialized democracies of the Western world. The surge was most dramatic and the cultural clash was most obvious in the United States, and the export of American mass culture—movies, cheap cars, the radio, and the wildly popular form of music that caused this era to be called "the Jazz Age"—began a global Americanization that is still under way.

Momentous, unsettling changes were meanwhile taking place in science. The discovery of X rays and radiation in 1898, Max Planck's work in quantum physics after 1900, and Albert Einstein's publication of his theories of relativity in 1905 and 1915 revolutionized how scientists saw the physical world. In the 1920s an often-bewildered public also became aware of these new visions of reality. ("Einstein Theory Puzzles Harding," read an understated *New York Times* headline.) Freudian psychological theory, which located the driving forces of human behavior in repressed childhood experiences and sexuality, in the 1920s ceased to seem scandalous and became a mainstream, even a fashionable, way to understand human nature—at least among educated laypeople. The Darwinian theory of evolution by this time had also gained general assent among sophisticated people, though in the United States Bible-believing fundamentalists tried to outlaw its teaching.

The Versailles treaty rankled Germans, and secretly the German government evaded its disarmament provisions. But after recovering from a devastating period of hyperinflation (which wiped out the savings of most of its middle-class citizens), Germany rebounded economically. Heavy infusions of American capital enabled Germany to meet its huge reparations bills to the victorious Allies. Unfortunately, however, the capitalist world had not absorbed the lesson that open markets and unimpeded international trade are essential for sustaining prosperity. High tariff barriers continued to be the rule, and both Great Britain and France sought to turn their vast overseas empires into "closed" trading areas, basically designed to benefit the home country and to discourage outside investment.

In October 1929 the international economic system that by then resembled a house of cards came tumbling down when the U.S. stock market collapsed. This event—actually a much-needed correction of an overheated, speculative run-up in stock prices—might not have led to a lasting disaster. But economic policy makers both in the United States and in Europe made almost every conceivable mistake in response to the crisis. They raised taxes and tariffs when they should have lowered them; they tightened credit when they should have loosened it; and they retreated into economic isolationism when they should have opened up international trade. As a result, the global economy plummeted downward, and by early 1933 the economic contraction and mass unemployment were threatening to plunge the industrialized world into chaos.

The Treaty of Versailles

Mark Mazower

World War I ended as it did because in the spring of 1917 the United States joined the fray, goaded into intervention by Germany's resort to sinking neutral vessels without warning on the Atlantic—a desperate action that the kaiser's Reich took in the hope of cutting off Great Britain's lifelines. Germany won the war in the east by forcing Russia to sign the Treaty of Brest-Litovsk in March 1918, but about that time fresh American troops began to arrive in France. When Germany made its last bid for victory on the western front, in the spring and summer of 1918, the American armies helped France and Britain withstand the offensive and counterattack. By November 11, 1918, the kaiser had fled the country and Germany agreed to an armistice. Meanwhile Austria-Hungary collapsed as various provinces declared their independence.

On June 28, 1919, delegates from the new, democratic German republic were forced to sign the Treaty of Versailles, formally ending the war. Germany lost territory to France, Poland, and other neighboring countries, gave up its colonial empire, was limited to a small army and practically no navy, and had to pay enormous reparations. Other peace treaties recognized the independence of the new countries that had arisen out of the wreckage of Austria-Hungary—Czechoslovakia, Yugoslavia, Poland, and an enlarged Romania—while Austria and Hungary were reduced to small rump states.

In subsequent years, many people besides those in the defeated countries questioned the wisdom of the Treaty of Versailles. Was it unduly harsh? Did it create too many weak little states in central Europe that could not resist when Germany and Russia recovered from the war? Was it all

Reprinted from "Two Cheers for Versailles," by Mark Mazower, *History Today*, vol. 49, July 1999. Reprinted with permission from *History Today*.

the product of the misplaced idealism of U.S. president Woodrow Wilson and the cynicism of the French, British, and Italian leaders with whom Wilson had negotiated for peace? British historian Mark Mazower answers these questions in the light of the subsequent history of the twentieth century—down to the recent tragedies in Bosnia and Kosovo, which demonstrated how violent antagonisms still divide some of eastern Europe's national minorities.

The Versailles Treaty settlement was, from the moment of its birth, unloved as few creations of international diplomacy have been before or since. Hitler and Churchill were united in its condemnation; so were commentators from the American anti-Soviet diplomat and historian George Kennan to the British Marxist E.H. Carr. One is hard put to find a school textbook with anything good to say about the achievements of the Paris peacemakers. Yet curiously we still live in the world they shaped: were the foundations laid more carefully by them than we like to think? The argument that the defects of Versailles led to the outbreak of another world war is commonplace; yet one might as easily argue that its virtues underpinned the peace after 1945.

Some suggest that Versailles was based on principles inconsistently applied. The charge is obviously true. The right of national self-determination was granted at Germany's expense, and the *Anschluss* with Austria, which Social Democrats in Vienna wanted in 1918, was prevented by the Great Powers and only achieved after the Nazis broke the League of Nations system and marched in twenty years later. But international affairs are not a matter of logic alone, and the principle of consistency must be matched against considerations of power politics or geography. National self-determination could never have been applied across the board; the basic issue is whether a better principle existed for the re-ordering of Europe.

More serious an accusation is that the peace settlement was not so much inconsistent as ineffective: it was based upon an inaccurate appraisal of the European balance of power and deprived of the means of its own defence by American withdrawal and British indifference. At Paris the Great Powers ignored the fact that the almost simultaneous collapse of Germany and Russia had produced an anomalous situation in eastern Europe. The French, who of all the Great Powers felt most immediately threatened, thought the only safeguard of their own security—if the League was not to be equipped with an army of its own—was alliance with grateful clients like the Baltic states, Poland, Czechoslovakia, Romania and Yugoslavia. But it should have been obvious that the newly independent states formed there would be unable alone to ensure stability in the region once these two Great Powers reasserted themselves. The Treaty of Brest Litovsk of early 1918 had shown what intentions the Germans of the *Kaiserreich* harboured in that area; after 1939, Hitler's New Order pushed the principle of German (and Russian) hegemony one brutal stage further. But this is less an argument against the Versailles settlement itself than against the refusal of the Great Powers who sponsored it to back it up with armed force before 1939.

Thirdly, it is often felt that the whole approach to Germany after the Treaty was flawed. The enemy was humiliated but not crushed, burdened by reparations yet unopposed when it rearmed and marched into the Rhineland. It is true that the contrast is striking with the policies pursued towards Germany after the Second World War when long-term economic assistance was provided and by governments not the markets, and when the *Bundeswehr* was quickly incorporated within west European defence arrangements. But the economic problem after 1919 was not so much reparations as the shaky structure of international lending and, in particular, the shock of the world depression. The Allies were helped to learn from the mistakes of the inter-war era by the Cold War, which divided Germany, and made Europe's German problem a question of reunification rather than of territorial expansion and *revanche* [revenge] in the East.

Finally, there is the accusation common to conservatives and Communists alike that the Versailles peace settlement was overly ideological. For some, it was an extension of nineteenth-century liberal moralising, a combination of British utilitarianism and American idealism—a basically philosophical approach to the world which lacked realism or understanding of the political passions which animated people in Europe.

Alternatively, it was—behind the veil of noble sentiments—an anti-Communist crusade whose liberalism masked a fundamentally reactionary and deeply conservative goal: the containment, if not the crushing, of Bolshevism. Outflanked gradually by other more determined and forceful anti-Communist movements of the right, European liberals lost their enthusiasm for defending the Versailles order and sat back to watch fascism take over the task of saving Europe from red revolution.

One question, however, confronts the critics of Versailles: what were the alternatives? It was not, after all, as if the Powers had willed this new liberal order of independent, democratic nation-states into existence. They had certainly not been fighting the Great War [World War I] to this end. On the contrary, as late as 1918 most Entente diplomats still favoured the preservation of the old empires in central Europe in the interests of continental stability. Of course, after 1919 the conflicts and tensions produced by the new states of the region made many people nostalgic for what the Austrian writer Stefan Zweig, looking back to the Habsburg era, called 'the world of yesterday'. Fragmentation since the war seemed to have harmed the region both politically and economically, especially once the world depression [of the 1930s] forced countries into an impoverished self-sufficiency.

Yet it was a rare blend of nostalgia and *realpolitik* which lay behind much of the antipathy to Versailles. The makers of America's new role in Europe after 1945, for example, who had grown up looking closely at these problems, held Versailles responsible for the instability of interwar Europe. Adolf Berle, [Franklin D.] Roosevelt's assistant secretary of state between 1938 and 1944, believed that French generals had been responsible for breaking up the Austro-Hungarian Empire and wanted some kind of reconstitution of that entity to ward off the Russians. Hitler, he advised the president on the eve of Munich [when, in 1938, Britain and France agreed to let Hitler begin to break up Czechoslovakia], was perhaps 'the only instrument capable of re-establishing a race and economic unit which can survive and leave Europe in balance.'

George Kennan, a younger man but more influential than Berle in defining the Cold War policy of containment, took a very similar view in the late 1930s. In his despatches from Prague he wrote:

> It is generally agreed that the breakup of the limited degree of unity which the Habsburg Empire represented was unfortunate for all concerned. Other forces are now at work which are struggling to create a new form of unity. . . . To these forces Czechoslovakia has been tragically slow in adjusting herself. . . . The adjustment—and this is the main thing—has now come.

It did not take long for someone as astute as Kennan to realise that the Nazi New Order was not going to stabilise central Europe in the way the Habsburgs had done. But the reason for this, in his mind, was not the apparently obvious one that Hitler's whole upbringing had turned him into a German nationalist critic of the Austro-Hungarian monarchy. It was, rather, what Kennan conceived as the excessively democratic character of Hitler's Germany and the limited involvement of Germany's aristocracy in the Third Reich. More aristocratic government was Kennan's answer to Europe's problems. It is hard to imagine a more far-fetched or unrealistic approach—the Habsburgs were marginalised between the wars even by Hungary's reactionary regent Admiral Horthy [the right-wing leader of Hungary], and the most successful Habsburg aristocrat of that era was the bizarre and premature proponent of European union, Count

Coudenhove-Kalergi. Perhaps only an American conservative intellectual like Kennan could have taken the prospect of a Habsburg restoration seriously. European conservatives, closer to the ground, had fewer illusions. 'The Vienna to Versailles period has run its course,' wrote the [British] historian Lewis Namier in February 1940.

> Whatever the weaknesses of the system created in 1919, a return to previous forms is impossible. They have been broken, and broken for good.

It was not aristocrats that had kept the old empires together but dynastic loyalty, and this had vanished.

If dynasticism no longer offered an alternative principle to the Versailles order, then what of the rival ideologies of right and left? This was where root-and-branch critics of Versailles had to bite the bullet. Most anti-Communists between the wars had no difficulty in swallowing the idea of an authoritarian revision of the Versailles settlement. What made them hesitate was a quite different proposition; the reality of life under the Nazi New Order. The difference between a right tolerable to most conservatives and an extreme and ideological fascism was that, for instance, between King Alexander's royal dictatorship in Yugoslavia, and Ante Pavelic's genocidal *Ustase* [Fascist] state in Croatia, or between King Carol's Romania and that of the Iron Guard, with its bloody pogroms, in the winter of 1940–41. Above all, the New Order was based on the idea of German racial superiority, and few anti-Communists could stomach this once they saw what it meant in terms of practical politics.

If one agreed with Namier that 'no system can possibly be maintained on the European Continent east of the Rhine which has not the support either of Germany or of Russia,' then the only ideological alternative to Nazism was Communism, or more precisely the extension of Russian rule westwards into Europe. Just as Versailles's critics on the right had seen Germany's move east after 1933 as confirmation of their own prejudices, so critics on the left similarly interpreted the course of events after 1943 as a happy necessity. Historians like E.H. Carr [a left-wing British historian] saw this as realism replacing the idealism of Versailles. It was apparently not felt to be realistic to point out that all the historical evidence pointed to the unpopularity of Communism among the majority of the populations who now had to endure it. In only one country in central Europe, Hungary, had a Bolshevik regime held power for any length of time before 1945, and that still brief experience—the Bela Kun regime of 1919—had only confirmed how unpropitious the soil was for such experiments. Today we are unlikely to see Communism as an attractive alternative to the principles embodied in the Versailles order: yesterday's 'realism' looks riddled with its own form of wishful thinking.

One of the reasons Bela Kun fell from power in 1919 was that he had not understood the strength of Hungarian nationalist feeling. So long as it had appeared to Hungarians that Bolshevik Russia might help them get back their traditional lands, they were prepared to tolerate Kun. But once it appeared that the Allies would not let this happen, Kun lost any popularity he had once enjoyed and he was easily defeated. The power of nationalism was the chief force to emerge from the First World War in Europe, and was the main political factor facing the architects of a new postwar settlement. From our perspective at the century's end, it hardly looks as though fascism and Communism were able to handle European nationalism better than the peacemakers at Versailles. Hitler's New Order proceeded by ignoring all nationalisms except the German, and lost Europe in consequence. Communism believed that eventually nationalist antipathies would vanish, subsumed within an internationalist struggle: but time ran out for the Communists before this happened. If we want to find guidance in the past for how to tackle the problems of nationalism that remain in Europe, we cannot do better than return to the diplomats who gathered in Paris eighty years ago.

In the Bukovina (a former province of the Habsburg empire), Paris seemed very far away in the spring of 1919. But events were occurring there which help us chart the trajectory of antisemitic violence from the unorganised pogroms of the nineteenth century to the more systematic population engineering of the twentieth. A manifesto was posted up in the village of Kamenestie, written in Romanian:

> Order to all the Jews in the village. Those Jews who are still in the village are asked to go to the city or somewhere else. You can leave in good condition [sic] and without fear in ten days. It will be made unbearable for those who stay beyond the limit.

Throughout the little villages of the Bukovina, pogroms were taking place in late 1918. 'Following the example of the neighbouring villages,' runs an account from Petroutz,

> The peasants decided to drive the Jews out of this place. On the night of November 17th, they attacked the Jewish families Hermann, Feller and Schubert, broke doors and windows and took away everything they found. A scroll of the Law was torn to pieces by the marauders. After the robbery they burned everything that remained. All three families fled to Suczawa.

The Jews were the chief targets of ethnic violence in the Bukovina, as they were elsewhere in eastern Europe, in Galicia [southern Poland] for instance, or in Lithuania. But the war of nationalities could not be reduced to antisemitism: Poles were fighting with Ukrainians, Germans and Lithuanians. Across much of Europe there fell a double shadow: ethnic as well as class war. Bolshevism was contained by a combination of land reform, reformist social democracy and the military defeat of the Red Army in the Russo-Polish war. But the nationalist enmities and suspicions which exploded into violence as the First World War ended, and which generated casualties on such a scale that some historians have compared them with the violence which erupted under Nazi rule after 1941, these proved harder to tackle.

Ethnic civil war emphasised in the most unmistakable way that the peacemakers in Paris were not sketching their maps on a *tabula rasa* [blank slate]. On the contrary, they were as much responding to circumstances as shaping them. East European critics of Great Power arrogance often forget today how far the Versailles settlement was brought into being, not by the Powers, but by local nationalist elites and their supporters. New nations were pressing their claims on paper, in the streets and by force of arms, as the war approached an end. Serb, Croat and Slovene delegates issued the Corfu Declaration in July 1917 and declared the new tripartite Yugoslav nation 'a worthy member of the new Community of Nations.'

The Provisional People's Government of the Polish Republic proclaimed 'the authority of Polish democracy' in its November 1918 manifesto. The Czech National Committee seized power in Prague as early as October 28th of the same year in the name of the infant Czechoslovak state. Much of the subsequent fighting from the Baltic to the Balkans was designed to conquer as much territory as possible for the new states, to see off rival claimants and to settle scores with Jews, Germans, Muslims and other hated, despised or feared peoples. Between 1920 and 1923, the Treaty of Sèvres was signed, scrapped and replaced by the Treaty of Lausanne as the struggle between Greece and Turkey shifted first one way then the other, culminating eventually in the forced population exchange of some two million people.

It is to the credit of the Versailles peacemakers that they confronted the problem of ethnic violence head on. They were aware of the chief defect of the Wilsonian principle of national self-determination— namely that if it was interpreted territorially and not merely as a grant of cultural autonomy, then on its own it ruled out either an equitable or a geographically coherent settlement of the problems of central and eastern Europe. No one, after all, was proposing to give the Kashubians, the Polesians, the Pomaks, or any of the other small ethnic groups of the region a state of their own. They, and several other larger peoples like the Jews, the Ukrainians and the Macedonians, would remain under the rule of others. In other words, the creation—or better, the recognition—of nation-states at Versailles was accompanied by its inescapable shadow, the problem of minorities.

Fearful in particular that Poland's appetite for territory might destabilise the whole area, the Powers obliged the reluctant Poles to sign a treaty granting the country's very sizeable minority population certain rights. The Polish treaty formed the basis for a series of similar treaties imposed in 1919 and 1920 upon most of the states of central and eastern Europe. The result was that for the first time an international organisation—the League of Nations—assumed the right to intervene in a member state's internal affairs on behalf of minority populations.

This right, however, was very limited and scarcely used at all by the League. Most countries feared doing away with the idea that a state was sovereign within its own borders, and even the Great Powers who had sponsored the Minority Rights Treaties trod warily. They had resisted calls to universalise the regime of minority rights on the grounds that 'the League cannot assume to guarantee good government in this matter throughout the world'. By 1929 they were very reluctant to act at all against member states accused of rights violations. British foreign secretary Austen Chamberlain warned that,

> We have not reached such a degree of solidarity in international affairs that any of us welcome even the most friendly intervention in what we consider to be our domestic affairs.

This attitude discouraged the most dynamic lobbyists for Europe's minorities, the Germans and the Jews. Until 1933, they worked together in the European Congress of Nationalities to try to give the Minority Treaties teeth. Thereafter their paths diverged. But Hitler's rise to power can be seen in the context of the failure of the League to protect Europe's minorities. Where the League's rather timid use of international law had failed, the Nazis used force; their 'solution' involved forced population transfer, resettlement and ultimately genocide. And after 1944 many of these instruments were turned on the Germans themselves as they were driven out of Poland and the former Habsburg lands.

Yet we should not write off the peacemakers of Versailles too quickly. Despite the horrors of the 1940s, which virtually eliminated both the Jews and the Germans from much of eastern Europe, many minorities remained across the region. However, instead of building on the League's tentative efforts to construct an international regime of minority rights, the architects of the post-war order enshrined in the United Nations deliberately retreated from the problem and tried to dress up its reluctance to deal with it with meaningless persiflage about 'human rights'. As a result, when issues of minority rights came to the fore after the collapse of Communism in eastern Europe in the decade after 1989, most obviously in the context of the disintegration of Yugoslavia, the international community possessed no coherent strategy for tackling the problem.

The consequences have been all too visible in Bosnia and Kosovo. The United Nations was less equipped to tackle the fundamental problem of minority rights than its predecessor, the League, had been. It delivered food and tried to keep the peace without a clear doctrine of what kind of peace it should keep. The contrast between the self-confident and articulate liberal universalism of the 1920s and the post-modern evasions of the 1990s was all too conspicuous. In Kosovo, too, the contrast with the Versailles generation does not flatter our own times. NATO intervention in Kosovo could, as articulated somewhat optimistically by [British prime minister] Tony Blair, be interpreted as marking a new doctrine of foreign affairs, according to which state sovereignty may be overridden to prevent massive violations of minority rights. Yet, NATO's attacks on the Serbs, in the absence of any UN mandate, do not indicate any great confidence in international law and institutions. The United States, which has been leading the charge, is, after all, opposed to the creation of an International Criminal Court. If inter-war Europe suffered because international guarantees were never acted upon, we may suffer in the 1990s through military action taken without any reference to international law at all, the late twentieth-century equivalent of gunboat diplomacy handled by a post-Holocaust generation of politicians.

The very least, then, that we can say for Versailles is that it recognised and articulated the major problems for European stability at that time. What was more, there was no palatable alternative to the nation-state then, or since. Where the peace was found wanting between the wars was in the will to uphold it. Today NATO is turning itself into the kind of force which the peacemakers of 1919 lacked. But do its political masters have a clear grasp of what kind of Europe they wish to defend? They could do worse than cast their eyes back to the work of their predecessors eighty years ago.

The Revolution in Physics

Fritjof Capra

During the seventeenth century, great scientists including Sir Isaac Newton worked out what for more than two hundred years were considered the immutable laws of physics. However, by the late 1880s and 1890s scientists working at the cutting edge of physics knew that the "Newtonian laws" did not adequately explain phenomena observed in experiments with electrodynamics, as well as the newly discovered X rays.

In 1905, the young German physicist Albert Einstein, employed by the Swiss government patent office, worked out his special theory of relativity. The new phenomena could only be understood, Einstein argued, if we abandoned the fundamental Newtonian principle that time and space were absolute. Einstein's theory relegated Newtonian physics to being a "special case," valid only for phenomena that we can readily observe in everyday life. However, in the vast realm of stars and galaxies, relativity prevails—just as, in the almost infinitesimally small realm of the atoms and electrons, we must accept the quantum theory that had been proposed in 1900 by another German physicist, Max Planck.

The work of Planck and Einstein at the beginning of the twentieth century forms the basis of modern physics and has fundamentally altered the way we see the universe. Their insights also paved the way for unleashing atomic power and for building the transistors on which modern computing rests.

Nuclear physicist Fritjof Capra has written a stimulating but somewhat controversial book, *The Tao of Physics,* in which he attempts to use the age-old spiritual insights of Chinese, Japanese, and Indian philosophy to help explain the theories of modern physics. In the excerpt that follows, however, Capra gives an exceptionally clear and reliable account of the conceptual breakthroughs achieved by European physicists from 1900 to the mid-1920s.

A t the beginning of the twentieth century, . . . physicists had two successful theories which applied to different phenomena: Newton's mechanics and Maxwell's electrodynamics. Thus the Newtonian model had ceased to be the basis of all physics.

The first three decades of our century changed the whole situation in physics radically. Two separate developments—that of relativity theory and of atomic physics—shattered all the principal concepts of the Newtonian world view: the notion of absolute space and time, the elementary solid particles, the strictly causal nature of physical phenomena, and the ideal of an objective description of nature. None of these concepts could be extended to the new domains into which physics was now penetrating.

At the beginning of modern physics stands the extraordinary intellectual feat of one man: Albert Einstein. In two articles, both published in 1905, Einstein initiated two revolutionary trends of thought. One was his special theory of relativity, the other was a new way of looking at electromagnetic radiation which was to become characteristic of quantum theory, the theory of atomic phenomena. The complete quantum theory was worked out twenty years later by a whole team of physicists. Relativity theory, however, was constructed in its complete form almost entirely by Einstein himself. Einstein's scientific papers stand at the beginning of the twentieth century as imposing intellectual monuments—the pyramids of modern civilization.

Einstein strongly believed in nature's inherent harmony and his deepest concern throughout his scientific life was to find a unified foundation of physics. He began to move towards this goal by constructing a common framework for electrodynamics and mechanics, the two separate theories of classical physics. This framework is known as the special theory of relativity. It unified and completed the structure of classical physics, but at the same time it involved drastic changes in the traditional concepts of space and time and undermined one of the foundations of the Newtonian world view.

According to relativity theory, space is not three-dimensional and time is not a separate entity. Both are intimately connected and form a four-dimensional continuum, 'space-time'. In relativity theory, therefore, we can never talk about space without talking about time and vice versa. Furthermore, there is no universal flow of time as in the Newtonian model. Different observers will order events differently in time if they move with different velocities relative to the observed events. In such a case, two events which are seen as occurring simultaneously by one observer may occur in different temporal sequences for other observers. All measurements involving space and time thus lose their absolute significance. In relativity theory, the Newtonian concept of an absolute space as the stage of physical phenomena is abandoned and so is the concept of an absolute time. Both space and time become merely elements of the language a particular observer uses for describing the observed phenomena.

The concepts of space and time are so basic for the description of natural phenomena that their modification entails a modification of the whole framework that we use to describe nature. The most important consequence of this modification is the realization that mass is nothing but a form of energy. Even an object at rest has energy stored in its mass, and the relation between the two is given by the famous equation $E = mc^2$, c being the speed of light.

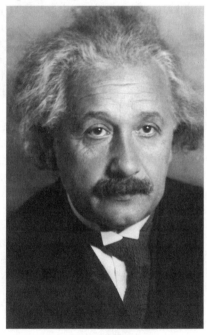

Albert Einstein

This constant c, the speed of light, is of fundamental importance for the theory of relativity. Whenever we describe physical phenomena involving velocities which approach the speed of light, our description has to take relativity theory into account. This applies in particular to electromagnetic phenomena, of which light is just one example and which led Einstein to the formulation of his theory.

In 1915, Einstein proposed his general theory of relativity in which the framework of the special theory is extended to include gravity, i.e. the mutual attraction of all massive bodies. Whereas the special theory has been confirmed by innumerable experiments, the general theory has not yet been confirmed conclusively. However, it is so far the most accepted, consistent and elegant theory of gravity and is widely used in astrophysics and cosmology for the description of the universe at large.

The force of gravity, according to Einstein's theory, has the effect of 'curving' space and time. This means that ordinary Euclidean geometry is no longer valid in such a curved space, just as the two-dimensional geometry of a plane cannot be applied on the surface of a sphere. On a plane, we can draw, for example, a square by marking off one metre on a straight line, making a right angle and marking off another metre, then making another right angle and marking off another metre, and finally making a third right angle and marking off one metre again, after which we are back at the starting point and the square is completed. On a sphere, however, this procedure does not work because the rules of Euclidean geometry do not hold on curved surfaces. In the same way, we can define a three-dimensional curved space to be one in which Euclidean geometry is no longer valid. Einstein's theory, now, says that three-dimensional space is actually curved, and that the curvature is caused by the gravitational field of massive bodies.

Wherever there is a massive object, e.g. a star or a planet, the space around it is curved and the degree of curvature depends on the mass of the object. And as space can never be separated from time in relativity theory, time as well is affected by the presence of matter, flowing at different rates in different parts of the universe. Einstein's general theory of relativity thus completely abolishes the concepts of absolute space and time. Not only are all measurements involving space and time relative; the whole structure of space-time depends on the distribution of matter in the universe, and the concept of 'empty space' loses its meaning.

The mechanistic world view of classical [Newtonian] physics was based on the notion of solid bodies moving in empty space. This notion is still valid in the region that has been called the 'zone of middle dimensions', that is, in the realm of our daily experience where classical physics continues to be a useful theory. Both concepts—that of empty space and that of solid material bodies—are deeply ingrained in our habits of thought, so it is extremely difficult for us to imagine a physical reality where they do not apply. And yet, this is precisely what modern physics forces us to do when we go beyond the middle dimensions. 'Empty space' has lost its meaning in astrophysics and cosmology, the sciences of the universe at large, and the concept of solid objects was shattered by atomic physics, the science of the infinitely small.

At the turn of the century, several phenomena connected with the structure of atoms and inexplicable in terms of classical physics were discovered. The first indication that atoms had some structure came from the discovery of X-rays [in 1896]; a new radiation which rapidly found its now well known application in medicine. X-rays, however, are not the only radiation emitted by atoms. Soon after their discovery, other kinds of radiation were discovered which are emitted by the atoms of so-called radioactive substances. The phenomenon of radioactivity gave definite proof of the composite nature of atoms, showing that the atoms of radioactive substances not only emit various types of radiation, but also transform themselves into atoms of completely different substances.

Besides being objects of intense study, these phenomena were also used, in most ingenious ways, as new tools to probe deeper into matter than had ever been possible before. Thus Max von Laue used X-rays to study the arrangements of atoms in crystals, and Ernest Rutherford realized that the so-called alpha particles emanating from radioactive substances were high-speed projectiles of subatomic size which could be used to explore the interior of the atom. They could be fired at atoms, and from the way they were deflected one could draw conclusions about the atoms' structure.

When Rutherford bombarded atoms with these alpha particles, he obtained sensational and totally unexpected results. Far from being the hard and solid particles they were believed to be since antiquity, the atoms turned out to consist of vast regions of space in which extremely small particles—the electrons—moved around the nucleus, bound to it by electric forces. It is not easy to get a feeling for the order of magnitude of atoms, so far is it removed from our macroscopic scale. The diameter of an atom is about one hundred millionth of a centimetre. In order to visualize this diminutive size, imagine an orange blown up to the size of the Earth. The atoms of the orange will then have the size of cherries. Myriads of cherries, tightly packed into a globe of the size of the Earth—that's a magnified picture of the atoms in an orange.

An atom, therefore, is extremely small compared to macroscopic objects, but it is huge compared to the nucleus in its centre. In our picture of cherry-sized atoms, the nucleus of an atom will be so small that we will not be able to see it. If we blew up the atom to the size of a football, or even to room size, the nucleus would still be too small to be seen by the naked eye. To see the nucleus, we would have to blow up the atom to the size of the biggest dome in the world, the dome of St Peter's Cathedral in Rome. In an atom of that size, the nucleus would have the size of a grain of salt! A grain of salt in the middle of the dome of St Peter's, and specks of dust whirling around it in the vast space of the dome—this is how we can picture the nucleus and electrons of an atom.

Soon after the emergence of this 'planetary' model of the atom, it was discovered that the number of electrons in the atoms of an element determine the element's chemical properties, and today we know that the whole periodic table of elements can be built up by successively adding protons and neutrons to the nucleus of the lightest atom—hydrogen*—and the corresponding number of electrons to its atomic 'shell'. The interactions between the atoms give rise to the various chemical processes, so that all of chemistry can now in principle be understood on the basis of the laws of atomic physics.

---

* The hydrogen atom consists of just one proton and one electron.

These laws, however, were not easy to recognize. They were discovered in the 1920s by an international group of physicists including Niels Bohr from Denmark, Louis De Broglie from France, Erwin Schrödinger and Wolfgang Pauli from Austria, Werner Heisenberg from Germany, and Paul Dirac from England. These men joined their forces across all national borders and shaped one of the most exciting periods in modern science, which brought them, for the first time, into contact with the strange and unexpected reality of the subatomic world. Every time the physicists asked nature a question in an atomic experiment, nature answered with a paradox, and the more they tried to clarify the situation, the sharper the paradoxes became. It took them a long time to accept the fact that these paradoxes belong to the intrinsic structure of atomic physics, and to realize that they arise whenever one attempts to describe atomic events in the traditional terms of physics. Once this was perceived, the physicists began to learn to ask the right questions and to avoid contradictions. In the words of Heisenberg, 'they somehow got into the spirit of the quantum theory', and finally they found the precise and consistent mathematical formulation of this theory.

The concepts of quantum theory were not easy to accept even after their mathematical formulation had been completed. Their effect on the physicists' imagination was truly shattering. Rutherford's experiments [around 1900] had shown that atoms, instead of being hard and indestructible, consisted of vast regions of space in which extremely small particles moved, and now quantum theory made it clear that even these particles were nothing like the solid objects of classical physics. The subatomic units of matter are very abstract entities which have a dual aspect. Depending on how we look at them, they appear sometimes as particles, sometimes as waves; and this dual nature is also exhibited by light which can take the form of electromagnetic waves or of particles.

This property of matter and of light is very strange. It seems impossible to accept that something can be, at the same time, a particle— i.e. an entity confined to a very small volume—and a wave, which is spread out over a large region of space. This contradiction gave rise to most of the . . . paradoxes which finally led to the formulation of quantum theory. The whole development started when Max Planck discovered [in 1900] that the energy of heat radiation is not emitted continuously, but appears in the form of 'energy packets'. Einstein called these energy packets 'quanta' and recognized them as a fundamental aspect of nature. He was bold enough to postulate that light and every other form of electromagnetic radiation can appear not only as electromagnetic waves, but also in the form of these quanta. The light quanta, which gave quantum theory its name, have since been accepted as bona fide particles and are now called photons. They are particles of a special kind, however, massless and always travelling with the speed of light.

The apparent contradiction between the particle and the wave picture was solved in a completely unexpected way which called in question the very foundation of the mechanistic world view—the concept of the reality of matter. At the subatomic level, matter does not exist with certainty at definite places, but rather shows 'tendencies to exist', and atomic events do not occur with certainty at definite times and in definite ways, but rather show 'tendencies to occur'. In the formalism of quantum theory, these tendencies are expressed as probabilities and are associated with mathematical quantities which take the form of waves. This is why particles can be waves at the same time. They are not 'real' three-dimensional waves like sound or water waves. They are 'probability waves', abstract mathematical quantities with all the characteristic properties of waves which are related to the probabilities of finding the particles at particular points in space and at particular times. All the laws of atomic physics are expressed in terms of these probabilities. We can never predict an atomic event with certainty; we can only say how likely it is to happen.

Quantum theory has thus demolished the classical concepts of solid objects and of strictly deterministic laws of nature. At the subatomic level, the solid material objects of classical physics dissolve into wave-like patterns of probabilities, and these patterns, ultimately, do not represent probabilities of things, but rather probabilities of interconnections. A careful analysis of the process of observation in atomic physics has shown that the subatomic particles have no meaning as isolated entities, but can only be understood as interconnections between the preparation of an experiment and the subsequent measurement. Quantum theory thus reveals a basic oneness of the universe. It shows that we cannot decompose the world into independently existing smallest units. As we penetrate into matter, nature does not show us any isolated 'basic building blocks', but rather appears as a complicated web of relations between the various parts of the whole. These relations always include the observer in an essential way. The human observer constitutes the final link in the chain of observational processes, and the properties of any atomic object can only be understood in terms of the object's interaction with the observer. This means that the classical ideal of an objective description of nature is no longer valid. The Cartesian partition between the I and the world, between the observer and the observed, cannot be made when dealing with atomic matter. In atomic physics, we can never speak about nature without, at the same time, speaking about ourselves.

The Great Depression: Unemployment

John A. Garraty

Economists and historians still argue over what caused the Great Depression, which began in 1929 and lasted until World War II. Informed explanations involve varying combinations of factors: the capitalist world's unhealthy dependence on a flow of American loans to Germany that enabled that country to pay reparations to Great Britain and France, which in turn used the money to repay their war debts to the United States; the failure of wages in industrial countries to keep pace with rising output, so that workers (who were also consumers) could not buy all that they produced, creating gluts of unsellable merchandise; the weak agricultural economies everywhere in North America and Europe; the speculation on world stock markets, tempting investors to pay unrealistically high prices for securities, often using borrowed money; the high tariff barriers that prevented international trade from moving freely and protected weak industries from foreign competition; and the blunders of central banks (especially America's Federal Reserve System), which seemed to do everything wrong. The crash of the New York stock market in October 1929 started a financial panic that rapidly spread through the rest of the capitalist world. Although the governments of Europe, North America, and Japan tried to deal with the crisis, none could restart the engines of prosperity that had hummed so reassuringly through most of the 1920s. Unemployment, poverty, and misery stalked the industrialized world, and in Germany the extremist Nazi movement was voted into power in 1933. Only a new arms race on the eve of World War II ended the crisis.

Excerpted from "What It Did to the Jobless," by John Garraty in *The Great Depression: An Inquiry into the Causes, Course, and Consequences of the Worldwide Depression of the 1930s.* Copyright © 1986 by John Garraty. Reprinted with permission from Harcourt, Inc.

American historian John A. Garraty has studied the worldwide economic crisis of the 1930s. In the following excerpt from his book *The Great Depression* he offers a comparative study of the impact of unemployment on its victims.

T o contemporaries, persistent, unprecedentedly high unemployment was the most alarming aspect of the Great Depression. In every industrial nation, more people were out of work than in any period in the past. It has been estimated that in 1933 about 30 million workers were jobless, about two-thirds of these in three countries— the United States, Germany, and Great Britain. If anything, this estimate is low.

But little can be gained by citing numbers. No accurate counts were made either before or during the depression. Furthermore, the estimates that were made were arrived at by different methods in different countries. B.R. Mitchell's authoritative *European Historical Statistics: 1750–1970* (1976) ends six pages of statistics on unemployment in nineteen nations with this caution: "The variety of different indicators of unemployment used is clear from the footnotes [25 in number]. This should serve as a warning against incautious comparisons."

Modern American economists have gone to great lengths in the effort to estimate the number of people unemployed in the United States in the twenties and thirties. They have used fragmentary contemporary evidence, much of it derived from labor union records. One recent student of the problem, Gene Smiley, has characterized the best of these records as "strikingly different and contradictory.". . .

The most useful way to express numerically the extent of unemployment during the Great Depression is to use the index of the International Labor Organization. According to the ILO index, if the world's unemployed population is taken as 100 in 1929, it was 235 by 1931, 291 in the autumn of 1932, and still about 200 as late as 1935. . . .

Beyond the difficulty in counting the unemployed, there are all sorts of variations to be considered that affected the significance of unemployment to the unemployed and to the societies they inhabited. It made a great difference whether a person was unemployed for a few weeks or months or for a longer period. Unemployment affected men differently in most cases than women, old people differently than the young, married people differently than single. Such obvious matters as the number of children in a breadwinner's family and the existence and amount of unemployment insurance or welfare also affected the meaning of joblessness for its victims. So did the amount of unemployment in the community.

Investigators, government and private, did a much better job of studying the effects of unemployment than of counting the number of people without work. Studies of the impact of unemployment on living conditions, school attendance, health, and other topics were carried out in many lands. . . .

Much valuable information was gathered in these ways, but by far the most interesting and useful investigations were those conducted by field workers who studied the jobless directly. Two now-classic examples were those of the sociologists E. Wight Bakke, an American, and Paul F. Lazarsfeld, an Austrian.

Bakke, at the time a Yale graduate student, spent six months in 1931 in the London suburb of Greenwich. He lived with a working-class family and spent many hours observing people in local pubs and employment offices. He went with jobless men as they made the rounds looking for work. In these ways, he got to know many un-employed people well. Some he interviewed repeatedly, recording carefully their changing moods—their attitudes toward themselves and English society, toward politics, and so on. He persuaded some of them to write day-by-day accounts of their activities and feelings. He published his conclusions in *The Unemployed Man* (1933), his doctoral dissertation.

Lazarsfeld was the head of a team of social scientists from the University of Vienna who spent the winter of 1931–32 in the village of Marienthal, not far from Vienna. Marienthal was a one-factory town. The factory, a textile mill, had gone bankrupt and closed down, so that just about everyone in the village of about 1,500 people was unemployed. For most the tiny relief payments supplied by the Austrian government were the only source of income.

The Lazarsfeld team used two kinds of data—what they called "natural" evidence obtained by observing the subjects, and "experimental" material designed by the team, such as questionnaires. The investigators lived among the villagers and followed their activities closely. They kept a file on each of the 478 families in Marienthal. . . .

Bakke's and Lazarsfeld's painstaking research projects were only the most original of many such investigations. Important studies were made by field workers in Italy, Czechoslovakia, Poland, France, England, and the United States. In America such analyses were almost without number. . . .

The unemployment studies of the 1930s varied a great deal in scope and quality—they were indeed a mixed bag. Jobless people and their families were subjected to batteries of tests. Some investigators sought to plumb the psyches of idle workers, hoping to isolate traits that might explain why they could not find work or why they reacted in the ways they did to their unfortunate condition. Some compared the unemployed with people in their trades and professions who were still working. There were studies of tramps and vagrants, of people on relief, of those employed on public works projects.

No single pattern or explanation emerged from these investigations. But an enormous amount was learned. It is surely correct to say that the people of that era knew more about the effects of unemployment than they did about the extent of unemployment or its causes.

Despite the physical and mental suffering that often resulted from prolonged joblessness, there is no evidence that the general health of society was affected by the depression. In the United States, the trend toward increased longevity (one that fortunately still continues) proceeded unchecked during the depression. Life expectancy was 57.1 years in 1929, 63.7 years in 1939. The death rate fell from 11.9 per thousand to 10.6 in those years. Trends in the European industrial countries were similar.

The trends of course obscure what was happening to many individuals. After all, the unemployed were a relatively small minority of the population. Furthermore, the steep decline of food prices, a result of the agricultural depression, meant that most people with jobs could improve their diets during the depression years. In some places the per capita consumption of fruit, milk, and meat increased. In France meat consumption rose by more than 10 percent between 1928 and 1936, milk consumption by 20 percent. This much conceded, it is certain that many unemployed people did not get enough to eat and that the quality of the food that the jobless and their dependents consumed was often poorer than what was necessary to maintain good health.

There were 20 known cases of starvation in New York City in 1931, though how many of these were related to unemployment is not clear. Such deaths could occur in places where there were no well-organized welfare systems. Starvation was everywhere rare, however. Highly colored accounts of mass malnutrition do not stand up to close investigation.

Field studies in a number of countries of what unemployed families actually ate show that in nearly all cases, people were getting enough calories to maintain body weight. Consumption ranged from about 2,600 to 2,900 calories per day for adult males, no more than 200 or 300 fewer than what working people were getting.

But in order to obtain *enough* to eat, unemployed people had to cut down on relatively expensive items like meat and fresh fruit. Even milk and other dairy products cost more than many could afford to buy in adequate amounts. In New York City, by December 1930, milk consumption was down by a million quarts a day. Meat consumption plummeted in Vienna in 1931–32. In Budapest, where relief agencies were swamped by hordes of rural people who had crowded in looking for jobs, conditions were even worse. An Australian doctor with a large practice among the unemployed reported in 1935 that many of the children he treated were undernourished. "None will complain of insufficient bread and meat, and in some cases they will admit that they have more bread than necessary," he reported. But they were not obtaining milk, vegetables, or fruit 'in sufficient quantities."

The failure of many poor people to manage their meager resources efficiently complicated the problem. Lazarsfeld reported that nearly half the residents of Marienthal had nothing to eat at their evening meal but bread and coffee—the coffee of course had no nutritional value whatsoever. In the depths of the depression, [British writer] George Orwell made a trip through the northern part of England, where unemployment was especially high. He reported his impressions in a fascinating book, *The Road to Wigan Pier.* Orwell was appalled by how much money unemployed people were spending on sweets, fried potatoes, and tea. (He called tea "the Englishman's opium.") Numbers of unemployed Belgians spent money raising pigeons—not to eat but in hopes of winning a worthless prize. Students of French unemployment complained that the jobless continued to spend a large part of their food budgets on coffee and wine.

It is probably true that some of this "inefficient" consumption was due to ignorance. But as George Orwell noted, it was also an understandable reaction on the part of people in straitened circumstances who had few other ways to relieve the tedium of day-to-day existence. "When you are unemployed," Orwell wrote, "you don't *want* to eat dull, wholesome food. You want something a little bit 'tasty.' " The German sociologist Siegfried Kracauer made a related observation in commenting on the tendency of idle German workers to spend money on movie tickets. They were doing so, he surmised, "less for pleasure than to drive away the ghost of bad times."

Furthermore, the margin for poor people was so thin that it was difficult even with the best management to provide a good diet. A study of 869 German families revealed that they were spending 45 percent of their incomes on food. A French estimate of a similar group reported the food percentage at 60, which is perhaps a comment on the French value system as much as on the limited resources of the subjects.

Routine medical and dental care tended to be neglected by the unemployed in favor of more pressing needs. A report of the German Welfare Ministry issued in 1931 noted that doctors were complaining about parents who were not bringing in their children soon enough when they were sick. According to a dentist in Muncie, Indiana, "working-class patients have tended to delay about two years longer in coming in, and then the tooth has become so bad that there is nothing left to do but to extract it." Orwell mentioned in *The Road to Wigan Pier* that people told him that to avoid toothaches "it is best to 'get shut of' your teeth as early in life as possible."

Many of the unemployed suffered from a lack of proper clothing and from poor housing. Social workers often reported that children of their clients could not go to school because they had no shoes. Many families suffered cruelly in winter because they had no money for coal or wood. It is true that landlords frequently allowed destitute families to remain in their flats out of pity or, the chance of finding another tenant being small, because they preferred having the places occupied in order to prevent them from being vandalized. But the press was full of stories of people evicted for nonpayment of rent or forced to part with their homes because they could not meet mortgage payments.

There was a big increase in vagrancy as people lost their homes and as the jobless took to the road in search of work. Lodging houses operated by local governments and by charitable organizations such as the Salvation Army took care of many of these unfortunates. On the borders of cities from Adelaide and Sydney in Australia to Buenos Aires in Argentina, shantytowns sprang up as groups of homeless people constructed ramshackle shelters on vacant land. One of the most elaborate of these places was the Village of Misery on the northwest outskirts of Vienna, with its shacks made of broken bricks, rusting stovepipes, and other discarded building materials.

The Australians gave these settlements names ranging from Hungry Mile to the sardonic Happy Valley; they called the shacks, constructed of packing cases, scrap lumber, and sheets of rusting metal, "humpies." At first Americans gave their shantytowns similar names—Hardluck-on-the-River for example, and Prosperity Park. But they soon began to call them Hoovervilles, an indication of what the result of the 1932 election was likely to be. . . .

The social and psychological effects of unemployment were studied at least as thoroughly as the material effects, and the results of these investigations make interesting reading. In few areas was there so much agreement; it did not seem to matter what the geographical, political, social, or cultural background—people who lost their jobs reacted in similar ways. Not every individual responded in exactly the same manner. But the patterns of the responses were few in number and not very different from one country to the next.

Statistics show that birth rates declined during the depression. In the United States, the rate went down by 10 percent, which was typical. Marriage rates were less uniformly affected. That rate fell by about 20 percent in the United States and France, still further, for example, in South Australia. But it remained unaffected in Great Britain, and in Germany the birth rate rose after the Nazis came to power. Divorce rates declined, most probably because of the high cost of divorce in most nations.

At least in America, the suicide rate rose during the depression, though . . . ruined investors did not jump out of the windows of skyscrapers in droves after Black Tuesday or at any time during the depression. The suicide rate also went up in Germany. Crime statistics show no clear trend, though it is obvious that many unemployed people stole things they needed but could not afford and committed crimes of many kinds because of the emotional strains they were enduring.

As for the psychological impact of unemployment on its victims, the number of studies of this subject made during the depression was almost infinite. . . . These . . . studies varied widely in scope, method, and scientific objectivity. . . . But their conclusions were remarkably uniform. The intelligence, nationality, and work experience of unemployed persons had little effect on how they reacted. In brief, when people lost their jobs, they responded first by searching energetically for new ones. If nothing turned up, they gradually became discouraged, perhaps emotionally distraught. But after some months of idleness, they either sank into apathy or adjusted to doing nothing, in either case leading extremely circumscribed existences in apparent calm.

One of the first to describe this pattern was E. Wight Bakke. The behavior of one of his informants, whom he called "A," is worth describing in some detail. A was a truck driver whom Bakke met at a political rally in Greenwich a few days after he was laid off. "There's plenty of jobs for a man with my experience," A told Bakke on that occasion. "I've never been out more than a week or so before. I'll soon be back."

But it did not work out that way. A answered want ads without success. To save money, he moved in with his parents. When Bakke saw him again a few weeks later, he had not given up hope, but he was getting discouraged. And after another five weeks, he told Bakke, "I'm beginning to wonder what is wrong with me." Three more weeks passed, and he said, "Either I'm no good, or there is something wrong with business around here. . . . Even my family is beginning to think I'm not trying." Finally A became despondent, complaining to Bakke of "the hopelessness of every step you take.". . .

Lazarsfeld's generalizations, reached after his work in Marienthal, dealt of necessity with how people reacted after long periods of idleness more than with the evolution of their reactions. He focused on the hundred poorest families in the village. He found four types.

Those least affected he called *unbroken.* They continued to seek work, made plans for the future, and had an optimistic outlook. Though poor by any standard, these people had a little more money than the others in the group. Next came those Lazarsfeld called the *resigned* (by far the largest segment, nearly half those studied). They had adjusted to a limited existence, made no plans, had few expectations. . . . Another quarter of the group Lazarsfeld called *despairing.* They were gloomy and full of undirected rage and given to frequent bouts of drunkenness. Finally there were the *apathetic.* These were the poorest of the poor. They had given up completely, apparently uninterested even in the present moment.

In a town such as Marienthal, the percentage of the people who were crushed by unemployment may have been higher than in less blighted communities. Lazarsfeld called Marienthal "*die müde Gemeinschaft,*" the tired community. "For hours on end," he wrote, "the men stand around in the street, alone or in small groups, leaning against the wall of a house or the parapet of the bridge. . . . They have forgotten how to hurry."

A mountain of other evidence demonstrates that apathy and despair were widespread among the unemployed. "You see that corner?" a Welsh miner asked an investigator. "My time is spent between here and that corner."

"I was one of a gang," a young Englishman explained. "We used to stay in bed late . . . so as not to need breakfast. . . . Then we would all go down to the library and read the papers. Then we went home for a bit of lunch, and then we met again at a billiard hall where you could watch the play for nothing. . . . In the evening we all used to go to the pictures. That was how we spent the dole money." This man added, showing that he had not completely surrendered to apathy, "In the end I thought I'd go mad if I went on like that.". . .

Unemployment, says a character in the English novel *Love on the Dole,* "got you slowly, with the slippered stealth of an unsuspected malignant disease. You fell into the habit of slouching, of putting your hands into your pockets and keeping them there; of glancing at people furtively, ashamed of your secret, until you fancied that everybody eyed you with suspicion." A German novelist made the same point somewhat differently. "If [the unemployed] speak of the future, they mean tomorrow or the next day. They do not think of anything beyond that. And if a year passes, that time becomes yesterday, the next year, tomorrow."

Siegfried Kracauer reported that the men at a German employment office scarcely listened to the announcements of jobs. They were "too numbed to believe in their chance of being chosen." The reports of American social workers who dealt with the unemployed are full of words like depression, indifference, lethargy, submission, and apathy. In Boston, one wrote, people on relief seemed emotionally flat. They expressed neither resentment at their condition nor gratitude for the government benefits they were receiving. As Lillian Wald of the Henry Street settlement house explained, the jobless lost "self-respect . . . ambition and pride."

Of course personal differences, the degree of suffering, and the kind of emotional support available from friends and relatives influenced how people reacted to long-term joblessness. Observers noted that people who had experienced periodic unemployment in the past could handle the inevitable psychological depression better than those for whom unemployment was a new experience. Hard-driving, ambitious types seemed less able than more relaxed people to resist the debilitating effect of being out of work for long periods.

Much discussion occurred during the depression as to whether or not being on relief or accepting charity of any kind encouraged idleness or undermined the recipient's eagerness to work. This was almost certainly not the case for most people. . . . Bakke found that about half the unemployed people that he studied in New Haven *never* applied for help, no matter how desperate their situations. . . . Social workers were almost unanimous in arguing that work relief programs were preferable to direct grants of money to the jobless. But the reason was their belief that work sustained people, not that a dole would make them lazy.

In the United States, people were supposed to be individualistic, self-reliant pioneer types. Accepting any kind of aid was thought to be an especially painful experience, what two sociologists called "a severe mental jolt." Dependency was indeed hard for most Americans to take, but all the evidence demonstrates that it was equally hard for the jobless of other industrial nations.

Observers everywhere were amazed by evidence that the jobless, despite the extent and duration of mass unemployment, tended to blame themselves for their inability to find work. "When for the first time I held out my hand for my 9 *zloty* of benefit I was filled with disgust for the whole of my previous existence," one of the [unemployed] Polish autobiographers wrote. . . .

How, then, to explain the tendency of observers to claim that many of the unemployed were deadbeats who should be compelled to work for any aid they received? Partly by the fact that some *were* lazy and happy to live off the labor of others. Partly also because some of the unemployed were true unemployables: the physical and mental misfits who exist in any community even in prosperous times. But mostly because many unemployed people suffered from the debilitating effects of long-term joblessness. . . .

The conclusions reached by the many investigators of family life during the depression were much less clearcut than those reached by students of the unemployed themselves, mostly because with more complex human relationships involved, the number of possible reactions increased enormously. Members of families that suffered serious financial setbacks substituted their own labor for goods and services previously obtained with money—the changes might range from baking a cake instead of buying one to discharging a servant and doing one's own housework. Boys who found jobs after school tended to become more appreciative of the value of money and be more "adult oriented.". . .

In some cases, unemployment caused trouble within families. In other instances, it brought family members closer together. Some men enjoyed having more time to be with their children. Others found that being around the children for prolonged periods drove them up the wall. Some men became absorbed in doing chores around the house; some took up new hobbies. Some took to drink. Others sulked.

One of the few general effects of unemployment on family life was its strong tendency to increase the influence of women, both as wives and as mothers. . . .

What form this influence took and its impact on husband-wife and mother-child relationships varied considerably. Some wives were very supportive of their jobless spouses, others scornful. Some found jobs, leaving their husbands to take care of home and children. All kinds of role reversals could occur, with unpredictable results. Much depended on the basic relationships between family members. When these were shaky to begin with, unemployment was likely to make them worse. . . .

Here are a few examples of the kinds of difficulties other investigators reported:

1. Male resentment at loss of dominance, especially if the woman became the breadwinner.

2. Loss of prestige (and the power to control by the dispensing of allowance money) in the eyes of children.

3. Social isolation, caused by lack of money to entertain, by shame, and eventually by apathy.

4. Sexual problems, caused by such things as decline in physical energy, apathy again, and fear of pregnancy.

Worldwide, in 1929 about one-third of all workers were women. Many of these women lost their jobs during the depression. But the statistics suggest (though like other unemployment figures of the period, they are not very reliable) that proportionately fewer women were laid off than men. This was true partly because most women were paid lower wages than men for the same work. Employers tended to keep them on when it was necessary to cut back. Also, the kinds of work that most women did were not as hard hit during the depression as the heavy industry and building trade work that was done by males.

On the other hand, many women workers were domestics, and unemployment among domestics was seldom recorded. Furthermore, the tendency of married women to look for work if their husbands were laid off meant that more of them found jobs. (Today this would raise the female unemployment rate because of the way joblessness is measured, but this was not the case in the 1930s.)

The question of whether they suffered the ravages of unemployment more or less frequently than men aside, the depression had many bad effects upon women. Massive efforts were made to get married women, especially those whose husbands were employed, out of the work force. Even before 1929, many countries had passed laws restricting the employment of married women. In some, women civil servants were expected to retire when they married. If their husbands were also employed by the government, in some countries laws against nepotism required that one or the other be discharged. In nearly every instance, the wife was the one to go.

The depression increased this pressure on women workers. A 1932 American antinepotism law for government workers did not stipulate which spouse must be discharged, but three out of every four who were let go under the law were females. An Austrian law stated specifically that the woman had to retire. . . .

Restrictions on women workers took extreme forms in Nazi Germany. To the Nazi way of thinking, women were supposed to concentrate their energies on household tasks and child raising. "A job will not bring happiness near. The home alone is your proper sphere" a Nazi slogan ran. Women were barred from certain professions. A quota of only 10 percent was placed on women entering the universities. Marriage loans provided to encourage population growth and stimulate industry were made conditional on the bride giving up work.

All these antifemale policies made little sense. In Germany before the depression, only about 30 percent of women workers were married. Three-quarters of these were helpers in family-run businesses, such as grocery stores and small craft enterprises. Many of the few who held true second jobs worked because their husbands were not earning enough money to support the family. Many of the rest were engaged in professions that men traditionally avoided, such as domestic service and nursing. As a study made by the United States Women's Bureau put it, most women worked "because they have to."

The Totalitarian Challenge, 1933–1940

PREFACE

The concept of totalitarianism has had a long, politically charged life. Between the late 1930s and the mid-1960s, European and American liberals used the word to sum up all that they found repulsive in the dictatorial regimes of Stalinist Russia, Nazi Germany, and Fascist Italy: these regimes' use of terror to maintain their power, their sweeping denial of all human and civil rights, their aggressive expansionism; in a word, their determination to exercise total power. After World War II, the same totalitarian label got attached to Communist China. But by the late 1960s the value of totalitarianism as an explanatory model was fading. Historians were learning that within the supposedly monolithic dictatorships of Benito Mussolini, Adolf Hitler, Joseph Stalin, and China's Mao Zedong had actually burrowed great swarms of competing party bosses; the dictators at the top, it seemed, had actually known little about what went on down below. With the Soviet Union evolving from a revolutionary state that terrorized its people to a gray, dull, economically stagnant oligarchy, comparisons to Nazi Germany no longer appeared apt. Nor did it seem to apply to China after Mao's Cultural Revolution faded in the mid-1970s. Totalitarianism as a description of twentieth-century dictatorships was no longer in scholarly fashion.

Today, however, people in the former Soviet Union, Eastern Europe, and China tend to use the concept of totalitarianism to describe the experience from which they have now emerged. Totalitarian regimes, they acknowledge, may never have exercised "total" control, but these dictatorships certainly *claimed* that no sphere of life was private and they certainly *aspired* to remold every aspect of human character. Selections later in this book will give evidence of such claims and intentions.

Mussolini Defines Totalitarianism

Benito Mussolini

Benito Mussolini (1883–1945), the Fascist dictator of Italy from 1922 until he was shot and publicly hung head-downwards by Communist revolutionaries at the end of World War II, was proud to call himself a totalitarian. In this selection from a 1935 statement of his regime's aims, he explicitly calls the Fascist movement he founded and headed the antithesis of liberal democracy.

L ike all sound political conceptions, Fascism is action and it is thought; action in which doctrine is immanent, and doctrine arising from a given system of historical forces in which it is inserted, and working on them from within. It has therefore a form correlated to contingencies of time and space; but it has also an ideal content which makes it an expression of truth in the higher region of the history of thought. . . . To know men one must know man; and to know man one must be acquainted with reality and its laws. There can be no conception of the State which is not fundamentally a conception of life: philosophy or intuition, system of ideas evolving within the framework of logic or concentrated in a vision or a faith, but always, at least potentially, an organic conception of the world.

Thus many of the practical expressions of Fascism—such as party organisation, system of education, discipline—can only be understood when considered in relation to its general attitude toward life. . . . A spiritual attitude. Fascism sees in the world not only those superficial, material aspects in which man appears as an individual, standing by

Excerpted from *Connecting with the Past: The D.C .Heath Document Sets for Western Civilization* (Lexington, MA: D.C. Heath & Co., 1995). Copyright © 1995 by Houghton Mifflin Co.

himself, self-centered, subject to natural law which instinctively urges him toward a life of selfish momentary pleasure; it sees not only the individual but the nation and the country; individuals and generations bound together by a moral law, with common traditions and a mission which suppressing the instinct for life closed in a brief circle of pleasure, builds up a higher life, founded on duty, a life free from the limitations of time and space, in which the individual, by self-sacrifice, the renunciation of self-interest, by death itself, can achieve that purely spiritual existence in which his value as a man consists.

The conception is therefore a spiritual one, arising from the general reaction of the century against the flaccid materialistic positivism of the XIXth century. . . .

In the Fascist conception of history, man is man only by virtue of the spiritual process to which he contributes as a member of the family, the social group, the nation, and in function of history to which all nations bring their contribution. . . . Outside history man is a nonentity. Fascism is therefore opposed to all individualistic abstractions based on eighteenth century materialism; and it is opposed to all Jacobinistic utopias and innovations. . . .

Anti-individualistic, the Fascist conception of life stresses the importance of the State and accepts the individual only in so far as his interests coincide with those of the State, which stands for the conscience and the universal will of man as a historic entity. It is opposed to classical liberalism which arose as a reaction to absolutism and exhausted its historical function when the State became the expression of the conscience and will of the people. Liberalism denied the State in the name of the individual; Fascism reasserts the rights of the State as expressing the real essence of the individual. And if liberty is to be the attribute of living men and not of abstract dummies invented by individualistic liberalism, then Fascism stands for liberty, and for the only liberty worth having, the liberty of the State and of the individual within the State. The Fascist conception of the State is all-embracing; outside of it no human or spiritual values can exist, much less have value. Thus understood, Fascism is totalitarian, and the Fascist State—a synthesis and a unit inclusive of all values—interprets, develops, and potentiates the whole life of a people.

Hitler

Alan Bullock

Without World War I and the Great Depression, the world would never have heard of the Austrian ne'er-do-well Adolf Hitler; he would doubtless have spent the rest of his days ranting against Jews in the slums of Vienna with only his fellow inmates of the city's flophouses to listen. But Germany's defeat in World War I gave him a cause on which he could begin to build a mass movement, and the agony of the Great Depression encouraged Germans by the millions to turn to him. In January 1933 he came to power legally, albeit with the aid of some unscrupulous intriguing among-right wing German politicians who naively or cynically thought that they could manipulate him. They were wrong: Hitler was one of the most gifted and evil demagogues of all time, and a clever, ruthless, and utterly fanatical politician. No one could control him. Before he finally killed himself in his bunker beneath the streets of a besieged Berlin on April 30, 1945, he caused the deaths of perhaps 20 million people and wrecked almost all of Europe.

British historian Alan Bullock wrote a biography of Hitler in the 1950s and revised it in 1962. Despite its age and the recent appearance of other fine biographies of the Nazi führer ("leader"), Bullock's *Hitler: A Study in Tyranny* remains a classic. Here, Bullock analyzes Hitler's ideas and his willingness to put them—murderously—into effect.

The basis of Hitler's political beliefs was a crude Darwinism. 'Man has become great through struggle. . . . Whatever goal man has reached is due to his originality plus his brutality. . . . All life is bound up in three theses: Struggle is the father of all things, virtue lies in blood, leadership is primary and decisive.' On another occasion he declared: 'The whole work of Nature is a mighty struggle

Excerpted from *Hitler: A Study in Tyranny*, by Alan Bullock. Copyright © 1962 by Alan Bullock. Reprinted with permission in the U.S. from HarperCollins Publishers, Inc. and in Canada from Curtis Brown, Ltd.

between strength and weakness—an eternal victory of the strong
over the weak. There would be nothing but decay in the whole of
Nature if this were not so. States which offend against this elementary law fall into decay.' It followed from this that 'through all the
centuries force and power are the determining factors. . . . Only force
rules. Force is the first law.' Force was more than the decisive factor in any situation; it was force which alone created right. 'Always
before God and the world, the stronger has the right to carry through
what he wills. History proves: He who has not the strength—him the
"right in itself" profits not a whit.'

The ability to seize and hold a decisive superiority in the struggle
for existence Hitler expressed in the idea of race, the role of which
is as central in Nazi mythology as that of class in Marxist. All that
mankind has achieved, Hitler declared in *Mein Kampf*, has been the
work of the Aryan race: 'It was the Aryan who laid the groundwork
and erected the walls of every great structure in human culture.' But
who were the Aryans?

Although Hitler frequently talked as if he regarded the whole German nation as of pure Aryan stock (whatever that may mean) his real
view was rather different. It was only a part of any nation (even of
the German nation) which could be regarded as Aryan. These constituted an élite within the nation (represented by the Nazi Party and
especially by the S.S.) which stamped its ideas upon the development of the whole people, and by its leadership gave this racial ag-
glomeration an Aryan character which in origin belonged only to a
section. Thus Hitler's belief in race could be used to justify both the
right of the German people to ride roughshod over such inferior peoples as the uncouth Slavs and the degenerate French, and the right
of the Nazis, representing an élite, sifted and tested by the struggle
for power, to rule over the German people. This explains why Hitler
often referred to the Nazi capture of power in Germany as a racial
revolution, since it represented the replacement of one ruling caste
by another. As Hitler told Otto Strasser in May 1930: 'We want to
make a selection from the new dominating caste which is not moved,
as you are, by any ethic of pity, but is quite clear in its own mind that
it has the right to dominate others because it represents a better race.'

In Hitler's and [S.S. chief Heinrich] Himmler's plans for the
S.S.—a racial élite selected with the most careful eye to Nazi eu-
genics—recruitment was to be open not only to Germans, but to
Aryans of other nations as well.

> The conception of the nation ([German writer Walter] Rauschning records
> Hitler saying) has become meaningless. We have to got rid of this false
> conception and set in its place the conception of race. The New Order
> cannot be conceived in terms of the national boundaries of the peoples
> with an historic past, but in terms of race that transcend these bound-

aries. . . . I know perfectly well that in the scientific sense there is no such thing as race. But you, as a farmer, cannot get your breeding right without the conception of race. And I, as a politician, need a conception which enables the order that has hitherto existed on an historic basis to be abolished, and an entirely new and anti-historic order enforced and given an intellectual basis. . . . And for this purpose the conception of race serves me well. . . . France carried her great Revolution beyond her borders with the conception of the nation. With the conception of race, National Socialism will carry its revolution abroad and recast the world.

I shall bring into operation throughout all Europe and the whole world this process of selection which we have carried out through National Socialism in Germany. . . . The active sections in nations, the militant, Nordic section, will rise again and become the ruling element over these shopkeepers and pacifists, these puritans and speculators and busybodies. . . . There will not be much left then of the clichés of nationalism, and precious little among us Germans. Instead there will be an understanding between the various language elements of the one good ruling race.

This is Hitler at his most flamboyant, and it is not to be taken too literally. Hitler was a master of nationalist appeal, and old-fashioned nationalism was very far from being played out in Europe. Hitler's foreign policy was nationalist in character, and nationalism, both that of the Occupied Countries and that of the Germans, cut across and wrecked the attempt to turn the Quislings [Nazi collaborators] and the S.S. into an international Nazi élite, just as it proved too strong for the Jacobins outside France in the 1790s. But it is also a passage characteristic of Hitler's way of talking: a straightforward claim to unlimited power was dressed up in the myth of a 'pure' race, just as on other occasions Hitler gave it a Wagnerian colouring and talked of founding a new Order of Knights.

What Hitler was seeking to express in his use of the word 'race' was his belief in inequality—both between peoples and individuals —as another of the iron laws of Nature. He had a passionate dislike of the egalitarian doctrines of democracy in every field, economic, political and international.

There are [he said in this speech to the Düsseldorf Industry Club] two closely related factors which we can time and time again trace in periods of national decline: one is that for the conception of the value of personality there is substituted a levelling idea of the supremacy of mere numbers—democracy— and the other is the negation of the value of a people, the denial of any difference in the inborn capacity, the achievement of individual peoples. . . . Internationalism and democracy are inseparable conceptions.

Hitler rejected both in favour of the superior rights of the *Herrenvolk* [Master Race] in international affairs and of the Nazi élite in the government of the state.

Just as he opposed the concept of 'race' to the democratic belief in equality, so to the idea of personal liberty Hitler opposed the superior claims of the *Volk*. [*Volk* is the German word for people, but it connotes a mystical concept of people united by blood and soil.]

National Socialism [Hitler declared] takes as the starting point of its views and its decisions neither the individual nor humanity. It puts consciously into the central point of its whole thinking the *Volk*. This *Volk* is for it a blood-conditioned entity in which it sees the God-willed building-stone of human society. The individual is transitory, the *Volk* is permanent. If the Liberal *Weltanschauung* [world view] in its deification of the single individual must lead to the destruction of the *Volk*, National Socialism, on the other hand, desires to safeguard the *Volk*, if necessary even at the expense of the individual. It is essential that the individual should slowly come to realize that his own ego is unimportant when compared with the existence of the whole people . . . above all he must realize that the freedom of the mind and will of a nation are to be valued more highly than the individual's freedom of mind and will.

In an interview with the *New York Times* [in 1933] Hitler summed up his view in the sentence: 'The underlying idea is to do away with egoism and to lead people into the sacred collective egoism which is the nation.'

The *Volk* not only gave meaning and purpose to the individual's life, it provided the standard by which all other institutions and claims were to be judged.

Party, State, Army, the economic structure, the administration of justice are of secondary importance, they are but a means to the preservation of the *Volk*. In so far as they fulfil this task, they are right and useful. When they prove unequal to this task they are harmful and must either be reformed or set aside or replaced by better means.

Here was the justification for the campaign of the Nazis and other Völkish [adjective derived from *Volk*] groups against the Weimar Republic: their loyalty had been, not to the Republican State, but to the *Volk*, for betraying the interests of which men like Rathenau and Erzberger had been assassinated. Justice, truth and the freedom to criticize must all be subordinated to the overriding claim of the *Volk* and its preservation.

The [economically] radical wing of the Party argued that if the same criterion were applied to the economic system it meant the socialist organization of the national economy in the interests of the *Volk*. Hitler's views about economics, however, were entirely opportunist. The truth is that he was not at all interested in economics. He preached the true doctrine of the totalitarian State—which the rulers of Soviet Russia also practised, but found it embarrassing to admit—the supremacy of politics over economics. It is not economics but power that is decisive. . . .

With Marxism there could be no compromise. 'When people cast in our teeth our intolerance we proudly acknowledge it—yes, we have formed the inexorable decision to destroy Marxism in Germany down to its very last root.' This was said in 1932, at a time when Hitler saw in the unbroken organization of the Social Democratic Party and the trade unions the most solid obstacle to his ambitions, and in the rival extremists of the German Communist Party, the only other German party whose votes mounted with his own.

Hitler regarded the Marxist conception of class war and of class solidarity cutting across frontiers as a particular threat to his own exaltation of national unity founded on the community of the *Volk*. The object of National Socialist policy was to create a truly classless society. 'The slogan, "The dictatorship of the bourgeoisie must make way for the dictatorship of the proletariat", is simply a question of a change from the dictatorship of one class to that of another, while we wish for the dictatorship of the nation, that is, the dictatorship of the whole community. Only then shall we be able to restore to the millions of our people the conviction that the State does not represent the interests of a single group or class, and that the Government is there to manage the concerns of the entire community.' This single-minded concept of the national interest was to be embodied in, and guaranteed by, the absolutism of the State, as it had been in the time of Frederick the Great [in the eighteenth century] and in the Prussian tradition of the State glorified by Hegel [a leading Prussian philosopher of the early nineteenth century].

Hitler's skills in manipulating people and circumstances brought the Nazi Party to power.

Just as Hitler ascribed to the 'Aryan' all the qualities and achievements which he admired, so all that he hated is embodied in another mythological figure, that of the Jew. There can be little doubt that Hitler believed what he said about the Jews; from first to last his anti-Semitism is one of the most consistent themes in his career, the master idea which embraces the whole span of his thought. In whatever direction one follows Hitler's train of thought, sooner or later one encounters the satanic figure of the Jew. The Jew is made the universal scapegoat. Democracy is Jewish—the secret domination of the Jew. Bolshevism and Social Democracy; capitalism and the 'interest-slavery' of the moneylender; parliamentarianism and the freedom of the Press; liberalism and internationalism; anti-militarism and the class war; Christianity; modernism in art (*Kultur-Bolschewismus* [cultural Bolshevism]), prostitution and miscegenation [race mixing]—all are instruments devised by the Jew to subdue the Aryan peoples to his rule. One of Hitler's favourite phrases . . . was: 'The Jew is the ferment of decomposition in peoples.' This points to the fundamental fact about the Jew in Hitler's eyes; unlike the Aryan, the Jew is incapable of founding a State and so incapable of anything creative. He can only imitate and steal—or destroy in the spirit of envy.

> The Jew has never founded any civilization, though he has destroyed hundreds. He possesses nothing of his own creation to which he can point. Everything he has is stolen. Foreign peoples, foreign workmen build him his temples; it is foreigners who create and work for him; it is foreigners who shed their blood for him. He has no art of his own; bit by bit he has stolen it all from other peoples. He does not even know how to preserve the precious things others have created. . . . In the last resort it is the Aryan alone who can form States and set them on their path to future greatness. All this the Jew cannot do. And because he cannot do it, therefore all his revolutions must be international. They must spread as a pestilence spreads. Already he has destroyed Russia; now it is the turn of Germany, and with his envious instinct for destruction he seeks to disintegrate the national spirit of the Germans and to pollute their blood.

From this early speech of 1922, through the Nuremberg Laws of 1935 and the pogrom of November 1938 to the destruction of the Warsaw Ghetto and the death camps of Mauthausen and Auschwitz, Hitler's purpose was plain and unwavering. He meant to carry out the extermination of the Jewish race in Europe, using the word 'extermination' not in a metaphorical but in a precise and literal sense as the deliberate policy of the German State—and he very largely succeeded. On a conservative estimate, between four and four and a half million Jews perished in Europe under Hitler's rule—apart from the number driven from their homes who succeeded in finding refuge abroad. [Historians today put the figure at about 6 million dead.] History records few, if any, crimes of such magnitude and of so cold-blooded a purpose.

Stripped of their romantic trimmings, all Hitler's ideas can be reduced to a simple claim for power which recognizes only one relationship, that of domination, and only one argument, that of force. 'Civilization,' the Spanish philosopher, Ortega y Gasset, once wrote, 'consists in the attempt to reduce violence to the *ultima ratio*, the final argument. This is now becoming all too clear to us, for direct action reverses the order and proclaims violence as the *prima ratio* [first argument], or rather the *unica ratio*, the sole argument. It is the standard that dispenses with all others.'

Hitler was not original in this view. Every single one of his ideas—from the exaltation of the heroic leader, the racial myth, anti-Semitism, the community of the *Volk*, and the attack on the intellect, to the idea of a ruling élite, the subordination of the individual and the doctrine that might is right—is to be found in anti-rational and racist writers (not only in Germany but also in France and other European countries) during the hundred years which separate the Romantic movement from the foundation of the Third Reich. By 1914 they had become the commonplaces of radical, anti-Semitic and pan-German journalism in every city in Central Europe, including Vienna and Munich, where Hitler picked them up.

Hitler's originality lay not in his ideas, but in the terrifying literal way in which he set to work to translate these ideas into reality, and his unequalled grasp of the means by which to do this. To read Hitler's speeches and table talk is to be struck again and again by the lack of magnanimity or of any trace of moral greatness. His comments on everything except politics display a cocksure ignorance and an ineradicable vulgarity. Yet this vulgarity of mind, like the insignificance of his appearance, the badly fitting raincoat and the lock of hair plastered over his forehead of the early Hitler, was perfectly compatible with brilliant political gifts.

Stalin Starves Ukraine

Robert Conquest

Lenin built the Soviet Union into a dictatorship controlled by the Communist Party, which he dominated by the sheer force of his personality. But after his death in 1924, leadership of the party was contested. Leon Trotsky, the most flamboyant Bolshevik of the Revolution and the creator of the Red Army, seemed to be Lenin's obvious heir, but as a Jew, a brilliant intellectual, and a latecomer to the Bolshevik movement he aroused strong opposition within the party. The seemingly colorless Joseph Stalin, who controlled the party bureaucracy, intrigued behind the scenes and by 1928 had thrust Trotsky aside, even labeling him and his supporters "enemies of the party." Stalin now dominated the Soviet government.

Having defeated Trotsky politically, Stalin adopted his rival's economic plan, calling for rapid industrialization with the cost borne by the Soviet Union's peasant majority. The first of the Four Year Plans, issued in 1929, aimed at building up Soviet heavy industry at breakneck speed. To ensure that the growing industrial towns had reliable food supplies, the peasant population was forced into vast state and collective farms (*kolkhozy*), from which the authorities demanded ever-increasing quotas of foodstuffs. Over heavy peasant resistance, most of Soviet agriculture was collectivized by 1932.

Stalin was not satisfied. Resistance had been fiercest among the peasants of Ukraine, the Soviet republic that was the USSR's "breadbasket" region and a land where substantial nationalist sentiment persisted. (Ukrainians, like Russians, are Slavs, but they speak a different language and have different cultural traditions.) Strong evidence suggests that Stalin

Excerpted from *The Harvest of Sorrow: Soviet Collectivization and the Terror-Famine,* by Robert Conquest (London: Hutchinson, 1986). Copyright © 1986 by Robert Conquest. Reprinted with permission from Curtis Brown, Ltd., London, on behalf of Robert Conquest.

decided deliberately to crush potential Ukrainian resistance to his rule, which was slowly becoming absolute. In 1932, the puppet government of Ukraine, dominated by Stalin's appointees, raised the grain-delivery quotas for the republic's collective farms so high that practically nothing was left for the peasantry to eat. When these seemingly unrealistic deliveries were not made, Stalin treated the failure as "sabotage" by the kulaks— theoretically "rich peasants" but actually any villager who disliked being collectivized and starved. British historian Robert Conquest, in his 1986 book *Harvest of Sorrow*, describes what happened next.

Although some foreign journalists knew what was going on, the Western press almost totally ignored the government-induced famine in Ukraine and other parts of the Soviet Union in the early 1930s, and "progressive" admirers of the "Soviet experiment" dismissed as hostile propaganda the reports that did surface. Thanks in part to Conquest's book, we now know that the famine in Ukraine was mass murder almost on the scale of the Nazi Holocaust of World War II, and not much different from later genocides that have occurred in Cambodia and Rwanda.

A s the winter wore on, things got worse and worse. On 20 November 1932 a decree of the Ukrainian government halted the remittance of any grain at all to the kolkhoz peasants in payment of their 'labour days' until the grain delivery quota had been met.

On 6 December 1932 a further decree of the Ukrainian Soviet Government and the Central Committee of the Ukrainian Communist Party named six villages (two each in Dnipropetrovsk, Kharkov and Odessa Provinces) as sabotaging grain deliveries. The sanctions imposed were:

Halt the supply of goods immediately, halt the local cooperative and state trading, and remove all visible supplies from the cooperative and state stores.

Prohibit completely all collective farm trading, equally for collective farms, members of collective farms and individual holders.

Terminate the advancing of credits, arrange foreclosures of credits and other financial obligations.

Examination and purging of all foreign and hostile elements from cooperative and state apparatus to be carried out by the organs of the Workers and Peasants Inspection.

Examination and purging of collective farms of the above villages, of all counter-revolutionary elements . . .

Many more followed; and Ukrainian villages that could not meet their quotas were literally blockaded, to prevent city products from reaching them.

On 15 December 1932, a list was even published of whole *districts* 'to which supplies of commercial products have been halted until they achieve a decisive improvement in fulfilment of grain collective plans'. There were eighty-eight of these (out of 358 in the whole Ukraine), in the Dnipropetrovsk, Donets, Chernihiv, Odessa and Kharkov Provinces. Inhabitants of these 'blockaded' districts were deported *en masse* to the North.

In spite of all the Party's efforts, at the end of 1932 only 4.7 million tons of grain had been delivered—only 71.8% of the plan.

An official list from the Krynychky district, of 'peasants with a high fixed tax in kind and their deliveries of corn up to 1 January 1933' covers eleven villages and seventy names. Only nine delivered their quota, most of the others finding only half, or a quarter, of the necessary grain. The one case of high over-delivery from an individual is explained: 'all his corn has been taken out of his pits: sentenced'. In all six had been 'sentenced' (plus a wife and a son in the absence of the two 'guilty' peasants) or arrested; thirty-nine had their property sold off; and twenty-one had 'escaped from the village'. And so it was throughout the Ukraine.

So, at the beginning of 1933, a third procurement levy was announced, and a further assault on the now non-existent reserves of the Ukrainian peasantry took place, in the most horrible conditions.

For Stalin and his associates had not looked kindly on the failure of the Ukraine to deliver grain which did not exist, and once again they exerted extreme pressure on the Ukrainian authorities.

At a joint sitting of the Moscow Politburo and Central Executive Committee on 27 November 1932, Stalin said that the difficulties encountered in the procurement of bread in the past year had been due to first, 'the penetration of the kolkhozes and sovkhozes [state farms] by anti-Soviet elements who organized sabotage and wrecking'; and, secondly, 'the incorrect, unMarxist approach of a significant part of our village communists towards the kolkhozes and sovkhozes . . .' He went on to say that these 'village and district communists idealize too much the kolkhozes', thinking that once one had been formed, nothing anti-Soviet or of a sabotage nature could arise, 'and if they have facts about sabotage and anti-Soviet phenomena, they pass these facts by . . . nothing tells them that such a view of the kolkhoz has nothing in common with Leninism!'

Pravda on 4 and 8 December 1932 called for a resolute struggle against the kulaks, especially in the Ukraine; and on 7 January 1933 it editorialized to the effect that the Ukraine was behind in its grain deliveries because the Ukrainian Communist Party permitted a situation in which 'the class enemy in the Ukraine is organizing itself'.

At a plenum of the All-Union Central Committee and the Central Executive Committee in January 1933, Stalin said that the 'causes of the difficulties connected with the grain collection' must be sought in the Party itself. The Kharkov first secretary, Terekhov, told him flatly that famine raged in the Ukraine. Stalin sneered at him as a romancer . . . , and all attempts even to discuss the matter were simply dismissed out of hand.

Kaganovich made a report, insisting again that 'in the village there are still representatives of kulakdom . . . kulaks who had not been deported, well-off peasants inclining to kulakdom, and kulaks who had escaped from exile and were being hidden by relatives, and occasionally by "tenderhearted" members of the party . . . in fact showing themselves traitors to the interests of the toilers'. And then there were 'representatives of the bourgeois-whiteguard, Petliuraist, cossack, SR-intelligentsia'. The rural 'intelligentsia' at this time consisted of teachers, agronomists, doctors and so on, and the naming of their groups as the targets of a purge of anti-Soviet elements is significant.

Once more the call was for war on the 'class enemy'. 'What,' Kaganovich asked, 'are the basic manifestations of the class struggle in the countryside? Above all, the organizing role of the kulak in sabotaging the collection of grain deliveries and of sowing'. He went on to blame sabotage at every stage, including 'some central agricultural organs'. He attacked breakdowns in labour discipline; he said that the kulak had made use of the petty bourgeois tendencies of 'yesterday's individual peasant'; and he accused these elements of 'terrorizing' the honest kolkhoz workers. . . .

People had been dying all winter [in 1932–1933]. But all reports make it clear that death on a mass scale really began in early March 1933.

> When the snow melted true starvation began. People had swollen faces and legs and stomachs. They could not contain their urine . . . And now they ate anything at all. They caught mice, rats, sparrows, ants, earthworms. They ground up bones into flour, and did the same with leather and shoe soles; they cut up old skins and furs to make noodles of a kind, and they cooked glue. And when the grass came up, they began to dig up the roots and eat the leaves and the buds; they used everything there was: dandelions, and burdock, and bluebells, and willowroot, and sedums and nettles . . .'

The linden, acacia, sorrel, nettles and so forth now much eaten do not contain protein. Snails, only common in some districts, were boiled, and the juices consumed, while the gristly meat was chopped fine, mixed with green leaves and 'eaten, or rather, bolted'. This helped prevent the swelling up of the body, and promoted survival. In the southern regions of the Ukraine, and in the Kuban, it was sometimes possible to survive by catching marmots and other small animals. In other areas fish could be caught, though families could be sentenced for catching fish in a river near their village. The swill from a local distillery at Melnyky, discarded as unfit for livestock, was eaten by neighbouring peasants.

Even late the following year foreign correspondents brought hor-rifying first-hand reports. One American, in a village twenty miles south of Kiev, found every cat and dog had been eaten: 'In one hut they were cooking a mess that defied analysis. There were bones, pigweed, skin and what looked like a boot top in the pot. The way the remaining half-dozen inhabitants (of a former population of forty) eagerly watched this slimy mess showed their state of hunger'.

At a Ukrainian village school the teacher reports that in addition to a pseudo-borshch made of nettles, beet tops, sorrel and salt (when available) the children were eventually also given a spoonful of beans—except for the children of 'kulaks'.

In a village in the Vinnyt-sia Province, an agronomist recalls, when the weeds came up in April the peasants 'started to eat cooked orrach, sorrel, nettles . . . But after consuming such wild plants, people suffered from dropsy and died from starvation in great numbers. In the second half of May the death rate was so great that a kolkhoz wagon was specially set aside for the purpose of carrying the dead each day to the cemetery' (the bodies were thrown into a common grave, without ceremonies). Another activist describes going with a sled-driver whose job was to ask at each house or each

Joseph Stalin

house still with inhabitants, if they had any dead to be carted off.

We have witnesses' reports of a variety of types, including that of victims, former activists, and Soviet authors who witnessed these events when young and wrote of them when it became possible years later. . . . One such . . . was able under [Nikita] Khrushchev [the Soviet leader after Stalin's death] to tell how 'in 1933 there was a terrible famine. Whole families died, houses fell to pieces, village streets grew empty'.

Another of the same period writes:

> Hunger: a terrible soul-chilling word of darkness. Those who have never experienced it cannot imagine what suffering hunger causes. There is

nothing worse for the man—the head of the family—than the sense of his own helplessness in the face of his wife's prayers, when she cannot find food for her hungry children. There is nothing more terrible for the mother than the sign of her emaciated, enfeebled children who through hunger have forgotten to smile.

If it were only for a week or a month, but it is for many months that most of the local families have nothing to put on the table. All the cellars were swept clean, not a single hen remained in the village: even the beetroot seeds have been consumed . . .

The first who died from hunger were the men. Later on the children. And last of all, the women. But before they died, people often lost their senses and ceased to be human beings.

A former activist comments:

On a battlefield men die quickly, they fight back, they are sustained by fellowship and a sense of duty. Here I saw people dying in solitude by slow degrees, dying hideously, without the excuse of sacrifice for a cause. They had been trapped and left to starve, each in his home, by a political decision made in a far-off capital around conference and banquet tables. There was not even the consolation of inevitability to relieve the horror.

The most terrifying sights were the little children with skeleton limbs dangling from balloon-like abdomens. Starvation had wiped every trace of youth from their faces, turning them into tortured gargoyles; only in their eyes still lingered the reminder of childhood. Everywhere we found men and women lying prone, their faces and bellies bloated, their eyes utterly expressionless.

In May 1933 one traveller noted six dead bodies on a twelve kilometre stretch between two villages in the Dnipropetrovsk Province. A foreign journalist, on an afternoon's walk in the country, came across nine dead bodies, including two boys of about eight and a girl of about ten.

A soldier reports that as his train puffed into the Ukraine he and his comrades were horrified. They passed food out to the begging peasants and were reported by the train commandant. However, the corps commander (Timoshenko) took very mild disciplinary action. When the units deployed, 'men, women, girls, children came to the road that led into the camp. They stood silently. Stood and starved. They were driven away but they reappeared in a different place. And again—stood and starved.' The political instructors had to work hard to bring the soldiers out of a state of gloom. When the manoeuvres started, the field kitchens were followed by the famished peasantry, and when meals were served, the soldiers handed over their rations. The officers and political commissars went away and pretended not to have noticed.

Meanwhile, in the village 'the poor begged from the poor, the starving begged from the starving', and those with children from those without. In early 1933 in the centre of one large Ukrainian village, 'close by the ruins of the church, which had been dynamited, is the village bazaar. All the people one sees have swollen faces. They are silent, and when they talk they can hardly whisper. Their movements are slow and weak because of swollen legs and arms. They trade in cornstalks, bare cobs, dried roots, bark of trees and roots of waterplants . . .'

One young girl in a village in Poltava Province which had not suffered as much as most describes her Easter in 1933. Her father had gone to trade 'the very last shirts in the family' (the linen and embroidery having gone already) 'for food for the holy day'. On his way back with ten pounds of corn and four of screenings, he was arrested for speculation (though released two weeks later), and the food confiscated. When he did not arrive, 'Mother made soup for us from two glassfulls of dried, crushed potato peelings and eight not very large potatoes'. The 'brigadier' then came in and ordered them out to work in the fields.

A woman in the village Fediivka, in the Poltava Province, whose husband had been given five years in camp as a member of the SVU, [a nationalist group] managed to keep her family fed in various ways until April 1933. Then her four-year-old son died. Even then the brigades did not leave her alone, and suspected that the grave she had dug for the boy was really a grain pit. They dug it up again, found the body, and left her to rebury it.

Everything ground to a halt.

At school the upper grades continued to attend classes until nearly spring. But the lower grades stopped during the winter. And in the spring the school shut down. The teacher went off to the city. And the medical assistant left too. He had nothing to eat. Anyway, you can't cure starvation with medicines. And all the various representatives stopped coming from the city too. Why come? There was nothing to be had from the starving . . . Once things reached the point where the state could not squeeze anything more out of a human being, he became useless. Why teach him? Why cure him?

Stalin's Great Terror

Robert Conquest

In the mid-1930s Stalin terrorized not only the peasantry but the Communist Party and indeed the entire Soviet Union. In his book *The Great Terror*, Robert Conquest describes how Stalin and his secret police (the NKVD, predecessor of what was later called the KGB) used the technique of guilty-by-association to enmesh the entire Soviet population in a desperate game of denouncing every possible "class enemy" before someone else denounced them. Conquest and other scholars believe that Stalin's aim was to "atomize" the population and thus build a totalitarian system—a form of government in which the state and the ruling single-party dominates every sphere of human activity. More controversially, Conquest also believes that Stalin realized that, because his collectivization policy had been a gigantic mistake, he had to forestall the party and the military from blaming him. Certainly the result was the destruction of most of the surviving "Old Bolsheviks," most of the higher officer corps, and vast numbers of ordinary Soviet citizens. In addition everyone—not just actual or potential enemies, but simply random victims—was cowed. His terror also opened career paths for countless younger Soviet citizens (like Nikita Khrushchev and Leonid Brezhnev) willing to step into positions of power over the bodies of their neighbors, friends, and coworkers.

It is very hard for the Western reader to envisage the sufferings of the Soviet people as a whole during that time. And in considering the Terror, it is precisely this moral and intellectual effort which needs to be made. To demonstrate the facts is no more than to provide the bare framework of evidence. It is not the province of the investigator to do more. Yet it cannot but be that these facts are offered for moral judgment. And however coolly we consider them we should think in terms of [Soviet poet and novelist Boris] Pasternak, breaking off his *Sketch for an Autobiography* before the Terror with the words 'To continue it would be immeasurably difficult. . . . One would have to talk in a manner which would grip the heart and make the hair stand on end.'

Thus far we have dealt with the Purge as it struck the Party. Information about this side of it, especially from Soviet sources, is much richer than for the larger but less dramatic fate of the ordinary Russian. Yet for every Party member who suffered—and many even of *them* were scarcely political in any real sense—eight or ten ordinary citizens went to the cells.

The Party figures . . . [who were eliminated during the purges] were consciously involved to a greater or lesser degree in a political struggle whose rules they understood. They had themselves in many cases been responsible for the imprisonment or death of peasants and others by the million in the course of collectivization. Our pity for their own sufferings should doubtless not be withheld, but it can at least be qualified by a sense of their having a lesser claim to sympathy than the ordinary people of the country. If Krylenko was to go to the execution cellars, he had himself sent to their deaths, on false charges, hundreds of others. If Trotsky was to be assassinated in exile, he had himself ordered the shooting of thousands of the rank and file, and gloried in it. [Nineteenth-century Russian poet Aleksandr] Pushkin once described an earlier generation of Russian revolutionaries as 'positively heartless men who care little for their own skins, and still less for those of others'. We may accept this about such people as Rosengolts [one of Stalin's victims in the Communist Party]. But it plainly does not apply to his wife. In her, we can already see the fate and the feelings of an ordinary non-Communist, caught up in the frightful tensions and agonies of the Great Purge.

The oppressive feeling that hung over everything is well illustrated in a comparison made by Dudorov, in [Pasternak's novel] *Doctor Zhivago:*

> It isn't only in comparison with your life as a convict, but compared to everything in the thirties, even to my favourable conditions at the university, in the midst of books and money and comfort; even to me there, the war came as a breath of fresh air, an omen of deliverance, a purifying storm. . . . And when the war broke out, its real horrors, its real dangers, its menace of real death, were a blessing compared with the inhuman power of the lie. . . .

It is difficult for those of us who have lived in fairly stable societies to make the imaginative effort of realizing that the heads of a

great State can be men who in the ordinary course of events would
be thought of as criminals. It is almost equally hard to get the feel of
life as it was for the Soviet citizen under the Great Terror. It is easy
to speak of the constant fear of the 4 a.m. knock on the door, of the
hunger, fatigue and hopelessness of the great labour camps. But to
feel how this was worse than a particularly frightful war is not so
simple.

Russia had undergone the Terror before. Lenin had spoken of it
frankly as an instrument of policy. During the Civil War period executions simply of 'class enemies' were carried out on a large scale. . . .

But Lenin's Terror was the product of the years of war and violence, of the collapse of society and administration, the desperate
acts of rulers precariously riding the flood, and fighting for control
and survival.

Stalin, on the contrary, attained complete control of the country at
a time when general conditions were calm. By the end of the twenties
the country had, however reluctantly, accepted the existence and stability of the Soviet Government. And that Government had in turn
made slight economic and other concessions which had led to comparative prosperity. It was in cold blood, quite deliberately and un-
provokedly, that Stalin started a new cycle of suffering. First had come
the Party's war on the peasantry. When this first Stalinist operation had
done its worst, and things were settling down again in the mid-thirties,
the Great Terror was again launched cold-bloodedly at a helpless population. And the cold-bloodedness was compounded by the other distinguishing quality of the Stalin purge—the total falsehood of all the
reasons given for it and accusations made during it. . . .

What is so hard to convey about the feeling of Soviet citizens
through 1936–38 is the . . . long-drawn-out sweat of fear, night after
night, that the moment of arrest might arrive before the next dawn.
The comparison is reasonable even as to the casualty figures. The
risk was a big enough one to be constantly present. And again, while
under other dictatorships arrests have been selective, falling on genuinely suspected enemies of the regime, in the Yezhov era, just as in
the mud-holes of Verdun and Ypres, anyone at all could feel that he
might be the next victim.

Fear by night, and a feverish effort by day to pretend enthusiasm for
a system of lies, was the permanent condition of the Soviet citizen.

Denunciation

For Stalin required not only submission but complicity. The moral
crisis arose in a form well described by Pasternak. In 1937 (he later
told Dr Nilsson),

> On one occasion they came to me . . . with something they wanted me to
> sign. It was to the effect that I approved of the Party's execution of the

Generals. In a sense this was a proof of their confidence in me. They did-
n't go to those who were on the list for liquidation. My wife was preg-
nant. She cried and begged me to sign, but I couldn't. That day I examined the pros and cons of my own survival. I was convinced that I would
be arrested—my turn had now come! I was prepared for it. I abhorred
all this blood. I couldn't stand things any longer. But nothing happened.
It was, I was told later, my colleagues who saved me indirectly. No one
dared to report to the hierarchy that I hadn't signed.

But few could match the moral grandeur of the great poet. Everyone was isolated. The individual, silently objecting, was faced with
vast meetings calling for the death 'like dogs' of the opposition leaders, or approving the slaughter of the generals. How could he know
if they were not genuine, or largely so? There was no sign of opposition or even neutrality; enthusiasm was the only visible phenomenon. Even the children and relatives of the arrested got up to denounce their parents.

The disintegration of family loyalty was a conscious Stalinist aim.
When, in November 1938, Stalin destroyed the leadership of the
Komsomol [Communist Youth League], headed by Kosarev, his
complaint was that the organization was not devoting itself to vigilance activities, but sticking to its statutory obligation as a political
training-ground for young Communists. Stalin's idea of a good
young Communist demanded not this sort of political training, but
the qualities of an enthusiastic young nark.

Many denunciations were made out of fear. If a Russian heard an
incautious word, and failed to report it, it might be himself who
would suffer. There are many accounts of Party members who were
unable to think of any enemies of the people among their acquaintances, being severely censured by their own branch secretaries as
'lacking in revolutionary vigilance'. There are many stories of conversations between old acquaintances which became too frank and
ended with each of them denouncing the other. Any conversation
that strayed even slightly from the orthodox could only be conducted
between old and trusted friends, and with great circumspection. [So-
viet writer] Ilya Ehrenburg's daughter had an old shaggy poodle
which had learned the trick of closing the dining-room door as soon
as the guests began to talk in a guarded way. As it was given a slice
of sausage for its vigilance, it became expert at guessing the type of
conversation.

Not every responsible citizen did his duty as a delator [de-
nouncer]. One director gave a lift to the mother of an enemy of the
people, an old woman, and was told by his chauffeur: 'Comrade Director, I may be a son of a bitch who must report everything he sees
and hears. Believe me or not, but I swear by my own mother that I
will not report this time. My own mother is just a plain woman, not

a fine lady like this one. But I love her and, anyhow, thank you, Victor Andreyevich, as one Russian to another.' And in fact this incident was never brought up against the director, though many less serious 'crimes' were to be alleged against him.

Nevertheless, just as Nazism provided an institutionalized outlet for the sadist, so Stalinist totalitarianism on the whole automatically encouraged the mean and malicious. Even now [the late 1960s], the Soviet press prints frequent stories of busybodies who report people to the police for imaginary offences, and still succeed in getting them deported. In Stalin's time this was routine. The carriers of personal or office feuds, the poison-pen letter-writers, who are a minor nuisance in any society, flourished and increased.

'I have seen' says Ehrenburg, 'how in a progressive society people allegedly dedicated to novel ideas committed dishonourable acts for personal advantage, betrayed comrades and friends, how wives disavowed their husbands and resourceful sons heaped abuse upon hapless fathers.' A recent Soviet story tells, as reasonably typical, of a geological student who denounced another because he heard him, at a dance, telling his girl friend that his father had been executed— a fact that he had failed to disclose at the Institute. On the first student reporting it, his colleague disappeared, to serve fifteen years in a labour camp.

Individual denouncers operated on an extraordinary scale. In one district in Kiev sixty-nine persons were denounced by one man, in another over a hundred. In Odessa a single Communist denounced 230 people. In Poltava a Party member denounced his entire organization.

At the XVIIIth Party Congress [1939], when the 'excesses' of the Purge period were being belatedly and peripherally criticized, one was now made to confess his methods, which had involved removing fifteen local Party Secretaries. Another well-known slanderer, in Kiev, applied for a free pass to a *kurort* [spa] on the grounds that he had worn out his strength in 'the struggle with the enemy', a remark which caused loud laughter in the Congress. . . .

But the NKVD did not, of course, leave denunciation on an amateur and voluntary basis. Everywhere it organized a special network —the *seksots,* recruited from among the general population.

Seksots were divided into two types: the voluntary—malicious degenerates out to injure their neighbours, together with 'idealists' who were convinced that they were working for the Cause; and the involuntary—who were drawn into it out of fear, or (very often) promises of the alleviation of the fate of an arrested member of the prospective *seksot*'s family. These last hoped that if they kept strictly to the truth and reported nothing disadvantageous about their friends, no harm would be done. But once started, they were trapped: the pressure became greater and greater. The *seksot* who failed to produce information was himself automatically suspect. As the population became more and more careful in its talk, more and more harmless acts and words had to be reported, misinterpreted, and finally invented, to slake the NKVD's insatiable appetite for plots. . . .

Every account of life in the Soviet office or institution, even before the Great Purge, is replete with intrigues. Such, doubtless, would be true of most other countries. But the resources available to a keen intriguer in Soviet conditions made it a far greater menace, since the normal method of getting on was to 'compromise' and have expelled from the Party, and as often as not arrested, either one's rival, or, if his position was for the time being too strong, one of his subordinates—through whom he could eventually be undermined. One rough estimate was that every fifth person in the average office was in one way or another an NKVD stool-pigeon. . . .

Right through the Purge Stalin's blows were struck at every form of solidarity and comradeship outside of that provided by personal allegiance to himself. In general, the Terror destroyed personal confidence between private citizens everywhere. The heaviest impact of all was, of course, on the organizational and communal loyalties which still existed in the country after eighteen years of one-party rule. The most powerful and important organization drawing loyalty to itself and its ideas rather than to the General Secretary himself was the Party—or rather its pre-Stalinist membership. Then came the Army. Then the intellectual class, rightly seen as the potential bearer of heretical attitudes. These special allegiances attracted particularly violent attention. But in proceeding to attack the entire people on the same basis, Stalin was being perfectly logical. The atomization of society, the destruction of all trust and loyalty except to himself and his agents, could only be carried through by such methods.

In fact the stage was reached which the writer Isaac Babel summed up: 'Today a man only talks freely with his wife—at night, with the blankets pulled over his head.' Only the very closest of friends could hint to each other of their disbelief of official views (and often not even then). The ordinary Russian had no means of discovering how far the official lies were accepted. He might be one of a scattered and helpless minority, and Stalin might have won his battle to destroy the idea of the truth in the Russian mind. Every man became in one sense what [English poet John] Donne says he is not, 'an island'.

Not that everyone blamed Stalin. His skill in remaining in the background deceived even minds like Pasternak and [Soviet theater director Vsevolod] Meyerhold. If men—albeit nonpolitical—of this calibre could feel so, it is clear that the idea must have been widespread. The fear and hatred of the population was concentrated on

Yezhov, who was thus unconsciously making himself ready to be the scapegoat, the eponym of the 'Yezhovshchina'.

Mass Terror

As 'the number of arrests based on charges of counter-revolutionary crimes grew tenfold between 1936 and 1937', the Purge extended itself outwards from the Party victims to include all their contacts, however slight. For example, in 1932 the Party Secretary in the Urals, Kabakov, had visited some workers' quarters and chanced to look in at an apartment where he found only the mother at home. She told him that her son had gone on a rest cure after being overworked, but had to do it at his own expense. Kabakov ordered the management of the trust employing the worker to pay the expenses. Five years later, when Kabakov was arrested . . . , someone informed the NKVD that he had visited this worker and given him protection. He was himself at once pulled in, and accused of 'bootlicking' Kabakov.

Thirteen accomplices had been found for Nikolayev, who had really acted alone. This became a general principle. 'Vigilance' was made the test of a good citizen or employee, as well as of a good Party member. The NKVD everywhere, and all public organizations and economic institutions, were under continual pressure to show their worth in uprooting the enemy. Every man arrested was pressed to denounce accomplices, and in any case all his acquaintances automatically became suspects.

In the show trials themselves, some of the confessions automatically implicated not just individuals, or groups of political associates, but wide circles completely outside the Party struggle. For example, in his evidence in the Bukharin Trial, Zelensky pleaded guilty to the fact that 15 per cent of the staff of the Central Co-operative Union 'consisted of former Mensheviks, Socialist-Revolutionaries, anarchists, Trotskyites, etc. In certain regions the number of alien elements, former members of other parties, Kolchak [pro-tsarist] officers and so on . . . was considerably higher.' These elements were, he said, assembled to 'act as a centre of attraction for all kinds of anti-Soviet elements'. The way this would snowball almost automatically, and throughout the country, is obvious.

Yet it was not only this process of association that gave the Purge its increasingly mass character. In the thirties, there were still hundreds of thousands who had been members of non-Bolshevik parties, the masses who had served in White [pro-tsarist Civil War] armies, professional men who had been abroad, nationalist elements in the local intelligentsias, and so on. The increasingly virulent campaign for vigilance against the hidden enemy blanketed the whole country, not merely the Party, in a press and radio campaign. And while the destruction of hostile elements in the Party was going forward, it must have seemed natural to use the occasion to break all remaining elements suspected of not being reconciled to the regime.

For this sizeable part of the population was already listed in the files of the Special Department of the NKVD, and its local branches, under various headings, such as:

AS anti-Soviet element
Ts active member of the Church
S member of a religious sect
P rebel—anyone who in the past was in any way involved in anti-Soviet uprisings
SI anyone with contacts abroad.

Such categories were not in themselves legal grounds for prosecution, but they automatically made those listed natural suspects, and almost automatic victims when an NKVD branch was called upon to show its merits by mass arrests. . . .

Thus by mid–1937 practically the entire population was potential Purge fodder. Few can have failed to wonder if their turn had come. Pasternak, in the bitterly matter-of-fact passage with which he ends the main body of *Doctor Zhivago*, gives the expectations of the time:

One day Lara [the novel's heroine] went out and did not come back. She must have been arrested in the street, as so often happened in those days, and she died or vanished somewhere, forgotten as a nameless number on a list which later was mislaid, in one of the innumerable mixed or women's concentration camps in the north. . . .

There were various methods of avoiding arrest. A well-known scholar avoided the first wave of the Purge by pretending to be a drunkard. Another, taking the same line a little further, got drunk and created a disturbance in a public park, thus getting six months for a minor criminal offence, and avoiding political trouble. By a curious irony, some genuine enemies of the regime—perhaps more prescient than most—escaped by simply fading into the background. For example, Nicholas Stasiuk, who had actually been Minister of Supply in the anti-Communist Rada Government in the Ukraine in 1918, survived in Mariupol working as a park attendant until the German occupation during the Second World War, when he became a leading figure in the nationalist movement in the area. . . .

In general, moving frequently was a certain protection, since it usually took 'at least six months or a year' before the local NKVD paid much attention or had accumulated enough evidence against a figure whom there was no exceptional reason to persecute. It also took a great deal of time before his personal documents from the NKVD of his previous place of residence were forwarded, 'particularly as all such documents were dispatched by special NKVD express messenger and not through the ordinary post'. Sometimes they never arrived at all. Siberia, in particular, was a good place to go. Comparatively speaking, the local authorities were glad to have settlers, hardly distinguishing between people in forced exile and those freely arriving. . . .

But such actions were open to few, and were often no more than temporary protection. The arrests came, eventually, in millions.

[Stalin's chief prosecutor Andrei] Vyshinsky's assistant, Roginsky, who got a fifteen-year sentence, continued to argue in camp that the regime was justified in isolating from the community large numbers of people who might cause trouble, and in continuing to exploit the labour to the maximum, regardless of any guilt or innocence, of those who were economically 'old and useless'. More sophisticated NKVD and Party members would defend the Purges on subtler grounds. Even if mild jokes or criticisms of the Government was all that had taken place, this was a potential for future active opposition, and the NKVD, by excising this group, was carrying out a justified preventive operation.

In the factories, public denunciation meetings of the established type spread to the workers as a whole. A recent Soviet novel describes such a works scene in 1937:

> A short man in a lambskin cap angrily announced 'My foreman Sereda failed to issue me with cement. I thought at the time this was suspicious. Yesterday I learned that Sereda was concealing his relationship to one of [Civil War anarchist] Makhno's followers who married his cousin!'

> 'The fitter Tsvirkun when taking up employment concealed the fact that his old man was an elder of the church!' announced a second speaker.

> A third speaker proceeded to expose his former comrade whose parents had been deprived of electoral rights for sabotage during the period of collectivization. . . .

The extension of the Purge throughout the country was not, as sometimes suggested, just the result of too much eagerness on the part of local NKVD officials who let things get out of control. On the contrary, it was insisted on from the centre. For example, on 29 November 1936 Vyshinsky was already ordering that within a month all 'criminal cases of major conflagrations, accidents and output of poor quality products be reviewed and studied with the aim of exposing a counter-revolutionary and saboteur background in them'. In certain areas, where few prosecutions on charges of counterrevolutionary activity had been brought, severe censure was issued from the Public Prosecutor's Office in Moscow. In 1937 only eight cases in this category were brought to court through a large part of Siberia, and Moscow blamed this on 'a weak and inadequate struggle to stamp out the nests of saboteurs'.

In general, occasional highly organized mass trials and much more frequent mass arrests marked the period. In May 1937 the [Soviet] Far Eastern press announced fifty-five death sentences in such trials, and in June another ninety-one, in July another eighty-three, and so on through the year. In Byelorussia [Belarus] from June onwards, hardly a week went by without wrecking and espionage being discovered in various industrial enterprises, the Academy of Sciences, the Polish [-language] theatre, the physical culture groups, the banks, the cement industry, the veterinary services, the bread supply organization, and the railways. (The local railway authorities were denounced on 8 October 1937 and charged with being not only Polish but also Japanese spies, in accordance with railway tradition.) In Central Asia it was the same: twenty-five executions were announced in Kazakhstan and eighteen in Uzbekistan in November. In January 1938 came twenty-six more in Kirghizia and another 134 in Uzbekistan. . . .

The cold-blooded administrative organization of such mass arrest and deportation comes out very clearly in Serov's Order No. 001233 for the Baltic States [annexed by Stalin in 1940]:

> Operations shall be begun at daybreak. Upon entering the home of the person to be deported, the senior member of the operative group shall assemble the entire family of the deportee into one room. . . . In view of the fact that a large number of deportees must be arrested and distributed in special camps and that their families must proceed to special settlements in distant regions, it is essential that the operations of removal of both the members of the deportee's family and its head shall be carried out simultaneously, without notifying them of the separation confronting them.

The New Deal: A Middle Way

Arthur M. Schlesinger Jr.

Responding to the crises of the 1930s, Nazi Germany and the Soviet Union became totalitarian states in which dictatorial power was wielded by a single political party (dominated in turn by one man) that justified its rule in the name of an *ideology*. Ideologies are tightly constructed sets of ideas—"laws," even—that, advocates insist, provide a reliable guide to political, social, economic, and cultural policy.

The administration led by President Franklin D. Roosevelt took power in the United States in March 1933 at one of the most desperate moments in the nation's history. The banking system was at the point of collapse. Unemployment may have reached one-third of the work-force, and even those who still had work were terrified of losing their jobs. Prospects for an economic revival seemed remote. Roosevelt asked for, and was virtually given by Congress, powers as sweeping as he would have needed had the country been invaded by a foreign army. Yet, despite some groundless complaints by his political opponents (and they were legion), nothing Roosevelt did threatened the nation's democratic institutions. His "New Deal" policies were the opposite of ideological: They represented a mix of pragmatic remedies. He was willing to try anything that might work, and many of his "solutions" worked at cross-purposes. In fact, his approach did not cure the Great Depression; only the military buildup as American involvement in World War II grew closer accomplished that goal. But ultimately, Roosevelt's New Deal preserved the American democratic capitalist system. The nation also was able to sustain a mighty war effort and a largely unbroken postwar economic ascent which has exerted an immense impact on the history of the world since 1941.

In the following excerpt from his three-volume work *The Age of Roosevelt,* historian Arthur M. Schlesinger Jr. pays tribute to the New Deal's "middle way": a path forged between the rigid ideological assumptions of dogmatic, old-fashioned conservatism and the collectivist, totalitarian solutions that Nazi Germany and Stalinist Russia pursued. Schlesinger is not an unbiased observer, however. His book fervently defended the Roosevelt administration, he served as a presidential aide to John F. Kennedy, and he remains one of the foremost spokesmen for modern American political liberalism.

W as no middle way possible between freedom and tyranny—no mixed system which might give the state more power than Herbert Hoover would approve, enough power, indeed, to assure economic and social security; but still not enough to create a Hitler or a Stalin? This was the critical question.

To this question the Hoovers, no less than the Hitlers and Stalins, had long since returned categorical answers. They all—the prophets of individualism and the prophets of totalitarianism—agreed on this if on nothing else: no modified capitalism was possible, no mixed economy, no system of partial and limited government intervention. One could have one thing or the other, but one could never, never, never mix freedom and control. There was, in short, no middle way.

If this conclusion were true, it would have the most fateful consequences for the future of the world.

The assumption that there were two absolutely distinct economic orders, capitalism and socialism, expressed, of course, . . . a conviction that reality inhered in theoretical essences of which any working economy, with its compromises and confusions, could only be an imperfect copy. If in the realm of essences capitalism and socialism were wholly separate phenomena based on wholly separate principles, then they must be rigorously kept apart. . . . Thus abstractions became more "real" than empirical reality: both doctrinaire capitalists and doctrinaire socialism fell victim to . . . the "fallacy of misplaced concreteness." Both ideological conservatism and ideological radicalism dwelt in the realm of either-or. Both preferred essence to existence.

The distinction of the New Deal lay precisely in its refusal to approach social problems in terms of ideology. Its strength lay in its preference of existence to essence. The great central source of its energy was the instinctive contempt of practical, energetic, and compassionate people for dogmatic absolutes. Refusing to be intimidated by abstractions or to be overawed by ideology, the New Dealers responded by doing things. Walt Whitman once wrote, "To work for Democracy is good, the exercise is good—strength it makes and lessons it teaches." The whole point of the New Deal lay in its faith in "the exercise of Democracy," its belief in gradualness, its rejection of catastrophism, its denial of either-or, its indifference to ideology, its conviction that a managed and modified capitalist order achieved by piecemeal experiment could best combine personal freedom and economic growth. "In a world in which revolutions just now are coming easily," said Adolf Berle, "the New Deal chose the more difficult course of moderation and rebuilding." "It looks forward toward a more stable social order," said [Treasury secretary Robert] Morgenthau, "but it is not doctrinaire, not a complete cut-and-dried program. It involves the courage to experiment." "The course that the new administration did take," wrote [Interior secretary Harold] Ickes, "was the hardest course. It conformed to no theory, but it did fit into the American system—to meet concrete needs, a system of courageous recognition of change." [Braintruster Rexford G.] Tugwell, rejecting laissez faire and Communism, spoke of the "third course."

Roosevelt hoped to steer between the extreme of chaos and tyranny by moving always, in his phrase, "slightly to the left of center." "Unrestrained individualism" had proved a failure; yet "any paternalistic system which tries to provide for security for everyone from above only calls for an impossible task and a regimentation utterly uncongenial to the spirit of our people." He deeply agreed with [British historian William] Macaulay's injunction to reform if you would preserve. Once, defending public housing to a press conference, he said, "If you had knowledge of what happened in Germany and England and Vienna, you would know that 'socialism' has probably done more to prevent Communism and rioting and revolution than anything else in the last four or five years."

Roosevelt had no illusions about revolution. Mussolini and Stalin seemed to him "not mere distant relatives" but "blood brothers." When [German anti-Nazi writer] Emil Ludwig asked him his "political motive," he replied, "My desire to obviate revolution. . . . I work in a contrary sense to Rome and Moscow." He said during the 1932 campaign:

> Say that civilization is a tree which, as it grows, continually produces rot and dead wood. The radical says: "Cut it down." The conservative says: "Don't touch it." The liberal compromises: "Let's prune, so that we lose neither the old trunk nor the new branches." This campaign is waged to teach the country to march upon its appointed course, the way of change, in an orderly march, avoiding alike the revolution of radicalism and the revolution of conservatism.

His "speech material" file contained a miscellany of material indexed according to the random categories of the President's mind. One

President Franklin D. Roosevelt used a personal tone in addressing the nation when broadcasting his famous fireside chats on the radio.

folder bore the revealing label: "Liberalism vs. Communism and Conservatism."

As Roosevelt saw it, he was safeguarding the constitutional system by carrying through reforms long overdue. "The principal object of every Government all over the world," he once said, "seems to have been to impose the ideas of the last generation upon the present one. That's all wrong." As early as 1930 he had considered it time for America "to become fairly radical for at least one generation. History shows that where this occurs occasionally, nations are saved from revolution." In 1938 he remarked, "In five years I think we have caught up twenty years. If liberal government continues over another ten years we ought to be contemporary somewhere in the late nineteen forties."

For Roosevelt, the technique of liberal government was pragmatism. Tugwell talked about creating "a philosophy to fit the Rooseveltian method"; but this was the aspiration of an intellectual. Nothing attracted Roosevelt less than rigid intellectual systems. "The fluidity of change in society has always been the despair of theorists," Tugwell once wrote. This fluidity was Roosevelt's delight, and he floated upon it with the confidence of an expert sailor, who could detect currents and breezes invisible to others, hear the slap of waves on distant rocks, smell squalls beyond the horizon and make infallible landfalls in the blackest of fogs. He respected clear ideas, accepted them, employed them, but was never really at ease with them and always ultimately skeptical about their relationship to reality.

His attitude toward economists was typical. Though he acknowledged their necessity, he stood in little awe of them. "I brought down several books by English economists and leading American economists," he once told a press conference. ". . . I suppose I must have read different articles by fifteen different experts. Two things stand out: The first is that no two of them agree, and the other thing is that they are so foggy in what they say that it is almost impossible to figure out what they mean. It is jargon; absolute jargon." Once Roosevelt remarked to [British economist John Maynard] Keynes of Leon Henderson, "Just look at Leon. When I got him, he was only an economist." (Keynes could hardly wait to repeat this to Henderson.) Roosevelt dealt proficiently with practical questions of government finance, as he showed in his press conferences on the budget; but abstract theory left him cold.

Considering the state of economic theory in the nineteen thirties, this was not necessarily a disabling prejudice. Roosevelt had . . . what was more important than theory, and surely far more useful than bad theory, a set of intelligent economic attitudes. He believed in government as an instrument for effecting economic change (though not as an instrument for doing everything: in 1934, he complained to the National Emergency Council, "There is the general feeling that it is up to the Government to take care of everybody . . . they should be told all the different things the Government can not do"). He did not regard successful businessmen as infallible repositories of economic wisdom. He regarded the nation as an estate to be improved for those who would eventually inherit it. He was willing to try nearly anything. And he had a sense of the complex continuities of history—that special intimacy with the American past which, as [Labor secretary] Frances Perkins perceptively observed, signified a man who had talked with old people who had talked with older people who remembered many things back to the War of the Revolution.

From this perspective, Roosevelt could not get excited about the debate between the First and Second New Deals. No one knew what he really thought about the question of the organic economy versus the restoration of competition. Tugwell, perhaps the most vigilant student of Roosevelt's economic ideas, could in one mood pronounce Roosevelt "a progressive of the nineteenth century in economic matters" (1946) who "clung to the Brandeis-Frankfurter view" (1950) and "could be persuaded away from the old progressive line only in the direst circumstances" (1950); in another, he could speak of Roosevelt's "preference for a planned and disciplined business system" (1957) and for "overhead management of the whole economy"

(1940), and question whether he ever believed in Brandeis (1957). Corcoran and Cohen, who helped persuade Roosevelt to the Second New Deal, thought he never really abandoned the NRA dream of directing the economy through some kind of central economic mechanism. Roosevelt himself, confronted with a direct question, always wriggled away ("Brandeis is one thousand per cent right in principle but in certain fields there must be a guiding or restraining hand of Government because of the very nature of the specific field"). He never could see why the United States has to be all one way or all the other. "This country is big enough to experiment with several diverse systems and follow several different lines," he once remarked to Adolf Berle. "Why must we put our economic policy in a single systemic strait jacket?"

Rejecting the battle between the New Nationalism and the New Freedom which had so long divided American liberalism, Roosevelt equably defined the New Deal as the "satisfactory combination" of both. Rejecting the [sharp] distinction between "capitalism" and "socialism," he led the way toward a new society which took elements from each and rendered both obsolescent. It was this freedom from dogma which outraged the angry, logical men who saw everything with dazzling certitude. Roosevelt's illusion, said Herbert Hoover, was "that any economic system would work in a mixture of others. No greater illusions ever mesmerized the American people." "Your President," said Leon Trotsky with contempt, "abhors 'systems' and 'generalities.' . . . Your philosophic method is even more antiquated than your economic system." But the American President always resisted ideological commitment. His determination was to keep options open within the general frame of a humanized democracy; and his belief was that the very diversity of system strengthened the basis for freedom.

Asia in Turmoil, 1931–1945

PREFACE

Throughout the 1930s, while Europe and North America were suffering through the Great Depression and while the Hitler and Stalin dictatorships were being consolidated in Germany and the Soviet Union, a century or more of European and American dominance in Asia was reaching a state of crisis.

Japan, which as an industrialized capitalist society also found the Great Depression traumatic, saw its political system fall under the growing influence of military men and extreme nationalists. In 1931 the Japanese military seized China's huge northern province of Manchuria, a region potentially rich in mineral resources and industrial potential. Having already won control of Korea, and having taken over Germany's interests in northern China before and during World War I, Japan, by its conquest of Manchuria, was taking its second major step toward building a large colonial empire in East Asia. "The Greater East Asia Co-Prosperity Sphere," the Japanese took to calling what they had in mind. Their explicit purpose was to exclude Western influence from East Asia and to harness the region's resources for Japan's benefit. Western (and Soviet) resistance to Japan's advance into Manchuria proved to be minimal. This emboldened the Japanese military to encroach further on the rest of China, although neither side really wanted a full-scale war. But in 1937 a minor military clash quickly escalated into an all-out Japanese invasion.

China had been in the throes of revolution since 1911, when the Ch'ing (or Manchu) dynasty collapsed under the weight of its inability to respond to the nation's economic stagnation, demographic explosion, and humiliation at the hands of the imperialist powers, both Western and Japanese. But the Chinese Republic, proclaimed in 1912, had been feeble and divided from the outset. Real power lapsed into the hands of regional warlords. Eventually, by the mid-1920s, one of these warlords, Chiang Kai-shek,[1] who had already gained control of the Nationalist Party (called the Kuomintang or Guomindang), tried to unify China under his rule. In 1927 his regime attempted to crush one of its potential challengers, the Soviet-trained Chinese Communist Party. Chiang failed to destroy the Communists, but he did force them out of their urban base in industrial cities like Shanghai and Canton (now Guangzhou) and drove them into China's

1. Jiang Jishei, as his name is spelled according to the Pinyin system of rendering Chinese words in the Roman alphabet that is now used in the People's Republic of China but not in Taiwan

bleak, impoverished northeast. There, effectively beyond reach of Chiang's armies, the Communists under the leadership of Mao Zedong reoriented their movement away from the industrial working class and toward the peasantry, carrying out an agrarian revolution in the areas they controlled. And because the Communists were now based in the north, they bore the brunt of the Japanese invasion beginning in 1937. Chiang armies, more concerned with protecting Kuomintang interests and in preparing for an eventual showdown with the Communists' People's Liberation Army, tried to husband their resources and thus generally pulled back as the Japanese advanced.

India (which before World War II also embraced present-day Pakistan, Bangladesh, Sri Lanka, and Burma, or Myanmar) was still under British rule throughout the interwar period, but the huge country was growing very restive. After the Great War a formidable Indian independence movement arose, led (at least in the areas dominated by India's Hindu majority) by the Congress Party. By 1930 Mohandas Gandhi had become a powerful influence within the independence movement and the Congress Party. Gandhi, a British-trained lawyer, believed in nonviolence, both as a practical strategy to gain self-rule and as a means for transforming Indian society and indeed all human relationships. Repeatedly the British authorities jailed Gandhi and his followers on account of their civil-disobedience protest activities, but Gandhi's austere image as a moral reformer and pacifist won him worldwide respect. Itself a law-abiding, constitutional state, Great Britain could never marshal the brute force that would have been needed to bludgeon into submission the Indian independence movement led by such a man as Gandhi. By the time World War II broke out, British rule in India seemed on the way to eventual extinction. The great question was whether an independent India would remain (as Gandhi hoped it would) a home in which Hindus, Muslims, Christians, and other religious groups would respectfully and peacefully coexist. It was to prove a vain hope, as events after World War II would show.

The Coming of the Pacific War

Kenneth B. Pyle

Beginning in 1931, Japan responded to the economic challenge of the Great Depression by attempting to carve out an empire for itself on the mainland of northeastern Asia. Having conquered the mineral-rich Chinese province of Manchuria, Japan hoped to force the rest of China into economic dependence. The island empire saw the Soviet Union as the major threat to its imperial ambitions. But these calculations were thrown off in 1937, when a minor military clash near Beijing escalated into an all-out war that eventually sucked Japanese troops deep into China's vast interior. To sustain this war effort, Japan—a nation that completely lacks such strategic resources as petroleum, rubber, and iron ore—saw no alternative but to seize the European colonies in Southeast Asia. After 1940, these prizes were ripe for the picking because of the defeats that Nazi Germany had inflicted on France and the Netherlands in Europe. But lunging for Southeast Asia also put Japan on a collision course with Great Britain and the United States, both of which also had colonial possessions in the region. To break out of this strategic logjam, the Japanese military devised and carried out a daring plan to destroy American naval power in the Pacific, hoping that the United States would be too stunned to strike back in time.

American historian Kenneth B. Pyle analyzes these fateful steps in the following excerpt from his book *The Making of Modern Japan*.

In the summer of 1937 Japan blundered into war with China. It was not a war that the [Japanese] army General Staff wanted. The truth is that even the most able of the total war planners were acutely

Excerpted from *The Making of a Modern Japan*, by Kenneth B. Pyle. Copyright © 1996 by Houghton Mifflin Company. Reprinted with permission from Houghton Mifflin Company.

aware that it would require considerably more time to develop and integrate an effective industrial structure before Japan would be prepared for all-out war. To them it was critical to avoid hostilities and concentrate on a fully coordinated effort to develop Japan's economy. But having chosen to abandon the principles of the [1921] Washington Treaty System, and operating in an atmosphere dominated by ultranationalist goals and a growing willingness to resort to military solutions, the government was ill-prepared to restrain itself. In June 1937 Konoe Fumimaro was chosen . . . to become prime minister. Prince Konoe was a widely respected figure from an old noble family, who might, it was thought, succeed in uniting the country and restraining the military. He spoke of achieving "social justice" in domestic affairs, but he proved a weak and ineffectual leader. It was during his first tenure as prime minister (June 1937–January 1939) that the nation stumbled into full-scale war with China and during his second tenure (July 1940–October 1941) that fateful steps were taken toward Pearl Harbor.

Since 1931 the general consensus held that if new conflict came, it would most likely be with the Soviet Union. A prime goal of the General Staff, therefore, was to concentrate on the economic development of Manchukuo [Japanese-ruled Manchuria] and its integration into the industrial complex of Japan so as to increase the strength of the military establishment. Conflict with the nationalist government in China was, therefore, to be avoided as a hindrance to the implementation of the plans designed to prepare for war with Russia. The General Staff in the spring of 1937 had, in fact, ordered Japanese commanders of military forces in north China to avoid incidents that might disrupt the status quo. When a minor skirmish broke out on July 7, 1937, between Chinese and Japanese troops stationed in the Marco Polo Bridge area, just outside of Peking, the Japanese army sought to achieve a quick local settlement. But the incident could not be so easily contained; instead it swiftly escalated into full-scale hostilities. Chiang Kai-shek, the [Chinese] nationalist leader, under immense pressure to resist Japanese encroachment, was doubtless determined not to allow any new pretext such as the Manchurian Incident of 1931 to serve the Japanese expansionist cause. He therefore responded to the Marco Polo Bridge Incident by dispatching four divisions to north China. Konoe responded with an ill-advised sword-rattling statement, which only served to confirm Chiang in his suspicions, and hopes of attaining a local settlement evaporated.

It is not easy, even in retrospect, to see how conflict between China and Japan could have been avoided. History sometimes brings nations into logjams from which they are extricated only by force. Chinese nationalism could no longer tolerate the status quo with

Japan. Yet Japanese of all persuasions looked at Japan's position in China as sanctioned by economic need and by their destiny to create "a new order in Asia" that would expel Western influence and establish a structure based upon Asian concepts of justice and humanity. Chiang's government was regarded as an obstruction that had to be overcome on the way to this "new order," and so in 1938 Konoe called for an all-out campaign to "annihilate" the nationalist regime. The expectation was that Chinese resistance would be short-lived: a "fundamental resolution of Sino-Japanese relations" could be achieved by compelling the nationalists to accept Japanese leadership in creating an Asian community of nations, free of Anglo-American capitalism and Soviet Communism. It was a fateful decision. It tragically underrated the difficulties involved, not least the strength of Chinese nationalism; it justified tighter controls at home and brought vastly heightened tensions with the United States. Atrocities committed against Chinese citizens, especially the pillaging and the rape and massacre of many tens of thousands at Nanking in early 1938, left a lasting outrage against the invaders. But Japanese leadership pushed ahead with supreme nerve justifying their goals with Pan-Asian slogans and, ultimately, with the vision of a Greater East Asia Coprosperity Sphere from which all vestiges of Western imperialism would be erased.

The dilemma that Japanese diplomacy had struggled with ever since the Manchurian Incident now became still more difficult, for as the China conflict expanded, the nation was the less prepared to deal with the Soviet army on the Manchurian border and the American fleet in the Pacific. A succession of border skirmishes with the Red Army revealed the vulnerability of the [Japanese] Kwantung Army; at the same time the U.S. Navy was now embarked on a resolute program of building additional strength in the Pacific. By the spring of 1940 the Japanese navy General Staff had concluded that America's crash program would result in its gaining naval hegemony in the Pacific by 1942, and that Japan must have access to the oil of the Dutch East Indies in order to cope with American power. Konoe's impulsive and unstable foreign minister, Matsuoka Yōsuke, set out to resolve the impasse by a swift demarche. In the autumn of 1940 he signed the Tripartite Pact with Germany and Italy, in which the signatories pledged to aid one another if attacked by a power not currently involved in the European war or the fighting in China. Matsuoka thereby hoped to isolate the United States and dissuade it from conflict with Japan, thus opening the way for Japan to seize the European colonies in Southeast Asia, grasp the resources it needed for self-sufficiency, and cut off Chinese supply lines. Furthermore, to free his northern flank he signed a neutrality pact with the Soviet Union in April 1941; and when Hitler attacked Russia in

June the Manchukuo-Soviet border seemed wholly secure. Within weeks Japanese troops entered Indochina.

American reaction to the Tripartite Pact was, to Matsuoka, unexpectedly strong. President Franklin D. Roosevelt forbade any further shipment of scrap iron to Japan, and after the entry into Indochina he embargoed oil. Negotiations between Secretary of State Cordell Hull and Ambassador Nomura Kichisaburō foundered in a morass of confusion and ineptness. It is doubtful that negotiations had much opportunity for success in any case at this juncture—given the positions taken by the two sides. Hull's insistence on Japanese withdrawal from China was seen as nullifying a decade of foreign policy and reducing Japan to a second-class power.

Rather than turn back, Japanese leaders were prepared to take risks. "Nothing ventured, nothing gained," Matsuoka concluded. "We should take decisive action." And the new prime minister, General Tōjō Hideki, was quoted as saying, "Sometimes people have to shut their eyes and take the plunge." The navy General Staff in particular pressed for war, arguing that oil reserves were limited and American naval strength increasing. Ultimately its reasoning was accepted, and the president of the Privy Council explained to the Emperor a month before Pearl Harbor, "It is impossible from the standpoint of our domestic political situation and of our self-preservation, to accept all of the American demands. . . . If we miss the present opportunity to go to war, we will have to submit to American dictation. Therefore, I recognize that it is inevitable that we must decide to start a war against the United States. I will put my trust in what I have been told: namely, that things will go well in the early part of the war; and that although we will experience increasing difficulties as the war progresses, there is some prospect of success."

The approach of war was accompanied by a crescendo of nationalist sentiment that had as its main theme a determination to establish not only Japan's strategic autonomy in East Asia but also its cultural autonomy and independence from the West and its own sphere of influence in which Japanese culture would predominate. This preoccupation with Japan's unique cultural identity had been a central theme in modern Japanese nationalism since the 1890s. Partly to compensate for the massive borrowing from the West that industrialization entailed, nationalism asserted Japanese moral superiority. The war brought to a culmination these themes of cultural self-determination. In a study of attitudes in the Pacific War, [American historian] John Dower found Japanese thinking characterized by an "intense self-preoccupation" that emphasized Japanese virtue and purity. Nationalists characterized Anglo-American values of individualism, liberalism, and capitalism as motivated by materialism and egocentrism. In contrast, Japanese society had its foundations in spiritual commitments of selfless loyalty to the welfare of the entire community. As a result, society attained a natural harmony and solidarity in which everyone found their proper place. This moral order had divine origins in the unique imperial line, and the Japanese consequently had a mission to extend its blessings to other peoples. Japan's purpose in the war was to create a "new world order" that would "enable all nations and races to assume their proper place in the world, and all peoples to be at peace in their own sphere." As the "leading race" of Asia, Japan should create a Coprosperity Sphere in which there would be a division of labor with each people performing economic functions for which their inherent capabilities prepared them. Nationalist writings often contained themes of Pan-Asianism and liberation of Asians from Western imperialism. A report produced by Japanese bureaucrats, however, privately described the goal of the new order as creation of "an economic structure which would ensure the permanent subordination of all other peoples and nations of Asia to Japan." Cultural policies throughout the Coprosperity Sphere stressed "Japanization," reverence for the Emperor, observance of Japanese customs and holidays, and use of Japanese as the common language.

Japan paid a terrible price for the bold gamble of its leaders in 1941. Abandoning the cautious realism that had traditionally characterized Japanese diplomacy, the nation entered into a conflict that cost it the lives of nearly 3 million Japanese, its entire overseas empire, and the destruction of one-quarter of its machines, equipment, buildings, and houses. Generations were left physically and psychologically scarred by the trauma.

The outcome was heavy with historic irony. War sentiment in Japan had been impelled by an ultranationalist ideology that sought to preserve the traditional values of the Japanese political order, that vehemently opposed the expansion of Bolshevik influence in Asia, and that wanted to establish the Japanese Empire. Instead, war brought a social-democratic revolution at home, the rise of Communism in China, and for the first time in Japan's history—occupation by an enemy force.

The Peasant Revolution in China

Jean Chesneaux

Japanese calculations that the weak, fragmented China of 1937 could easily be subjugated went wrong. True, China was in the throes of a civil war between Communist forces led by Mao Zedong and the corrupt nationalist government headed by Chiang Kai-shek, but the Japanese invasion galvanized the peasantry of northern China, where Communist rebels were already entrenched, into redoubled efforts to achieve both social revolution and national liberation.

French historian Jean Chesneaux sees the Communist-led peasant resistance movement of the 1930s and 1940s as the most recent manifestation of a long chain of events in Chinese history. Repeatedly, he points out, when China's central government fell into weakness or corruption that encouraged outsiders to invade the land, the nation's hardy peasantry became the reservoir out of which forces of regeneration emerged. Chesneaux's understanding of the Chinese revolution is sympathetic: He insists that, unlike the Stalinist Communists of the Soviet Union, the Chinese Communists respected the peasantry and based their movement on the peasantry's inherent drive for personal and national dignity. (It is indeed significant that Stalin disliked Mao, expected him to fail, gave him relatively little help, and feared for the future when in 1949 the Communist movement finally triumphed in China.) In the excerpt that follows from his book *Peasant Revolts in China 1840–1949*, Chesneaux explains how the Chinese Communist Party assumed the leadership of

Excerpted from *Peasant Revolts in China*, by Jean Chesneaux, translated and edited by C.A. Curwen. Copyright © 1973 by Thames & Hudson, Ltd., London. Reprinted with permission from W.W. Norton & Co. Inc.

peasant resistance to the Japanese and thus laid the foundation for China's reemergence as a major power in the second half of the twentieth century.

In July 1937 the Japanese launched a general invasion of China. Very quickly they seized all the major industrial and railway towns of north China. The Kuomintang [Chinese nationalist government of Chiang Kai-shek] took refuge in the distant plateaux and basins of the south-west where for eight years they were content with a military strategy of waiting.

From this moment, the struggles of the Chinese peasants under the leadership of the Chinese Communists changed in character. The strategic principle remained the same—prolonged armed struggle demanding the formation of small insurgent bases, of which the main social base was necessarily the peasantry—but from now on these bases were devoted to resistance against Japan, which took priority over the fight against the landlords and the Kuomintang. The Long March of 1934–35 had been initially a desperate measure to avoid complete liquidation of the peasant soviets of Kiangsi, to save at least the cadres and the future of the peasant revolution. But on arrival in . . . north-west China, where the Communists took refuge, there occurred a remarkable change in the historical situation. The Communists . . . were in a better position than the Kuomintang to keep an eye on Japanese-occupied zones, they were in direct contact with the peasants of north China who were bearing the whole weight of the Japanese occupation and could therefore be mobilized for armed resistance.

From 1937 onwards the Japanese occupied all the major urban centres of north China; but they could not avoid the extension of their operations into the countryside, and a clash with the peasantry. They had to recruit by force the civil labour and military auxiliaries they needed, in particular the 'puppet troops', officially commanded by the pro-Japanese government installed in Nanking. They were forced to react against the latent hostility of the population and organize the suppression of the guerilla bands which were beginning to form. Japanese mopping-up campaigns, the measures of the 'rural pacification movement', and, above all, the extermination campaigns became more and more harsh as peasant resistance developed. In 1942 the Japanese General Okamura formulated his policy of *Sanko Seisaku* ('three alls'—burn all, kill all and destroy all). The very severity of the Japanese occupation left the peasants no choice but to rise up on a mass scale. . . .

The latent and spontaneous hostility of the peasantry towards the

Japanese invaders would not have found historical expression if it had not been for the existence of an organizing force—the Communist survivors of the Long March. From 1938 onwards the Eighth Route Army (the name adopted by the Communist forces in the north-west after the agreement reached with the Kuomintang in July 1937 to resist Japan) organized guerilla bases in the Japanese rear. . . . All these bases . . . were situated . . . in areas which were relatively easy to defend. . . .

For eight years, armed struggle against Japan was carried on by these guerilla bases under extremely difficult conditions. The Japanese enjoyed absolute superiority in heavy equipment, such as artillery, armoured vehicles and the like; but the Communists had the advantage of a very flexible organization on three levels: the regular army, the peasant militia and the local guerillas. Their high degree of mobility, the ease with which they could obtain supplies from the towns, their excellent intelligence system—in sum, the constant support they received from the peasantry—allowed them to evade Japanese attempts to surround them, to survive the 'mopping-up', 'nibbling-up' and 'village-combing' campaigns, and even take the offensive. . . . The Communist-led struggle against Japan is one of the most perfect examples of a 'people's war', based on the intimate unity of the armed forces with a peasant population which gives them complete *political* and therefore military support.

The demands of the agrarian revolution were temporarily subordinated to the resistance against Japan and the policy of 'national salvation'. New broad political alliances became necessary, although the poor peasantry of north China continued to be the main social base for the Communist movement. The theory behind these new alliances was propounded by Mao Tse-tung in 1940 in his article *On New Democracy*; they were to constitute a new form of political structure, different from both 'bourgeois democracy' and the Soviet type of democratic socialism. 'New democracy' was based on the alliance of the 'four revolutionary classes'—the proletariat, the poor and middle peasants, the petty bourgeoisie (including intellectuals and so on) and the 'national capitalists'. These four classes were associated together in the same historical mission: to defeat imperialism—by fighting the Japanese—and to destroy feudalism. In the 'liberated areas' controlled by the guerillas, political power was organized on this basis. Local governments were set up on the 'three-three-three' principle: that is, three Communists, three members of the centre parties (eventually including the Kuomintang) and three non-party progressives. Indeed, the political alliance went even further, and landlords were encouraged to participate actively in the struggle against Japan, in spite of their social position as the natural enemies of the peasants. Priority given to resistance against Japan made them at least temporary allies of the peasantry; hence the term 'enlightened landlords' (*k'ai-ming ti-chu*), which underlined the necessity of an alliance between the poor peasantry and their age-old adversaries. . . .

During the war, Communist agrarian policy in the liberated zones and guerilla bases was one of calculated moderation. Its essential elements were the reduction of land rent (by 25 per cent) and the limitation of interest on loans 'to a reasonable level', which would neither ruin the debtor nor discourage the potential creditor. Particular emphasis was put on production, and the 'production campaigns' of 1938 and 1941–42 aimed at making the liberated areas [economically] self-sufficient. . . .

It would be quite wrong to consider that the period of the anti-Japanese resistance was one of retreat for the peasant movement. The policy of rent and interest reduction was pursued with vigour, with the deliberate intention of reducing the economic power of the landlords. In Shansi, for example, where many peasants had fallen heavily into debt during the agricultural depression of the thirties, interest rates were fixed at 10 per cent, and the families of soldiers in the people's army, that is to say the poorest families, enjoyed a complete moratorium on their debts. The fiscal policy of the popular committees set up in the liberated areas was also very hard on the landlords. Taxes paid by peasants were considerably reduced, if not completely abolished; those paid by landlords were increased, in accordance with the slogan, 'Those with wealth must contribute money, those with muscle—their strength'—a new form of the ancient slogan of peasant rebels, 'Hit the rich and help the poor!'

Even more important is the fact that the development of armed resistance against Japan led to a radical change in the political balance of power between the gentry and the poor peasants, even if this was not at the time the result of radical land reform measures. Taking arms against Japan and contributing the main war effort, the peasants inevitably became conscious of their historical power and developed confidence in their own strength. They knew, and the landlords knew as well, that their arms could serve in the future to defend their class interests and not just their country. Moreover, because of the traditional solidarity of the 'forces of law and order' and the fear of compromising their material interests, the gentry naturally tended to collaborate with the enemy, or at least to maintain a policy of 'wait and see'. 'Enlightened landlords' were exceptional and although the emphasis between 1937 and 1945 was upon patriotic resistance to Japan rather than on the social struggle, the peasants often found themselves in the opposite camp to the landlords. In the final analysis the term 'collaborator' had as much a class significance as a patriotic one.

Even if the temporary needs of political strategy led to a postponement of the agrarian revolution, the Chinese Communist Party remained, in the eyes of the peasants of north China, the party of the poor. The peasantry of Shansi called the Eighth Route Army 'the good army that does not harm people or do evil things', 'our army, the army of the poor'.

During the eight years of resistance against Japan, a real 'social model' was created at Yenan and in the other Border Regions. It was the image of a new society founded on new political and human relations, with a new culture and a new type of militant revolutionary. It was a rural society, and the fruit of peasant struggles. The headquarters of the Chinese revolution was henceforth a peasant headquarters, and remained so until 1949.

The peasant society of Yenan was a military society, in which armed resistance was closely integrated with the everyday life of everyone, and in which the traditional aspects of peasant life were adapted for military purposes. The land was dug, not merely for planting crops, but also for making tunnels and planting mines; munitions, and not just the harvest, were transported in the peasants' carts; children might be sent from village to village to carry messages concerning guerilla action and not just to transmit village or family gossip. Peasants are accustomed to keep quiet about what goes on in their heads, so they knew how to keep quiet about the movements of the Eighth Route Army. The American journalist, Harrison Forman, who visited the liberated zones of north China in 1944, wrote:

> That village was one of the most belligerent I have ever seen. Every approach, every trail, was heavily mined; and the mines were set not only on the trails but also in the fields, where the wary Japs might be expected to move. This was a precaution against possible Jap reinforcements. Warning notices, easy to remove should the enemy approach, were stuck into the ground over every mine. It gave you a goose-pimply sensation to zigzag your horse carefully in and out between those marked mines—you hoped they hadn't missed marking any!

> Even the village entry was mined. The villagers moved about nonchalantly, as though oblivious of death underfoot. Every one carried a weapon of some sort—a rifle over his back, a potato-masher grenade at his hip. This weapon carrying had grown so natural that even the little boys and girls wore dummy grenades dangling from their waists.

> In pre-war days, this village was locally famed for the manufacture of firecrackers, and the inhabitants had now turned their firecracker-making skill to the making of mines. In one courtyard I saw men, women and children at work making black powder, casting mine-molds, and piling-up loaded mines in neat heaps. Because of the shortage of metal for the mine-casings, some of the villagers were hollowing out big rocks to make

stone mines; others were filling bottles, jugs, and even teapots; and one
man was fashioning a wooden cannon of his own invention.

The significance of all this lay not in the effectiveness of such primitive
weapons; it lay in their clear reflection of the fighting spirit of the people. A people must needs be brave who would match such puny con-
trivances against the deadly weapons of the enemy.

The society of Yenan was also a democratic society, in which the
traditional opposition between the organs of power—military as well
as civil—and more recently between members of the Party and ordinary people was reduced to the minimum. The civil and military
cadres shared the simple life of the peasants and soldiers, lived like
them in caves cut out of the loess hills, and bore no insignia of rank
or power. The army was profoundly linked with the peasantry; not
only because it enjoyed their constant support in military operations
and drew recruits from the villages, but also because the army
helped with work in the fields, instead of living at the expense of the
villages like the armies of the past. . . .

The same kind of equality was to be found in the relationships between men and women. Except for those who had joined secret societies in the old days, peasant women had always been kept in a situation of family dependence and social subordination. Now they
participated actively in the work of the peasant committees, in
guerilla operations, in the production campaigns; they formed their
own groups, the Women's Associations, the better to mobilize and
keep an eye open for the recurrence of 'male chauvinism'.

The atmosphere of close unity between the people and its organized advance guard, the army and Party owed its existence to the
deep crisis which shook the Communist Party between 1940 and
1942, in the 'rectification campaign'. The object of this was to teach
Communists to break with élitist practices, with the dogmatism and
sectarianism of the Comintern period, with the habit of relying on
authoritarian measures and ready-made formulas. Mao Tse-tung said
in 1938, '. . . empty and abstract talk must be stopped and doctri-
nairism must be buried to make way for the fresh and lively things
of Chinese style and Chinese flavour which the common folk of
China love to see and hear.'

The revolutionary militants from the towns, the intellectuals and
cadres, had to go to the school of the peasantry, to learn its language
and to draw on its rich traditions and colourful imagery. The 'rectification' of the Communist Party was accompanied by the elaboration of a new popular culture, fed by peasant tradition and at the
same time integrated with the revolutionary struggle. The vitality of
this new culture was one of the characteristics of the Yenan period.
In 1942 a forum of writers and artists was held there, at which intellectuals were encouraged to form closer links with the ordinary

peasants, to live among them and express their aspirations. Several writers came from Shanghai or other great cities, completely ignorant of peasant life, and in response to this call immersed themselves in village life and took part in one way or another in the revolutionary struggles of the time. But no one captured the atmosphere of rural life better than Chao Shu-li. His book, *The Rhymes of Li Yu-tsai* (1943), portrays a sharp and perceptive peasant, who observes in silence the oppression of the peasants by the landlords, the peculations of the village bigwigs and the errors of inexperienced Communist cadres; but in the rhymes which he improvises he poses discreetly yet trenchantly the political problems which the peasants must themselves understand before they can resolve them. . . .

Yenan was not a return to some idealized, pre-industrial rural life, it was not an escape from the hard realities of the twentieth century. If the peasantry became the main social support of the Communist revolution, if in taking refuge deep in the fertile 'yellow earth' the Communists found the strength to recover from the defeat of the Kiangsi soviet, it was because the peasantry and the land itself had become an integral part of Communist strategy and Marxist ideology. The peasant movement had been able to fuse so perfectly into the Chinese revolution only by overcoming its own limitations, since the catalyst which had started the movement was the military and economic expansion of the great industrial powers of the twentieth century, and the resistance to this expansion was led by the organized forces which came from outside the rural world, the Communist Party and the Red Army.

In 1945, at the time of the Japanese collapse, the liberated areas had a total area of some 950,000 square kilometres and a population of nearly a million; the regular army was 950,000 strong and the militia 2,200,000 strong, while the village self-defence units could boast ten millions. There were nineteen liberated areas. The oldest and strongest were in north China. . . . The liberated areas of central China were located in the valleys of the Yangtze and its tributaries; they were less extensive and politically less stable. In south China there were two small guerilla zones. . . .

In comparison with the period between 1935 and 1937, the situation had turned in favour of the Chinese revolutionary movement. The Communists now had considerable political and military power and were in a position to play a decisive role in Chinese politics. They nevertheless sought first of all a political solution. Mao Tse-tung, who visited Chiang Kai-shek in Chungking in October 1945, and Chou En-lai, who resided in Nanking as soon as the nationalist government returned there, attempted to arrive at a formula for a coalition government, which both the Kuomintang and the Americans favoured, at least in principle. But disagreement was fundamental. The Kuomintang insisted that the armed forces of the Communists must be disbanded before they could be allowed to share power. The Communists insisted on preserving their armed forces, which they regarded as the sole guarantee of real democratization of Chinese political life and the end of Kuomintang dictatorship. At most, as a last attempt at conciliation, the Communists agreed to evacuate their armies from eight of the liberated areas which they controlled at the time of the Japanese surrender, those in the south. But civil war was resumed in July 1946, and the participation of the peasantry, right up until the final defeat of the Kuomintang in 1949, was to be as large-scale and as decisive as it had been in the war of resistance against Japan.

In the new political situation the Communists no longer had any reason to subordinate the aims of the agrarian revolution to the exigencies of the united front and national resistance to Japan, as they had been obliged to do between 1937 and 1945. On the contrary, it was now indispensable to mobilize the peasantry more widely than ever before to fight against the Kuomintang and its landlord allies in the countryside. An official directive in May 1946 and the agrarian programme of October 1947 prepared the way for the concentration of forces in the areas under Communist control and the renewal of the class struggle of the poor peasantry. The significance of these two documents lies in the fact that they gave expression to the political situation as it was, to the upsurge of a semi-spontaneous popular movement, one which was, at the same time, led and encouraged by the Communist Party. . . .

The peasants took revenge for countless humiliations and miseries by primitive violence, by the brutality with which they treated the accused landlords. Their confiscation of goods and luxuries from the houses of the rich was symbolic of the revenge of the exploited upon the exploiters. Liberation consisted above all in the fact of speaking up, of expressing oneself, of having the moral courage to stand up to the enemy. The peasants became conscious of their collective strength through reasoned examination of the condition of each one of them. [A sympathetic Western writer,] Jack Belden described how villagers settled accounts with a landlord called Wang:

> Suddenly, someone said: 'Maybe Wang will run away.'
> 'Let's get him tonight,' said several farmers at once.
>
> After some discussion, they all trooped out of the cave and started a march on Landlord Wang's home. Among the thirty men, there was one rifle and three hand grenades.
>
> The marching farmers separated into two groups. One climbed on the top of the cliffs and worked along the cave roofs until they were over the courtyard. Others marched directly to the gate, knocked loudly and commanded the landlord to open up.

Wang's wife answered the door and announced that her husband was not at home. Refusing to believe her, the peasants made a search and discovered a secret passage behind a cupboard. Descending through an underground tunnel, they found Wang cowering in a subterranean cave. They took him away and locked him up overnight. . . .

In the course of the morning and afternoon, the crowd accused the landlord of many crimes, including betrayal of resistance members to the Japanese, robbing them of grain, forcing them into labour gangs. At last he was asked if he admitted the accusations.

'All these things I have done,' he said, 'but really it was not myself who did it, but the Japanese.'

He could not have chosen worse words. Over the fields now sounded an angry roar, as of the sea, and the crowd broke into a wild fury. Everybody shouted at once, proclaiming against the landlord's words. Even the non-participating bystanders warmed to something akin to anger.

Then above the tumult of the crowd came a voice louder than the rest, shouting: 'Hang him up!'

The chairman of the meeting and the cadres were disregarded. For all that the crowd noticed they did not exist.

The crowd boiled around Wang, and somewhere a rope went swishing over a tree. . . .

In this incident the anger of the peasants had not merely been aroused by the memory of all the crimes and exactions of the Wangs as landlords and collaborators; it stemmed also from the discovery of the murderer of Old Li, one of the first peasants who had dared to speak out when the others were still silent.

The reaction of the landlords to peasant anger was both brutal and cunning, and always very determined—the resistance of a privileged class with centuries of experience. This was real class struggle, carried on without mercy. The landlords attempted to corrupt the most determined of the peasants, to seduce them by means of their daughters or young servants, to intimidate them by sorcery and superstition and by assassinating cadres from the towns. The landlords hid their goods, recruited peasants by terror and attempted to slander the militants by nosing into their pasts.

The agrarian reforms of May 1946 and October 1947 took place against this background of collective violence and the awakening of the consciousness of the oppressed. The directive of May 1946 returned to the slogan of 'land to the tiller'; landlords' holdings were compulsorily purchased, not with money, but by bonds issued by the local governments of the liberated areas. Heavier taxes were imposed, and reduction of land rent applied retroactively, so that landlords were obliged to pay back considerable sums to their tenants.

By themselves these measures did not change the relations of production in the countryside; but combined with the mass struggles about which we have spoken above, they implied a return to agrarian radicalism.

The land programme of October 1947 completed this evolution. All debts were written off without compensation and landlords' ownership rights were annulled. Their lands and other goods became the property of the Poor Peasants' Association, for distribution to the peasants. The rich peasants only had their surplus land confiscated. Clearly the Communists were still on their guard against 'left excesses', that is to say, against the killing of landlords, looting, violent attacks on rich and even middle peasants. In an article dated February 1948 Mao Tse-tung called for 'correction of leftist deviations in land reform propaganda'. He condemned excessively harsh measures against rich peasants, in order to preserve the political alliance with marginal elements and safeguard production and the economic balance of the liberated areas. References were still made (by Mao Tse-tung in March 1948, for example) to 'enlightened landlords', rural gentry who supported the political struggle of the Communists against the Kuomintang as they had supported them against the Japanese, which shows that priority was still given to political objectives.

The same flexibility of approach can be seen in the distinction between 'old liberated areas' and 'new liberated areas'. Radical agrarian policies were applied only in the former, where the peasant movement had strong roots. In areas recently conquered by the Communist armies in the course of the war against the Kuomintang, there was only reduction of rents and interest rates on loans, measures which would not preclude the development of a real political movement among the peasantry. But the essential trend was that of return to agrarian radicalism. One hundred million peasants received the land upon which they and their ancestors had toiled. In the villages social, moral and political relationships were fundamentally transformed, and this was of greater significance than a mere change in land ownership.

Throughout these violent agrarian struggles between 1946 and 1948 the emphasis upon 'changing man' was more marked than during the Yenan period and the war of resistance against Japan. The idea of *fan-shen* (literally, to turn over the body) is almost an exact parallel to St Paul's 'put off the old man and put on the new'. The term *fan-shen* was used of peasants who dared look the landlords in the face, who dared to stand up against their power and prestige. It was also applied to Communist cadres. Towards 1947-48 there was a natural recrudescence of bureaucratic practices in the liberated areas. Some of the peasant militants who had become cadres tended to abuse their power, to enrich themselves and to engage in intrigue;

they had arms and were inclined to take privileges for themselves. . . .

This is why the Communist Party, whose initiatives coincided with the impatience of the ordinary peasants, launched a 'purification' campaign. Each cadre came up before public examination by the people under his administration and only the ones who 'passed the gate' were confirmed in their jobs. This internal shake-up 'in the Party was a foretaste, on a smaller scale, of the violent 'rectifications' of the Cultural Revolution twenty years later.

Without the explosions of the peasant struggle in the liberated areas in 1946–48 the Communist armies would not have been able to hold out against the Kuomintang, whose military superiority had even enabled them to take Yenan and hold it for a time in 1947; nor would they have been able to launch their great counter-offensive of 1948. The same principles of 'people's war' as had been proved in resistance against Japan were now put in operation against Chiang Kai-shek: cooperation between the regular army, guerilla and militia units, the dialectic of 'the fish and the water', deep politicization of the army and so forth. The Kuomintang was progressively driven out of all the rural areas of north China towards the end of 1948 and the major cities were then surrounded.

The military success of the Communists had been greatly facilitated by internal crisis within Kuomintang-held territory, in which there were strikes, student unrest and political discontent among the middle class. For the first time in several decades, the peasant movement was able to coordinate its action effectively with that of other social forces.

However, the very rapidity of the Kuomintang débâcle in 1948–49 created regional, geopolitical distortions which the People's Republic was to inherit. In the rural regions of the north the popular regime was the result of the bitter struggle which had been conducted for ten or fifteen years by the poor peasants against Japan, against the Kuomintang and against the landlords. Consequently its mass base was very solid. But Communist power in the 'new liberated areas' in the south, and in the cities and towns, was the fruit of a sudden victory which was almost premature. It had not been based on the slow accumulation of popular energy in the course of a prolonged struggle, on the gradual maturing of an internal situation leading to the radical defeat of the enemy and the destruction of his social base. The imbalance which resulted from this was still evident much later: the Cultural Revolution was most active in the 'old liberated areas'. The revolutionary process was more painful and slower in regions like Hunan or Szechuan, where Communist power had been established in 1949 on the basis of a sudden rallying of the middle and even of the privileged classes, and not as the result of a prolonged political and military struggle at village level. The transfer of power here had operated directly at the provincial level.

In the spring of 1949, after twenty years of struggle in the countryside, the Communists returned to the towns. Robert Guillain, correspondent of [the French newspaper] *Le Monde,* who watched their peasant armies enter Shanghai, marching at dawn past the luxurious shops in Nanking Road, imagined the arrival of Martians.

On 1 October 1949 Mao Tse-tung proclaimed the foundation of the People's Republic of China. The Chinese peasantry, whose fight for liberation through the ages had been so many times and so bloodily defeated, now stood among the victors; not as marginal and mistrusted allies, rapidly to be pushed aside as they had been in 1911, but as the main social force of the revolutionary movement. The feudal system of peasant exploitation had survived in the countryside after the fall of the Ch'ing dynasty and the imperial regime, and this agrarian conservatism had condemned the republican revolution to failure. It was the collapse of the feudal regime, consummated by the struggle of the peasants themselves in their villages, which had paved the way and made inevitable the collapse of the Kuomintang.

Settling Scores in a Chinese Village, 1945

William Hinton

Fanshen is a Chinese word meaning "to turn over," but in revolutionary China, as American author William Hinton explains, "it meant to stand up, to throw off the landlord's yoke, . . . to throw off superstition and study science, . . . to cease considering women as chattels, . . . to enter a new world." Or so Hinton believed, after years of studying the Chinese Revolution and interviewing Chinese people who had lived through it. His book *Fanshen*, published in the United States in 1965, is a documentary record both of how the revolution transformed a village called Long Bow in northern China and of how an enthusiastic (but perhaps naïve) Westerner reacted to it during the 1960s.

The selection that appears below is Hinton's account of how the villagers of Long Bow "settled scores" with their landlord and other "rich" people after the Communist People's Liberation Army swept through in 1945. It is based on interviews with the villagers, which Hinton conducted through Communist Party–approved interpreters.

Wang Ch'ung-lai's wife returned to Long Bow late in 1945. Driven out by the family that bought her as a child wife and forced into beggary, she and her husband had lived in another village for 20 years. When they heard that the landlords would be brought to account

Excerpted from *Fanshen: A Documentary of Revolution in a Chinese Village,* by William Hinton. Copyright © 1966 by William Hinton. Reprinted with permission from the University of California Press.

and old debts repaid, they hurried home only to be met by a stone wall of hostility from the local cadres. T'ien-ming, Fu-yuan, Kuei-ts'ai, and Cheng-k'uan had never heard of the couple. They were reluctant to let them join the struggle for they didn't want to share the "fruits" with outsiders. When Ch'ung-lai's wife went to the district office and protested, Fu-yuan was directed to call in Wang Lai-hsun's mother for questioning.

The old lady denied that Ch'ung-lai was her son. "I only borrowed him," she said. "He lived here half a year and then he ran away. I never ill-treated him."

"Then why did you buy a wife for him?" cried Ch'ung-lai's wife in anger. "And why, if he was not your adopted son, did I live in your family and suffer six years of beatings? Everyone in this village knows how Ch'ung-lai worked hard for more than ten years like a hired laborer in your family. Can you cover the sky with your hand?"

Fu-yuan believed her then, but since she and her husband were still strangers to most of the younger people, the Peasants' Association gave them no property. They were allowed to live in part of Lai-hsun's house and to farm one and one-half acres of Lai-hsun's land, but nothing was turned over to them as their own. Ch'ung-lai and his wife had waited a long time; they could wait some more. They moved into their borrowed quarters and looked forward to the day when the struggle against Lai-hsun would come. They did not have long to wait.

Wang Lai-hsun followed Kuo Fu-wang to the tribune. When he appeared before his tenants and laborers, Ch'ung-lai's wife was standing in the front row. She was the first to speak.

"How was it that you stayed at home while we were driven out?" she asked, stepping in front of the astounded landlord on her small bound feet.

"Because Ch'ung-lai had a grandfather. He had another place to live," said Lai-hsun looking at the ground. He did not have the courage to look her in the face.

"But you too had in-laws. You too had a place to go. Why did you drive us out and make beggars of us? During the famine year we came to beg from you, our own brother, but you gave us nothing. You drove us away with a stick and beat me and the children with an iron poker."

"I remember that day," said Lai-hsun.

"Why?" shouted Ch'ung-lai's wife, tears rolling down her dirt-stained face. "Why?"

"I was afraid if you returned you would ask to divide the property with me."

This answer aroused the whole meeting.

"Beat him, beat him," shouted the crowd.

Ch'ung-lai's wife then took a leather strap from around her wasting body and she and her son beat Lai-hsun with the strap and with their fists. They beat him for more time than it takes to eat a meal and as they beat him Ch'ung-lai's wife cried out, "I beat you in revenge for six years of beatings. In the past you never cared for us. Your eyes did not know us. Now, my eyes do not know you either. Now it is my turn."

Lai-hsun cringed before them and whimpered as the blows fell on his back and neck, then he fainted, fell to the ground, and was carried to his home.

After that meeting, Ch'ung-lai and his family were given outright the ten sections of house and the acre and a half of land that had only been loaned to them up until that time.

Wang Lai-hsun's debt to the people added up to a very large sum but the militia found very little wealth in his home. In addition to the land and the houses he had only a few bags of grain. Even when beaten severely he insisted that he had not hidden silver or gold. He was a heroin addict, he said. He had spent all his money on heroin.

The peasants did not believe him, however, and, after getting nowhere by beating him, decided to carry the struggle to his wife. The meeting that day was held in the temple. When the people questioned Lai-hsun's wife, she said that she did have some coins but that she had given them to Ch'ung-lai's wife for safekeeping. This angered everyone. The militia ran to find Ch'ung-lai's wife. When they brought her to the temple they asked her, "Why did you hide money for that landlord?"

"I never did," said Ch'ung-lai's wife. "Who told you that?"

"She did," said the cadres, pointing to Lai-hsun's wife.

Ch'ung-lai's wife went livid with rage and rushed at the woman who had been her bitterest enemy for so long. But the cadres tore her from her victim and questioned her further. They didn't believe her story. They thought she had fooled them.

"Tell us where you have the money," they demanded.

When she answered, "How could I do such a thing? She is my enemy!" they started to beat her. Chin-chu, one of the poor peasants who had been a hired laborer for Lai-hsun, got out a pair of scissors and cut her flesh with them. Blood gushed out over her tunic.

But Ch'ung-lai's wife screamed and fought back. "She didn't even hide a needle in my home. She hates me because we moved back into the courtyard that she ruled for so long. She is accusing me to make trouble and you believe her!"

At last the young men decided that Ch'ung-lai's wife was telling the truth. They let her go. Wang Lai-hsun and his family were driven from the courtyard just as they themselves had driven out the other half of the family so long ago. Now it was their turn to go and live in abandoned temples and beg for food. But they could not stand such a life. After a few weeks they left Long Bow altogether. All their land, property, houses, clothes, tools, and furniture were confiscated. Only the old lady, Lai-hsun's and Ch'ung-lai's foster mother, remained in the village. She stayed in an abandoned hovel just off the main street. One day she came to Ch'ung-lai's home to beg a little food. The boy, her grandson by adoption, remembered her. He ran into the street and beat her with a stick, saying, "I'll give you some of your own medicine."

This old woman finally maimed herself badly trying to get warm in front of some burning straw. A gust of wind set her clothes on fire. Large areas of her skin were scorched. The pain was so great that she could no longer go out to beg. She died of starvation.

Thus were old scores settled one by one. The brutality of the old system echoed again and again in the convulsions of its demise.

Nonviolence on Trial: Gandhi Responds to World War II

B.R. Nanda

Mohandas Gandhi (1869–1948), called by his fellow Hindus (and later by the whole civilized world) *Mahatma*, or "Great Soul," was one of the truly saintly figures in the public life of the twentieth-century world. A British-educated lawyer who entered politics while he was living among the Indian minority in South Africa and there experienced firsthand the evil effects of racial discrimination, Gandhi found a way to mobilize his fellow Indians in a *nonviolent* movement for national independence from British rule. Although a lifelong Hindu, Gandhi drew inspiration from the spiritual messages of the Christian Gospels and the Islamic Qur'an, as well as from the American thinker Henry David Thoreau (1817–1862) and the Russian novelist and religious prophet Leo Tolstoy (1828–1910). Back in India, in 1919 he joined the independence movement but insisted that it could only succeed if it upheld the sanctity of life. The strategy he developed was peaceful civil disobedience (*satyagraha*)—a principled refusal to obey unjust laws. In 1930 he gained international prominence for himself and his Congress Party by leading a nonviolent march to the sea to protest a British tax on salt (a vital commodity that ordinary Indians used to preserve food), in the course of which more than sixty thousand Indian protesters were jailed.

Excerpted from *Mahatma Gandhi: A Biography,* by B.R. Nanda (Delhi: Oxford University Press, 1998). Copyright © 1998 by B.R. Nanda. Reprinted with permission from the author.

Gandhi himself willingly enduring imprisonment and hunger fasts; he sought and won the moral high ground for the *satyagraha* struggle. Although most of his followers (including Jarwaharlal Nehru, later the first prime minister of independent India) regarded his doctrines primarily as tactics in a political and social struggle, Gandhi always insisted that the *satyagraha* was a religiously inspired guide to life. When, just as India was finally winning its independence, Gandhi was assassinated by a fanatical Hindu who opposed his attempt to reconcile the nation's Hindu majority and Muslim minority, the Mahatma died a martyr's death to the cause of nonviolence.

B.R. Nanda, an Indian historian and biographer of Gandhi, describes how Gandhi, the leader of the Indian freedom movement and an advocate of pacifism and nonviolent civil disobedience, responded as the globe was drifting into World War II.

The clouds of war were hovering over Europe in 1938. The World War of 1914–18 had not proved 'a war to end war'; the peace treaty created more problems than it solved. The system of 'collective security' through the League of Nations had belied the hopes built on it. The League was handicapped by the absence of the United States, the exclusion of Russia and the reluctance of its members to subordinate national interests to international considerations. The first challenge of national defiance from Japan had revealed the helplessness of the League. The invasion of Abyssinia by Italy, the occupation of the demilitarized zone, and the annexation of Austria by Germany and the foreign intervention in the Spanish Civil War revealed that the law of the jungle was being applied to international relations. Political democracy and individual liberty were at a discount. Authoritarian governments, which had crushed all opposition at home, and regimented their resources for war, were preparing for adventures abroad. The smaller nations of Europe lived in daily dread, not knowing when and where the next blow would fall. A thick pall of fear seemed to settle over the civilized world and men wondered if a new dark age had set in.

How did nationalist India react to these events? Internationalism, writes Jawaharlal Nehru, develops in a free country as 'subject condition is like a cancerous growth inside the body politic which not only prevents any limb from becoming healthy but is a constant irritant to the mind and colours all thought and action'. That Indian nationalism, as represented by the Indian National Congress, was sensitive to what was happening on the world stage was largely due to Nehru himself, who had, by study and travel, kept himself abreast of developments abroad. Nehru had reacted sharply to the make-believe diplomacy of the period of 'appeasement', and discounted hopes of buying of dictators with concessions. Under his inspiration, the Indian National Congress had denounced every act of aggression by Japan, Germany and Italy, and condemned the suppression within these countries of civil liberties, the stifling of intellect and conscience, the persecution of religious and racial minorities, the liquidation of political opponents and the brazen display of naked force for the coercion of weaker neighbours.

In 1931, during Gandhi's visit to England, the *Star* had published a cartoon which showed him in a loin cloth beside Mussolini, Hitler, [Irish president Eamon] De Valera and Stalin, who were clad in black, brown, green, and red shirts, respectively.The caption, 'And he ain't wearin' any bloomin' shirt at all,' was not only literally, but figuratively true. For a man of non-violence, who believed in the brotherhood of man, there was no facile division of nations into good and bad, allies and adversaries. This did not, however, mean that Gandhi did not distinguish between the countries which inflicted and the countries which feared violence. Briefed by Nehru in international affairs, it was only natural that his sympathies should be with the victims of aggression. But Gandhi's own life had been one long struggle against the forces of violence. For more than thirty years he had been evolving a technique which, while eschewing violence, would nevertheless be effective in solving individual and group problems.

Gandhi's ideas on non-violence, and his technique of Satyagraha had matured over many years. In the Boer War and the First World War he had raised ambulance units and collected recruits for the British Indian Army. The fact that he had not handled a gun himself made no material difference. As he confessed later: 'There is no defence for my conduct only in the scales of non-violence (Ahimsa). I draw no distinction between those who wield weapons of destruction, and those who do Red Cross work. Both participate in war and advance its cause. Both are guilty of the crime of war. But even after introspection during all these years, I feel that in the circumstances in which I found myself, I was bound to adopt the course I did.'

The Indians whom Gandhi led in the battlefronts of the Boer War, or whom he exhorted to join the British Indian Army in 1918, did not believe in non-violence; it was not repugnance to violence, but indifference or cowardice which had held them back from participating on their own in the war. Believing, as he did in those days, in the British Empire as a benign institution, Gandhi also considered that, as citizens of the Empire, Indians had duties as well as rights, and one of those duties was to participate in the defense of the Empire.

In the two decades which spanned the first and second World Wars, Gandhi's faith in the British Empire had been irrevocably shaken; his own belief in the power of non-violence had grown with greater reflection and experience, and the people of India, thanks to three major Satyagraha campaigns and his extensive countrywide tours, had become familiar with the cult of non-violence. Such was the emphasis which Gandhi had placed on non-violence in the struggle for political freedom that it sometimes looked as if he regarded the means as more important than the goal. In November 1931 he had gone so far as to say: 'And I would like to repeat to the world, times without number, that I will not purchase my country's freedom at the cost of non-violence. My marriage to non-violence is such an absolute thing that I would rather commit suicide than be deflected from my position.' He wished India to give a successful demonstration of non-violence and to set an example to the rest of the world.

As the threat of war grew and the forces of violence gathered momentum, Gandhi reasserted his faith in the efficacy of nonviolence. He felt more strongly than ever that at that moment of crisis in world history he had a message for India and India had a message for the bewildered humanity. Through the pages of *Harijan* he expounded the non-violent approach to military aggression and political tyranny. He advised the weaker nations to defend themselves not by seeking protection from better-armed States, nor by increasing their own fighting potential, but by non-violent resistance to the aggressor. A non-violent Abyssinia, he explained, needed no arms and no succour from the League of Nations; if every Abyssinian man, woman, and child refused co-operation with the Italians, willing or forced, the latter would have to walk to victory over the dead bodies of their victims and to occupy the country without the people.

It may be argued that Gandhi was making a heavy overdraft upon human endurance. It required supreme courage for a whole people to die to the last man, woman, and child, rather than surrender to the enemy. Gandhi's non-violent resistance was thus not a soft doctrine—a convenient refuge from a dangerous situation. Nor was it an offer on a silver platter to the dictators of what they plotted to wrest by force. Those who offered non-violent resistance had to be prepared for the extreme sacrifice.

Early in 1939, Gandhi told Dr Kagawa, a Japanese expert on co-operatives who claimed to be a pacifist, that it was his duty, if he felt that the war against China was unjust, to declare himself against it and to face the consequences: I would declare my heresies and be shot. I would put the co-operatives and all your work in one scale, and put the honour of your nation in the other, and if you found that the honour was being sold, I would ask you to declare your views against Japan and in so doing make Japan live through your death.' One wonders what Kagawa thought of this advice; the mantle of Socrates does not fit everyone. The melancholy fact was that while millions could be persuaded to kill or be killed in war, not even a few hundred pacifists were willing to die for their convictions in peace.

The fact that the governments and the peoples of the world could not bring themselves to accept Gandhi's technique did not in his eyes detract from its value. Few of his critics understood the implications and the potentialities of this technique. Unfortunately the word non-violence was an inadequate English translation of Gandhi's ideas. Questioned by some visitors in January 1939 as to whether non-violence had a positive quality, Gandhi explained: "If I had used the word love, which non-violence is in essence, you would not have asked this question. But perhaps love does not express my meaning fully. The nearest word is charity. We love friends as equals. But the reaction that a ruthless dictator sets up in us is either that of awe or pity according respectively as we react to him violently or non-violently.'

Those who offered non-violent resistance and refused to return violence with violence, or hatred with hatred, posed a problem to the opponent. He might at first mistake this restraint for cowardice, but before long he would discover he was being made to fight on a new ground which was not of his choosing. The reaction of the aggressor to successful non-violent resistance would be progressively one of surprise, ridicule, indignation, and finally of inner doubt and conversion. In a non-violent struggle there are no victors or vanquished; the object is not to humiliate the opponent but to convert him; there is no aftermath of anger, hatred, or revenge to breed fresh conflicts. Satyagraha thus viewed offers a superior alternative to war for resolving disputes and making adjustments inevitable in a dynamic world-order.

The events of 1938–39 had put the faith of many pacifists in Europe to a severe test. [British Socialist] G.D.H. Cole eloquently expressed the anguish of his soul in an article in the *Aryan Path:* 'Until two or so years ago, I believed myself opposed to war, and death-dealing violence under all circumstances. But today, hating war, I would risk war to stop these horrors. I would risk war, and yet even now that second self of mine shrinks back appalled at the thought of killing a man. Personally, I would sooner die than kill. But may it not be my duty to kill rather than die?'

New horrors were being let loose on humanity. The engines of destruction were being progressively perfected; the aeroplane had extended the range of attack. Yet, however terrible the instruments of war, it was a human hand which wielded them and it was a human mind which directed that hand. Those who plotted war did so for a definite purpose—to exploit men and materials of the territories they set out to conquer. The aggressor's effort was to apply terrorism in a sufficient measure to bend the adversary to his will. 'But supposing,' wrote Gandhi: 'a people make up their mind that they will never do the tyrant's will, nor retaliate with the tyrant's own method, the tyrant will not find it worth his while to go on with his terrorism. If all the mice in the world held conference together and resolve that they would no more fear the cat but all run into her mouth, the mice will live.'

Gandhi was aware of the apotheosis of violence which Nazi and Fascist régimes represented, but he did not accept that Hitler and Mussolini were beyond redemption. A fundamental assumption in the non-violent technique was that human nature in essence was one and must ultimately respond to love. 'If the enemy realized,' wrote Gandhi, 'that you have not the remotest thought in your mind of raising your hand against him even for the sake of your life, he will lack the zest to kill you. Every hunter has had this experience. No one has heard of anyone hunting cows.'

When Czechoslovakia was blackmailed into submission in September 1938, Gandhi commended his non-violent method to the unfortunate Czechs: 'There is no bravery greater than a resolute refusal to bend the knee to an earthly power, no matter how great, and that without bitterness of spirit and in the fulness of faith that the spirit alone lives, nothing else does.'

To those who considered such heroism impossible, Gandhi's answer was that they were underrating the powers of the human spirit. The line between the possible and the impossible was, moreover, not a fixed one. Gandhi was fond of giving an analogy from his school days: 'Till my eyes of geometrical understanding had been opened my brain was swimming as I read and re-read the twelve axioms of Euclid. After the opening of my eyes, geometry seemed to be the easiest science to learn. Much more so is the case with non-violence. It is a matter of faith and experience not of argument beyond a point.'

Non-violence was, moreover, not merely a method to meet aggression; it represented a way of life. The motive power of Nazi and Fascist militarism was the desire to carve new empires, and behind it all was a ruthless competition to annex new sources of raw materials and fresh markets. Wars were thus rooted in the overweening greeds of men, as also in a purblind tribalism which enthroned nationalism above humanity. If the world was to get rid of this recurring menace of war, it had to shake off not only militarism, but competitive greed and fear and hatred which fed it.

In an article in the *Aryan Path* in September 1938, John Middleton Murry described Gandhi as the greatest Christian teacher in the modern world and wrote: 'Assuredly I see absolutely no hope for western civilization except the kindling of a vast and consuming flame of Christian Love. The choice appears to be between that or a mass-murder on a scale at which the imagination sickens.'

In fact there was no kindling of a flame of Christian Love. The lights went out one by one until the war broke out in September 1939.

World War II, 1939–1945

PREFACE

In some respects World War II was a continuation of the Great War, but the stakes were raised even higher on account of the evil intentions of the man who had come to rule Germany. Although historians still debate the question of responsibility for the struggle that broke out in 1914, no one doubts that the decision to send armies into battle in September 1939 was Adolf Hitler's alone, fully supported by his weird band of Nazi henchmen. Hitler intended not only to win the victory that had been denied to Germany in the Great War but also to go far beyond the rather traditional war aims of Kaiser Wilhelm's Reich—that is, Hitler planned to establish a Eurasian empire ruled by the German (or Aryan) "race," which would dominate the globe and either subordinate or exterminate non-Aryans according to where these lower grades of human beings stood on the Nazi hierarchy of racial qualities.

Before 1939 few people in the world really understood how dangerous Hitler was and how essential it was to maintain the peace settlement (flawed as it might be) that had been defined by the Treaty of Versailles. Distracted by the Great Depression, divided by internal class struggles, and disillusioned by the supposed hollowness of Great War–era "idealism," the people of the Western democracies (including the isolationist United States) hoped that by appeasing Hitler's aggressive demands peace could be preserved.

Appeasement did not work. The more Hitler took—rearmament, occupation of the demilitarized Rhineland, and the annexations of Austria and Czechoslovakia—the more he demanded. In August 1939 Joseph Stalin made his own contribution to appeasement by signing a nonaggression pact with Hitler, giving the Nazi dictator a free hand to attack Poland and partitioning that hapless country and the Baltic republics between Germany and the USSR. Freed from the danger of a two-front war, Hitler sent his highly mechanized army against Poland on September 1, 1939. Britain and France declared war, but they did nothing to help their Polish ally, which was overwhelmed by German (and Soviet) troops within one month. Then, still unchecked by threats from his rear, in the spring and early summer of 1940 Hitler conquered western Europe from Norway to France. But he failed either to cajole Great Britain into making a "compromise" peace or to batter the island into submission by aerial attacks. He had little trouble, however, in bringing the Balkan Peninsula under German control by the spring of 1941.

Then Hitler made the first of his fateful mistakes. Despite the Hitler-Stalin Pact, the Nazi dictator's ultimate aim had always been to conquer Russia, destroy bolshevism, and turn the Soviet Union's people into slaves of the Aryan race. Frustrated by his inability to knock Britain out of the war, in early 1941 Hitler revived his long-standing plans to attack Russia. Stalin ignored many secret warnings from his own intelligence service and from the British and American governments, and he refused to take seriously the danger that Hitler might break his word. On June 22, 1941, Hitler struck, sending huge armies of German and allied troops into the USSR. His forces stunned the Red Army and sent it reeling in retreat. But Hitler had overconfidently expected the war to be over within a few months, and so he had not even equipped his armies for winter warfare. When his overextended troops faltered, unable to take Moscow in the late fall of 1941, the oncoming Russian winter dealt the Germans a severe setback. A year later a second massive German offensive in southern Russia was first stopped and then crushingly defeated in the epic Battle of Stalingrad in February 1943.

Stalingrad marked the war's real turning point, while more or less simultaneously American forces were turning the tide in the war that by now was raging in the Pacific between the United States and Japan.

Hitler's war in Europe and Japan's war with China had merged to form the global world war in December 1941. By launching a surprise attack on the American naval base at Pearl Harbor, Hawaii, on December 7, 1941, Japan brought the hitherto resolutely isolationist United States into the Pacific war. Hitler and his comrade-in-arms, Benito Mussolini, had no obligation to support Japan under these circumstances, but both dictators impulsively declared war on the United States. It was another fatal mistake, for the American public's wrath was focused on Japan, and President Franklin Roosevelt would almost certainly have failed to persuade Congress to bring the United States into the Anglo-Russian war against Nazism and fascism. But had American forces limited themselves to avenging Pearl Harbor, it is difficult to see how the war in Europe would have ended in an Allied victory.

One of Hitler's war aims was to establish the Thousand-Year Reich for the benefit of the Aryan race, but this goal depended on winning on the battlefield. Yet even if he failed to win militarily, he could meanwhile accomplish his other primary goal: to exterminate the Jewish people, or at least all of the Jews who had fallen under his power. That is the true meaning of—and the reason for—the Holocaust. The "final solution" of "the Jewish question," meaning genocide, was set in motion by the Nazi state soon after Hitler invaded the Soviet Union. The effort continued as long as the Nazi regime endured, even when toward the end of the war it represented a serious diversion of resources from the defense of the German homeland. As Red Army troops closed in on his underground bunker amid the ruins of Berlin on April 30, 1945, Hitler committed suicide, still railing against "the Jewish conspiracy" that (he said) had brought on the war. What was left of the German government surrendered to the Allies a week later.

While the Nazis were mobilizing to carry out their so-called final solution, another enterprise of enormous scope and fateful consequences was getting under way in the United States: the Manhattan Project to build a nuclear weapon. Ironically, many of the most important scientists involved in this joint Anglo-American venture were Jews or political dissidents, driven from Germany and other central European countries by Nazism and fascism. This immense concentration of genius and talent, plus the infusion of practically unlimited but strictly secret U.S. government money, enabled physicists and engineers to produce for the first time in human history a controlled nuclear reaction and (by June 1945) a working nuclear device. After the device was tested in the New Mexico desert, President Harry S. Truman ordered two atom bombs dropped on Japan, on August 6 and August 9, 1945. Japan, fearfully bloodied as American forces closed in on the home islands but still defiant and unreconciled to defeat, now had to surrender. World War II was over, at a hideous cost.

The Battle of
Britain

Winston S. Churchill

World War II broke out in Europe on September 1, 1939, when Nazi Germany attacked Poland. In March 1940, after months in which little fighting had occurred in the West, Nazi forces seized Denmark and Norway, and in April they struck a sudden, massive blow against France and the Low Countries. By June of that year they had swept through western Europe. With the Soviet Union still neutral (and in fact helping Hitler), Great Britain now stood alone to face the Nazi war machine. Hitler hoped that the British would agree to a compromise peace leaving him in control of the Continent. When Britain refused, Hitler furiously ordered Hermann Goering, the commander of his numerically superior air force, the Luftwaffe, to batter the island into submission and prepare the way for a German invasion. The first step in the campaign was to destroy Britain's Royal Air Force (RAF).

Great Britain's wartime prime minister, Winston S. Churchill, had been an outspoken critic of the prewar government's "appeasement" policy, which had attempted to buy peace by giving in to Hitler's demands. Churchill, a conservative man who had been in politics since before World War I, had a record of opposing women's suffrage and Indian independence. But his inspiring tenacity, his soaring eloquence, and his ability to work with erstwhile socialist and liberal opponents in a coalition government made him the ideal leader in a time of grave national peril.

In *Their Finest Hour*, one volume of the series of books he later wrote describing his leadership of Britain during World War II, Churchill uses his powerful command of the English language to tell from his perspective how the outnumbered RAF beat back the Luftwaffe's assault between mid-July and mid-September 1940, and thereby probably saved Britain—and the whole civilized world—from defeat at Hitler's hands. Considering what was at stake and the narrow margin of the victory that was won, the Battle of Britain surely ranks among the most significant turning points in world history.

O ur fate now depended upon victory in the air. The German leaders had recognised that all their plans for the invasion of Britain depended on winning air supremacy above the Channel and the chosen landing places on our south coat. The preparation of the embarkation ports, the assembly of the transports, the minesweeping of the passages, and the laying of the new minefields were impossible without protection from British air attack. For the actual crossing and landings, complete mastery of the air over the transports and the beaches was the decisive condition. The result, therefore, turned upon the destruction of the Royal Air Force and the system of airfields between London and the sea. We now know that Hitler said to Admiral Raeder[chief of the German Navy] on July 31: "If after eight days of intensive air war the Luftwaffe has not achieved considerable destruction of the enemy's air force, harbours, and naval forces, the operation will have to be put off till May 1941." This was the battle that had now to be fought.

I did not myself at all shrink mentally from the impending trial of strength. I had told Parliament on June 4: "The great French Army was very largely, for the time being, cast back and disturbed by the onrush of a few thousand armoured vehicles. May it not also be that the cause of civilisation itself will be defended by the skill and devotion of a few thousand airmen?" And to [South African prime minister J.C.] Smuts, on June 9: "I see only one sure way through now—to wit, that Hitler should attack this country, and in so doing break his air weapon." The occasion had now arrived. . . .

[T]he main features and the outline of this famous conflict, upon which the life of Britain and the freedom of the world depended, are not in dispute.

The German Air Force . . . required a period of weeks or months for recovery [from the French campaign]. This pause was convenient to us too, for all but three of our fighter squadrons had at one time or another been engaged in the Continental operations. Hitler could not conceive that Britain would not accept a peace offer after the collapse of France. . . . He did not understand the separate, aloof resources of an island state, and . . . he misjudged our will-power. . . .

During June and early July, the German Air Force revived and regrouped its formations and established itself on all the French and

Belgian airfields from which the assault had to be launched, and by reconnaissance and tentative forays sought to measure the character and scale of the opposition which would be encountered. It was not until July 10 that the first heavy onslaught began, and this date is usually taken as the opening of the battle. Two other dates of supreme consequence stand out, August 15 and September 15. There were also three successive but overlapping phases in the German attack. First, from July 10 to August 18, the harrying of British convoys in the Channel and of our southern ports from Dover to Plymouth; whereby our Air Force should be tested, drawn into battle, and depleted; whereby also damage should be done to those seaside towns marked as objectives for the forthcoming invasion. In the second phase, August 24 to September 27, a way to London was to be forced by the elimination of the Royal Air Force and its installations, leading to the violent and continuous bombing of the capital. This would also cut communications with the threatened shores. But in Goering's view there was good reason to believe that a greater prize was here in sight, no less than throwing the world's largest city into confusion and paralysis, the cowing of the Government and the people, and their consequent submission to the German will. Their Navy and Army Staffs devoutly hoped that Goering was right. As the situation developed, they saw that the R.A.F. was not being eliminated, and meanwhile their own urgent needs for the "Sea Lion" [invasion] adventure were neglected for the sake of destruction in London.

And then when all were disappointed, when invasion was indefinitely postponed for lack of the vital need, air supremacy, there followed the third and last phase. The hope of daylight victory had faded, the Royal Air Force remained vexatiously alive, and Goering in October resigned himself to the indiscriminate bombing of London and the centres of industrial production.

In the quality of the fighter aircraft there was little to choose. The Germans' were faster, with a better rate of climb; ours more manoeuvrable, better armed. Their airmen, well aware of their greater numbers, were also the proud victors of Poland, Norway, the Low Countries, France; ours had supreme confidence in themselves as individuals and that determination which the British race displays in fullest measure when in supreme adversity. . . .

By August, the Luftwaffe had gathered 2669 operational aircraft, comprising 1015 bombers, 346 dive-bombers, 933 fighters, and 375 heavy fighters. The Fuehrer's Directive Number 17 authorised the intensified air war against England on August 5. Goering never set much store by "Sea Lion"; his heart was in the "absolute" air war. His consequent distortion of the arrangements disturbed the German Naval Staff. The destruction of the Royal Air Force and our aircraft industry was to them but a means to an end: when this was accomplished, the air war should be turned against the enemy's warships and shipping. They regretted the lower priority assigned by Goering to the naval targets, and they were irked by the delays. . . .

The continuous heavy air fighting of July and early August had been directed upon the Kent promontory [southeastern England] and the Channel coast. Goering and his skilled advisers formed the opinion that they must have drawn nearly all our fighter squadrons into this southern struggle. They therefore decided to make a daylight raid on the manufacturing cities north of the Wash [northeastern England]. The distance was too great for their first-class fighters, the M.E. 109's. They would have to risk their bombers with only escorts from the M.E. 110's, which, though they had the range, had nothing like the quality, which was what mattered now. This was nevertheless a reasonable step for them to take, and the risk was well run.

Accordingly, on August 15, about a hundred bombers, with an escort of forty M.E. 110's, were launched against Tyneside[in northern Britain]. At the same time a raid of more than eight hundred planes was sent to pin down our forces in the South, where it was thought they were already all gathered. But now the dispositions which Dowding had made of the Fighter Command were signally vindicated. The danger had been foreseen. Seven Hurricane or Spitfire squadrons had been withdrawn from the intense struggle in the South to rest in and at the same time to guard the North. They had suffered severely, but were nonetheless deeply grieved to leave the battle. The pilots respectfully represented that they were not at all tired. Now came an unexpected consolation. These squadrons were able to welcome the assailants as they crossed the coast. Thirty German planes were shot down, most of them heavy bombers (Heinkel 111's, with four trained men in each crew), for a British loss of only two pilots injured. The foresight of Air Marshal Dowding in his direction of Fighter Command deserves high praise, but even more remarkable had been the restraint and the exact measurement of formidable stresses which had reserved a fighter force in the North through all these long weeks of mortal conflict in the South. We must regard the generalship here shown as an example of genius in the art of war. Never again was a daylight raid attempted outside the range of the highest-class fighter protection. . . .

August 15 was the largest air battle of this period of the war; five major actions were fought, on a front of five hundred miles. It was indeed a crucial day. In the South all our twenty-two squadrons were engaged, many twice, some three times, and the German losses, added to those in the North, were seventy-six to our thirty-four. This was a recognisable disaster to the German Air Force.

It must have been with anxious minds that the German Air Chiefs measured the consequences of this defeat, which boded ill for the future. The German Air Force, however, had still as their target the port of London, all that immense line of docks with their masses of shipping, and the largest city in the world which did not require much accuracy to hit.

During these weeks of intense struggle and ceaseless anxiety, Lord Beaverbrook [a member of the coalition government] rendered signal service. At all costs the fighter squadrons must be replenished with trustworthy machines. This was no time for red tape and circumlocution, although these have their place in a well-ordered, placid system. All his remarkable qualities fitted the need. His personal buoyancy and vigour were a tonic. I was glad to be able sometimes to lean on him. He did not fail. This was his hour. His personal force and genius, combined with so much persuasion and contrivance, swept aside many obstacles. Everything in the supply pipeline was drawn forward to the battle. New or repaired airplanes streamed to the delighted squadrons in numbers they had never known before. All the services of maintenance and repair were driven to an intense degree. . . .

Another Minister I consorted with at this time was [Socialist] Ernest Bevin, Minister of Labour and National Service, with the whole man-power of the nation to manage and animate. All the workers in the munitions factories were ready to take his direction. . . . The trade-unionists cast their slowly framed, jealously guarded rules and privileges upon the altar where wealth, rank, privilege, and property had already been laid. . . .

I was most anxious to form a true estimate of the German losses. With all strictness and sincerity, it is impossible for pilots fighting often far above the clouds to be sure how many enemy machines they have shot down, or how many times the same machine has been claimed by others. . . . On August 20 I could report to Parliament:

> The enemy is of course far more numerous than we are. But our new production already largely exceeds his, and the American production is only just beginning to flow in. Our bomber and fighter strengths now, after all this fighting, are larger than they have ever been. We believe that we should be able to continue the air struggle indefinitely and as long as the enemy pleases, and the longer it continues, the more rapid will be our approach first towards that parity, and then into that superiority, in the air, upon which in large measure the decision of the war depends.

Up till the end of August, Goering did not take an unfavourable view of the air conflict. He and his circle believed that the English ground organisation and aircraft industry and the fighting strength of the R.A.F. had already been severely damaged. They estimated that since August 8 we had lost 1115 aircraft against the German losses of 467. But of course each side takes a hopeful view, and it is in the interest of their leaders that they should. There was a spell of fine weather in September, and the Luftwaffe hoped for decisive results. Heavy attacks fell upon our aerodrome [airport] installations round London, and on the night of the 6th, sixty-eight aircraft attacked London, followed on the 7th by the first large-scale attack of about three hundred. On this and succeeding days, during which our anti-aircraft guns were doubled in numbers, very hard and continuous air fighting took place over the capital, and the Luftwaffe were still confident through their overestimation of our losses. But we now know that the German Naval Staff, in anxious regard for their own interests and responsibilities, wrote in their diary on September 10: "There is no sign of the defeat of the enemy's air force over Southern England and in the Channel area. . . ."

As by this time Hitler had been persuaded by Goering that the major attack on London would be decisive, the Naval Staff did not venture to appeal to the Supreme Command; but their uneasiness continued. . . .

I stated in a broadcast on September 11:

Whenever the weather is favourable, waves of German bombers, protected by fighters, often three or four hundred at a time, surge over this island, especially the promontory of Kent, in the hope of attacking military and other objectives by daylight. However, they are met by our fighter squadrons and nearly always broken up; and their losses average three to one in machines and six to one in pilots.

This effort of the Germans to secure daylight mastery of the air over England is, of course, the crux of the whole war. So far it has failed conspicuously. It has cost them very dear, and we have felt stronger, and actually are relatively a good deal stronger, than when the hard fighting began in July. There is no doubt that Herr Hitler is using up his fighter force at a very high rate, and that if he goes on for many more weeks he will wear down and ruin this vital part of his air force. That will give us a great advantage.

On the other hand, for him to try to invade this country without having secured mastery in the air would be a very hazardous undertaking. Nevertheless, all his preparations for invasion on a great scale are steadily going forward. Several hundreds of self-propelled barges are moving down the coasts of Europe, from the German and Dutch harbours to the ports of Northern France; from Dunkirk to Brest; and beyond Brest to the French harbours in the Bay of Biscay.

Besides this, convoys of merchant ships in tens and dozens are being moved through the Straits of Dover into the Channel, dodging along from port to port under the protection of the new batteries which the Germans have built on the French shore. There are now considerable gatherings of shipping in the German, Dutch, Belgian, and French harbours—all the way from Hamburg to Brest. Finally, there are some preparations made of ships to carry an invading force from the Norwegian harbours.

Behind these clusters of ships or barges there stand large numbers of German troops, awaiting the order to go on board and set out on their very dangerous and uncertain voyage across the seas. We cannot tell when they will try to come; we cannot be sure that in fact they will try at all; but no one should blind himself to the fact that a heavy full-scale invasion of this island is being prepared with all the usual German thoroughness and method, and that it may be launched now—upon England, upon Scotland, or upon Ireland, or upon all three.

If this invasion is going to be tried at all, it does not seem that it can be long delayed. The weather may break at any time. Besides this, it is difficult for the enemy to keep these gatherings of ships waiting about indefinitely while they are bombed every night by our bombers, and very often shelled by our warships which are waiting for them outside.

Therefore, we must regard the next week or so as a very important period in our history. It ranks with the days when the Spanish Armada was approaching the Channel, and Drake was finishing his game of bowls; or when Nelson stood between us and Napoleon's Grand Army at Boulogne. We have read all about this in the history books; but what is happening now is on a far greater scale and of far more consequence to the life and future of the world and its civilisation than those brave old days.

In the fighting between August 24 and September 6, the scales had tilted against [the British] Fighter Command. During these crucial days the Germans had continuously applied powerful forces against the airfields of South and Southeast England. Their object was to break down the day fighter defence of the capital, which they were impatient to attack. Far more important to us than the protection of London from terror-bombing was the functioning and articulation of these airfields and the squadrons working from them. In the life-and-death struggle of the two air forces, this was a decisive phase. We never thought of the struggle in terms of the defence of London or any other place, but only who won in the air. . . . It was therefore with a sense of relief that Fighter Command felt the German attack turn on to London on September 7, and concluded that the enemy had changed his plan. Goering should certainly have persevered against the airfields, on whose organisation and combination the whole fighting power of our air force at this moment depended. By departing from the classical principles of war, as well as from the hitherto accepted dictates of humanity, he made a foolish mistake.

This same period (August 24 to September 6) had seriously drained the strength of Fighter Command as a whole. The Command had lost in this fortnight 103 pilots killed and 128 seriously wounded, while 466 Spitfires and Hurricanes had been destroyed or seriously damaged. Out of a total pilot strength of about a thousand, nearly a quarter had been lost. Their places could only be filled by 260 new, ardent, but inexperienced pilots drawn from training units, in many cases before their full courses were complete. The night attacks on London for ten days after September 7 struck at the London docks and railway centres, and killed and wounded many civilians, but they were in effect for us a breathing space of which we had the utmost need.

During this period I usually managed to take two afternoons a week in the areas un-

Winston Churchill

der attack in Kent or Sussex in order to see for myself what was happening. For this purpose I used my train, which was now most conveniently fitted and carried a bed, a bath, an office, a connectible telephone, and an effective staff. I was thus able to work continuously, apart from sleeping, and with almost all the facilities available at Downing Street.

We must take September 15 as the culminating date. On this day the Luftwaffe, after two heavy attacks on the 14th, made its greatest concentrated effort in a resumed daylight attack on London.

It was one of the decisive battles of the war, and, like the Battle of Waterloo, it was on a Sunday. I was at Chequers [the prime minister's official country residence]. . . . The weather on this day seemed suitable to the enemy, and accordingly I drove over to Uxbridge and arrived at the Group Headquarters. . . . My wife and I were taken down to the bomb-proof Operations Room, fifty feet below ground. All the ascendancy of the Hurricanes and Spitfires would have been fruitless but for this system of underground control centres and telephone cables, which had been devised and built before the war by the Air Ministry under Dowding's advice and impulse. . . .

The Group Operations Room was like a small theatre, about sixty feet across, and with two storeys. We took our seats in the dress circle. Below us was the large-scale map-table, around which perhaps twenty highly trained young men and women, with their telephone assistants, were assembled. Opposite to us, covering the entire wall, where the theatre curtain would be, was a gigantic blackboard divided into six columns with electric bulbs, for the six fighter stations, each of their squadrons having a sub-column of its own, and also divided by lateral lines. Thus, the lowest row of bulbs showed as they were lighted the squadrons which were "Standing By" at two minutes' notice, the next row those "At Readiness," five minutes, then "At Available," twenty minutes, then those which had taken off, the next row those which had reported having seen the enemy, the next—with red lights—those which were in action, and the top row those which were returning home. On the left-hand side, in a kind of glass stage-box, were the four or five officers whose duty it was to weigh and measure the information received from our Observer Corps, which at this time numbered upwards of fifty thousand men, women, and youths. Radar was still in its infancy, but it gave warning of raids approaching our coast, and the observers, with field-glasses and portable telephones, were our main source of information about raiders flying overland. Thousands of messages were therefore received during an action. . . .

On the right hand was another glass stage-box containing Army officers who reported the action of our anti-aircraft batteries, of which at this time in the Command there were two hundred. At night it was of vital importance to stop these batteries firing over certain areas in which our fighters would be closing with the enemy. . . . All was now fused together into a most elaborate instrument of war, the like of which existed nowhere in the world.

"I don't know," said Park, as we went down, "whether anything will happen today. At present all is quiet." However, after a quarter of an hour the raid-plotters began to move about. An attack of "40 plus" was reported to be coming from the German stations in the Dieppe area. The bulbs along the bottom of the wall display panel began to glow as various squadrons came to "Stand By." Then in quick succession "20 plus," "40 plus" signals were received, and in another ten minutes it was evident that a serious battle impended. On both sides the air began to fill.

One after another signals came in, "40 plus," "60 plus"; there was even an "80 plus." On the floor table below us the movement of all the waves of attack was marked by pushing discs forward from minute to minute along different lines of approach, while on the blackboard facing us the rising lights showed our fighter squadrons getting into the air, till there were only four or five left "At Readiness." These air battles, on which so much depended, lasted little more than an hour from the first encounter. The enemy had ample strength to send out new waves of attack, and our squadrons, having gone all out to gain the upper air, would have to refuel after seventy or eighty minutes, or land to rearm after a five-minute engagement.

If at this moment of refuelling or rearming, the enemy were able to arrive with fresh unchallenged squadrons, some of our fighters could be destroyed on the ground. It was, therefore, one of our principal objects to direct our squadrons so as not to have too many on the ground refuelling or rearming simultaneously during daylight.

Presently the red bulbs showed that the majority of our squadrons were engaged. A subdued hum arose from the floor, where the busy plotters pushed their discs to and fro in accordance with the swiftly changing situation. Air Vice-Marshal Park gave general directions for the disposition of his fighter force, which were translated into detailed orders to each fighter station by a youngish officer in the centre of the dress circle, at whose side I sat. . . . He now gave the orders for the individual squadrons to ascend and patrol as the result of the final information which appeared on the map-table. The Air Marshal himself walked up and down behind, watching with vigilant eye every move in the game, supervising his junior executive hand, and only occasionally intervening with some decisive order, usually to reinforce a threatened area. In a little while all our squadrons were fighting, and some had already begun to return for fuel. All were in the air. The lower line of bulbs was out. There was not one squadron left in reserve. At this moment Park spoke to Dowding at Stanmore, asking for three squadrons from Number 12 Group to be put at his disposal in case of another major attack while his squadrons were rearming and refuelling. This was done. They were specially needed to cover London and our fighter aerodromes, because Number 11 Group had already shot their bolt.

The young officer, to whom this seemed a matter of routine, continued to give his orders, in accordance with the general directions of his Group Commander, in a calm, low monotone, and the three reinforcing squadrons were soon absorbed. I became conscious of the anxiety of the Commander, who now stood still behind his subordinate's chair. Hitherto I had watched in silence. I now asked, "What other reserves have we?" "There are none," said Air Vice-Marshal Park. In an account which he wrote about it afterwards, he said that at this I "looked grave." Well I might. What losses should we not suffer if our refuelling planes were caught on the ground by further raids of "40 plus" or "50 plus"! The odds were great; our margins small; the stakes infinite.

Another five minutes passed, and most of our squadrons had now descended to refuel. In many cases our resources could not give them overhead protection. Then it appeared that the enemy were going home. The shifting of the discs on the table below showed a continuous eastward movement of German bombers and fighters. No new attack appeared. In another ten minutes the action was ended. We climbed again the stairways which led to the surface, and almost as we emerged the "All Clear" sounded.

"We are very glad, sir, you have seen this," said Park. "Of course, during the last twenty minutes we were so choked with information that we couldn't handle it. This shows you the limitation of our present resources. They have been strained far beyond their limits today." I asked whether any results had come to hand, and remarked that the attack appeared to have been repelled satisfactorily. Park replied that he was not satisfied that we had intercepted as many raiders as he had hoped we should. It was evident that the enemy had everywhere pierced our defences. Many scores of German bombers, with their fighter escort, had been reported over London. About a dozen had been brought down while I was below, but no picture of the results of the battle or of the damage or losses could be obtained.

It was 4.30 P.M. before I got back to Chequers, and I immediately went to bed for my afternoon sleep. I must have been tired by the drama of Number 11 Group, for I did not wake till eight. When I rang, John Martin, my principal private secretary, came in with the evening budget of news from all over the world. It was repellent. This had gone wrong here; that had been delayed there; an unsatisfactory answer had been received from so-and-so; there had been bad sinkings in the Atlantic. "However," said Martin, as he finished this account, "all is redeemed by the air. We have shot down a hundred and eighty-three for a loss of under forty."

Although post-war information has shown that the enemy's losses on this day were only fifty-six, September 15 was the crux of the Battle of Britain. That same night our Bomber Command attacked in strength the shipping in the ports from Boulogne to Antwerp. At Antwerp particularly heavy losses were inflicted. On September 17, as we now know, the Fuehrer decided to postpone "Sea Lion" indefinitely. It was not till October 12 that the invasion was formally called off till the following spring. In July, 1941, it was postponed again by Hitler till the spring of 1942, "by which time the Russian campaign will be completed." This was a vain but an important imagining. On February 13, 1942, Admiral Raeder had his final interview on "Sea Lion" and got Hitler to agree to a complete "stand-down." Thus perished "Operation Sea Lion." And September 15 may stand as the date of its demise. . . .

Yet the Battle of London was still to be fought out. Although invasion had been called off, it was not till September 27 that Goering gave up hope that his method of winning the war might succeed. In October, though London received its full share, the German effort was spread by day and night in frequent small-scale attacks on many places. Concentration of effort gave way to dispersion; the battle of attrition began. Attrition! But whose? . . .

No doubt we were always oversanguine in our estimates of enemy scalps. In the upshot we got two to one of the German assailants, instead of three to one, as we believed and declared. But this was enough. The Royal Air Force, far from being destroyed, was triumphant. A strong flow of fresh pilots was provided. The aircraft factories, upon which not only our immediate need but our power to wage a long war depended, were mauled but not paralysed. The workers, skilled and unskilled, men and women alike, stood to their lathes and manned the workshops under fire, as if they were batteries in action—which, indeed, they were. At the Ministry of Supply, Herbert Morrison spurred all in his wide sphere. "Go to it," he adjured, and to it they went. Skilful and ever-ready support was given to the air fighting by the Anti-Aircraft Command under General Pile. Their main contribution came later. The Observer Corps, devoted and tireless, were hourly at their posts. The carefully wrought organisation of Fighter Command, without which all might have been vain, proved equal to months of continuous strain. All played their part.

At the summit the stamina and valour of our fighter pilots remained unconquerable and supreme. Thus Britain was saved. Well might I say in the House of Commons, "Never in the field of human conflict was so much owed by so many to so few."

The Holocaust: A Revolution

Daniel Jonah Goldhagen

Historian Daniel Jonah Goldhagen in 1997 published a highly controversial book about one of the greatest horrors in human history: the Nazis' deliberate murder of some 6 million European Jews. Goldhagen states the book's thesis in his title: *Hitler's Willing Executioners: Ordinary Germans and the Holocaust*. According to Goldhagen, virulent anti-Semitism had penetrated so deeply into the European—and particularly the German—spirit in the early twentieth century that great numbers of ordinary people under Nazi rule either turned a blind eye to the wholesale murder going on around them or else actively aided and abetted the murderers. Betraying Jews' hiding places, taking part in the "conveyor belt" that delivered Jews to the Nazi death camps, or profiting from the distribution of deported and killed Jews' property: All these and more were ways of being complicit in the Holocaust.

Other scholars, equally acquainted with the documentary evidence, have questioned the sweep of Goldhagen's indictment. Daily life in a totalitarian society, say critics, gave ordinary people no opportunity to oppose the horrors going on around them, and every incentive to keep their mouths shut. Although many Germans (*how* many, no one can truly say) may have disliked Jews, other critics maintain, few indeed would have ever wanted to launch the "Final Solution." Probably we will never know the complete truth.

In the epilogue to his book (excerpted here), however, Goldhagen offers a thesis that is less controversial—but no less chilling. The Holocaust, he says, can only be understood as the Nazis' massive attempt to reorder German and European society, based on the sole criterion of racial hierarchy. Human solidarity, compassion, ethics, conscience it-self—all the foundations of the Judeo-Christian value system—were to be destroyed. The Nazis were trying to carry out nothing less than a to-tal revolution in the way Western society and culture are constituted. It is frightening to think how close the world came to the triumph of such a pure form of evil.

This study of the Holocaust and its perpetrators assigns to their beliefs paramount importance. . . . Its conclusion that the elim-inationist antisemitic German political culture, the genesis of which must be and is explicable historically, was the prime mover of both the Nazi leadership and ordinary Germans in the persecution and ex-termination of the Jews, and therefore was the Holocaust's principal cause, may at once be hard to believe for many and commonsensical to others. The evidence that so many ordinary people did maintain at the center of their worldview palpably absurd beliefs about Jews like those that Hitler articulated in *Mein Kampf* is overwhelming. And the evidence has been available for years, indeed available to any observer in Germany during the 1930s. But because the beliefs have seemed to us to be so ridiculous, indeed worthy of the ravings of madmen, the truth that they were the common property of the German people has been and will likely continue to be hard to ac-cept by many who are beholden to our common-sense view of the world, or who find the implications of this truth too disquieting.

Germany during the Nazi period was inhabited by people ani-mated by beliefs about Jews that made them willing to become con-senting mass executioners. The study of the perpetrators, especially of police battalions, who were a representative cross section of Ger-man men—and therefore are indicative of what ordinary Germans were like regarding Jews—compels us, precisely because they were representative of Germans, to draw this conclusion about the Ger-man people. Being ordinary in the Germany that gave itself to Nazism was to have been a member of an extraordinary, lethal po-litical culture. That German political culture was producing such vol-untaristic killers suggests, in turn, that perhaps this was a society that had undergone other important and fundamental changes, particu-larly cognitive and moral ones. The study of the Holocaust's perpe-trators thus provides a window through which German society can be viewed and examined in a new light. It demands that important features of the society be conceived anew. It suggests further that the Nazis were the most profound revolutionaries of modern times and that the revolution that they wrought during their but brief suzerainty in Germany was the most extreme and thoroughgoing in the annals of western civilization. It was, above all, a cognitive-moral revolution which reversed processes that had been shaping Europe for centuries. This book is ultimately not only about the perpetrators of the Holocaust. Because the perpetrators of the Holocaust were Germany's representative citizens, this book is about Germany during the Nazi period and before, its people and its culture.

The Nazi German revolution, like all revolutions, had two fundamental, related thrusts: a destructive enterprise, which was a thoroughgoing revolt against civilization, and a constructive enterprise, which was a singular attempt to make a new man, a new body social, and a new Nazified order in Europe and beyond. It was an unusual revolution in that, domestically, it was being realized—the repression of the political left in the first few years notwithstanding—without massive coercion and violence. The revolution was primarily the transformation of consciousness—the inculcation in the Germans of a new ethos. By and large, it was a peaceful revolution willingly acquiesced to by the German people. Domestically, the Nazi German revolution was, on the whole, consensual.

While it was consensual at home, the Nazi German revolution was the most brutal and barbarous revolution of modern western history for those who would be excluded from the new Germany and Europe, namely the tens of millions whom the Germans marked for subjugation, enslavement, and extermination. The essential nature of the revolution—how it was transforming the mental and moral substance of the German people and how it was destroying, to use [Heinrich] Himmler's formulation, the "human substance" of non-Germans—was to be discerned in Germany's emblematic institution during its Nazi period: the camp.

The camp was not merely the paradigmatic institution for the Germans' violent domination, exploitation, and slaughter of those whom they designated as enemies, for the Germans' most uninhibited self-expression of mastery, and for the Germans' molding of their victims according to their "subhuman" image of them. The camp's essence was not reducible to these particular features . . . , because the camp was above all else a revolutionary institution, one that Germans actively put to ends that they understood to be radically transformative.

The revolution was one of *sensibility and practice*. As a world of unrestrained impulses and cruelty, the camp system allowed for the expression of the new Nazi moral dispensation, one which was in its essential features the antithesis of Christian morality and Enlightenment humanism—"those stupid, false, and unhealthy ideals of humanity," as [Hermann] Göring called them. The camp system denied in practice the Christian and Enlightenment belief in the moral equality of human beings. In the Nazi German cosmology, some humans, by reason of their biology, ought to be killed; others were fit for slavery, and they too could be killed if the Germans deemed them to be superfluous. The camp system was predicated upon the existence of superiors and inferiors, of masters and slaves. Both its theory and practice mocked the Christian admonition to love one's brother, to feel pity for the downtrodden, to be guided by empathy. Instead, the ethos of the camp preached and was animated by the hatred of others, banished pity from its discourse and practice, and inculcated not an empathetic emotional reverberation for the suffering of others, but a hardened disdain, if not a gleeful enjoyment of it.

Suffering and torture in the German camp world was, therefore, not incidental, episodic, or a violation of rules, but central, ceaseless, and normative. Gazing upon a suffering or recently slaughtered Jew or, for that matter, a suffering Russian or Pole, did not elicit and, according to the moral life of the camp, should not have elicited sympathy, but was indeed greeted, as it ought to have been according to the Nazi German morality, by German hardness and satisfaction in having furthered the reconstructive destructive vision for the new Germany and the new German-ruled Europe.

The ideal guiding the Germans' treatment of the most hated of the camp world's prisoners, the Jews, was that it ought to be a world of unremitting suffering which would end in their deaths. A Jew's life ought to be a worldly hell, always in torment, always in physical pain, with no comfort available. It is worth emphasizing that this was a profound alteration, a revolutionary alteration, in sensibility occurring in mid-twentieth-century Europe. So brutal was the German revolutionary practice that Chaim Kaplan was already struck by it in late 1939—before the formal program of extermination had begun:

> The horrible persecutions of the Middle Ages are as nothing in face of the terrible troubles in which the Nazis enmesh us. In primitive times, methods of torture were also primitive. The oppressors of the Middle Ages knew only two alternatives: life or death. As long as a man lived, even if he were a Jew, they let him live. He also had an opportunity to live out his days by choosing conversion or exile. The Nazi inquisition, however, is different. They take a Jew's life by throttling his livelihood, by "legal" limitations, by cruel edicts, by such sadistic tortures that even a tyrant of the Middle Ages would have been ashamed to publicize them. It was part of the concept of that generation to burn a sinning soul, but it was not their habit to torture a man because he was born "in sin," according to the hangman's ideas.

The regression to barbarism, the logic of modern German antisemitism, and the tasks to which the Nazi leadership put it were such that Kaplan and, presumably, many other Jews would have preferred to live not in this German twentieth century, with its exemplary institution of the camp, but under some benighted medieval tyrant.

The second goal for which the Germans employed the camp world was the *revolutionary transformation of society* in a manner that denied basic premises of European civilization. The Nazi German revolution sought to reconstitute and reshape the European social landscape according to its racial biological principles, by killing millions of people deemed, according to its racial fantasies, dangerous or expendable, and thereby to increase the proportion of the "superior races" and strengthen the overall biological stock of humanity and, complementing this, to reduce the danger to the "superior races" by the more numerous "inferior" ones. The ethos of the vast, regressive reconstructive enterprise that Nazism envisaged for a German-dominated Europe was frequently declaimed by Himmler, who was spearheading the revolution: "Whether nations live in prosperity or starve to death interest me only insofar as we need them as slaves for our *Kultur,* otherwise it is of no interest to me." Eastern Europe would become a German colony populated by German settlers and Slavic slaves.

The camp world was revolutionary because it was the main instrument for the Germans' fundamental reshaping of the social and human landscape of Europe. The camp world and the *system* of German society which it composed was understood to have been guided by principles which stood on its head the body of principles that had previously informed the public morality and (the many exceptions notwithstanding) the conduct of German and European society. The establishment of this new world would have meant the end of western civilization as it was known, which would have included and been symbolized by the destruction of Christianity itself. The camp system was also revolutionary because it was itself already a microcosm of that world, the social model that was to be imposed on a large part of Europe and the moral model that was to become the foundation for the European society which the Germans were forging. Indeed, the ever-growing camp system was the embryo of the new Germanic Europe, which essentially would have become a large concentration camp, with the German people as its guards and the remaining European peoples (with the exception of the "racially" privileged) as its corpses, slaves, and inmates.

Already in the fall of 1940, Hans Frank, the German Governor of Poland outlined clearly this vision of Europe, though he spoke directly only of his jurisdictional area of Poland. "We think here in imperial terms, in the most grandiose style of all times. The imperialism that we develop is incomparable with those miserable attempts that previous weak German governments have undertaken in Africa." Frank reported to his audience that "the *Führer* has further said explicitly" that Poland is (in Frank's paraphrase) "destined" to be a "gigantic work camp, where everything that means power and independence is in the hands of the Germans." No Pole would receive higher education, and "none may rise to a rank higher than foreman." In Hitler's and Frank's view, the Polish state would never be restored. The Poles would be permanently "subjugated" to the master race. Frank's elaboration upon this vision of the concentration camp as the model for Poland was not done in secret but expressed in two speeches to the heads of the departments of his administration. Frank was imparting the governing ethos to the people who were governing Poland.

The camp system was a defining feature of German society during its Nazi period, and the camp was the society's emblematic institution. It was the institution that most prominently set Germany apart from other European countries, that to a large extent gave it its distinctive murderous character. The camp system was also the largest and most important institutional innovation of Nazism, forming an entire new subsystem of society. The first few camps of 1933, set up shortly after Hitler's ascension to power, laid the foundation for this new system of society, which continually expanded geographically in the number of its installations (reaching over ten thousand) and in the size of its population. The camp system was the greatest growth institution during this period of German history, and it would only have increased in size and importance had Germany not been defeated. Finally, it was defining and emblematic because manifold features of camps represented and symbolized distinctive central aspects of Germany during its Nazi period. The camp system was the site where the Nazi German world was most unreservedly, most unabashedly being created. Nazi ideology, which cannot be doubted to have been the source of and the driving force behind the murderous and transformative German policies under Hitler, was most fully expressed in the camp world. The type of society and values which Nazi ideology called for, which the German educational system was inculcating in Germany's young, and which Hitler and Himmler made clear they were working to create, was realized first and found its closest empirical referent in the camp world. Thus, it was in the camps that the essential features of the Nazi German revolution and the revolution's new German man, the character of its refashioned body social, and the nature of the intended European order could most clearly be seen.

The camp world taught its victims firsthand lessons and therefore teaches us secondhand lessons about the essential nature of Germany during the Nazi period. The camp system exposes not just Nazism's but also Germany's true face. The notion that Germany during the Nazi period was an "ordinary," "normal" society which had the misfortune to have been governed by evil and ruthless rulers who, using the institutions of modern societies, moved people to commit

acts that they abhorred, is in its essence false. Germany during the
Nazi period was a society which was in important ways fundamentally different from ours today, operating according to a different [set
of fundamental values], inhabited by people whose general understanding of important realms of social existence was not "ordinary"
by our standards. The notion, for example, that an individual's defining characteristics were derived from his race and that the world was
divided into distinct races—whose respective capacities and moral
worth were biologically determined and widely variable—was, if not
quite an axiom of German society during the Nazi period, then an
extremely widespread belief. That the world ought to be organized
or reorganized according to this conception of an immutable hierarchy of races was an accepted norm. The possibility of peaceful coexistence among the races was not a central part of the cognitive
landscape of the society. Instead, races were believed to be inexorably competing and warring until one or another triumphed or was
vanquished. Life within the camp system demonstrated how radically ordinary Germans would implement the racist, destructive set
of beliefs and values that was the country's formal and informal public ideology. The camp—Germany's distinguishing, distinctive, indeed, perhaps, central institution—was the training ground for the
masterly conduct of the ordinary new German "superman," and it revealed his nature. The camp reveals that Himmler's *Kultur* had, to a
great extent, already become the *Kultur* of Germany.

The ever-expanding camp world was the principal site of central
aspects of the Nazi German revolution. The Germans' mass murder,
their reintroduction of slavery on the European continent, their adoption of free license to treat "subhumans" however they wished without any restraints—all suggest that the camp was the emblematic institution of Germany during its Nazi period and the paradigm for the
Thousand Year Reich. The camp world reveals the essence of the
Germany that gave itself to Nazism, no less than the perpetrators reveal the slaughter and barbarism that ordinary Germans were willing to perpetrate in order to save Germany and the German people
from the ultimate danger—DER JUDE ["The Jew"].

A Last Letter
from Stalingrad

Author unknown

The turning point of World War II was the Battle of Stalingrad, fought between gigantic armies of Nazi Germany and the Soviet Union amid the rubble of a key city named for Joseph Stalin between November 1942 and February 1943. Stalingrad, on Russia's Volga River, marked the deepest penetration of Hitler's forces into the USSR, and it was here that Stalin drew the line and made his stand. A massive Red Army counterattack cut off the bulk of Hitler's forces as they fought their way into Stalingrad, and Hitler—for whom Stalingrad was as much a symbol as it was for Stalin—forbade the German troops even to attempt a retreat. Surrounded, freezing, their supplies and ammunition running out, the German soldiers were slowly pummeled into submission. On February 2, 1943, less than 100,000 of what had originally been 600,000 men surrendered. Only a few thousand of them would ever—twelve years later—return home from the Arctic prison camps into which they were herded.

In January 1943 the last German planes flew out of besieged Stalingrad, carrying sacks of what the men of the doomed Nazi army knew would be their last letters home. The following is one of those letters.

W ell, now you know that I shall never return. Break it to our parents gently. I am deeply shaken and doubt everything. I used to be strong and full of faith; now I am small and without faith. I will never know many of the things that happen here; but the little that I have taken part in is already so much that it chokes me. No one can

Excerpted from *Last Letters from Stalingrad,* translated by Franz Schneider and Charles Gullans (New York: Morrow & Co., 1961). Copyright © 1961 by The Hudson Review, Inc.

tell me any longer that the men died with the words "Deutschland" or "Heil Hitler" on their lips. There is plenty of dying, no question of that; but the last word is "mother" or the name of someone dear, or just a cry for help. I have seen hundreds fall and die already, and many belonged to the Hitler Youth as I did; but all of them, if they still could speak, called for help or shouted a name which could not help them anyway.

The Führer made a firm promise to bail us out of here; they read it to us and we believed in it firmly. Even now I still believe it, because I have to believe in something. If it is not true, what else could I believe in? I would no longer need spring, summer, or anything that gives pleasure. So leave me my faith, dear Greta; all my life, at least eight years of it, I believed in the Führer and his word. It is terrible how they doubt here, and shameful to listen to what they say without being able to reply, because they have the facts on their side.

If what we were promised is not true, then Germany will be lost, for in that case no more promises can be kept. Oh, these doubts, these terrible doubts, if they could only be cleared up soon!

Einstein Alerts Roosevelt About Nuclear Weaponry

Richard Rhodes

Albert Einstein, the genius who worked out the theory of relativity and contributed enormously to uncovering the secrets of atomic energy, was a gentle, eccentric man: a German Jew who fled Nazi Germany, a socialist, and a pacifist who admired Mahatma Gandhi. Nevertheless, he and other leading physicists took alarm when they learned that in the spring of 1939, as war clouds were piling up in Europe, German researchers in Berlin discovered how to achieve nuclear fission—to "split" a uranium atom by bombarding it with electrons, releasing the enormous natural force that binds atomic particles together. This ominous news reached the United States through a communication from Danish scientist Niels Bohr to a brilliant Hungarian-born nuclear physicist named Leo Szilard (pronounced "Síl-ard"). Szilard quickly enlisted his younger colleagues and fellow-Hungarians Eugene Wigner and Edward Teller in a scheme to warn the Belgian government against selling Germany uranium from the Belgian Congo, the world's leading source of the relatively rare metal. This improbable threesome of émigré scientists (humorously calling themselves "the Hungarian conspiracy") decided that their best way of contacting the Belgian government was through Einstein, who then was teaching at Princeton University. Their bumbling efforts to get in touch with Einstein eventually succeeded, and they persuaded Einstein to write a letter about the danger that nuclear fission represented should it be incorporated into a bomb.

Through roundabout ways, Einstein's letter was eventually delivered not to the queen of Belgium, whom Einstein knew personally, but to the president of the United States, Franklin D. Roosevelt, in October 1939—a little over a month after World War II had broken out. The United States was still officially neutral, but Roosevelt took the warning seriously, and by 1941 (before the Japanese attack on Pearl Harbor) the ultra-secret Manhattan Project was under way: the Anglo-American crash program to build a nuclear weapon before Hitler's scientists could do the job.

American historian Richard Rhodes has written a fascinating book that traces the story of nuclear research from the time European physicists first began investigating the subject at the end of the nineteenth century until the United States exploded two atom bombs over Hiroshima and Nagasaki in August 1945. In this excerpt, Rhodes describes how Einstein got involved in the "conspiracy" and how word of the awesome new power available to humankind was finally brought to Roosevelt.

Despite his Olympian ego not even Leo Szilard felt capable of saving the world entirely alone. He called on his Hungarian compatriots now for moral support. Edward Teller had moved to Manhattan for the summer to teach physics at Columbia; Eugene Wigner came up from Princeton to conspire with them. In . . . a letter he wrote on August 15, 1939, [Szilard] offers reliable contemporary testimony: "Dr. Wigner is taking the stand that it is our duty to enlist the cooperation of the [Roosevelt] Administration. A few weeks ago he came to New York in order to discuss this point with Dr. Teller and me." Szilard had shown Wigner his uranium-graphite calculations. "He was impressed and he was concerned." Both Teller and Wigner, Szilard wrote in a background memorandum in 1941, "shared the opinion that no time must be lost in following up this line of development and in the discussion that followed, the opinion crystallized that an attempt ought to be made to enlist the support of the Government rather than that of private industry. Dr. Wigner, in particular, urged very strongly that the Government of the United States be advised."

But the discussion slipped away from that project into "worry about what would happen if the Germans got hold of large quantities of the uranium which the Belgians were mining in the Congo." Perhaps Szilard emphasized the futility of the government contacts that he and [Italian physicisist Enrico] Fermi had already made. "So we began to think, through what channels could we approach the Belgian government and warn them against selling any uranium to Germany?"

It occurred to Szilard then that his old friend Albert Einstein knew the Queen of Belgium. Einstein had met Queen Elizabeth in 1929 on a trip to Antwerp to visit his uncle; thereafter the physicist and the sovereign maintained a regular correspondence, Einstein addressing her in plainspoken letters simply as "Queen."

The Hungarians were aware that Einstein was summering on Long Island. Szilard proposed visiting Einstein and asking him to alert Elizabeth of Belgium. Since Szilard owned no car and had never learned to drive he enlisted Wigner to deliver him. They . . . learned he was staying at a summer house on [Long Island]. . . .

Wigner picked up Szilard on the morning of Sunday, July 16, and drove out Long Island to Peconic. They reached the area in early afternoon but had no luck soliciting directions to the house until Szilard thought to ask for it in Einstein's name. "We were on the point of giving up and going back to New York"—two world-class Hungarians lost among country lanes in summer heat—"when I saw a boy aged maybe seven or eight standing on the curb. I leaned out of the window and I said, 'Say, do you by any chance know where Professor Einstein lives?' The boy knew that and he offered to take us there."

[British writer] C.P. Snow had visited Einstein at the same summer retreat two years before, also losing his way, and makes the scene familiar:

> He came into the sitting room a minute or two after we arrived. There was no furniture apart from some garden chairs and a small table. The window looked out on to the water, but the shutters were half closed to keep out the heat. The humidity was very high.
>
> At close quarters, Einstein's head was as I had imagined it: magnificent, with a humanizing touch of the comic. Great furrowed forehead; aureole of white hair; enormous bulging chocolate eyes. I can't guess what I should have expected from such a face if I hadn't known. A shrewd Swiss once said it had the brightness of a good artisan's countenance, that he looked like a reliable old-fashioned watchmaker in a small town who perhaps collected butterflies on a Sunday.
>
> What did surprise me was his physique. He had come in from sailing and was wearing nothing but a pair of shorts. It was a massive body, very heavily muscled: he was running to fat round the midriff and in the upper arms, rather like a footballer in middle-age, but he was still an unusually strong man. He was cordial, simple, utterly unshy. The large eyes looked at me, as though he was thinking: what had I come for, what did I want to talk about? . . .

Similarly settled, Szilard told Einstein about the Columbia secondary-neutron experiments and his calculations toward a chain reaction in uranium and graphite. Long afterward he would recall his surprise that Einstein had not yet heard of the possibility of a chain reaction. When he mentioned it Einstein interjected, *"Daran habe ich gar nicht gedacht!"*—"I never thought of that!" He was nevertheless, says Szilard, "very quick to see the implications and perfectly willing to do anything that needed to be done. He was willing to assume responsibility for sounding the alarm even though it was quite possible that the alarm might prove to be a false alarm. The one thing most scientists are really afraid of is to make fools of themselves. Einstein was free from such a fear and this above all is what made his position unique on this occasion."

Einstein hesitated to write Queen Elizabeth but was willing to contact an acquaintance who was a member of the Belgian cabinet. Wigner spoke up to insist again that the United States government should be alerted, pointing out, Szilard goes on, "that we should not approach a foreign government without giving the State Department an opportunity to object." Wigner suggested that they send the Belgian letter with a cover letter through State. All three men thought that made sense.

Einstein dictated a letter to the Belgian ambassador, a more formal contact appropriate to their State Department plan, and Wigner took it down in longhand in German. At the same time Szilard drafted a cover letter. Einstein's was the first of several such compositions—they served in succession as drafts—and the origin of most of the statements that ultimately found their way into the letter he actually sent.

Wigner carried the first Einstein draft back to Princeton, translated it into English and on Monday gave it to his secretary to type. When it was ready he mailed it to Szilard. Then he left Princeton to drive to California on vacation.

A message from [a German émigré friend named] Gustav Stolper awaited Szilard. . . . "He reported to me," Szilard wrote Einstein on July 19, "that he had discussed our problems with Dr. Alexander Sachs, a vice-president of the Lehman Corporation, biologist and national economist, and that Dr. Sachs wanted to talk to me about this matter." Eagerly Szilard arranged an appointment.

Alexander Sachs, born in Russia, was then forty-six years old. He had come to the United States when he was eleven, graduated from Columbia in biology at nineteen, worked as a clerk on Wall Street, returned to Columbia to study philosophy and then went on to Harvard with several prestigious fellowships to pursue philosophy, jurisprudence and sociology. He contributed economics text to Franklin Roosevelt's campaign speeches in 1932; beginning in 1933 he worked for three years for the National Recovery Administration, joining the Lehman Corporation in 1936. He had thick curls and a receding chin and looked and sounded like the comedian Ed Wynn. His associates at the NRA used to point him out to visiting firemen under that *nom de guerre* as ultimate proof, if the NRA itself was not sufficient, of Roosevelt's gift for radical innovation. Sachs communicated in dense, florid prose (he had been thinking that spring of writing a book entitled *The Inter-War Retreat from Reason as Exemplified in the Mis-history of the Recent Past and in the Contemporaneous Conduct of International Political and Economic Affairs by the United States and Great Britain*) but could coruscate [sparkle] in committee.

Sachs heard Szilard out. Then, as Sand wrote Einstein, he "took the position, and completely convinced me, that these were matters which first and foremost concerned the White House and that the best thing to do, also from the practical point of view, was to inform Roosevelt. He said that if we gave him a statement he would make sure it reached Roosevelt in person." Among those who valued Sachs' opinions and called him from time to time for talks, it seems, was the President of the United States.

Szilard was stunned. The very boldness of the proposal won his heart after all the months when he had confronted caution and skepticism: "Although I have seen Dr. Sachs once," he told Einstein, "and really was not able to form any judgment about him, I nevertheless think that it could not do any harm to try this way and I also think that in this regard he is in a position to fulfill his promise."

Szilard met Sachs shortly after returning from Peconic—between Sunday and Wednesday. Unable at midweek to reach Wigner en route to California, he tracked down Teller, who thought Sachs' proposal preferable to the plan they had previously worked out. Drawing on the first Einstein draft, Szilard now prepared a draft letter to Roosevelt. He wrote it in German because Einstein's English was insecure, added a cover letter and mailed it to Long Island. "Perhaps you will be able to tell me over the telephone whether you would like to return the draft with your marginal comments by mail," he proposed in the cover letter, "or whether I should come out to discuss the whole thing once more with you." If he visited Peconic again, Szilard wrote, he would ask Teller to drive him, "not only because I believe his advice is valuable but also because I think you might enjoy getting to know him. He is particularly nice."

Einstein preferred to review a letter to the President in person. Teller therefore delivered Szilard to Peconic, probably on Sunday, July 30, in his sturdy 1935 Plymouth. "I entered history as Szilard's chauffeur," Teller aphorizes the experience. They found the Princeton laureate in old clothes and slippers. Elsa Einstein served tea. Szilard and Einstein composed a third text together, which Teller wrote down. "Yes, yes," Teller remembers Einstein commenting, "this would be the first time that man releases nuclear energy in a direct form rather than indirectly." Directly from fission, he meant, rather than indirectly from the sun, where a different nuclear reaction produces the copious radiation that reaches the earth as sunlight.

Einstein apparently questioned if Sachs was the best man to carry the news to Roosevelt. On August 2 Szilard wrote Einstein hoping "at long last" for a decision "upon whom we should try to get as middle man." He had seen Sachs in the interim; the economist, who certainly coveted the assignment of representing Albert Einstein to the President, had generously listed the financier Bernard Baruch or Karl T. Compton, the president of MIT, as possible alternates. On the other hand, he had strongly endorsed Charles Lindbergh; though he must have known that Roosevelt despised the famous aviator for his outspoken pro-German isolationism. Szilard wrote that he and Sachs had discussed "a somewhat longer and more extensive version" of the letter Einstein had written with Szilard at their second Peconic meeting; he now enclosed both the longer and shorter versions and asked Einstein to return his favorite along with a letter of introduction to Lindbergh.

Einstein opted for the longer version, which incorporated the shorter statement that had originated with him but carried additional paragraphs contributed by Szilard in consultation with Sachs. He signed both letters and returned them to Szilard in less than a week with a note hoping "that you will finally overcome your inner resistance; it's always questionable to try to do something too cleverly." That is, be bold and get moving. "We will try to follow your advice," Szilard rejoined on August 9, "and as far as possible overcome our inner resistances which, admittedly, exist. Incidentally, we are surely not trying to be too clever and will be quite satisfied if only we don't look too stupid."

Szilard transmitted the letter in its final form to Sachs on August 15 along with a memorandum of his own that elaborated on the letter's discussion of the possibilities and dangers of fission. He had not given up contacting Lindbergh—he drafted a letter to the aviator the following day—but he seems to have decided to try Sachs in the meantime, probably in the interest of moving the project on; he pointedly asked Sachs either to deliver the letter to Roosevelt or to return it.

One of the discussions Szilard had added to the longer draft that Einstein chose concerned who should serve as liaison between "the Administration and the group of physicists working on chain reactions in America." In his letter of transmittal to Sachs, Szilard now tacitly offered himself for that service. "If a man, having courage and imagination, could be found," he wrote, "and if such a man were put—in accordance with Dr. Einstein's suggestion—in the position to act with some measure of authority in this matter, this would certainly be an important step forward. In order that you may be able to see of what assistance such a man could be in our work, allow me please to give you a short account of the past history of the case." The short account that followed, an abbreviated and implicit *curriculum vitae*, essentially outlined Szilard's own role since Bohr's announcement of the discovery of fission seven crowded months earlier.

Szilard's offer was as innocent of American bureaucratic politics as it was bold. It was surely also the apotheosis of his drive to save the world. By this time the Hungarians at least believed they saw major humanitarian benefit inherent in what Eugene Wigner would describe in retrospect as "a horrible military weapon," explaining:

> Although none of us spoke much about it to the authorities [during this early period]—they considered us dreamers enough as it was—we did hope for another effect of the development of atomic weapons in addition to the warding off of imminent disaster. We realized that, should atomic weapons be developed, no two nations would be able to live in peace with each other unless their military forces were controlled by a common higher authority. We expected that these controls, if they were effective enough to abolish atomic warfare, would be effective enough to abolish also all other forms of war. This hope was almost as strong a spur to our endeavors as was our fear of becoming the victims of the enemy's atomic bombings.

From the horrible weapon which they were about to urge the United States to develop, Szilard, Teller and Wigner—"the Hungarian conspiracy," Merle Tuve was amused to call them—hoped for more than deterrence against German aggression. They also hoped for world government and world peace, conditions they imagined bombs made of uranium might enforce.

Alexander Sachs intended to read aloud to the President when he met with him. He believed busy people saw so much paper they tended to dismiss the printed word. "Our social system is such," he told a Senate committee in 1945, "that any public figure [is] punch-drunk with printer's ink. . . . This was a matter that the Commander in Chief and the head of the Nation must know. I could only do it if I could see him for a long stretch and read the material so it came in by way of the ear and not as a soft mascara on the eye." He needed a full hour of Franklin Delano Roosevelt's time. . . .

The German atomic bomb project was [already] well begun.

It may have been no less complicated by humanitarian ambiguities than the project the Hungarians in the United States proposed. One young but highly respected German physicist involved in the work from near the beginning was Carl Friedrich von Weizsäcker, the son of the German Undersecretary of State. In a 1978 memoir von Weizsäcker remembers discussing the possibility of a bomb with Otto Hahn in the spring of 1939. Hahn opposed secrecy then partly on the grounds of scientific ethics but also partly because he "felt that if it were to be made, it would be worst for the entire world, even for Germany, if Hitler were to be the only one to have it." Like Szilard, Teller and Wigner, von Weizsäcker remembers realizing in discussions with a friend "that this discovery could not fail to radically change the political structure of the world":

> To a person finding himself at the beginning of an era, its simple fundamental structures may become visible like a distant landscape in the flash of a single stroke of lightning. But the path toward them in the dark is long and confusing. At that time [i.e., 1939] we were faced with a very simple logic. Wars waged with atom bombs as regularly recurring events, that is to say, nuclear wars as institutions, do not seem reconcilable with the survival of the participating nations. But the atom bomb exists. It exists in the minds of some men. According to the historically known logic of armaments and power systems, it will soon make its physical appearance. If that is so, then the participating nations and ultimately mankind itself can only survive if war as an institution is abolished.

Both sides might work from fear of the other. But some on both sides would be working also paradoxically believing they were preparing a new force that would ultimately bring peace to the world.

[On September 1, 1939, World War II began with Nazi Germany's attack on Poland.]

As September extended its violence Szilard grew impatient. He had heard nothing from Alexander Sachs. Pursuing Sachs' previous suggestions and his own leads, he arranged for Eugene Wigner to give him a letter of introduction to MIT president Karl T. Compton; recontacted a businessman of possible influence whom he had once interested in the Einstein-Szilard refrigerator pump; read a newspaper account of a Lindbergh speech and reported to Einstein that the aviator "is in fact not our man." Finally, the last week in September, he and Wigner visited Sachs and found to their dismay that the economist still held Einstein's letter. "He says he has spoken repeatedly with Roosevelt's secretary," Szilard reported to Einstein on October 3, "and has the impression that Roosevelt is so overburdened that it would be wiser to see him at a later date. He intends to go to Washington this week." The two Hungarians were ready to start over: "There is a distinct possibility that Sachs will be of no use to us. If this is the case, we must put the matter in someone else's hands. Wigner and I have decided to accord Sachs ten days' grace. Then I will write you again to let you know how matters stand."

But Alexander Sachs did indeed travel to Washington, not that week but the next, and on Wednesday, October 11, presented himself, probably in the late afternoon, at the White House. Roosevelt's aide, General Edwin M. Watson, "Pa" to Roosevelt and his intimates . . . reviewed Sachs' agenda. When he was convinced that the information was worth the President's time, Watson let Sachs into the Oval Office.

"Alex," Roosevelt hailed him, "what are you up to?"

Sachs liked to warm up the President with jokes. His sense of humor tended to learned parables. Now he told Roosevelt the story of the young American inventor who wrote a letter to Napoleon. The inventor proposed to build the emperor a fleet of ships that carried no sail but could attack England in any weather. He had it in his power to deliver Napoleon's armies to England in a few hours without fear of wind or storm, he wrote, and he was prepared to submit his plans. Napoleon scoffed: ships without sails? "Bah! Away with your visionists!"

The young inventor, Sachs concluded, was Robert Fulton. Roosevelt laughed easily; probably he laughed at that.

Sachs cautioned the President to listen carefully: what he had now to impart was at least the equivalent of the steamboat inventor's proposal to Napoleon. Not yet ready to listen, Roosevelt scribbled a message and summoned an aide. Shortly the aide returned with a treasure, a carefully wrapped bottle of Napoleon brandy that the Roosevelts had preserved in the family for years. The President poured two glasses, passed one to his visitor, toasted him and settled back.

Sachs had made a file for Roosevelt's reading of Einstein's letter and Szilard's memorandum. But neither document had suited his sense of how to present the information to a busy President. "I am an economist, not a scientist," he would tell friends, "but I had a prior relationship with the President, and Szilard and Einstein agreed I was the right person to make the relevant elaborate scientific material intelligible to Mr. Roosevelt. No scientist could sell it to him." Sachs had therefore prepared his own version of the fission story, a composite and paraphrase of the contents of the Einstein and Szilard presentations. Though he left those statements with Roosevelt, he read neither one of them aloud. He read not Einstein's subsequently famous letter but his own eight-hundred-word summation, the first authoritative report to a head of state of the possibility of using nuclear energy to make a weapon of war. It emphasized power production first, radioactive materials for medical use second and "bombs of hitherto unenvisaged potency and scope, third. It recommended making arrangements with Belgium for uranium supplies and expanding and accelerating experiment but imagined that American industry or private foundations would be willing to foot the bill. To that end it proposed that Roosevelt "designate an individual and a committee to serve as a liaison" between the scientists and the Administration.

Sachs had intentionally listed the peaceful potentials of fission first and second among its prospects. To emphasize the "ambivalence" of the discovery, he said later, the "two poles of good and evil" it embodied, he turned near the end of the discussion to Francis Aston's 1936 lecture, "Forty Years of Atomic Theory"—it had been published in 1938 as part of a collection, *Background to Modern Science,* which Sachs had brought along to the White House— where the English spectroscopist had ridiculed "the more elderly and apelike of our prehistoric ancestors" who "objected to the innovation of cooked food and pointed out the grave dangers attending the use of the newly discovered agency, fire." Sachs read the entire last paragraph of the lecture to Roosevelt, emphasizing the final sentences:

> Personally I think there is no doubt that sub-atomic energy is available all around us, and that one day man will release and control its almost infinite power. We cannot prevent him from doing so and can only hope that he will not use it exclusively in blowing up his next door neighbor.

"Alex," said Roosevelt, quickly understanding, "what you are after is to see that the Nazis don't blow us up."

"Precisely," Sachs said.

Roosevelt called in Watson. "This requires action," he told his aide. Meeting afterward with Sachs, Watson went by the book. He proposed a committee consisting initially of the director of the Bureau of Standards, an Army representative and a Navy representative. The Bureau of Standards, established by Act of Congress in 1901, is the nation's physics laboratory, charged with applying science and technology in the national interest and for public benefit. Its director in 1939 was Dr. Lyman J. Briggs, a Johns Hopkins Ph.D. and a government scientist for forty-three years who had been nominated by Herbert Hoover and appointed by FDR. The military representatives were Lieutenant Colonel Keith F. Adamson and Commander Gilbert C. Hoover, both ordnance experts.

"Don't let Alex go without seeing me again," Roosevelt had directed Watson. Sachs met the same evening with Briggs, briefed him and proposed he and his committee of two get together with the physicists working on fission. Briggs agreed. Sachs saw the President again and declared himself satisfied. That was good enough for Roosevelt.

Truman Drops
the Bomb

Alonzo Hamby

The Manhattan Project succeeded brilliantly. At the cost of secret expenditures of more than $2 billion (a colossal sum at the time), a team of American, British, and exiled European scientists discovered how to control nuclear fission and then constructed a nuclear device. Fortunately for the rest of the world, the Germans' own nuclear program had been caught in a technological blind alley and thus lost its initial advantage. By the time the Manhattan Project had a device ready to test, the war in Europe was over (had a bomb been available, it would almost certainly have been used on Germany), but the war in the Pacific was still raging. A new president also sat in the Oval Office—Harry S. Truman, Franklin Roosevelt's untested vice president, who took office on FDR's death in April 1945. On Truman fell the awesome responsibility of deciding whether to use the bomb to force Japan into surrender. His decisions to obliterate Hiroshima and Nagasaki constitute the only use (so far) of nuclear weaponry in combat.

Truman's decision has been bitterly criticized from many perspectives. Was he acting out of racial prejudice against the nonwhite Japanese? Did he intend to intimidate Stalin, who was increasingly perceived as a dangerous antagonist to the Western democracies? American historian Alonzo Hamby, the author of an acclaimed recent biography of Truman and a lifelong student of his presidency, weighs the alternatives that Truman faced.

H arry S. Truman had been President of the United States for less than two weeks on April 25th, 1945, when Secretary of War Henry L. Stimson delivered to him a full report on the most expen-

Reprinted from "Truman and the Bomb," by Alonzo Hamby, *History Today,* vol. 45, August 1995.
Reprinted with permission from *History Today.*

sive and secret American enterprise of the Second World War. The document began with the chilling words, 'Within four months, we shall in all probability have completed the most terrible weapon ever known in human history'. From that point until he received word of its successful test in mid-July, the atomic bomb was at the back of Truman's mind as he attempted to cope with the manifold problems accompanying the end of the greatest war in human history.

On May 8th, Truman's sixty-first birthday, Germany surrendered unconditionally. It was still necessary to achieve final victory in the Pacific and manage a multitude of diplomatic difficulties with the Allies, especially the Soviet Union, not yet at war with Japan and (so it seemed) desperately needed for the final campaigns in the Pacific conflict.

Truman's attitude to the war was heavily motivated by his own experience as a combat artilleryman in the First World War, in his perceptions of Japanese fanaticism, and in forming his identity as a politician attempting to establish the limits of his discretion. Revisionist scholars, motivated by a pacifist revulsion against the horrors of nuclear war, have criticised his eventual use of the atomic bomb as unnecessary; some have asserted that he cynically sacrificed Japanese lives in an effort to intimidate the Soviet Union. Such charges have little merit. An examination of the available evidence, considered within the context of 1945 rather than 1995, reveals a president who made imperfect judgements and was shaken by the destruction he wrought, but who could rightly think he was acting simply to end a terrible war being fought against an implacable enemy.

Diplomatic issues stemming from the termination of the European war and the establishment of the United Nations necessarily occupied much of Truman's attention during his first three months in office, but the struggle against Japan was never far from his attention. On April 1st, just eleven days before he took office, American troops had landed on Okinawa, 400 miles from the southernmost Japanese island of Kyushu. Allied forces, mostly American but including a British naval contingent, had overwhelming superiority. Okinawa was smaller than Rhode Island: nevertheless, the battle that followed lasted nearly three months. More than 100,000 Japanese troops defended the island, fighting with suicidal tenacity. Waves of kamikaze planes attacked the American fleet, inflicting greater losses than the Japanese navy had managed over the past year.

As Truman read daily battle reports, he surely thought of his own combat experiences and of those of his close friends in the Argonne area and then to the east of Verdun during the Great War: finding himself in No Man's Land while acting as a forward observer for his artillery regiment; his cousin, Captain Ralph Truman, pulling a shattered infantry force together against a German counterattack; Major

John Miles, a close comrade, holding his artillery battalion firm in the same action; corpses along dusty roads; a dying freckle-faced kid with a leg blown off; the scattered remains of unknown soldiers heaved from shallow graves by German artillery shells. And he must have thought of two friends who had served under him in that war, Eddie McKim and Abie Burkhart, both of whom had already lost sons in the current war. And he surely thought of his four nephews, all of them in uniform, one of them a sailor on the USS Missouri, off Okinawa.

Despite his willingness to assume full and sole responsibility for use of the atomic bomb in later years, Truman dealt with the impending event in the fashion of a circumspect chairman of the board. He appointed a committee. Headed by Stimson and containing James Byrnes (soon to be appointed Secretary of State) as his personal representative, the Interim Committee, as it was called, saw the bomb, however terrible, as a proxy for the thousand-plane raids that had already devastated numerous German and Japanese cities. None of the committee members, scientists and politicians alike, fully understood the horrifying radioactive side-effects of nuclear warfare. On June 1st, citing all the uncertainties of employing an unprecedented (and as yet untested) weapon, the Interim Committee recommended use of the bomb against Japan without warning. No one doubted that Truman would accept the advice.

On June 18th, the president met with his top military officials to discuss the possible scenarios for ending the war against Japan. They recommended an invasion of Kyushu no later than November 1st. The operation would be enormous: 766,000 American assault troops engaging an estimated 350,000 Japanese defenders. It would be followed in 1946 by a decisive campaign near Tokyo on the main island of Honshu.

Would the Kyushu operation, Truman asked, be 'another Okinawa closer to Japan'? With questionable optimism, the military chiefs of staff predicted the casualties would be somewhat lighter. Still their estimate for the first thirty days was 31,000 casualties. Truman gave his reluctant approval, but not without saying he hoped 'there was a possibility of preventing an Okinawa from one end of Japan to another'.

In fact, Pentagon planners were at work on estimates that projected 132,000 casualties (killed, wounded, missing) for Kyushu, another 90,000 or so for Honshu. Of these, probably a quarter would be fatalities. The figures were not wholly worked out by the June 18th meeting but they would be given to Truman in due course and would constitute the estimates upon which he acted. In later years, he exaggerated them, but they required no magnification to make the atomic bomb a compelling option.

The June 18th meeting also explored ways in which the war might be concluded without either the Kyushu invasion or the atomic bomb. Should the United States, could it, accept less than unconditional surrender from Japan? The president's personal military chief of staff, Admiral William D. Leahy was most emphatic in asserting that it should. Transfixed by the fanaticism of Japanese resistance, fearful that American losses would exceed Pentagon estimates, doubtful that the bomb would ever work, Leahy declared that Japan could not menace the United States in the foreseeable future. Stimson and Assistant Secretary of War John J. McCloy favoured giving the Japanese guarantees that they could keep the emperor.

Truman appeared somewhat sympathetic, said he had left the door open for Congress to alter the unconditional surrender policy, but felt he could not take action to change public opinion. He apparently did not believe that an utterly defeated Japan might be allowed to retain the emperor under terms that still could be called 'unconditional surrender' and that the American people would prefer so minor a compromise to another year of war.

Should the United States warn the Japanese of its atomic capability, perhaps even arrange some sort of demonstration? McCloy alone argued for doing so. Other military leaders argued the shock value of surprise. The Interim Committee had explicitly rejected such proposals. Byrnes, who was formally named Secretary of State on July 3rd, strongly favoured both rigid unconditional surrender and total surprise.

Truman had been presented with a wide consensus from an interlocking directorate composed of the men who had won the war: the Interim Committee, his top military leaders, and his most important Cabinet members. He would feel a need to talk of using the atomic bomb against strictly military targets, but that, which he probably realised was not realistic, was his only inhibition.

The four weeks after June 18th were intensely busy for the new president. In addition to a budget message for Congress, he faced a wide range of military and diplomatic matters—the San Francisco conference to establish the United Nations, myriad conflicts with the Soviet Union in occupied Germany and Eastern Europe, numerous squabbles with the French and British, the shape of the post-war Far East. Above all, so long as the atomic bomb remained a prospect, rather than an accomplished reality, he had to nail down Soviet participation in the war against Japan.

Many of these issues came to a head when he met at Potsdam with Stalin and Churchill. (Near the end of the conference, after the Conservative election defeat, Clement Attlee replaced Churchill). Truman arrived on July 15th; the conference would last until August

2nd. During his time away from the negotiations—his spare time, astonishingly—he would grapple with the bomb as an actuality and make the final decisions required.

On July 15th, Truman toured the rubble of Berlin. 'What a pity that the human animal is not able to put his moral thinking into practice!' he mused. 'I fear that machines are ahead of morals by some centuries'. Perhaps thinking of the bomb, he added, 'We are only termites on a planet and maybe when we bore too deeply into the planet there'll be a reckoning—who knows?'

He may well have written those lines after meeting between 7.30 and 8.00 pm with Secretary Stimson, who presented him with a top secret message he had just received from his closest aide, George Harrison. Tersely and obliquely, it indicated that the first atomic test, near Alamogordo in the New Mexico desert, had been a great success. On the morning of July 18th, Stimson gave Truman another message from Harri-

Winston Churchill, President Truman, and Joseph Stalin at the Potsdam Conference

son in Washington: the flash of the explosion had been visible for 250 miles, the sound of the blast had carried 50 miles. Truman, Stimson wrote in his diary, was 'highly delighted . . . evidently very greatly reinforced'.

Truman confided some thoughts to his own diary that day. Since they have been badly distorted by at least one writer, they are worth quoting in full:

> Discussed Manhattan (it is a success). Decided to tell Stalin about it. Stalin had told PM [Churchill] of telegram from Jap Emperor asking for peace. Stalin also read his answer to me. It was satisfactory. Believe Japs will fold up before Russia comes in.
>
> I am sure they will when Manhattan appears over their homeland. I shall inform Stalin about it at an opportune time.

Truman clearly assumed that the bomb would be used, that it would compel Japan to surrender, and that Soviet participation might not be necessary after all. But what of the emperor's telegram 'asking for peace'? Were the Japanese ready to surrender? And if so, why was the war permitted to continue for another month? The 'emperor's telegram', drafted by the Japanese Foreign Office, asked

Stalin to receive Prince Fumimaro Konoye on an unspecified mission related to the termination of the war. The nature of the petition reflected gridlock in Tokyo. The Japanese military bitterly opposed surrender. Civilian officials who talked about it risked assassination. In the absence of an agenda or a basis for discussion, the request was meaningless. The Konoye mission never materialised.

US Intelligence was intercepting and decoding diplomatic transmissions between Japanese Foreign Minister Shigenori Togo and Ambassador Naotake Sato in Moscow; they revealed the unreal hopes in Tokyo. Truman was briefed on and probably saw copies of Sato's telegram to Togo, dated July 12th. With a bold directness and despairing eloquence, Sato declared that the time was past for negotiation, that the Japanese homeland was in peril, that the Soviets would be of no help. 'We ourselves must firmly resolve to terminate the war', he declared:

> Is there any meaning in showing that our country has reserve strength for a war of resistance, or in sacrificing the lives of hundreds of thousands of conscripts and millions of other innocent residents of cities and metropolitan areas?

Asking Togo's pardon and begging for his understanding, Sato concluded, 'in international relations there is no mercy, and facing reality is unavoidable'. Togo responded curtly and specifically warned Sato against giving the impression that Japan was ready to surrender unconditionally. After reading such an exchange, Truman and those around him had to think that Japan planned to fight to the end.

On July 21st, a much fuller report of the Alamogordo test by General Leslie Groves arrived at Potsdam. It contained specific data on the explosion: a force of 15-20,000 tons of TNT, a fireball lasting several seconds and shining as brightly as several midday suns, a mushroom cloud rising to 41,000 feet above sea level, secondary explosions within it, a 1,200-foot crater, the evaporation of the 100-ft tower from which the bomb had been suspended, the destruction of a 70-ft steel tower a half-mile away. General Thomas Farrell wrote of the blast's 'strong, sustained, awesome roar which warned of doomsday and made us feel that we puny things were blasphemous to dare tamper with the forces heretofore reserved to The Almighty'.

Stimson read the report to Truman and Byrnes. 'They were immensely pleased', he wrote shortly afterwards:

> The president was tremendously pepped up by it and spoke to me of it again and again when I saw him. He said it gave him an entirely new feeling of confidence and he thanked me for having come to the Conference and being present to help him in this way.

Because the British had been partners in the Manhattan Project, Churchill was fully informed. Gunpowder, the prime minister declared, had become trivial and electricity meaningless; the bomb was 'the Second Coming in Wrath'. Truman told himself: 'It may be the fire destruction prophesied in the Euphrates Valley Era after Noah and his fabulous Ark'.

The bomb had given Truman a sense of enormous power. At a stroke, it had changed his position from that of a supplicant in quest of an ally against Japan to a more-than-equal partner now able to be indifferent. Churchill had observed on July 21st that the president was markedly more assertive and considerably firmer in rejecting Soviet demands. Now he understood why. A consensus quickly developed among the British and Americans that the USSR should be told as little as possible. On July 24th, at the conclusion of the day's negotiations, Truman walked over to Stalin and, as he later would tell it, 'casually mentioned . . . that we had a new weapon of unusual destructive force'.

Stalin, poker-faced, said that he hoped the United States would make good use of it, asked no questions, and made no further comments. Of course, thanks to his espionage ring at Los Alamos, he was actually well-informed about the Manhattan Project, although he may not yet have learned of the successful test. The Americans, many of them puzzled at his lack of interest, did not realise that they had witnessed the first display of an interim Soviet strategy for dealing with the bomb—to behave as if it were irrelevant—until the USSR could produce one of its own.

As Truman remembered it in 1952, he asked his top advisers once again about likely casualties in the planned invasions of Kyushu and Honshu and received from General George Marshall an estimate of about 250,000 Americans and at least an equal number of Japanese. Of those with whom he talked, no one was more important than Stimson, who had his total respect and was directly responsible for the atomic project.

When Stimson insisted on dropping Kyoto from the target list, Truman concurred (in Stimson's words) 'with the utmost emphasis'. The military saw Kyoto as a prime industrial target; Stimson saw it as a city of shrines and cultural centres that could not be destroyed without alienating the Japanese population. Stimson was probably also the key figure, if only through his silence, in leading Truman to accept a strategy of dropping the first two bombs in rapid succession. The idea was to convince the Japanese that the United States had a large stockpile.

As to use of the bomb, there was no dissent among the primary advisers. On July 25th, Truman gave the final go-ahead. Sometime during the first ten days of August, the bomb would be used against Hiroshima, Kokura, or Nigata in that order of choice—unless Japan surrendered unconditionally.

On July 26th, the United States, Great Britain and China issued a proclamation from Potsdam demanding the unconditional surrender of Japan. The alternative would be 'the inevitable and complete destruction of the Japanese armed forces and . . . the utter devastation of the Japanese homeland'. Following the decisions already made in Washington, the ultimatum did not mention an atomic bomb. Nor did it specifically state that Japan would be allowed to retain the emperor; instead, it promised to recognise 'in accordance with the freely expressed will of the Japanese people a peacefully inclined and responsible government'.

On July 28th, Japan rejected the proclamation with a verb that could be translated as 'treat with silent contempt' or 'ignore entirely'. The government, Prime Minister Suzuki asserted, would 'resolutely fight for the successful conclusion of this war'.

For most Americans, 'unconditional surrender' had become a wartime objective carved in stone; having obtained it from Germany, no American president could appear to negotiate anything less with Japan, which in turn surely bore the burden of responsibility for ending a war it had started. Still, the United States could have made it clear, either publicly or through diplomatic backchannels, that unconditional surrender would not mean removal of the emperor. Whether Japan would have responded to such an initiative cannot be known, but one can only regret that it did not crystallise in Truman's mind before the obliteration of two cities.

As it was, the president allowed things to go forward, buoyed by a belief that the war would soon be ended without a massive invasion, yet not entirely comfortable with what he had done. Writing in his diary, he portrayed his orders to Stimson in terms that in his heart he had to know were unrealistic:

> I have told the Sec. of War, Mr Stimson, to use it so that military objectives and soldiers and sailors are the target and not women and children. Even if the Japs are savages, ruthless, merciless and fanatic, we as the leader of the world for the common welfare cannot drop this terrible bomb on the old Capitol [Kyoto] or the new [Tokyo].
>
> He & I are in accord. The target will be a purely military one . . .

At approximately 8.11 am on August 6th, a B-29, the *Enola Gay,* piloted by Colonel Paul Tibbets, dropped an atomic bomb over the city of Hiroshima from an altitude of 31,600 feet. The explosion occurred at 2,000 feet. Observers in a trailing B-29 witnessed the blinding fireball, the shock wave, the mushroom cloud rising miles into the sky. The central city, built on a level plain, was instantly in flames; almost nothing remained standing within a one-mile radius of 'ground zero'. Perhaps 75,000 people, mostly civilians, were killed at once; more tens of thousands would eventually die from the effects of radiation. No single device in the history of warfare had killed so many people so indiscriminately.

The news reached Truman as he was returning from Potsdam aboard the cruiser *Augusta*. Elated, convinced that the war would soon be over, and cognisant of the unprecedented military and sci- entific implications, he declared: 'This is the greatest thing in his- tory'. Some would criticise the statement as callous, but Truman was celebrating the end of a war; and, if by 'greatest', he meant 'most important', who will say he was wrong?

The *Augusta* docked at Newport News on August 7th. The next day, Truman conferred with Stimson, who showed him photographs de- tailing the damage at Hiroshima. After examining them thoroughly, he remarked that the destruction placed a terrible responsibility upon him- self and the War Department. Stimson expressed his hope that the United States would make it as easy as possible for Japan to surrender and would treat the defeated enemy with tact and leniency. That after- noon, Truman announced to White House reporters that the USSR had declared war on Japan. With no surrender offer, no word at all, com- ing from Tokyo, he did not interfere with the use of the second bomb. On August 9th, at 11.00 am, it hit Nagasaki, a tertiary target selected because of bad weather and poor observation conditions at Kokura and Nigata. The death and devastation was perhaps half that at Hiroshima; yet it was still beyond imagination.

Would the Japanese have surrendered had they been given more time to contemplate the totality of Hiroshima? Or conversely were they more impressed by the Soviet declaration of war than by the bombs? No one can say. We know they realised an event of unique horror had occurred at Hiroshima and that the United States had an- nounced the use of an atomic bomb. We know that civilian officials wanted to surrender but that the military leaders found the prospect unbearable. Just before midnight on August 9th, the civilian-military Supreme War Council met in the presence of the emperor. After each side made its presentation, Hirohito declared emotionally and firmly, 'I swallow my own tears and give my sanction to the proposal to ac- cept the Allied proclamation'.

The Japanese surrender offer put before Truman on August 10th, still insisted on retention of the emperor. Only Secretary of State Byrnes was reluctant to accept it. Truman opted for a response as- serting that the Japanese message met American terms with the un- derstanding that the emperor would be subject to the Allied supreme commander. At a Cabinet meeting, he declared there would be no more atomic bombings. Secretary of Commerce Henry Wallace recorded his attitude: 'He said the thought of wiping out another 100,000 people was too horrible. He didn't like the idea of killing, as he said, "all those kids"'.

The Allies gave their approval to American terms. Japan remained silent. On August 13th, Truman authorised one last terrible 1,000-plane raid on Tokyo. Presiding over a final meeting of his War Council, Hirohito demanded acceptance of the United States offer. Within twenty-four hours die-hard army officers attempted a coup d'etat that was barely suppressed. On August 14th, late in the afternoon, the United States received Japanese acceptance of American surrender terms. That evening, Truman announced that the Second World War was over and declared a two-day holiday. For a moment it was possible to hope that the destruction of the enemy meant the birth of a hopeful new world.

At the August 10th Cabinet meeting, Truman declared ('most fiercely', according to Wallace) that he expected the Russians to stall on the surrender in order to grab as much of Manchuria as possible, and that if China and Britain agreed to the American terms, he would not wait for the Russians. Scholars of the Left invoke such bits and pieces of anti-Soviet rhetoric as proof that the bombs were dropped not to compel a Japanese surrender but to intimidate the USSR. Yet there is no credible evidence in Truman's personal contemporary writings or his later accounts that he saw the *use* of the bomb as a way of making a point to the Russians—although he clearly thought its *existence* would strengthen the hand of the United States.

Truman acted on the certainty that the longer the war lasted, the more American fatalities would occur. Some critics have suggested that he should have engaged in a grim calculus, that he should have accepted an additional 45–50,000 American deaths rather than kill many more Japanese with the bomb. But no conceivable US president in the summer of 1945 would have done that. The critics also believe that Japan, hammered by cumulative defeats, facing an unbreakable naval blockade, and shocked by Soviet intervention, would have shortly surrendered anyway. But a brute certainty remains. Japan did not muster the will to surrender until two atomic bombs had been dropped.

Most veterans of the Pacific war felt a sense of physical salvation. One of them was Army Second Lieutenant Francis Heller, a young man whose parents had fled Austria a decade earlier. Assigned to the first wave of the invasion of Honshu, Heller instead found himself wading ashore with his men on a quiet beach. 'I thought this is where I would have been killed if not for the atomic bomb', he recalls. The thought must have entered his mind many times nine years later when he helped Harry Truman write his memoirs.

Truman, the old artilleryman who had seen the horrors of the 1914–18 War close-up, understood from his own experience the hopes and fears of the Francis Hellers of the world—young combat officers dreaming of families and futures, just as he had done a generation earlier. They were the ultimate vindication of his decision.

The Cold War Years, 1945–1969

The United States possessed the atomic bomb in 1945, although until at least 1949 it had very few operational nuclear weapons at its disposal and few means of delivering them over great distances. Then, in 1949, the Soviet Union also successfully tested its first nuclear device. In 1952 the United States detonated its first thermonuclear weapon, the hydrogen bomb, which was far more powerful than the atom bombs dropped on Japan. Soon the Soviet Union did so, too, and by the mid-1950s both sides were developing ballistic missile systems capable of delivering nuclear weapons over intercontinental, medium-range, and short-range distances.

The Cold War cannot be understood without grasping the important shift in strategic thinking that accompanied the invention of sophisticated rocketry and nuclear weaponry. In the past—for example, in the years leading up to the Great War—arms races and the spread of hostile alliance systems had culminated in major wars. War, including *total* war, was considered a normal part of international relations. Total war had meant that every possible resource would be mobilized for victory, and that to prevail, armies and navies would use almost every available weapon. "Almost"—because during World War II both sides had refrained from using poison gas and biological weapons, realizing that the enemy would retaliate in kind. After 1945 that same logic convinced military planners that total war involving nuclear weapons would probably mean the end of civilization, if not human life itself. A grim joke of the time predicted that if World War III was fought with nuclear bombs, World War IV would be fought with sticks and stones.

Even as allies against Nazi Germany during World War II, the Western democracies and Joseph Stalin's Soviet Union had been deeply suspicious of each other. Each worried that the other might make a separate peace with Adolf Hitler. Winston Churchill never trusted the Soviet Union, though he was willing to deal with it cynically on the basis of an old-fashioned division of territorial spheres of influence. Franklin Roosevelt thought that if he dangled offers of American aid, he could persuade Stalin to cooperate in the postwar period, and he set great store by the United Nations (UN) as an international peacekeeper. Stalin wanted to get American aid in rebuilding the USSR, but he also demanded a wide Soviet-dominated "buffer zone" in Eastern Europe and he was suspicious of his allies simply because they were capitalists and were thus hostile to the Soviet Union's socialist order. As a Marxist-Leninist, he also believed that sooner or later a showdown between the capitalist and socialist camps, would end in the worldwide victory of socialism.

Amid this mutual suspicion—but also in an environment in which both sides understood that escalation to all-out war would be catastrophic—the Cold War unfolded after 1945. At first the main issue was Stalin's demand for effective control (through a puppet regime) of Poland, which the Western democracies were reluctant to concede because it denied self-determination to Poland, in whose defense the West had gone to war in 1939. Later, beginning in 1947, the defining East-West issue was whether occupied Germany should be reunified and neutralized (which the West feared would leave the country vulnerable to Soviet pressure) or partitioned, with the West keeping the larger and more industrialized part of the country out of Stalin's orbit. By 1949 most of the important countries of Western Europe had joined the United States and Canada in an alliance system known as the North Atlantic Treaty Organization (NATO) while the Soviet-dominated countries of Eastern Europe formed an alliance called the Warsaw Pact. Largely because "hot" war was strategically unthinkable, however, even the most dangerous Soviet-Western confrontation—the Berlin blockade of 1947–1949—did not end in shots being fired. Journalists called this a "cold war," and the name stuck.

By 1950 the Cold War had become a global confrontation. The Communist victory in the Chinese civil war and the proclamation of the People's Republic of China in October 1949 brought at least half a billion more people under Marxist-Leninist rule and precipitated a furious debate in the United States about who lost China. In June 1950 Communist North Korea invaded American-backed South Korea, and when the United States spearheaded a UN intervention on the South's behalf, the Cold War threatened to turn hot. China intervened to protect North Korea, and the war ended in 1953 in a stalemate, but the Soviet Union prudently stayed out. During the 1950s the United States concluded alliances and other mutual-defense commitments to numerous countries on the periphery of China and the Soviet Union, and on several occasions crises erupted between the two rival power blocks. For the United States, the most difficult phase of the Cold War began in 1965, when it was sucked into a long, unwinnable war to defend its client state, South Vietnam, against an internal Communist movement supported by North Vietnam. Yet even this conflict, which killed more than fifty thousand Americans and more than a million Vietnamese, remained a local, limited war. What American strategists called the "deterrence effect"—or the Mutual Assured Destruction (MAD) doctrine—kept the peace between the nuclear-armed superpowers.

In the Western democracies, the Cold War left its mark on many aspects of public and private life. Anxiety about a potential nuclear holocaust and, at times, about internal subversion were widespread public concerns in the late 1940s and throughout the 1950s, and these concerns were reflected in everything from movies and popular music to education and career paths. Especially in the United States, enormous political power devolved on what President Dwight Eisenhower (1953–1961) called the military-industrial complex, by which he meant the vote-seeking politicians, the news media, the defense industry, the military establishment, and the research institutes that were involved in developing and promoting military preparedness. The space race, which began when the Soviet Union launched its first Sputnik satellite in 1957, ran until American astronauts stepped onto the lunar surface twelve years later, always containing a strong dose of great-power rivalry.

The Cold War climaxed in October 1962, when American spy planes detected the rapid building of Soviet missile bases in Cuba, where a pro-Communist revolution led by Fidel Castro had occurred three years earlier. As the world waited breathlessly, President John F. Kennedy and Soviet leader Nikita Khrushchev went to the brink of nuclear war before finding a face-saving resolution.

Frightened by this near-catastrophe, for the rest of the 1960s the Western public allowed its obsession with the Cold War to wane. In part, this shift reflected the rise of new concerns: the civil rights and feminist movements, a rebellious youth culture, and permissive new attitudes in cultural and social life. Revisionist historians in the West reexamined the origins of the Cold War and found Anglo-American policy makers at least as responsible for the postwar global polarization as their Soviet counterparts. The growing opposition of the Western public (and above all of American young people) to the Vietnam War involved a wholesale rejection of anti-Communist Cold War rhetoric. All these trends had an anti-authoritarian bent and accorded little room for concern about an external Marxist-Leninist threat, orchestrated by devious schemers in the Kremlin. So did the sympathy that many young people in the West felt for the ex-colonial Third World's (and for Maoist China's) struggle to break free from Western imperialism, capitalism, and racism. By contrast, the post-Stalinist Soviet Union was quickly losing its aura of revolutionary dynamism; by the late 1960s it seemed gray, boring, predictable, and unattractive. The fact that it was also becoming heavily armed with missiles, a "blue-water" navy, and a huge inventory of nuclear warheads was more a concern for the Pentagon and Richard Nixon than for the Western public. Although the Soviet-Western confrontation would continue (and occasionally still seems dangerous) through the presidency of Ronald Reagan (1980–1989), the Cold War was fading into history.

Who Started the Cold War?

John Lewis Gaddis

The Cold War—the confrontation pitting the United States and its Western allies against the Soviet Union, China, and the other Marxist-Leninist states and revolutionary movements—was the defining public event of the second half of the twentieth century. It shaped so much else that happened in the period: the development of nuclear power and the arms race; the pace of technological change; political relationships in all the countries involved; the dynamics of decolonization; and indeed many contours of contemporary cultural life.

How the Cold War began, and whether one side or the other bore particular responsibility for it, are questions that historians have debated vigorously for at least a generation. Between the 1960s and the 1980s, many scholars in the United States and Western Europe placed much blame on the Western powers for not understanding Soviet needs for security after having suffered so badly in the Nazi German invasion. Other historians pointed to Western (and particularly American) leaders' determination never again to be surprised by an expansive power dominating the heartland of Europe, as Hitler had surprised them. Communist historians, inside and outside the Soviet Union, insisted that the Cold War had resulted from the aggressive moves of worldwide capitalism, led by the "ruling circles" who determined U.S. policy.

Since the fall of Soviet communism in the late 1980s and early 1990s, the former Soviet archives have been opened enough so that historians can at last assess the Cold War's origins more objectively. (Opening of these archives has not been complete, and many questions remain unanswered.) American historian John Lewis Gaddis, a veteran authority on Cold War history, was able to draw upon a considerable amount of new information from the Soviet side (including interviews with Stalin's foreign minister Vyacheslav Molotov, then in his late nineties) to write a fascinating 1997 book entitled *We Now Know: Rethinking Cold War History*. Gaddis assigns to Stalin the major responsibility for causing the breakdown of the East-West relationship. An excerpt from Gaddis's book follows.

S talin as well as Roosevelt and Churchill miscalculated when they assumed that there could be *friendly* states along an *expanded* Soviet periphery. For how could the USSR absorb the Baltic States entirely and carve off great portions of Germany, Poland, Romania, and Czechoslovakia, while still expecting the citizens of those countries to maintain cordial attitudes toward the state that had done the carving? It is of course true that the Finns, who were also carved upon, did somehow manage it. But not everyone else was like the Finns: if allowed free elections, it was by no means certain that Poles and Romanians would show the same remarkable qualities of self-control for which their northern neighbor would become famous. Nor was it obvious, even where the Russians permitted other Eastern Europeans to make a choice, that Moscow would follow its own Finnish example and stay out of their internal affairs: these states did have Germany, not Sweden, on the other side of them, and that surely made a difference.

But there was more to the matter than just geography: compounding it was a growing awareness of the particular system Stalin had imposed upon his own people and might well export elsewhere. The war was ending with the defeat of fascism, but not authoritarianism. The price of relying upon one authoritarian to conquer another had been that both would not simultaneously disappear. However vast the moral capital the Soviet Union—and the European communist parties—had accumulated in fighting the Germans, it could not obscure the fact that Stalin's government was, and showed every sign of continuing to be, as repressive as Hitler's had ever been. A movement that had set out, a century earlier, to free the workers of the world from their chains was now seeking to convince its own workers and everyone else that the condition of being in chains was one of perfect freedom. People were not blind, though, and victory over German authoritarianism brought fears of Soviet authoritarianism out into the open.

Worried that this might happen, Roosevelt and Churchill had hoped to persuade the Europeans that Stalin himself had changed: that he meant what he said when he denied any desire to extend his own system beyond its borders; that they could therefore safely accept the boundary changes he demanded and the sphere of influence within which he proposed to include so many of them. But this strategy required Stalin's cooperation, for it could hardly succeed if the Soviet leader failed to match his deeds with the Atlantic Charter's words. Unless the Soviet Union could show that it had shifted from a unilateral to a multilateral approach to security, there could be little basis for consent from Europeans certain to fall under its control. That situation, in turn, would place the Americans and the British in the painful position of being able to cooperate with Moscow only by publicly abandoning principles they themselves had proclaimed, and that Stalin himself appeared to have endorsed.

Authoritarians tend to see ends as justifying means, and are generally free to act accordingly. Democracies rarely allow that luxury, even if their leaders might, in their darker moments, wish for it. What people think does make a difference, and yet nothing in Stalin's experience had prepared him for this reality. Thus it was that although the objective he sought *appeared* to correspond with what his allies wanted—a secure postwar world—the *methods* by which he pursued that goal proved profoundly corruptive of it. Poland best illustrates the pattern.

Presumably Stalin had security in mind when he authorized the murder, at Katyn and elsewhere in the spring of 1940, of at least 15,000 Polish officers captured during the invasion that followed the Nazi-Soviet Pact. He apparently hoped to avoid disturbances that might endanger his relationship with Hitler, to clear out overcrowded camps, and perhaps also to eliminate potential leaders of a future Poland who might be unsympathetic to Soviet interests. He cannot have given the matter much thought, for he was only meting out to the Poles the kind of treatment he had already accorded several million Soviet citizens, and would extend to many others in the future.

What Stalin did not anticipate was that he would need to repair his relations with the Poles after Hitler attacked the Soviet Union in 1941, that he would find it necessary to recognize the Polish government-in-exile in London and reconstitute a Polish army on Soviet soil to fight the Germans, and that the Nazis, in 1943, would reveal the Katyn atrocity to the world. Rather than admit responsibility, Stalin chose to break off relations with the London Poles, who had called for an international investigation. He then created a puppet regime of his own in Lublin and begin treating it as the legitimate government of Poland, a maneuver he backed with force as the Red Army moved into that country in 1944. Stalin subsequently failed to support, or even to allow the Americans and the British to supply by air, an uprising of the Polish resistance in Warsaw, with the result that the Germans wound up completing, on a far more massive scale, the purge of Polish anti-communists he himself had started at Katyn four years earlier. This tragic sequence of events reflected Stalin's tendency, when confronting the prospect of insecurity, to try to redesign the future rather than admit that his own past behavior might have contributed to the problem in the first place.

Stalin in the end got the acquiescent Polish government he wanted, but only at enormous cost. The brutality and cynicism with which he handled these matters did more than anything else to exhaust the goodwill the Soviet war effort had accumulated in the West, to raise doubts about future cooperation in London and Washington, and to create deep and abiding fears throughout the rest of Europe. He also earned the enduring hostility of the Poles, thereby making their country a constant source of *insecurity* for him and for all of his successors. The most effective resistance to Soviet authority would eventually arise in Poland—effective in the sense that the Kremlin never found a way to suppress it. And in an entirely appropriate aftermath, the belated official acknowledgement of Stalin's responsibility for Katyn, which came only in 1990, turned out to be one of the ways in which the last Soviet government acknowledged, not only the illegitimacy of the sphere of influence Stalin had constructed half a century before, but its own illegitimacy as well.

It used to be thought that authoritarian leaders, unfettered by moral scruples, had powerful advantages over their democratic counterparts: it was supposed to be a source of strength to be able to use all means in the pursuit of selected ends. Today this looks much less certain. For the great disadvantage of such systems is the absence of checks and balances: who is to tell the authoritarian in charge that he is about to do something stupid? The killings Stalin authorized, the states he seized, the boundary concessions he insisted upon, and the sphere of influence he imposed provided no lasting security for the Soviet Union: just the opposite. His actions laid the foundations for a resistance in Europe that would grow and not fade with time, so that when a Soviet leader appeared on the scene who was not prepared to sustain with force the system Stalin had constructed, the Soviet empire, and ultimately the Soviet Union itself, would not survive the experience.

Social psychologists make a useful distinction between what they call "dispositional" and "situational" behavior in interpreting the actions of individuals. Dispositional behavior reflects deeply rooted personal characteristics which remain much the same regardless of the circumstances in which people find themselves. One responds inflexibly—and therefore predictably—to whatever happens. Situational behavior, conversely, shifts with circumstances; personal traits are less important in determining what one does. Historians need to be careful in applying this insight, though, because psychologists know how tempting it can be to excuse one's own actions by invoking situations, while attributing what others do to their dispositions. It would be all too easy, in dealing with so controversial a matter as responsibility for the Cold War, to confuse considered judgment with that most satisfying of sensations: the confirmation of one's own prejudices.

By the end of 1945 most American and British leaders had come around—some reluctantly, others eagerly—to a dispositional explanation of Stalin's behavior. Further efforts to negotiate or compromise with him were likely to fail, or so it seemed, because success would require that he cease to be what he was. One could only resolve henceforth to hold the line, remain true to one's own principles, and wait for the passage of time to bring a better world. Such at least was the view of . . . George Kennan [an analyst of Soviet politics in the U.S. Foreign Service], whose top secret "long telegram" from Moscow of 22 February 1946, would shape American policy over the next half century more profoundly than his distant relative's denunciations of tsarist authoritarianism had influenced it during the preceding one. Nor was "containment" just an American strategy: Frank Roberts, the British *chargé d'affaires* in the Soviet capital, was dispatching similar arguments to London even as former prime minister Winston Churchill, speaking at Fulton, Missouri, was introducing the term "iron curtain" to the world. It was left to Kennan, though, to make the dispositional case most explicitly in a lesser-known telegram sent from Moscow on 20 March: "Nothing short of complete disarmament, delivery of our air and naval forces to Russia and resigning of powers of government to American Communists" would come close to alleviating Stalin's distrust, and even then the old dictator would probably "smell a trap and would continue to harbor the most baleful misgivings."

If Kennan was right, we need look no further in seeking the causes of the Cold War: Stalin was primarily responsible. But how can we be sure that this perspective and the policies that resulted from it did not reflect the all too human tendency to attribute behavior one dislikes to the *nature* of those who indulge in it, and to neglect the *circumstances*—including one's own behavior—that might have brought it about? Is there a test historians can apply to avoid this trap?

One might be to check for evidence of consistency or inconsistency, within a particular relationship, in each side's view of the other. Attitudes that show little change over the years, especially when circumstances have changed, suggest deep roots and hence dispositional behavior. Trees may bend slightly before the wind, but they stay in place, for better or for worse, until they die. Viewpoints that evolve with circumstances, however, reflect situational behavior. Vines, after all, can creep, climb, adhere, entwine, and if necessary retreat, all in response to the environment that surrounds them.

Roosevelt's vine-like personality is universally acknowledged, and needs no further elaboration here: there could hardly have been a *less* dispositional leader than the always adaptable, ever-elusive F.D.R. But what about Stalin? Was he capable of abandoning, in world politics, the paranoia that defined his domestic politics? Could he respond to conciliatory gestures, or was containment the only realistic course?

Stalin's behavior toward fellow-authoritarians did twist and turn. He gave Hitler the benefit of the doubt at several points, but viewed him as an arch-enemy at others. His attitudes toward Josef Broz Tito in Yugoslavia and Mao Zedong in China would evolve over the years, albeit in opposite directions. But Stalin's thinking about democratic capitalists remained rooted to the spot: he always suspected their motives. "Remember, we are waging a struggle (negotiation with enemies is also struggle) . . . with the whole capitalist world," he admonished Molotov as early as 1929. He dismissed Roosevelt's and Churchill's warnings of an impending German attack in 1941 as provocations designed to hasten that event. He authorized penetration, by his spies, of the Anglo-American atomic bomb project as early as June 1942, long before his allies made the formal but by then futile decision to withhold such information from him. He placed repeated obstacles in the path of direct military cooperation with the Americans and the British during the war. He not only arranged to have Roosevelt's and Churchill's living quarters at the Tehran Conference bugged; he also had Beria's son, a precocious linguist, translate the tapes daily and report to him on what was said. "Churchill is the kind who, if you don't watch him, will slip a kopeck out of your pocket," Stalin famously warned on the eve of the landings in Normandy in June 1944, surely the high point of allied cooperation against the Axis. "Roosevelt is not like that. He dips in his hand only for bigger coins."

A compliment? Perhaps, in Stalin's grudging way, but hardly an expression of trust. The Soviet leader is on record as having expressed compassion—once, at Yalta—for the president's physical infirmity: "Why did nature have to punish him so? Is he any worse than other people?" But the very novelty of the remark impressed Gromyko, who heard it: his boss "rarely bestowed his sympathy on anybody from another social system." Only a few weeks later the same Stalin astounded and infuriated the dying Roosevelt by charging that secret Anglo-American negotiations for the surrender of Hitler's forces in Italy were really a plot to keep the Red Army out of Germany. Many years later a Soviet interviewer would suggest to Molotov that "to be paralyzed and yet to become president of the United States, and for three terms, what a rascal you had to be!" "Well said," the old Bolshevik heartily agreed.

If anyone knew Stalin's mind it was Molotov, the ever-faithful *apparatchik* who came to be known, for the best of reasons, as "his master's voice." Even into his nineties, Molotov's recollections of F.D.R. were clear, unrepentant, and unvarnished. A Roosevelt request for the use of Siberian air bases to bomb Japanese targets had been an excuse "to occupy certain parts of the Soviet Union instead of fighting. Afterward it wouldn't have been easy to get them out of there." The President's larger intentions were transparent:

> Roosevelt believed in dollars. Not that he believed in nothing else, but he considered America to be so rich, and we so poor and worn out, that we would surely come begging. "Then we'll kick their ass, but for now we have to keep them going." That's where they miscalculated. They weren't Marxists and we were. They woke up only when half of Europe had passed from them.

"Roosevelt knew how to conceal his attitude toward us," Molotov recalled, "but Truman—he didn't know how to do that at all." Charm, though, could not hide facts: "Roosevelt was an imperialist who would grab anyone by the throat."

If Stalin's wartime attitude toward Roosevelt was half as distrustful as Molotov's in retirement, then a significant pattern emerges: neither American nor British sources reveal anything approaching such deep and abiding suspicion on the Anglo-American side. Churchill subsequently credited himself, to be sure, with having warned of Soviet postwar intentions; but the archives have long since revealed a more complex pattern in which his hopes alternated with his fears well into 1945. In the case of Roosevelt, it is difficult to find *any* expressions of distrust toward Stalin, public or private, until shortly before his death. If he had doubts—surely he had some—he kept them so carefully hidden that historians have had to strain to find traces of them. Kennan first put forward his dispositional explanation of Stalin's actions in the summer of 1944. But in contrast to Molotov, he found no sympathy at the top, nor would he for some time to come.

From this perspective, then, one has to wonder whether the Cold War really began in 1945. For it was Stalin's disposition to wage cold wars: he had done so in one form or another throughout his life, against members of his own family, against his closest advisers and their families, against old revolutionary comrades, against foreign communists, even against returning Red Army war veterans who, for whatever reason, had contacts of any kind with the West in the course of defeating Nazi Germany. "A man who had subjected all activities in his own country to his views and to his personality, Stalin could not behave differently outside," [dissident Yugoslav communist Milovan] Djilas recalled. "He became himself the slave of the despotism, the bureaucracy, the narrowness, and the servility that he imposed on his country." [Nikita] Khrushchev put it more bluntly: "No one inside the Soviet Union or out had Stalin's trust."

Roosevelt's death in April 1945, then, is not likely to have altered the long-term course of Soviet-American relations: if Stalin had never trusted him, why should he have trusted that "noisy shopkeeper" Harry S. Truman, or the harder-line advisers the new president came to rely upon? The Labour Party's subsequent victory in the British general election produced no improvement in Anglo-Soviet relations either: Stalin was entirely ecumenical in the range of his suspicions, and if anything detested European socialists more than he did European conservatives. Khrushchev describes him going out of his way at the December 1945 Moscow Foreign Ministers' Conference to insult both Truman—who fortunately was not present—and British Foreign Secretary Ernest Bevin: "What caused Stalin to behave that way? This is difficult to explain. I think he believed he could run the policy of the whole world. That's why he behaved in such an unrestrained way toward representatives of countries that were our partners."

If doubts remained about Stalin's disposition, he thoroughly dispelled them in his first major postwar address, made on the eve of his own "election" to the Supreme Soviet in February 1946. The speech was not, as some Americans regarded it, a "declaration of World War III." It was, though, like Molotov's reminiscences, a revealing window into Stalin's mind. World War II, the Kremlin leader explained, had resulted *solely* from the internal contradictions of capitalism, and *only* the entry of the Soviet Union had transformed that conflict into a war of liberation. Perhaps it might be possible to avoid future wars if raw materials and markets could be "periodically redistributed among the various countries in accordance with their economic importance, by agreement and peaceful settlement." But, he added, "that is impossible to do under present capitalist conditions of the development of world economy." What all of this meant, Stalin's most perceptive biographer has argued, was nothing less than that "the postwar period would have to be transformed, in idea if not in actual fact, into *a new prewar period.*"

"There has been a return in Russia to the outmoded concept of security in terms of territory—the more you've got the safer you are." The speaker was former Soviet foreign minister and ambassador to the United States Maxim Litvinov, who [in 1933] had personally negotiated the establishment of Soviet-American diplomatic relations with Franklin D. Roosevelt. The occasion was an interview, given in Moscow to CBS correspondent Richard C. Hottelet a few months after Stalin's [February 1946] speech. The cause, Litvinov explained, was "the ideological conception prevailing here that conflict between Communist and capitalist worlds is inevitable." What would happen, Hottelet wanted to know, if the West should suddenly grant all of the Soviet Union's territorial demands? "It would lead to the West's being faced, after a more or less short time, with the next series of demands."

Litvinov managed, remarkably enough, to die in bed. His views on the breakdown of wartime cooperation, though, had hardly been a secret: his colleagues regularly listened to recordings of his conversations acquired, as Molotov put it, "in the usual way." Why was the old diplomat not arrested, charged with treason, and shot? Perhaps his public advocacy of collective security and cooperation with the West, paradoxically, shielded him: Stalin did, from time to time, worry about how his regime looked to the outside world. Perhaps his boss kept Litvinov alive in case the Soviet Union ever again needed the West's assistance. Perhaps he was just lucky, an explanation his successor as foreign minister favored. "Litvinov remained among the living," Molotov recalled with his usual grim clarity, "only by chance."

The 1950s: Emergence of the Western Youth Culture

Richard Welch

In the United States the 1950s was a decade of unparalleled affluence—a tremendous change after the bleak experience of the Great Depression in the 1930s and the anxieties of World War II and the early Cold War in the 1940s. But there was another side to the decade, too: racial tensions, the considerable injustices experienced by racial minorities and poor whites, and the nagging fears born of the nuclear arms race that, for example, made "bomb drills" a recurrent reality for school children.

Out of this combination of affluence and anxiety was born the cultural revolution epitomized by rock 'n' roll. Rock music burst like a bombshell upon the affluent American white world in the years 1954–1956. Teens and subteens embraced the new music enthusiastically; their parents, teachers, and ministers usually recoiled in stunned amazement. With rock so pervasive and "normal" a part of today's cultural scene, it is difficult to grasp how new and challenging it sounded in the mid-fifties. The common popular culture that young people and their parents had shared during the Great Depression and World War II, when everyone went to the same movies, listened to the same radio programs, and shared the same hopes and fears, was shattered: Rock was

Reprinted from "Rock 'n' Roll and Social Change," by Richard Welch, *History Today,* vol. 40, February 1990. Reprinted with permission from *History Today.*

youth's style, and young people flaunted it. Its infectious rhythms traveled around the world. Today there is hardly a corner of the world
where it does not reach: It has become the standard of popular culture.

In the article that follows, historian Richard Welch analyzes how the
rock revolution began and the large social, cultural, and political implications that the coming of rock music signified for the United States
in the 1950s.

R evolutions are not delicate operations. People experiencing them
usually realise they are passing through tumultuous times. The
changes are noted and recorded. Both casual observers and scholars
can detect remote and immediate causes. The focal points of the revolutions are located and the results analysed. Yet one of the most
profound cultural changes in American history is seldom credited
for what it was and did. In the mid-1950s this enormous cultural
revolution swept aside prevailing notions of American popular music, blended black and white musical traditions and integrated black
performers into the pantheon of musical superstars in an unprecedented fashion. In such a way, this revolution both presaged and encouraged the desegregation movement of the 1956–64 period. More
generally, this revolution created a music which became the common property not only of two generations of Americans, but millions
throughout the world, creating the most ubiquitous, and perhaps,
most influential form of American popular culture. The revolution
was rock 'n' roll.

The startling success of rock 'n' roll in transforming American
popular music and culture owed much to the phenomenon of the
mass-market adolescent subculture. While adolescence is normally
a time of some rebellion against adult authority and mores, nothing
seen before in history was quite as dramatic as the transformation of
adolescents from an age group to a virtual class after the Second
World War. To some degree this was a consequence of the increasingly large number of teenagers, especially in the United States. By
1970 half the population of the United States would be twenty-five
or under. Additionally, post-1945 American teenagers enjoyed an
unprecedented level of affluence. Their taste in film, music, literature and entertainment was backed up by enormous purchasing
power which record producers and film-makers were quick to sat-
isfy.

By 1950 there were growing signs that American teenagers were
rejecting, consciously or not, the quasi-official popular culture which
had flourished during the Depression and war years. With some significant exceptions, the purveyors of popular culture and entertain-

ment during the 1930s and 1940s presented a highly idealised, romanticised picture of family and national life. Once television became common, it too projected a monochromatic, self-congratulatory depiction of America. This sterile version of American life was increasingly scorned by teenagers seeking to deal with an increasingly atomised family life and domestic and international tensions. Some idea of the growing alienation of American adolescents could be gauged by the almost instantaneous popularity they gave J.D. Salinger's unrelentingly anti-adult *Catcher in the Rye.*

Additionally, American teenagers sought alternative explanations to their questions about American life from beyond the mainstream. They began to seek satisfaction for their longings for something new and different in the various subcultures which had always been present in the United States. One of these, the criminal, had long been a staple of folk myth in American popular culture. In the 1930s, Hollywood increased the reach and impact of mythic gangsters and outlaws, especially when they were played by attractive actors capable of projecting a sense of integrity and honour. In the 1950s three films which depicted youthful outlaws as alienated loners shaped and furthered the adolescent consciousness of themselves as a separate culture group and greatly influenced the look, if not the sound, of rock 'n' roll.

The first of these formative films was *City Across the River* (1951) which dealt with youth gangs in Brooklyn. Tony Curtis' characterisation of a hard but honest youth created an adolescent archetype. Moreover, his perfectly sculpted, swept-back, teetering pompadour 'duck's ass' hair style would start a major trend among teenage boys after it was flaunted by Elvis Presley in 1955. The second movie, *The Wild One,* about motorcycle gangs in California, featured Marlon Brando as the laconic, distant, rebellious, but ultimately honourable gang leader. Brando's motorcycle anti-hero came across as infinitely more attractive than the ignorant, wishy-washy or brutal adults with whom he dealt. The last movie, *Rebel Without A Cause,* starring the still legendary James Dean, focused not on an outlaw, but a troubled, alienated young man trying to find his own truth in a world where adults provide little guidance. Dean's performance electrified the nation, especially teenagers. Certainly, Dean's portrayal of teenage anomie fed off the same impulses which were simultaneously creating rock 'n' roll. Underlining the interrelationship between Dean and rock 'n' roll, Nicholas Ray, the director of *Rebel Without A Cause,* remembered that when he first met Elvis Presley in Hollywood '. . . [Elvis] knew I was a friend of Jimmy's so he got down on his knees before me and began to recite whole passages from the script. Elvis must have seen *Rebel* a dozen times by then and he remembered every one of Jimmy's lines'.

In addition to the criminal, outlaw and social fringe groups, American teenagers increasingly turned to the black sub-culture as an alternative to homogenised America. Black slang, and to a lesser degree, clothing styles, became increasingly common among American teenagers after 1950. Some whites had registered their dissatisfaction with the then current mass culture by becoming jazz cultists in the 1930s and 1940s. While some whites continued in this direction after 1950, the black music which found the largest audience among young whites was the hard driving, visceral rhythm and blues whose typical twelve-bar structure became rock 'n' roll's most common format.

By 1953, the growing fascination of young whites with black music came to the attention of a Cleveland, Ohio, disc jockey. Alan Freed, who certainly popularised the term 'rock 'n' roll' though he did not invent it, was alerted to the phenomenon by a record-shop owner. He had been doing a classical music programme, but asked to do a rock 'n' roll segment after his usual stint. The new programme caught on and Freed quickly became the most popular disc jockey in Cleveland. In March, 1953, he organised a stage show featuring black rhythm-and-blues acts. Two-thirds of the 30,000 who showed up were white. The inter-racial attraction of the music was apparent and the implications of growing numbers of young whites appreciating black music and attending integrated performances were enormous. Ruth Brown, a rhythm-and-blues vocalist, remembered that when performing in the still segregated South in the 1950s a rope was strung down the centre of the theatres to keep the races apart. Brown also recalled that by the time the show was over the rope was frequently gone and the audiences mixing freely. The effect of the increasing integration of musical tastes and resulting racial mixing is difficult to gauge. It seems likely that such developments predisposed at least a majority of young whites to accept the Supreme Court's outlawing of legal segregation in 1954.

Two other musical sub-cultures lured young whites. The first was folk music, generally derived from British and Irish sources, which had survived in the Appalachian areas of the country. The 'folk movement,' however, did not become powerful until 1960, and its practitioners and adherents were initially hostile to rock 'n' roll. After the mid-1960s, performers such as Bob Dylan and The Byrds grafted folk onto existing rock 'n' roll styles producing yet another rock variant. Far more popular, but originally more geographically confined was country and western music. This music was derived from Anglo-American ballad and dance music though black influences were also present. Country was primarily popular in the South and Southwest among working- and lower-middle-class whites. Whites higher up the social scale often denigrated it as 'hillbilly music'. After the late 1940s, maverick country singers, most especially

Hank Williams, gave country music a harder, driving sound, and an edge which in some ways paralleled the emotions blacks were putting into rhythm and blues. Clearly, a music which could combine elements of black rhythm and blues and white country—musical styles distinct but alike in their choice of primitive power and raw emotion over sophistication, musical styles which were scorned by mainstream culture pundits, musical traditions conceived from the point of view of a disadvantaged outsider—would prove very attractive to the American teenager.

The music which resulted from the combination of the two racial musical traditions, rock 'n' roll, emerged in different places and in somewhat different styles. Not surprisingly, however, many of its pioneer practitioners came from the margins of society where the major subcultures existed side by side in uneasy love-hate relationships. Consequently, much of what became rock 'n' roll appeared first in the American South, and few places proved so fertile to the development of the new music as Memphis, Tennessee, where the Sun Record Company unleashed the singer who came to epitomise everything people loved or hated about the new music.

Sun Records was founded by Sam Phillips whose experiments in musical hybridisation are now legendary. Phillips, a former radio engineer from Florence, Alabama, started his company in 1950. Originally, he recorded black bluesmen such as Howlin' Wolf and BB King. Phillips understood that young, white people were dissatisfied with the popular music of the time, typified by songs like *How Much Is That Doggie In the Window?* Like Freed and a few other independent producers, Phillips became convinced that the restless white youth market could be tapped by someone with a black-based musical style. Not many people in the record industry believed him. Nevertheless, Phillips persevered in his convictions, realising that if he were to win the young white record buyers his fortune would be made. Phillips also seemed to have a genuine personal commitment towards the discovery of artists who could seize the best of white and black musical styles. 'I was in it to record something I loved, something I felt, something I thought other people ought to hear' is the way he later explained it. In the summer of 1954 Phillips found what he was looking for.

The man whom Phillips used to start the revolution was an unlikely candidate. Elvis Aaron Presley came from decidedly humble origins. His father had done time for forgery and the family lived much of the time in public housing. When he first came to Sun the man whose swagger, leer and exuberant sexuality would delight and dismay in near equal numbers was remembered by Phillips as 'the most introverted person that came into that studio'. Presley was a loner, heavily attached to his mother and had few real friends. He compensated for his isolation by listening to everything that came out of the radio. He was, in fact, a repository for almost every musical form in America, white country, black blues, black and white gospel and Tin Pan Alley crooning. After his career took off he described how two of the influences affected him.

> I'd play along with the radio or phonograph. We were a religious family going around to sing together at camp meetings and revivals, and I'd take my guitar with us when I could. I also dug the real, low-down Mississippi singers, mostly Big Bill Broozy and Big Boy Crudup, although they would scold me at home for listening to them. 'Sinful music' the townfolk in Memphis said it was. Which never bothered me I guess.

At the time of his first meeting with Phillips, Presley was a truck driver. He came to the studio ostensibly to make a record for his mother's birthday. He might actually have been looking for a way to audition. However shy, lonely and isolated Presley might have been, his ambition was enormous. Phillips was impressed by what he heard.

> I knew he had the fundamentals of what I wanted. He was the first one I had seen who had that potential. He had a different type of voice. And this boy had listened to a lot of different music . . .

Before he left the studio, Presley agreed to return if Phillips found a song he thought suitable for him.

In the meantime, Phillips began assembling the back-up band which became an essential part of Elvis' early sound. The pivotal instrument was the electric guitar which was the cutting edge of both blues and country music. For Presley's lead guitar player Phillips chose Scotty Moore, a veteran of country swing bands. Moore's clean, sharp, and sometimes haunting solos helped define the early Presley sound, and rock 'n' roll guitar playing in general. Bill Black, 'the best slap bass player in the city' originally provided the rhythm along with Elvis' acoustic guitar. Later D.J. Fontana introduced drums, and the archetypical rock 'n' roll combo was created.

In August, 1954, Phillips came up with a song called *Without Love* which he thought might suit Presley's style. Moore, Black and Presley worked through the night trying to get a satisfactory take, but nothing seemed to jell. Taking a break from their frustrations, Presley and the two back-up players went into a blues number, *That's Allright Mama*. Phillips heard the song in the recording booth. He had found his singer.

What the 'damned thing' was was something no one had ever quite heard before. In fact, it was so bizarre for the time that many had trouble knowing how to react to it. Like most early rock 'n' roll, *That's Allright Mama* was based on a blues pattern, though not the standard twelve-bar variety. This led, and still leads, some to contend that Presley was simply a white man singing black blues. If he were just the first white man to do this successfully, he would still be notable. However, Presley and the Sun sound, and the best of rock 'n' roll in general, were much more. *That's Allright Mama* was originally written and sung by black bluesman Arthur 'Big Boy' Crudup. Even a quick listening of the two versions reveals the difference between blues and rock 'n' roll. Presley took the song, and the strong rhythmic element in it, but kicked it out of the heavy, almost ponderous groove Crudup used. What Presley succeeded in doing was injecting the blues with an abandoned hillbilly attitude characteristic of what Southerners sometimes indelicately refer to as 'shit kickin' music'. The result was a musical hybrid, destined to prove more exciting than either its blues or country parents while retaining elements of both. While Black and Moore were certainly important in the new music, the emerging style owed the most to Presley's own creative intuitions. And he knew it. 'I don't sing like nobody', the young singer once explained to Phillips.

Some recognised the revolutionary quality of the new music almost immediately. Marion Keisker, Phillip's secretary, decided it was '. . . like a giant wedding ceremony. It was like two feuding clans who had been brought together by marriage'. When Presley first began exciting his growing audiences at live performances, his fans saw a white man, playing black-based music with clear country influences. What else could he be but the 'Hillbilly Cat' the sobriquet used on his early tours. And while all the emerging black-influenced music was being called rock 'n' roll, Sun Records became the home of a distinctive sub-genre—rockabilly. And Presley was its prophet. The record appeared first on WDAI, the most influential black station in the South, then began its climb into the charts, crossing over from blues to country and then into the pop categories.

The year after August 1954 was perhaps the most creative in Elvis Presley's career. *Good Rockin' Tonight, Baby Let's Play House, Milkcow Blues Boogie* and the near-atavistic *Mystery Train* were all products of this dazzling year. The legend of the Hillbilly Cat spread throughout the South and rumours of his dynamic, charismatic performances were being heard in the North. Those with an eye and an ear for musical trends and markets began to take notice. Most significantly, American teenagers found in the music and Presley's public persona precisely what they had been looking for. Embracing the new music as their own, teenagers made rock 'n' roll a badge of their identity and distinctiveness from the adults who generally hated it. In one year, 1955–56, American popular music was transformed by dollar-propelled teenage musical preferences. Post-1955 record charts were, and remain, dominated by rock 'n' roll and rock influenced music.

Teenage enjoyment of rock 'n' roll was greatly enhanced by the condemnations heaped upon it by the adult population, especially the guardians of conventional popular culture. To many, rock 'n' roll was too loud, too raucous, too sexual, or too black. The earthiness of many of the lyrics, the pounding back-beat rhythm, not to mention Presley's leering sensuality, rendered the music objectionable to many. This dislike was most pronounced among the more fundamentalist churches in the South. Ministers railed against rock 'n' roll as obscene, and sometimes branded Presley as an agent of the devil. Television critic John Crosby denounced Presley as an 'unspeakably untalented, vulgar young entertainer. . . . Where do you go from Elvis Presley short of obscenity—which is against the law.' In early 1956, the *New York Times* reported that a white Southern church group wanted rock 'n' roll suppressed, claiming it was a plot by the National Association of Colored People to corrupt white youth. All in all the furore was wonderful publicity. '. . . now if I hadn't affected people like that I might have been in trouble' was Sam Phillips wry appraisal of the anti rock 'n' roll movement.

Elvis Presley's burgeoning popularity attracted the attention of RCA Victor. They contacted Phillips who, despite the success of Presley's records, was having financial difficulties. The end result was that Phillips sold Presley's contract to RCA for $35,000, plus $4–5,000 that Phillips owed the singer.

Even before Elvis had left, Phillips signed a young man from Jackson, Tennessee, whose first hit put Sun solidly in the black. Carl Perkins, next in line of Sun's major artists, came from a background more impoverished and racially mixed than Presley's:

> I was raised on a plantation in the flatlands of Lake County, Tennessee, and we were the only white people on it. . . . The night I was born my mom lay in a bed with no doctor but a granny lady named Mary. My daddy had double pneumonia on the next bed and almost died. He was always in bad health after that, later had a lung removed. They wouldn't give him good land on account of his health but he did all he could.

Like Presley, Perkins was exposed to heavy doses of black music, along with the white country traditionally available to young southern whites.

> The man who taught me guitar was an old colored man. I can see him now sitting on his porch. . . . I'd ask him in the field 'Uncle John, you gonna play tonight? Maybe, if my back ain't too tired', he'd say. My daddy'd let me go over for an hour. Uncle John'd get his old guitar out and fill a pot with oily rags to keep the mosquitos away. John Westbrook was his name, the champion cotton picker on the plantation. He taught me to pick cotton too. I could pick 300 pounds a day and, man that's grabbin'. . .

Things picked up somewhat for the Perkins family when they left Lake County for Jackson. A few years later when he first attempted to get a Sun contract, Phillips, who seemed to believe Presley had a monopoly on rock 'n' roll, was not overly interested. He finally signed Perkins, but had him do a different type of music from the rockabilly style he had developed. After Presley left, Perkins told him he had written a song called *Blue Suede Shoes*.

> The easiest song I ever wrote, got up at 3.00 a.m. to write it when my wife Valda and me were living in a project. Had the idea in my head seeing kids by the bandstand so proud of their new city shoes—you gotta be real poor to care about new shoes like I did—and that morning I went downstairs and wrote out the words on a potato sack . . .

Potato sack or no, *Blue Suede Shoes* became Perkins' first hit, transcending racial lines by running up the charts in blues, country and pop categories.

Perkins, who, unlike Presley, wrote his own material, was not a one-shot hit maker. *Boppin' the Blues, Your True Love* and *Matchbox* (with Jerry Lee Lewis on the piano) all sold well and had enormous influence on the young musicians learning from his records. Yet Perkins never quite became a superstar. Elvis was already king, and Perkins lacked Presley's charisma and physical presence. Being married also distanced him from young female fans whose record-buying habits did much to determine who the next stars would be. Worse, at the height of his own popularity, Perkins was in a serious accident which put him out of commission for months. In 1959, Perkins left Sun for Columbia which totally misunderstood his music, pushing him away from his infectious rockabilly and casting him into the role of a hard rocker for which he was unsuited.

Perkins' career at Sun overlaps with the third giant in Phillips stable, the wildest of them all, and the man Phillips himself described as the most talented person he ever knew. Jerry Lee Lewis had looks, a pounding roadhouse piano style and a sense of theatricality exceeding even Presley. Lewis grew up on a farm in Ferriday, Louisiana, and turned to music at an early age. He learned a little guitar from his father, but turned to piano which proved natural for him. Lewis once said he didn't see how anyone influenced him. 'God, man, I just got with it, you know, I created my own style'. Nevertheless, he was exposed to the same multiple influences as Presley and Perkins, particularly the country-blues combination.

Like the other two Sun artists, what he did with these influences was highly individual and he sounded as distinctive from them as they did from each other. Lewis' background was more religious than most of the other Sun singers. He was an active member of the Holiness Church, Meeting of God Assembly, and even went to the South West Bible School. Consequently, Lewis also did a large amount of gospel singing. 'We sang it with a beat . . . we always sang it with a beat'. That did not stop him from frequenting less spiritual establishments where he found earthier sources of inspiration. 'Well, I used to hang around Haney's Big House', he recollected in 1971. 'That was a colored establishment where they had dances and stuff. . . . Haney was this little colored fellow and we was just kids, we wasn't allowed in. So we'd slip around to the back and sneak in whenever we could. I saw a lot of 'em there, all those blues players. . . .' Lewis' attempts to begin a recording career were rocky at first. He'd been rejected by every label in Louisiana when he sold all the eggs on his father's farm to pay for a trip to Memphis.

As soon as he heard Lewis, Phillips did not hesitate. Lewis' first Sun release *Crazy Arms* became a medium hit and *Whole Lotta Shakin' Goin On* took the country by storm. Follow up records like *Great Balls of Fire, Breathless* and *High School Confidential* turned Lewis into a major rock 'n' roll star, a rival to Elvis himself. And while Elvis' originality was being eroded by fame and suffocating management, Lewis' manic, leering vocalisations, exuding a primordial *joie de vivre* served to remind everyone what rock 'n' roll was all about.

And then it stopped. In 1958, with three monster hits behind him, Lewis married a thirteen-year-old cousin. Many fans, disc jockeys and much of the media turned on him. For three years he wandered in an entertainment wilderness, his marriage the mark of Cain. When he began to re-emerge the decisive moment had passed for him, too.

The golden age of Sun Records lasted about four years, from Elvis' first records to Jerry Lee's personal debacle. Sun continued to have the occasional hit with singers such as Charlie Rich, but Phillips, who did not personally produce a record after 1963, seemed to grow tired of the game. Apprehensive about the way the record giants were buying talent away from the independent labels, Phillips came to believe the majors 'would eat me alive'. Though he could have been a producer with one of the mega-companies, Phillips had no desire to work for another company. He sold Sun in 1969.

More than any other group of rock pioneers the Sun artists created not only some of the best rock 'n' roll records, but the very image of rock 'n' roll itself—the abandoned, somewhat frenzied guitar slinger 'letting it all loose' about women and fast times. This image, made irreversible by Presley, became fixed in the public mind. The basic rock 'n' roll band unit of singer, lead and rhythm guitars, bass and drums became standard to a large degree because of Sun rockers. And the risqué, sometimes overtly sexual nature of the music, which has proved a perennial source of controversy, was there from the beginning as well. Not that the Sun singers did it all themselves. Even within rockabilly, distinctive versions could soon be heard from Gene Vincent in Virginia, Buddy Holly in Texas and lesser groups from almost everywhere.

A permanent legacy of the Sun rockabillies and their colleagues was the injection of black musical influences into mainstream American music in an unprecedented fashion. Certainly, black rock artists played their part in the development, but equally clearly the use of black musical idiom by Presley, Perkins and Lewis greatly enhanced the prospects for black performers. The merged black and white musical traditions of the early white rock 'n' rollers, most especially Presley, introduced the entire nation to elements of black music. Storming through the gap blasted by Presley and his compatriots, seminal black artists such as Chuck Berry, Little Richard and Fats Domino achieved great success and financial renumeration. Certainly several black rockers and bluesmen realised the role white audiences played in elevating them to a stardom that would otherwise have been impossible.

Thinking back on this period black rock 'n' roll pioneer Chuck Berry, whose distinctive style incorporated elements of country music, remarked 'It seems to me that the white teenagers of the forties and fifties helped launch black artists in to mainline of popular music'. Many, if not most, of the whites credited by Berry with opening the door to black rockers were themselves first drawn to the new black influenced music by Presley and his compatriots. It is difficult not to give some credit to rock 'n' roll for the growing white appreciation of both black culture and black grievances in a segregated society.

Certainly, the rise of rock 'n' roll as the predominant form of popular music overlaps with the appearance of the black civil rights movement as a major force in American society and politics. By the time the Southern Christian Leadership Conference initiated its 'Freedom Rides', voter registration drives and lunch-counter boycotts, young whites had experienced five years of musical integration via rock 'n' roll. The increased mixing in music seems to have anticipated, indeed, sometimes initiated, greater contacts between the races. On an early tour in the South in 1956, Chuck Berry saw ropes used to divide theatres into black and white sections. Nevertheless, he also witnessed more whites than blacks coming up on stage after a show to talk with black performers.

The stunning rise of rock 'n' roll as America's predominant popular music not only transformed the nation's prevailing musical norms, but signalled the triumph of the emerging youth culture. Despite the opposition and antagonism of the entrenched leaders of the music and entertainment industries, not to mention the desultory efforts at suppression by some religious and parental groups, American teenagers had imposed their will on the nation's airwaves, record stores and concert halls. The hitherto inchoate alienation of American adolescents coalesced to weld two cultural forms of 'outsider' groups.

Borrowing heavily from the musical traditions of blacks and white southerners, the rock 'n' roll pioneers of the mid-fifties fused elements of both to create a music which consciously rejected the conventions of the time and yet proved successful beyond the wildest dreams of its creators. The powerful black element in the music heralded new possibilities in interracial relations. Certainly rock 'n' roll made possible greater acceptance, appreciation, and a wider audience for black culture. But ultimately the triumph of rock 'n' roll signalled the coming of age of a new generation, one whose norms, culturally, intellectually and politically, often stood in sharp contrast to those of the generation immediately preceding it. The strength of the rock 'n' roll generation's break with previous attitudes, which first manifested itself musically, would reach full fruition in the social and political upheavals of the sixties.

President Eisenhower Warns of the Military- Industrial Complex

Dwight D. Eisenhower

The term *military-industrial complex*, referring to the concentration of great power that is wielded in the U.S. government by the Pentagon, the defense industry, and the politicians who benefit from military spending, was first coined by Dwight D. Eisenhower (1890–1969) three days before his presidential term ended in January 1961. This nationally broadcast speech, billed as his "farewell address," is excerpted here.

Many people, both then and now, are surprised that it was Eisenhower who gave the warning. Was he not the best-liked general to have emerged from World War II, the man to whom Americans entrusted the presidency during the height of the Cold War (1953–1961), the man who seemed to personify the popular soldier-politician in twentieth-century America? Yet a lifetime in the military, capped by eight years as president, had taught Eisenhower the dangers of allowing any concentration of power, "sought or unsought," to grow unchallenged in a democratic society.

As Eisenhower delivered his farewell address, vigorous and glamorous young John F. Kennedy was preparing to take over the presidency.

Excerpted from the *Public Papers of President Dwight D. Eisenhower, 1960–61* (Washington D.C.: National Archives and Records Service, 1961).

Kennedy had run on the slogan of "get the country moving again." He had warned of a "missile gap" developing between the United States and the USSR, and he intended to rev up the American economy, to carry out a long list of domestic reforms, and at the same time to confront communism overseas. Many of those who voted for Kennedy had dismissed Eisenhower as too cautious, too conservative, too apt to get tangled in words at his press conferences, and too much inclined to spend his spare time golfing.

Historians now know that Eisenhower cannot be dismissed (as he often was in the 1960s) as a "do-nothing" president. He was in fact a shrewd leader who preferred to operate with a "hidden hand." The complicated syntax with which he answered questions from the press was deliberately chosen to prevent unwanted information from getting out. He feared that Kennedy and politicians like him were too enamored of military power and of powerful, "activist" government—that they would lead the nation into risky ventures at home and abroad and would spend more money on armaments than the nation could afford. He knew that Kennedy's "missile gap" did not exist, though he could not say so publicly because that would signal to the Soviet Union what America's sources of military intelligence were. He genuinely feared for the future of American democracy if "big government" continued to grow. His 1961 "farewell address" must be read with this longer perspective in mind.

Good evening, my fellow Americans:

First, let me express my gratitude to the radio and television networks for the opportunity to express myself to you during these past eight years and tonight.

Three days from now, after half a century in the service of our country, I shall lay down the responsibilities of office as, in traditional solemn ceremony, the authority of the President is vested in my successor.

This evening I come to you with a message of leave-taking and farewell, and to share a few final thoughts with you, my countrymen. . . .

We now stand ten years past the midpoint of a century that has witnessed four major wars among great nations. Three of these involved our own country. Despite these holocausts America is today the strongest, the most influential, and most productive nation in the world. Understandably proud of this pre-eminence, we yet realize that America's leadership and prestige depend, not merely upon our unmatched material progress, riches, and material strength, but on how we use our power in the interests of world peace and human betterment.

Throughout America's adventure in free government, our basic purposes have been to keep the peace; to foster progress in human achievement; and to enhance liberty, dignity, and integrity among people and among nations. To strive for less would be unworthy of a free and religious people. Any failure traceable to arrogance, or our lack of comprehension or readiness to sacrifice would inflict upon us grievous hurt both at home and abroad.

Progress toward these noble goals is persistently threatened by the conflict now engulfing the world [the Cold War]. It commands our whole attention, absorbs our very beings. We face a hostile [Marxist-Leninist] ideology—global in scope, atheistic in character, ruthless in purpose, and insidious in method. Unhappily the danger it poses promises to be of indefinite duration. To meet it successfully, there is called for, not so much the emotional and transitory sacrifices of crisis, but rather those which enable us to carry forward steadily, surely, and without complaint the burdens of a prolonged and complex struggle—with liberty the stake. Only thus shall we remain, despite every provocation, on our chartered course toward permanent peace and human betterment.

Crises there will continue to be. In meeting them, whether foreign or domestic, great or small, there is a recurring temptation to feel that some spectacular and costly action could become the miraculous solution to all current difficulties. A huge increase in newer elements of our defense; development of unrealistic programs to cure every ill in agriculture; a dramatic expansion in basic and applied research—these and many other possibilities, each possibly promising in itself, may be suggested as the only way to the road we wish to travel.

But each proposal must be weighed in the light of a broader consideration: the need to maintain balance in and among national problems—balance between the private and the public economy, balance between cost and hoped for advantage—balance between the clearly necessary and the comfortably desirable; balance between our essential requirements as a nation and the duties imposed by the nation upon the individual; balance between actions of the moment and the national welfare of the future. Good judgment seeks balance and progress; lack of it eventually finds imbalance and frustration.

The record of many decades stands as proof that our people and their government have, in the main, understood these truths and have responded to them well, in the face of stress and threat. But threats, new in kind or degree, constantly arise. I mention two only.

A vital element in keeping the peace is our military establishment. Our arms must be mighty, ready for instant action, so that no potential aggressor may be tempted to risk his own destruction.

Our military organization today bears little relation to that known by any of my predecessors in peacetime, or indeed by the fighting men in World War II or Korea.

Until the latest of our world conflicts [World War II], the United States had no armaments industry. American makers of plowshares could, with time and as required, make swords as well. But now we can no longer risk emergency improvision of national defense; we have been compelled to create a permanent armaments industry of vast proportions. Added to this, three and a half million men and women are directly engaged in the defense establishment. We annually spend on military security more than the net income of all United States corporations.

This conjunction of an immense military establishment and a large arms industry is new in American experience. The total influence—economic, political, even spiritual—is felt in every city, every state house, every office of the federal government. We recognize the imperative need for this development. Yet we must not fail to comprehend its grave implications. Our toil, resources and livelihood are all involved; so is the very structure of our society.

In the councils of government, we must guard against the acquisition of unwarranted influence, whether sought or unsought, by the military-industrial complex. The potential for the disastrous rise of misplaced power exists and will persist.

We must never let the weight of this combination endanger our liberties or democratic processes. We should take nothing for granted. Only an alert and knowledgeable citizenry can compel the proper meshing of the huge industrial and military machinery of defense with our peaceful methods and goals, so that security and liberty may prosper together.

Akin to, and largely responsible for the sweeping changes in our industrial-military posture, has been the technological revolution during recent decades.

In this revolution, research has become central; it also becomes more formalized, complex, and costly. A steadily increasing share is conducted for, by, or at the direction of, the federal government.

Today, the solitary inventor, tinkering in his shop, has been overshadowed by task forces of scientists in laboratories and testing fields. In the same fashion, the free university, historically the fountainhead of free ideas and scientific discovery, has experienced a revolution in the conduct of research. Partly because of the huge costs involved, a government contract becomes virtually a substitute for intellectual curiosity. For every old blackboard there are now hundreds of new electronic computers.

The prospect of domination of the nation's scholars by federal employment, project allocations, and the power of money is ever present and is gravely to be regarded.

Yet, in holding scientific research and discovery in respect, as we should, we must also be alert to the equal and opposite danger that public policy could itself become the captive of a scientific-technological elite.

It is the task of statesmanship to mold, to balance, and to integrate these and other forces, new and old, within the principles of our democratic system—ever aiming toward the supreme goals of our free society.

Another factor in maintaining balance involves the element of time. As we peer into society's future, we—you and I, and our government—must avoid the impulse to live only for today, plundering, for our own ease and convenience, the precious resources of tomorrow. We cannot mortgage the material assets of our grandchildren without risking the loss also of their political and spiritual heritage. We want democracy to survive for all generations to come, not to become the insolvent phantom of tomorrow.

Down the long lane of the history yet to be written America knows that this world of ours, ever growing smaller, must avoid becoming a community of dreadful fear and hate, and be, instead, a proud confederation of mutual trust and respect.

Such a confederation must be one of equals. The weakest must come to the conference table with the same confidence as we do, protected as we are by our moral, economic, and military strength. That table, though scarred by many past frustrations, cannot be abandoned for the certain agony of the battlefield.

Disarmament, with mutual honor and confidence, is a continuing imperative. Together we must learn how to compose differences, not with arms, but with intellect and decent purpose. Because this need is so sharp and apparent I confess that I lay down my official responsibilities in this field with a definite sense of disappointment. As one who has witnessed the horror and the lingering sadness of war—as one who knows that another war could utterly destroy this civilization which has been so slowly and painfully built over thousands of years—I wish I could say tonight that a lasting peace is in sight.

Happily, I can say that war has been avoided. Steady progress toward our ultimate goal has been made. But, so much remains to be done. As a private citizen, I shall never cease to do what little I can to help the world advance along that road.

So—in this my last good night to you as your President—I thank you for the many opportunities you have given me for public service in war and peace. I trust that in that service you find some things worthy; as for the rest of it, I know you will find ways to improve performance in the future.

You and I—my fellow citizens—need to be strong in our faith that all nations, under God, will reach the goal of peace with justice. May we be ever unswerving in devotion to principle, confident but humble with power, diligent in pursuit of the nation's great goals.

To all the peoples of the world, I once more give expression to America's prayerful and continuing aspiration:

We pray that peoples of all faiths, all races, all nations may have their great human needs satisfied; that those now denied opportunity shall come to enjoy it to the full; that all who yearn for freedom may experience its spiritual blessings; that those who have freedom will understand, also, its heavy responsibilities; that all who are insensitive to the needs of others will learn charity; that the scourges of poverty, disease, and ignorance will be made to disappear from the earth, and that, in the goodness of time, all peoples will come to live together in a peace guaranteed by the binding force of mutual respect and love.

Now on Friday noon I am to become a private citizen. I am proud to do so. I look forward to it.

Eyeball to Eyeball: The Cuban Missile Crisis

Aleksandr Fursenko and Timothy Naftali

Many historians believe that the Cold War reached its climax in the 1962
Cuban missile crisis, when for more than a week the world hovered on
what seemed like the brink of nuclear war. During the summer of 1962,
the Soviet Union had secretly begun to build facilities in the territory of
its ally, Fidel Castro's Cuba, that could be used to launch intermediate-
range, nuclear-tipped missiles against the United States. In the fall, the Soviets started to bring in nuclear warheads, which could serve both as aggressive weapons against the United States and as defensive weapons
should American forces invade the island. Apparently the Soviet strategy,
as devised by the Kremlin's dominant leader, Nikita Khrushchev, was to
complete the missile buildup on Cuba and then demand important American concessions. He was taking what U.S. president John F. Kennedy
would soon call "one hell of a gamble."

Using high-flying U-2 spy planes, the Americans saw what was happening, although at the time they did not know that the Soviet commander in Cuba had authorization to use tactical nuclear weapons in the event
of a U.S. attack. On October 21, after having been assured by the Soviet
government that no such weapons buildup was under way, Kennedy startled the world by going on U.S. television to reveal what was actually happening, to demand that the Soviets remove the missiles that were already
in place, and to impose a naval "quarantine" on Cuba to prevent the arrival of any more Soviet missiles or weapons. (He did not use the word

blockade because under international law a blockade is an act of war, but the "quarantine" was in effect a blockade.) As Soviet ships steamed toward the island laden with more weaponry (and as one, the *Aleksandrovsk*, carrying nuclear warheads, actually got through), the whole world held its breath. Many of Kennedy's military and political advisers recommended bombing the Soviet missile sites and landing troops within two weeks. Kennedy, despite being wracked by a painful nerve disease for which he was being treated with cortisone injections (something not known outside his immediate family), kept his cool. Through back channels, the idea was floated that the withdrawal of Soviet missiles could (later) be compensated with the closure of some aging U.S. missile installations in Turkey. Khrushchev, too, realized that his gamble was threatening to precipitate World War III, and flinched at the last moment. Kennedy publicly accepted a more conciliatory offer that Khrushchev made, while ignoring a more bellicose, rambling letter that the Soviet leader also sent. "We're eyeball to eyeball," Secretary of State Dean Rusk said at the time, "and I think the other fellow just blinked." Castro, however, was furious at Khrushchev's "betrayal."

Russian scholar Aleksandr Fursenko and American writer Timothy Naftali collaborated in writing a dramatic account of the Cuban missile crisis, using newly revealed Soviet sources. An excerpt from their 1997 book *"One Hell of a Gamble": Khrushchev, Castro, and Kennedy, 1958–1964*, follows. It describes what happened in Washington and Moscow as the crisis reached its climax.

R obert Kennedy returned to the White House in time for Saturday's third Ex Comm session. More than half of the members did not know that the president had authorized this special meeting with the Soviet ambassador. Even those who knew, however, shared the general sense that a negotiated settlement was at best a fifty-fifty proposition.

Many in the Cabinet Room wanted the United States to respond forcefully if another U-2 was destroyed on Sunday. "Well, I think the point is," argued McNamara, "that if our planes are fired on tomorrow, we ought to fire back." Kennedy had other considerations in mind. "Let me say," he began, "I think we ought to wait till afternoon, to see whether we get any answer . . ." Kennedy did not finish this sentence. He did not say so; but he was obviously thinking in terms of giving Khrushchev time to digest his brother's conversation with [Anatoly] Dobrynin.

McNamara also spoke for those who believed an invasion was inevitable, whatever the administration's diplomatic efforts. Turning to Robert Kennedy, McNamara said, "I think the one thing, Bobby, we ought to . . . we need to have two things ready, a government for

Cuba, because we're going to need one . . . and secondly, plans for how to respond to the Soviet Union in Europe, because sure as hell they're going to do something there." President Kennedy understood McNamara's concerns. The vulnerability of U.S. allies had constrained Kennedy's actions regarding Cuba throughout this crisis. If the Turkish trade was not enough, the United States would have no choice but to intensify the pressure on Moscow. Then Italy, Berlin, and Turkey might face retribution. Kennedy crossed his fingers that there would be a peaceful way out of this quagmire.

Moscow, Sunday, October 28, 10:45 A.M. (2:45 A.M., EST)

At 10:45 A.M. on Sunday morning, [Soviet defense minister Rodion] Malinovsky briefed Khrushchev on what had occurred while he was sleeping. Khrushchev did not leave the Kremlin that night, but it had been decided not to wake him when the report arrived after midnight that an American reconnaissance plane had been shot down over Cuba. [Soviet foreign minister Andrei] Gromyko also had important news to report. Fidel Castro was panicking in Havana. He had written a letter that seemed to advocate the use of strategic nuclear weapons against the United States. [A] summary of the letter had arrived at about 1 A.M. But the news from the Foreign Ministry was not all bad. The Kennedy administration had also sent word via two channels that it was ready to negotiate an end to the crisis along the lines of the Kremlin's October 26 letter. The KGB chief in Washington, [Aleksandr] Feklisov, had met with an American journalist named [John] Scali, who claimed to have a White House proposal to end the crisis. The Foreign Ministry had considered the proposal barely credible because Scali had never been used before to send private messages to the Kremlin. But this morning a new letter had arrived from Kennedy; it offered essentially the same deal to Khrushchev. Apparently the Americans wanted to ignore the Soviet demand regarding the Jupiter missiles and to concentrate instead on providing a pledge not to invade Cuba.

The destruction of the American U-2 worried Khrushchev. It was just the type of incident that the Pentagon would use to force Kennedy's hand. To prevent something like this, he had cautioned Castro the day before not to use his antiaircraft guns. Now one of his own [Soviet] commanders had destroyed a U-2. What was especially infuriating was that this incident came on the heels of what appeared to be an excellent diplomatic proposal from the Kennedys. Khrushchev studied Kennedy's letter and Feklisov's report. The essence of the White House's proposal was contained in the central paragraph of the letter:

1) You would agree to remove these weapons systems from Cuba under appropriate United Nations observation and supervision; and undertake, with suitable safeguards, to halt the further introduction of such weapons systems into Cuba.

2) We, on our part, would agree—upon the establishment of adequate arrangements through the United Nations to ensure the carrying out and continuation of these commitments—(a) to remove promptly the quarantine measures now in effect and (b) to give assurances against an invasion of Cuba. I am confident that other nations of the Western Hemisphere would be prepared to do likewise.

This was not all that Khrushchev had asked for on October 27, but it was consistent with the Presidium's minimum terms for pulling out the missiles. This was an acceptable beginning. Anticipating that a decision would have to be made that day, Khrushchev ordered the entire Presidium, its members and candidate members, and even the relevant secretaries of the Central Committee to meet him at noon at a government dacha [country house] in Novo-Ogarevo, a Moscow suburb.

In opening the session, Khrushchev dramatically portrayed the danger facing the Soviet experiment. War was in the air, and under these conditions he needed the Presidium to take a difficult but necessary decision.

There was a time, when we advanced, like in October 1917; but in March 1918 we had to retreat, having signed the Brest-Litovsk agreement with the Germans. Our interests dictated this decision—we had to save Soviet power. Now we found ourselves face to face with the danger of war and of nuclear catastrophe, with the possible result of destroying the human race. In order to save the world, we must retreat. I called you together to consult and debate whether you are in agreement with this kind of decision.

Khrushchev was preparing to ask the Presidium to support him in accepting Kennedy's letter of October 27. It would have been better to have obtained the removal of the Jupiter missiles; but with the situation moving out of control in Cuba it was prudent to accept what Moscow could get. Khrushchev's previous doubts about Washington had returned, and he was no longer convinced that the threat of a U.S. invasion had passed. The Soviet military had picked up a rumor that Kennedy was preparing to deliver a nationally broadcast speech that night.

Before turning to the difficult discussion of acceptable terms for ending the crisis, the Presidium prepared for the possibility that the United States might launch a strike against Cuba that day. It was decided to allow General Pliyev [the Soviet commander in Cuba] to use force to defend himself. Although it said nothing in its decision about the use of tactical nuclear weapons, the Presidium hinted at the possibility that Pliyev might still receive authorization to use those under his command. "If the attack is provoked," the Presidium decided, "it is ordered to repel it with a responsive blow."

At this point Oleg Troyanovsky, one of Khrushchev's assistants who was also at the dacha, received a telephone call from the Foreign Ministry. A report from Anatoly Dobrynin had just arrived that described an interesting meeting with the president's brother. With an ear cocked to the telephone, Troyanovksy noted down the essentials. Regarding trading the Turkish missiles: he "doesn't see any insurmountable difficulties." Regarding the pace of future negotiations: "[This is] a request . . . not an ultimatum." One part to all of this, however, worried Troyanovsky. Apparently the American president was under severe pressure from the Pentagon to act. Robert Kennedy stressed that the Americans needed an answer from Moscow on Sunday, that very day: "[T]here is very little time to resolve this whole issue. . . . [E]vents are developing too quickly." His notes complete, Troyanovsky entered the hall and interrupted the session: "I . . . began to read my notes on Dobrynin's report. They [Khrushchev and the others] asked me to read the notes again. It goes without saying that the contents of the dispatch increased the nervousness in the hall by some degrees."

There was no time to waste. Khrushchev called a stenographer over and began to dictate in the meeting hall his acceptance of the White House's proposals:

> I have received your message of October 27. I express my satisfaction and thank you for the sense of proportion you have displayed. . . .
>
> In order to eliminate as rapidly as possible the conflict which endangers the cause of peace . . . the Soviet Government, in addition to earlier instructions on the discontinuation of further work on weapons construction sites, has given a new order to dismantle the arms which you described as offensive, and to crate and return them to the Soviet Union.

In addition to the public letter, Khrushchev sent two private messages to Kennedy, which Dobrynin was to convey orally to Robert Kennedy. The first confirmed what Kennedy would soon hear on the radio:

> The views which R. Kennedy expressed at the request of the President in the meeting with Dobrynin in the evening of October 27, are known in Moscow. Today the response will be given by radio to the president and this response will be positive. In the main, the issue that agitates the president—namely, the removal of the missile bases from Cuba under international control—does not meet with any objections and will be explicated in detail in the message of N.S. Khrushchev.

The second, a more secret message, explained that the Kremlin expected the White House to keep its promise to withdraw the Turkish missiles. Khrushchev explained that he took Robert Kennedy's statement that "it would take 4–5 months to remove the missile bases from Turkey" and his subsequent request that all discussion of a resolution of the Turkish issue be kept highly confidential to mean that the Kennedy administration had accepted his Turkish demand.

> In my letter to you of October 28, which was designed for publication, I did not touch on this matter because of your wish, as conveyed by Robert Kennedy. But all of the offers, which were included in this letter, were given on account of your having agreed to the Turkish issue raised in my letter of October 27 and announced by Robert Kennedy, from your side, in his meeting with the Soviet ambassador that same day.

Though pleased with how well the negotiations were turning out, Khrushchev feared a last-minute surprise. Concerned that some third party—a trigger-happy antiaircraft gunman in Cuba or a disgruntled general in the Pentagon—might undermine a settlement the Presidium decided, as it had on Saturday, to have the main letter to Kennedy read over Radio Moscow so that it would be received quickly in Washington. Khrushchev instructed Leonid F. Ilichov, one of the Central Committee secretaries, to rush a copy of the letter to Radio Moscow for immediate broadcast. He also wanted the Soviet command in Cuba to exercise better control over the situation on the island. "We think that you were in a hurry to shoot down a U.S. reconnaissance U-2 plane," Khrushchev cabled to Pliyev. Moscow now strictly forbade Pliyev to use the SA-2 [antiaircraft] missiles and grounded all Soviet jets in Cuba "to avoid a clash with U.S. reconnaissance planes."

Now that a negotiated settlement was within reach, Khrushchev also had to confront the problem of what to do about Castro. From Castro's late-night message he had concluded that the Cuban had lost all sense of proportion and was advocating nuclear suicide. What else could Castro have meant in calling this "the moment to eliminate such danger [of U.S. invasion] forever"? Khrushchev intended to set Castro straight at some later date on why he had been wrong to react the way he did. But the needs of this day required a calming letter that would discourage Castro from doing anything rash to upset the final stages of the negotiations. With the explanation that militarists in Washington would seize upon any opportunity to wreck the diplomatic agreement with Kennedy, Khrushchev asked Castro, in a letter that he hastily dictated along with the rest, to refrain from opening fire against American planes.

At 4:00 P.M.—or 8:00 A.M., EST—an hour before Radio Moscow beamed Khrushchev's letter around the world, Malinovsky ordered

Pliyev to begin dismantling the R-12 [missile] sites. The nuclear deterrent that Khrushchev had worked so hard to create in the Caribbean, and which had only just now become fully operational, was to be destroyed.

Washington, Sunday Morning, October 28, 9:00 A.M. EST (5 P.M., Moscow Time)

Maxwell Taylor [chairman of the Joint Chiefs of Staff] convened an early-morning meeting of the Joint Chiefs on Sunday to discuss the next American move if Khrushchev rejected the proposals contained in the president's October 27 letter. The chiefs, who had not been told about Robert Kennedy's private session with the Soviet ambassador on Saturday evening, felt they had good reason to believe that military action of some sort was inevitable. "Monday will be the last time to attack the missiles before they become fully operational," said [U.S. Air Force chief of staff] Curtis LeMay, who had been ready for days to send his air force into battle. "I want to see the President later today," LeMay insisted. Taylor was about to explain the reconnaissance flights over Cuba that had been prepared that day, when an assistant entered with a ticker tape of uncommon importance. At 9 A.M. Radio Moscow broadcast Khrushchev's acceptance of the Kennedy formula.

Looking over the text of the Kremlin leader's statement, the air force chief was not impressed: "The Soviets may make a charade of withdrawal and keep some weapons in Cuba." The grumbling among the chiefs continued until Defense Secretary McNamara and two of his assistants joined the discussion a short while later. The civilians were satisfied with Khrushchev's statement, arguing that it left the United States "in a much stronger position." LeMay remained unimpressed and again insisted on seeing President Kennedy later that day. Whereas before Khrushchev's statement LeMay had allies, now his fellow chiefs fell silent. It was best to await the latest batch of reconnaissance photographs. They would be the proof of the new pudding.

Meanwhile, the White House was relieved when news of the broadcast from Moscow reached the president. All of the messy contingencies, considered in the expectation that Robert Kennedy's secret mission might fail, could be shelved. Back-channel diplomacy seemed to have succeeded. Robert Kennedy went to see the Soviet ambassador to express the U.S. government's satisfaction. At the Ex Comm meeting that started at 11:10 A.M., [Kennedy's national security adviser McGeorge] Bundy remarked that "everyone knew who were the hawks and who were the doves, but . . . today was the doves' day."

On its own, CIA headquarters ordered a halt to "all action, maritime, and black infiltration." The message was sent to the CIA's

Miami station at Opa Locka at 1:30 P.M. Later that afternoon the
White House made the same request, and the CIA repeated the halt
order at 4:30. Operation Mongoose was frozen. [Operation Mongoose was an assassination plot aimed at Fidel Castro.]

Havana, Sunday Afternoon, October 28

Not having expected Moscow to back down, Fidel Castro was furious when he heard the news broadcast over Radio Moscow. His missiles were going—and for what? For a verbal promise from his antagonist John Kennedy that he would not invade. Castro called a
meeting of his military and political high command at 2:00
P.M. . . . With the Soviet representative in attendance, Castro pronounced a valedictory on the Soviet missile project.

"Cuba will not lose anything by the removal of the missiles, because she has already gained so much," Castro stated confidently. The
missile crisis had focused international attention on the plight of his
country. The fact that the Soviet Union had to go to such great lengths
to protect him demonstrated the extent of American imperialism; and
Castro hoped that as a result he might receive some international assistance in eliminating the American economic blockade.

Castro's search for a silver lining did not make him any less angry at Moscow. He thought Khrushchev had mishandled the resolution of the crisis. It was not only the substance of Khrushchev's
diplomacy that he found annoying; it was the fact that Moscow had
cut a deal without any consultation of Havana. . . . Consequently,
Castro argued that Moscow had committed a grave "political mistake" by first publicly demanding the removal of the Jupiters and
then dropping the requirement, apparently without any compensation, a day later.

Castro vowed not to make a resolution of the crisis any easier for
Khrushchev. "We won't find a better time to demand the liquidation
of the American military base at Guantánamo," he told his military.
Castro intended to inform Washington that if it wanted to inspect the
dismantled Soviet missile sites, the U.S. Navy would have to leave
Guantánamo. Kennedy had indicated in his October 27 letter that
these inspections were part of the package and that Khrushchev had
already indicated his agreement. But Castro intended to exercise a
veto over the agreement if Cuban demands were not met. . . .

Nikita Khrushchev may have averted a war with the United
States. But if the removal of the missiles from Cuba alienated Fidel
Castro, then the Kremlin's entire strategy in the Caribbean had
failed. On October 29 Khrushchev decided to send Anastas Mikoyan
to Havana to reassure the Cubans.

Man Lands on the Moon

John Noble Wilford

President John F. Kennedy set as America's goal the landing of a man on the moon by the end of the 1960s, and although neither he nor his brother Robert lived to see it (he was assassinated in 1963, as was Robert in 1968), the goal was won on July 20, 1969, when two American astronauts stepped from their landing capsule onto the powdery lunar soil. John Noble Wilford's *New York Times* story reporting that historic event, which millions worldwide witnessed on television as it happened, appears here.

It is appropriate to include this document within a chapter on the world in the Cold War era because so much of the "space race" of the 1950s and 1960s was driven by the Soviet-American rivalry—just as were the match-ups between the two countries' athletes every four years at the Olympic Games. The space race had begun in earnest in October 1957 when the Soviet Union used a powerful rocket to launch Sputnik, the world's first artificial satellite. Although President Eisenhower played down this achievement as a stunt, and although (after some embarrassing failures) the United States soon matched the Soviet success, both sides in the Cold War understood that prowess in developing the rocketry needed to lift large payloads into orbit or on their way to other celestial bodies meant prowess in building and deploying the nuclear-tipped intercontinental ballistic missiles (ICBMs) with which World War III would be fought.

It was not well understood at the time, but by 1969, when the first American astronauts walked on the moon, the Soviet Union had lost its economic and revolutionary dynamism; the first signs of the stagnation that would bring the whole Leninist system crashing down exactly twenty years later were already evident. The United States, too, had lost its inno-

Reprinted from "Men Walk on Moon," by John Noble Wilford, *The New York Times*, July 21, 1969. Reprinted with permission.

cence: It was trapped in an unwinnable war against a poor Southeast Asian nation; its soul was about to be tried by a sordid scandal in the White House and by corrosive inflation; it could no longer count on the cheap energy and the international system of currency exchange that it dominated in order to keep its engine of prosperity humming. The year 1969 was a milestone in more ways than most people then realized.

Houston, Monday, July 21—Men have landed and walked on the moon.

Two Americans, astronauts of Apollo 11, steered their fragile four-legged lunar module safely and smoothly to the historic landing yesterday at 4:17:40 P.M., Eastern daylight time.

Neil A. Armstrong, the 38-year-old civilian commander, radioed to earth and the mission control room here:

"Houston, Tranquility Base here. The Eagle has landed."

The first men to reach the moon—Mr. Armstrong and his co-pilot, Col. Edwin E. Aldrin Jr. of the Air Force—brought their ship to rest on a level, rock-strewn plain near the southwestern shore of the arid Sea of Tranquility.

About six and a half hours later, Mr. Armstrong opened the landing craft's hatch, stepped slowly down the ladder and declared as he planted the first human footprint on the lunar crust:

"That's one small step for man, one giant leap for mankind."

His first step on the moon came at 10:56:20 P.M., as a television camera outside the craft transmitted his every move to an awed and excited audience of hundreds of millions of people on earth.

Tentative Steps Test Soil

Mr. Armstrong's initial steps were tentative tests of the lunar soil's firmness and of his ability to move about easily in his bulky white spacesuit and backpacks and under the influence of lunar gravity, which is one-sixth that of the earth.

"The surface is fine and powdery," the astronaut reported. "I can pick it up loosely with my toe. It does adhere in fine layers like powdered charcoal to the sole and sides of my boots. I only go in a small fraction of an inch, maybe an eighth of an inch. But I can see the footprints of my boots in the treads in the fine sandy particles.

After 19 minutes of Mr. Armstrong's testing, Colonel Aldrin joined him outside the craft.

The two men got busy setting up another television camera out from the lunar module, planting an American flag into the ground, scooping up soil and rock samples, deploying scientific experiments and hopping and loping about in a demonstration of their lunar agility.

John F. Kennedy's goal of landing a man on the moon was realized on July 20, 1969.

They found walking and working on the moon less taxing than had been forecast. Mr. Armstrong once reported he was "very comfortable."

And people back on earth found the black-and-white television pictures of the bug-shaped lunar module and the men tramping about it sharp and clear as to seem unreal, more like a toy and toy-like figures than human beings on the most daring and far-reaching expedition thus far undertaken.

Nixon Telephones Congratulations

During one break in the astronauts' work, President Nixon congratu-0lated them from the White House in what, he said, "certainly has to be the most historic telephone call ever made."

"Because of what you have done," the President told the astronauts, "the heavens have become a part of man's world. And as you talk to us from the Sea of Tranquility it requires us to redouble our efforts to bring peace and tranquility to earth.

"For one priceless moment in the whole history of man all the people on this earth are truly one—one in their pride in what you have done and one in our prayers that you will return safely to earth."

Mr. Armstrong replied:

"Thank you Mr. President. It's a great honor and privilege for us to be here representing not only the United States but men of peace of all nations, men with interests and a curiosity and men with a vision for the future."

Mr. Armstrong and Colonel Aldrin returned to their landing craft and closed the hatch at 1:12 A.M., 2 hours 21 minutes after opening the hatch on the moon. While the third member of the crew, Lieut. Col. Michael Collins of the Air Force, kept his orbital vigil overhead in the command ship, the two moon explorers settled down to sleep.

Outside their vehicle the astronauts had found a bleak world. It was just before dawn, with the sun low over the eastern horizon behind them and the chill of the long lunar nights still clinging to the boulders, small craters and hills before them.

Colonel Aldrin said that he could see "literally thousands of small craters" and a low hill out in the distance. But most of all he was impressed initially by the "variety of shapes, angularities, granularities" of the rocks and soil where the landing craft, code-named Eagle had set down.

The landing was made four miles west of the aiming point, but well within the designated area. An apparent error in some data fed into the craft's guidance computer from the earth was said to have accounted for the discrepancy.

Suddenly the astronauts were startled to see that the computer was guiding them toward a possibly disastrous touchdown in a boulder-filled crater about the size of a football field.

Mr. Armstrong grabbed manual control of the vehicle and guided it safely over the crater to a smoother spot, the rocket engine stirring a cloud of moon dust during the final seconds of descent.

Soon after the landing, upon checking and finding the spacecraft in good condition, Mr. Armstrong and Colonel Aldrin made their decision to open the hatch and get out earlier than originally scheduled. The flight plan had called for the moon walk to begin at 2:12 A.M.

Flight controllers here said that the early moon walk would not mean that the astronauts would also leave the moon earlier. The lift-off is scheduled to come at about 1:55 P.M. today.

Their departure from the landing craft out onto the surface was delayed for a time when they had trouble depressurizing the cabin so that they could open the hatch. All the oxygen in the cabin had to be vented.

Once the pressure gauge finally dropped to zero, they opened the hatch and Mr. Armstrong stepped out on the small porch at the top of the nine-step ladder.

"O.K., Houston, I'm on the porch," he reported, as he descended.

On the second step from the top, he pulled a lanyard that released a fold-down equipment compartment on the side of the lunar module. This deployed the television camera that transmitted the dramatic pictures of man's first steps on the moon.

Ancient Dream Fulfilled

It was man's first landing on another world, the realization of centuries of dreams, the fulfillment of a decade of striving; a triumph of modern technology and personal courage, the most dramatic demonstration of what man can do if he applies his mind and resources with single-minded determination.

The moon, long the symbol of the impossible and the inaccessible, was now within man's reach, the first port of call in this new age of spacefaring.

Immediately after the landing, Dr. Thomas O. Paine, administrator of the National Aeronautics and Space Administration, telephoned President Nixon in Washington to report:

"Mr. President, it is my honor on behalf of the entire NASA team to report to you that the Eagle has landed on the Sea of Tranquility and our astronauts are safe and looking forward to starting the exploration of the moon."

The landing craft from the Apollo 11 spaceship was scheduled to remain on the moon about 22 hours, while Colonel Collins of the Air Force, the third member of the Apollo 11 crew, piloted the command ship, Columbia, in orbit overhead.

"You're looking good in every respect," Mission Control told the two men of Eagle after examining data indicating that the module should be able to remain on the moon the full 22 hours.

Mr. Armstrong and Colonel Aldrin planned to sleep after the moon walk and then make their preparations for the lift-off for the return to a rendezvous with Colonel Collins in the command ship.

Apollo 11's journey into history began last Wednesday from launching pad 39-A at Cape Kennedy, Fla. After an almost flawless three-day flight, the joined command ship and lunar module swept into an orbit of the moon yesterday afternoon.

The three men were awake for their big day at 7 A.M. when their spacecraft emerged from behind the moon on its 10th revolution, moving from east to west across the face of the moon along its equator.

Their orbit was 73.6 miles by 64 miles in altitude, their speed 3,660 miles an hour. At that altitude and speed, it took about two hours to complete a full orbit of the moon.

The sun was rising over their landing site on the Sea of Tranquility.

"We can pick out almost all of the features we've identified previously," Mr. Armstrong reported.

After breakfast, on their 11th revolution, Colonel Aldrin and then Mr. Armstrong, both dressed in their white pressurized suits, crawled through the connecting tunnel into the lunar module.

They turned on the electrical power, checked all the switch settings on the cockpit panel and checked communications with the command ship and the ground controllers. Everything was "nominal," as the spacemen say.

LM Ready for Descent

The lunar module was ready. Its four legs with yard-wide footpads were extended so that the height of the 16 $1/2$-ton vehicle now measured 22 feet and 11 inches and its width 31 feet.

Mr. Armstrong stood at the left side of the cockpit, and Colonel Aldrin at the right. Both were loosely restrained by harnesses. They had closed the hatch to the connecting tunnel.

The walls of their craft were finely milled aluminum foil. If anything happened so that it could not return to the command ship, the lunar module would be too delicate to withstand a plunge through earth's atmosphere, even if it had the rocket power.

Nearly three-fourths of the vehicle's weight was in propellants for the descent and ascent rockets—Aerozine 50 and nitrogen oxide, which substituted for the oxygen, making combustion possible.

It was an ungainly craft that creaked and groaned in flight. But years of development and testing had determined that it was the lightest and most practical way to get two men to the moon's surface.

Before Apollo 11 disappeared behind the moon near the end of its 12th orbit, Mission Control gave the astronauts their "go" for undocking—the separation of Eagle from Columbia.

Colonel Collins had already released 12 of the latches holding the two ships together at the connecting tunnel. He did this when he closed the hatch at the command ship's nose. While behind the moon, he was to flip a switch on the control panel to release the three remaining latches by a spring action.

At 1:50 P.M., when communication signals were reacquired, Mission Control asked: "How does it look?"

"Eagle has wings," Mr. Armstrong replied.

The two ships were then only a few feet apart. But at 2:12 P.M., Colonel Collins fired the command ship's maneuvering rockets to move about two miles away and in a slightly different orbit from the lunar module.

"It looks like you've got a fine-looking flying machine there, Eagle, despite the fact you're upside down," Colonel Collins commented watching the spidery lunar module receding in the distance.

"Somebody's upside down," Mr. Armstrong replied.

What is "up" and what is "down" is never quite clear in the absence of landmarks and the sensation of gravity's pull.

Mr. Armstrong and Colonel Aldrin rode the lunar module back around to the moon's far side, the rocket engine in the vehicle's lower stage was pointed toward the line of flight. The two pilots were leaning toward the cockpit controls, riding backwards and facing downward.

"Everything is 'go,'" they were assured by Mission Control.

Their on-board guidance and navigation computer was instructed to trigger a 29.8-second firing of the descent rocket, the 9,870-pound-thrust throttable engine that would slow down the lunar module and send it toward the moon on a long, curving trajectory.

The firing was set to take place at 3:08 P.M., when the craft would be behind the moon and once again out of touch with the ground.

Suspense built up in the control room here. Flight controllers stood silently at their consoles. Among those waiting for word of the rocket firing were Dr. Thomas O. Paine, the space agency's administrator, most of the Apollo project officials and several astronauts.

At 3:46 P.M., contact was established with the command ship.

Colonel Collins reported, "Listen, baby, things are going just swimmingly, just beautiful."

There was still no word from the lunar module for two minutes. Then came a weak signal, some static and whistling, and finally the calm voice of Mr. Armstrong.

"The burn was on time," the Apollo 11 commander declared.

When he read out data on the beginning of the descent, Mission Control concluded that it "looked great." The lunar module had already descended from an altitude of 65.5 miles to 21 miles and was coasting steadily downward.

Eugene F. Kranz, the flight director, turned to his associates and said, "We're off to a good start. Play it cool."

Colonel Aldrin reported some oscillations in the vehicle's antenna, but nothing serious. Several times the astronauts were told to turn the vehicle slightly to move the antenna into a better position for communications over the 230,000 miles.

"You're 'go' for PDI," radioed Mission Control, referring to the powered descent initiation—the beginning of the nearly 13-minute final blast of the rocket to the soft touchdown.

When the two men reached an altitude of 50,000 feet, which was approximately the lowest point reached by Apollo 10 in May, green lights on the computer display keyboard in the cockpit blinked the number 99.

This signaled Mr. Armstrong that he had five seconds to decide whether to go ahead for the landing or continue on its orbital path back to the command ship. He pressed the "proceed" button.

The throttleable engine built up thrust gradually, firing continuously as the lunar module descended along the steadily steepening trajectory to the landing site about 250 miles away.

"Looking good," Mission Control radioed the men.

Four minutes after the firing the lunar module was down to 40,000 feet. After five and a half minutes, it was 33,500 feet. At six minutes, 27,000 feet.

"Better than the simulator," said Colonel Aldrin, referring to their practice landings at the spacecraft center.

Seven minutes after the firing, the men were 21,000 feet above the surface and still moving forward toward the landing site. The guidance computer was driving the rocket engine.

The lunar module was slowing down. At an altitude of about 7,200 feet, with the landing site still about five miles ahead, the computer commanded control jets to fire and tilt the bag-shaped craft almost upright so that its triangular windows pointed forward.

Mr. Armstrong and Colonel Aldrin then got their first close-up view of the plain they were aiming for. It was then about three and a half minutes to touchdown.

The brownish-gray panorama rushed below them—the myriad craters, hills and ridges, deep cracks and ancient rubble on the moon, which Dr. Robert Jastrow, the space agency scientist, called the "Rosetta Stone of life."

"You're 'go' for landing," Mission Control informed the two men.

The Eagle closed in, dropping about 20 feet a second, until it was hovering almost directly over the landing area at an altitude of 500 feet.

Its floor was littered with boulders.

It was when the craft reached an altitude of 300 feet that Mr. Armstrong took over semimanual control for the rest of the way. The computer continued to have control of the rocket firing, but the astronaut could adjust the craft's hovering position.

He was expected to take over such control anyway, but the sight of a crater looming ahead at the touchdown point made it imperative.

As Mr. Armstrong said later, "The auto-targeting was taking us right into a football field–sized crater, with a large number of big boulders and rocks."

For about 90 seconds, he peered through the window in search of a clear touchdown point. Using the lever at his right hand, he tilted the vehicle forward to redirect the firing of the maneuvering jets and thus shift its hovering position.

Finally, Mr. Armstrong found the spot he liked, and the blue light on the cockpit flashed to indicate that five-foot-long probes, like curb feelers, on three of the four legs had touched the surface.

"Contact light," Mr. Armstrong radioed.

He pressed a button marked "Stop" and reported, "okay, engine stop."

There were a few more cryptic messages of functions performed.

Then Maj. Charles M. Duke, the capsule communicator in the control room, radioed to the two astronauts:

"We copy you down, Eagle."

"Houston, Tranquility Base here. The Eagle has landed."

"Roger, Tranquility," Major Duke replied. "We copy you on the ground. You got a bunch of guys about to turn blue. We are breathing again. Thanks a lot."

Colonel Aldrin assured Mission Control it was a "very smooth touchdown."

The Eagle came to rest at an angle of only about four and a half degrees. The angle could have been more than 30 degrees without threatening to tip the vehicle over.

The landing site, about 120 miles southwest of the crater Maskelyne, is on the right side of the moon as seen from earth. The position: Lat. 0.799 degrees N., Long. 23.46 degrees E.

Although Mr. Armstrong is known as a man of few words, his heartbeats told of his excitement upon leading man's first landing on the moon.

At the time of the descent rocket ignition, his heartbeat rate registered 110 a minute—77 is normal for him—and it shot up to 156 at touchdown.

At the time of the landing, Colonel Collins was riding the command ship Columbia about 65 miles overhead.

Mission Control informed the colonel, "Eagle is at Tranquility."

"Yea, I heard the whole thing," Colonel Collins, the man who went so far but not all the way, replied. "Fantastic."

When the Apollo astronauts landed on the Sea of Tranquility, the temperature at their touchdown site was about zero degrees Fahrenheit in the sunlight, even colder in the shade.

During a lunar night, which lasts 14 earth days, temperatures plunge as low as 280 degrees below zero. Unlike earth, the moon, having no atmosphere to act as a blanket, is unable to retain any of the day's warmth during the night.

During the equally long lunar day, temperatures rise as high as 280 degrees. By the time of Eagle's departure from the moon, with the sun higher in the sky, the temperatures there will have risen to about 90 degrees.

This particular landing site was one of five selected by Apollo project officials after analysis of pictures returned by the five Lunar Orbiter unmanned spacecraft.

All five sites are situated across the lunar equator on the side of the moon always facing the earth. Being on the equator reduces the maneuvering for the astronauts to get there. Being on the near side of the moon, of course, makes it possible to communicate with the explorers.

The Revolt Against Hegemony, 1960–1980

PREFACE

J ust as the Great War of 1914–1918 sowed the seeds in Europe of totalitarianism and World War II, so the Second World War did much to spawn the resurgence of the Third World. The globe's major colonial powers, Great Britain and France (and especially the latter), suffered massive material losses in the war with Adolf Hitler's Germany and almost equally grave blows to their prestige in the eyes of their non-Western subjects. These losses made it almost impossible to restore the full rigor of colonial rule after World War II ended. The Soviet Union openly encouraged colonized peoples to rebel, and the United States frequently criticized imperialism in all of its forms. The cause of anticolonialism gained legitimacy worldwide because of the towering moral stature of Mohandas Gandhi. The realization that racial prejudice had fueled Nazi anti-Semitism forced many individuals of European cultural heritage to reexamine the unthinking superiority with which they had generally regarded all non-Western people before World War II.

Hegemony means domination in any form. The years between 1945 and approximately 1980 constitute an important era in global history because during this relatively brief span the vast empires that European powers had been accumulating for centuries almost entirely disintegrated. In their place arose almost a hundred new sovereign nations, most of them former colonies, ranging in size from gigantic India to minuscule islands in the Caribbean and South Pacific. China, for more than a century mired in poverty and humiliated by foreigners, "stood up" (in the words of Mao Zedong) and reemerged as a proud if not always powerful new force in the world—and as the globe's most populous country. Muslims felt an intense religious renewal that sometimes—most notably in Iran in 1979—produced revolutions against every form of Western influence and restored an austere Islamic way of life.

Except for civil wars such as China's, the postwar liberation from Western hegemony was surprisingly peaceful. However, when European or European-descended states tried by force to oppose former colonial peoples' drives for independence—as did France in Algeria and Indochina, Portugal in its African colonies, and the United States in Vietnam—they suffered humiliating military defeats.

Within the United States and South Africa, the postwar rejection of hegemony came in still different ways. Nonwhites formed minority populations in the United States, but as late as the early 1950s racial discrimination against these people was the rule rather than the exception. Spearheading a movement that would later serve as a model for Hispanic Americans, Asian Americans, and Native Americans, the leaders of the African American community almost unanimously pursued a peaceful strategy of demanding dignity and full civil rights for their people. This strategy depended crucially both on Gandhi's philosophy of nonviolent civil disobedience and on litigation and legislation within the American constitutional system. Although discrimination was not completely eliminated, by 1980 all racial and ethnic minorities within the United States had made enormous gains. In South Africa, nonwhites constituted the vast majority of the population, but European-descended people completely controlled the country's wealth and government. Whites there used their power to maintain a cruel system of total racial segregation, called apartheid—and the African liberation struggle was longer, more bitterly contested, and occasionally more violent than in the United States. In 1980 white rule still seemed deeply entrenched. Yet by that time world opinion was mobilizing against the apartheid regime, and its end would come within fifteen years.

Economic change also shook Western global hegemony. A crucial source of energy, as well as a key manufacturing component, for the modern industrial world is petroleum. The drilling and refining of petroleum throughout most of the twentieth century were capital-intensive processes almost wholly controlled by European and American corporations. But by the early 1970s the most easily extracted oil fields in the world were not producing as abundantly or as cheaply as they once had. Energy was becoming more expensive, and Third World producer nations found the leverage they needed to make Westerners pay a great deal more for the oil they could not live without. The so-called energy crisis that began in 1973, the skillful tactics by which Arab producers used an oil boycott to force Israel and the Western nations that supported it to begin negotiating a withdrawal from occupied lands, and the sharp escalation of petroleum prices in 1973 and 1979 (when the Islamic revolution swept Iran)— all of these were dramatic and painful lessons to the West that the days when it could dictate terms to non-Western societies were over.

Martin Luther King Jr. Goes to Jail

Taylor Branch

In 1954 the courtroom strategy of the American black civil rights movement yielded the great milestone of the Supreme Court decision *Brown v. Board of Education*, which outlawed school segregation. But the legal and social barriers enforcing racial discrimination in the United States did not fall immediately, and a powerful white backlash arose, especially in the South. In 1955 a young African American minister named Martin Luther King Jr., came to prominence by leading a boycott movement aimed at integrating the public transportation system in Montgomery, Alabama. Five years later, in 1960, African American college students initiated the sit-in campaign to desegregate lunch counters, and a year later black and white activists braved violence and even death in a struggle to destroy segregation in interstate bus travel. The philosophical basis of this peaceful struggle for dignity and full legal rights was Gandhi's civil-disobedience campaign in India, which King had carefully studied and eloquently articulated. His Southern Christian Leadership Conference (SCLC), a coalition of black clergy, spearheaded the movement, alongside the student-led Student Non-Violent Coordinating Committee (SNCC, pronounced "Snick"), an outgrowth of the sit-ins.

In the spring of 1963 the SCLC targeted Birmingham, Alabama, probably the most rigidly segregated city in the South. An African American boycott movement consisting of picketing downtown businesses was fiercely resisted by the city's white police chief, Eugene "Bull" Connor, who used fire hoses and police dogs to break up the peaceful demonstrations. King's leadership was on the line: Should he allow himself to be arrested, or should he tour the North making fund-raising speeches to sympathetic white audiences? His father, the Reverend Martin Luther King Sr. ("Daddy King"), a powerful black preacher from Atlanta, counseled him to play it safe.

Taylor Branch, who has written a Pulitzer Prize–winning biography of King entitled *Parting the Waters: America in the King Years, 1954–1963,* analyzes how King applied the lessons of Gandhi's satyagraha movement to maintain the moral high ground of the African American struggle, and how this experience inspired King's "Letter from Birmingham Jail"—a classic in the literature of principled nonviolence.

B y staying away from the Thursday-night mass meeting at the Sixth Avenue Baptist Church, King avoided making any more promises. In the crisis, Daddy King rushed over from Atlanta to preach in his place, just as a new development promised to keep his son out of jail after all. The city notified the movement's bail bondsman that he had reached the limit of established credit, which amounted to a bankruptcy notice for the jail project. No longer could volunteers be assured that the movement would provide bail, and now the poorest of them might wind up in jail for six months instead of six days. Until late in the night, King and his advisers paddled around among a hundred ramifications. Could they warn potential jailgoers of this sad state without ruining what spirit remained? Was King's first obligation to fulfill his promise of going to jail, or should he, as the SCLC's only proven fund-raiser, tour the country to recharge the bail funds? If he took the latter course, would there be any movement left when he returned to Birmingham? . . .

Norman Amaker, an NAACP lawyer from New York, briefed King and some two dozen movement leaders early on Good Friday morning, April 12. Crowded into the sitting room of King's Room 30, the only suite in the Gaston Motel, they heard Amaker say that the Jenkins injunction was probably unconstitutional, but that anyone who violated it would probably be punished regardless. Whatever King decided to do, Amaker said in closing, the NAACP's Legal Defense Fund would stand behind him in court. King himself set a gloomy tone for what followed, saying he did not want to spend the rest of his life in jail. He did not know what to do, and felt trapped between conflicting obligations. While he did not want to let the injunction make him renege on his promises to carry on the Birmingham movement, neither did he want to lead new people blindly into jail, especially since he did not know how the movement could make bond for those already there. Then he called on his friends for suggestions. After a silence, one said that King could not go to jail, because the movement would die without new money.

Daddy King recommended that his son not break the injunction. A lawyer boasted implausibly that if King went to jail, he would spring him by getting the injunction quashed. Andrew Young and several others said they would support whatever King decided. Significantly, no one, including Shuttlesworth and Abernathy, suggested that other leaders go to jail in King's place. They were in a downward spiral; King recalled that "our most dedicated and devoted leaders were overwhelmed by a feeling of hopelessness."

He did not reply to any of the suggestions. When they died out, he simply withdrew into the bedroom and shut the door, acutely conscious that at the moment his closest associates formed an inert mass. Before him in one direction was the abyss of jail, with exaggerated martyr's hopes that his arrest would ignite both the Kennedy White House and Birmingham's Negroes. In the other direction were press conferences and elaborate explanations why a fund-raising detour was necessary for a sounder movement, with exaggerated hopes of a triumphant return—and silent fears that this was the end, that a leader could not duck out behind his followers. When King stepped back into the other room a few minutes later, he wore a work shirt, blue jeans that were crisply new and rolled up at the cuffs, and a new pair of "clodhopper" walking shoes. It was a startling sight, as some of those in the room had never seen King wear anything but a dark business suit.

This first glimpse of him announced that he would go to jail, which hushed the room. "I don't know what will happen," he said. "I don't know where the money will come from. But I have to make a faith act.". . . [King persuaded a reluctant Abernathy to join him in going to jail. When they subsequently appeared among the civil rights demonstrators, King and Abernathy were promptly arrested. King was thrown into a solitary-confinement cell, lacking even a mattress and without access to a telephone.]

On Monday afternoon, King was overjoyed to see the handsome face of Clarence Jones at his cell door. Jones, hoping to ward off hostile treatment from the Birmingham jailers, was decked out in his finest New York lawyer clothes. He greeted King with the words he most wanted to hear: "Harry has been able to raise fifty thousand dollars for bail bonds." And Belafonte had said he was good for more, for "whatever else you need." [Harry Belafonte was a popular black singer of the day.] King wrote later that these few words from Jones "lifted a thousand pounds from my heart." They meant that those who wanted out of jail could get out, and that King could not now be second-guessed for going to jail instead of raising money.

Jones also told King that Belafonte and Walker were organizing a phone and telegram campaign to pressure the Kennedy Administration to seek decent treatment for King in the jail. So far King remained isolated in his cell, allowed no phone calls. He had no mattress or linen, and was sleeping on metal slats. Hearing of these conditions from Wyatt Walker, Belafonte had called Robert Kennedy. As King knew, the Attorney General strongly opposed the entire Birmingham campaign, let alone King's going to jail, and Kennedy had further reason to feel put upon because he knew that King could relieve his suffering at any time by posting bond and walking out of jail. Under these circumstances, Jones reported, Kennedy's response to Belafonte had been testy, but leavened with humor. "Tell Reverend King we're doing all we can," Kennedy had told Belafonte, "but I'm not sure we can get into prison reform at this moment."

After Jones departed, the jailers led King out of his cell to the prisoners' pay phone, saying it was time for him to call his wife. King, who had enough jail experience to know that guards normally do not nurture an inmate's family communications, suspected correctly that the sudden kindness was really for the convenience of the police department's wiretap stenographers. When Coretta promptly informed him that the President had just called her, King did not reply. Stalling—caught between his hunger for her news and his reluctance to let Bull Connor know what President Kennedy was doing—King made small talk with his two older children. His evasive manner alerted Coretta.

"Are you being guarded?" she asked.

"Yes," he replied.

"Did they give you a time limit?"

"Not exactly, but hear everything, you know," King said pointedly. "Who did you say called you?"

"Kennedy," said Coretta. "The President."

"Did he call you direct?"

"Yes. And he told me you were going to call in a few minutes. It was about thirty minutes ago."

This was significant news, potentially a replay of President Kennedy's famous phone call before the 1960 election. "Let Wyatt know," King instructed. ". . . Do that right now."

Coretta recounted her conversation with President Kennedy, saying, "He told me the FBI talked with you last night. Is that right?"

"No, no," said King. He told her again to get word of Kennedy's phone call to Walker so that Walker could issue a statement. Coretta did not agree to do so outright, sensing perhaps that she was in a bind because she had issued her own statement to *The New York Times,* whereas King wanted Walker to handle the matter. She kept adding details of President Kennedy's expressed concern, and of two earlier phone calls from Robert Kennedy, while King kept asking her to tell it all to Walker.

When the news did reach Birmingham, Walker seized hopefully

on the White House involvement to proclaim the beginning of phase two in Birmingham—the national phase. Responses outside the mass meeting proved to be far less enthusiastic. News stories pointed out that President Kennedy had not initiated the phone contact, as he had done during the 1960 campaign. Instead, Kennedy had returned Coretta's urgent phone calls to the White House switchboard. This made Kennedy seem less resolutely sympathetic to King, and therefore made King's cause seem less worthy. Other, less subtle discrepancies appeared. With the Birmingham police department denying that FBI agents had visited King or that President Kennedy's influence had produced better treatment for King—and Chief Moore going so far as to declare that it had been his idea for King to call his wife, because he, Moore, was concerned about Coretta's postnatal condition—most newspapers concentrated their skepticism on the least authoritative party: Coretta. Reports tended to portray her as an anxious new mother who may have confused her White House fantasies with reality. She bore the brunt of condescension even though her version of the episode was closest to the truth. In Washington, the *Star* dismissed her entire story in a lead editorial entitled "Just a Bit Phony."

General press reaction to the Birmingham campaign was no more favorable. *Time* called it a "poorly timed protest": "To many Birmingham Negroes, King's drive inflamed tensions at a time when the city seemed to be making some progress, however small, in race relations." A Washington *Post* editorial attacked King's Birmingham strategy as one of "doubtful utility," and speculated that it was "prompted more by leadership rivalry than by the real need of the situation." *The New York Times,* while playing down President Kennedy's phone call to Coretta, devoted a great deal of space to a press conference in which Burke Marshall said the federal government had no authority to take action in Birmingham. By contrast, the *Times* was almost gushingly optimistic about Birmingham's prospects under its new mayor, Albert Boutwell, who was sworn in on April 15 as Clarence Jones was visiting King in jail. . . .

Martin Luther King Jr. leads a civil rights march.

In an editorial declaring that it did not expect enlightenment to come to Birmingham "overnight," the *Times* added that Martin Luther King "ought not to expect it either.". . .

King read these press reactions as fast as Clarence Jones could smuggle newspapers into his cell. They caused him the utmost dismay, especially since a diverse assortment of friends and enemies were using the same critical phrases almost interchangeably. King could have addressed his "Letter from Birmingham Jail" to almost any of these—to Mayor Boutwell or Burke Marshall or A.G. Gaston, to the Birmingham *News* or *The New York Times*. He gave no thought to secular targets, however, after he saw page 2 of the April 13 Birmingham *News*. There, beneath two photographs of him and Abernathy on their Good Friday march to jail, appeared a story headlined "White Clergymen Urge Local Negroes to Withdraw from Demonstrations." After attacking the Birmingham demonstrations as "unwise and untimely," and commending the news media and the police for "the calm manner in which these demonstrations have been handled," the clergymen invoked their religious authority against civil disobedience. "Just as we formerly pointed out that 'hatred and violence have no sanction in our religious and political traditions,'" they wrote, "we also point out that such actions as incite hatred and violence, however technically peaceful those actions may be, have not contributed to the resolution of our local problems. We do not believe that these days of new hope are days when extreme measures are justified in Birmingham."

The thirteen short paragraphs transfixed King. He was being rebuked on his own chosen ground. And these were liberal clergymen. Most of them had risked their reputations by criticizing Governor Wallace's "Segregation Forever!" inauguration speech in January. They were among the minority of white preachers who of late had admitted Andrew Young and other Negroes to specially roped off areas of their Sunday congregations. Yet to King, these preachers never had risked themselves for true morality through all the years when Shuttlesworth was being bombed, stabbed, and arrested, and even now could not make themselves state forthrightly what was just. Instead, they stood behind the injunction and the jailers to dismiss his spirit along with his body. King could not let it go. He sat down and begin scribbling around the margins of the newspaper. "Seldom, if ever, do I pause to answer criticism of my work and ideas," he began.

By the time Clarence Jones visited the jail again that Tuesday, King had pushed a wandering skein of ink into every vacant corner. He surprised Jones by pulling the newspaper surreptitiously out of his shirt. "I'm writing this letter," he said. "I want you to try to get it out, if you can." To Jones, the "letter" was an indistinct jumble of biblical phrases wrapped around pest control ads and garden club news. He regarded the surprise as a distraction from the stack of urgent business he had brought with him—legal questions about King's upcoming criminal trials, plus money problems, Belafonte and Kennedy reports, and a host of movement grievances assembled by Walker. Waving these away, King spent most of the visit showing a nonplussed Jones how to follow the arrows and loops from dead ends to new starts. "I'm not finished yet," King said. He borrowed a number of sheets of note paper from Jones, who left with a concealed newspaper and precious few answers for those awaiting King's dispositions at the Gaston Motel.

King wrote several scattered passages in response to the criticism that his demonstrations were "untimely." He told the white clergymen that "time is neutral," that waiting never produced inevitable progress, and that "we must use time creatively, and forever realize that the time is always ripe to do right." He feared that "the people of ill-will have used time much more effectively than the people of good will," and pointed out that Negroes already had waited more than three hundred years for justice. "I guess it is easy for those who have never felt the stinging darts of segregation to say, 'Wait.'" Then, in a sentence of more than three hundred words, he tried to convey to the white preachers a feeling of time built upon a different alignment of emotions:

> But when you have seen vicious mobs lynch your mothers and fathers at will and drown your sisters and brothers at whim; when you have seen hate-filled policemen curse, kick, brutalize and even kill your black brothers and sisters with impunity; when you see the vast majority of your twenty million Negro brothers smothering in an air-tight cage of poverty in the midst of an affluent society; when you suddenly find your tongue twisted and your speech stammering as you seek to explain to your six-year-old daughter why she can't go to the public amusement park that has just been advertised on television, and see tears welling up in her little eyes when she is told that Funtown is closed to colored children, and see the depressing clouds of inferiority begin to form in her little mental sky, and see her begin to distort her little personality by unconsciously developing a bitterness toward white people; when you have to concoct an answer for a five-year-old son asking in agonizing pathos: "Daddy, why do white people treat colored people so mean?"; when you take a cross-country drive and find it necessary to sleep night after night in the uncomfortable corners of your automobile because no motel will accept you; when you are humiliated day in and day out by nagging signs reading "white" and "colored"; when your first name becomes "nigger" and your middle name becomes "boy" (however old you are) and your last name becomes "John," and when your wife and mother are never given the respected title "Mrs."; when you are harried by day and

haunted by night by the fact that you are a Negro, living constantly at a
tip-toe stance, never quite knowing what to expect next, and plagued
with inner fears and outer resentments; when you are forever fighting a
degenerating sense of "nobodiness"; then you will understand why we
find it difficult to wait.

King assumed a multitude of perspectives, often changing voice
from one phrase to the next. He expressed empathy with the lives of
millions over eons, and with the life of a particular child at a single
moment. He tried to look not only at white preachers through the
eyes of Negroes, but also at Negroes through the eyes of white
preachers ("The Negro has many pent-up resentments and latent frustrations. . . . So let him march sometime, let him have his prayer pil-
grimages"). To the white preachers, he presented himself variously as
a "haunted," suffering Negro ("What else is there to do when you are
alone for days in the dull monotony of a narrow jail cell other than
write long letters, think strange thoughts, and pray long prayers?"), a
pontificator ("Injustice anywhere is a threat to justice everywhere"), a
supplicant ("I hope, sirs, you can understand . . ."), and a fellow bigshot
("If I sought to answer all of the criticisms that cross my desk, my secretaries would be engaged in little else"). He spoke also as a teacher:
"How does one determine when a law is just or unjust? . . . To put
it in the terms of Saint Thomas Aquinas, an unjust law is a human
law that is not rooted in eternal and natural law. . . . All segregation
statutes are unjust because segregation distorts the soul and damages
the personality. . . . Let me give another explanation . . ." And he
spoke as a gracious fellow student, seeking common ground: "You
are exactly right in your call for negotiation . . . I am not unmindful
of the fact that each of you has taken some significant stands on this
issue."

By degrees, King established a kind of universal voice, beyond
time, beyond race. As both humble prisoner and mighty prophet, as
father, harried traveler, and cornered leader, he projected a character of nearly unassailable breadth. When he reached the heart of his
case, he adopted an authentic tone of intimacy toward the very targets of his wrath—toward men who had condemned him without
mentioning his name. Almost whispering on the page, he presented
his most scathing accusations as a confession:

> I must make two honest confessions to you, my Christian and Jewish
> brothers. First, I must confess that over the last few years I have been
> gravely disappointed with the white moderate. I have almost reached the
> regrettable conclusion that the Negro's great stumbling block is not the
> White Citizen's Council-er or the Ku Klux Klanner, but the white mod-
> erate who is more devoted to "order" than to justice, who prefers a neg-
> ative peace which is the absence of tension to a positive peace which is
> the presence of justice, who constantly says "I agree with you in the goal

you seek, but I can't agree with your methods of direct action," who paternalistically believes that he can set the timetable for another man's freedom . . .

Back at the Gaston Motel, deciphering what he called King's "chicken-scratch handwriting," Wyatt Walker became visibly excited by these passages. "His cup has really run over with those white preachers!" Walker exclaimed. Long frustrated by what seemed to him King's excessive forbearance, Walker thrilled to see such stinging wrath let loose. He knew that the history of the early Christian church made jail the appropriate setting for spiritual judgments— that buried within most religious Americans was an inchoate belief in persecuted spirituality as the natural price of their faith. Here was the early church reincarnate, with King rebuking the empire for its hatred, for its fearful defense of worldly attachments. For this, Walker put aside his clipboard. Long into the night, he dictated King's words to his secretary for typing. . . . [A typed version of this letter was smuggled back to King in his jail cell.]

"I need more paper," King told Clarence Jones. Sometimes directly, and sometimes with the clandestine help of an old Negro trusty in the jail, he exchanged the new handwritten original for the typed draft. By then the smuggling relay was exasperating Jones, for whom the letter was a toothless appeal to white clergymen who did not matter. But he saw the letter-writing as a mental health exercise for King. "I figured he was entitled to it—you know, a man in jail," Jones later recalled. "But Lord have mercy, I thought he had lost his perspective." Among the few business decisions Jones managed to wrest from King was an order to evict Hosea Williams from the Gaston Motel. Williams had responded to King's request for help by driving over from Savannah with a carload of assistants, who were running up a motel bill on the SCLC's tab. Walker found this not only expensive but unseemly, as the outside staff people far outnumbered the Birmingham volunteers going to jail every day. King agreed.

The two confessions filled the second half of what turned out to be a twenty-page letter. At first King formally denounced the white preachers for their shortcomings, as though speaking from a pulpit. "I have heard numerous religious leaders of the South call upon their worshippers to comply with a desegregation decision because it is the *law*," he wrote, "but I have longed to hear white ministers say, 'follow this decree because integration is morally *right* and the Negro is your brother.'" As he continued with his usual themes on the failures of the church, his wrath turned slowly into a lament: "I have wept over the laxity of the church. But be assured that my tears have been tears of love." In supreme irony, the prisoner in the hole mourned over the most respectable clergymen in Alabama as lost sheep who were unable to find the most obvious tenets of their faith.

"Maybe again, I have been too optimistic," King added, as though it may have been folly to expect better. ". . . Maybe I must turn my faith to the inner spiritual church, the church within the church, as the true *ecclesia* and the hope of the world." Even if the prelates excluded themselves and all their authority from the cause of justice, King said he would not despair, because for him the inner church was a stream of belief intermingled with the religious core of the American creed. If all men were created equal, then all were brothers and sisters, and these fundamental beliefs tilted history toward the affirming conclusion that the universe was on the side of justice. "We will reach the goal of freedom in Birmingham and all over the nation," wrote King, "because the goal of America is freedom. . . . If the inexpressible cruelties of slavery could not stop us, the opposition we now face will surely fail. We will win our freedom because the sacred heritage of our nation and the eternal will of God are embodied in our echoing demands."

In this letter, as in his sermons, King pulled back from an initial peroration. Almost as an aside, he mentioned the part of the Carpenter statement that expressed thanks to the Birmingham authorities for downplaying the demonstrations with muffling restraint. "I don't believe you would so quickly commend the policemen if you would observe their ugly and inhuman treatment of Negroes here in the city jail," King wrote. Conceding that the police had performed with professional discipline in public, King raised the question he thought should have occurred to the white preachers. "But for what purpose?" he asked them, and he answered his own question: "To preserve the evil system of segregation." For all his nonviolent preaching about how it was wrong to use immoral means to attain moral ends, King wrote, "it is just as wrong, or even more so, to use moral means to preserve immoral ends." He quoted [British poet] T.S. Eliot to that effect.

Then he returned soulfully to his lament. "I wish you had commended the Negro sit-inners and demonstrators of Birmingham for their sublime courage, their willingness to suffer and their amazing discipline in the midst of the most inhuman provocation," he wrote. "One day the South will recognize its real heroes. . . . One day the South will know that when these disinherited children of God sat down at lunch counters, they were in reality standing up for the best in the American dream and the most sacred values in our Judeo-Christian heritage, and thusly, carrying our whole nation back to those great wells of democracy which were dug deep by the founding fathers."

Late at night, an exhausted Willie Pearl Mackey literally fell asleep over her typewriter. Failing to revive her, Wyatt Walker lifted his secretary by the arms, placed her in another chair, and sat down at the typewriter himself. Against his sharply defined sense of ex-

THE REVOLT AGAINST HEGEMONY, 1960–1980   **279**

ecutive hierarchy, only the rarest emergency could compel the descent into clerical duty, but this time Walker pecked to the end. He could not bear to leave undone so exquisite a blend of New Testament grace and Old Testament wrath. Near his closing, King groped consciously toward the mixture. "If I have said anything in this letter that is an overstatement of the truth and is indicative of an unreasonable impatience, I beg you to forgive me," he wrote to Bishop Carpenter and the others. "If I have said anything in this letter that is an understatement of the truth and is indicative of my having a patience that makes me patient with anything less than brotherhood, I beg God to forgive me."

The "Letter from Birmingham Jail" did not spring quickly to acclaim. It remained essentially a private communication for some time, in spite of Wyatt Walker's labors to attract the attention of the passing world. Its Gandhian themes did impress some of James Lawson's contacts, who offered to publish the letter in the June issue of *Friends,* the Quaker journal, but ordinary reporters saw no news in what appeared to be an especially long-winded King sermon. Not a single mention of the letter reached white or Negro news media for a month. In hindsight, it appeared that King had rescued the beleaguered Birmingham movement with his pen, but the reverse was true: unexpected miracles of the Birmingham movement later transformed King's letter from a silent cry of desperate hope to a famous pronouncement of moral triumph.

"Gotta Be This or That": The End of Colonialism

Raymond F. Betts

The 1950s and early 1960s were a period of liberation not only for African Americans but also for millions of Asians and Africans living in European colonies. World War II had weakened the European powers' hold on their overseas empires, and the postwar awareness among many Europeans and Americans that nonwhite peoples around the globe had a right to control their own destiny helped undermine the legitimacy of colonialism. When the colonies gained their freedom, political power almost always passed to the educated nonwhite men (and a few women) who had led the independence movements and impatiently awaited the day when they could fill the bureaucratic positions of the departing white colonial officials.

Particularly in Africa, the experience of the former colonies that gained their independence in the mid–twentieth century has often been unhappy. American historian Raymond F. Betts, a lifelong student of imperialism and colonialism, analyzes why this has been so in the excerpt that follows from his recent book *Decolonization*.

There was one particular resplendent moment in the early years of decolonization. It occurred on March 6, 1957, when Ghana obtained its independence. At one minute after midnight the Union Jack was lowered and the red, green, and gold flag of Ghana raised.

Later, at the official ceremonies during the bright light of day, the Duchess of Kent, representing Queen Elizabeth, declared: "My government in the United Kingdom have ceased from today to have any authority in Ghana." Kwame Nkrumah, new prime minister, responded: "We part from the former imperial power." Two thousand official representatives from all over the world attended the lavish independence day celebrations. In the evening, on the marbled floor of the new State House, the Duchess and the Prime Minister briefly danced together to the song, "Gotta Be This or That."

The general assumption of all there gathered was that it "gotta be this": independence, improvement, beneficial rule for all. Here was to be a "revolution of expectations," a popular phrase of the period describing the high hopes for a new postcolonial order. Nkrumah gave rhetorical emphasis to this change through his use of the traditional nautical metaphor by which he concluded his autobiography, published in the year of independence:

> And I, as I proudly stand on the bridge of that lone vessel as she confidently sets sail, I raise a hand to shade my eyes from the glaring African sun and scan the horizon. There is so much more beyond.

Within nine years the Nkrumah government was shipwrecked, overthrown as inefficient, corrupt, and authoritarian. The experience of Ghana was neither unique nor unusual. Throughout Africa and much of Asia in the next two decades, the final ones of decolonization, the cultural landscape was bleak. Disorder and oppression, the military *coup d'état* and dictatorship were frequent, almost commonplace. Human rights were violated and massive repressive measures were not unusual. Poverty and urban unemployment increased. Most economies performed poorly and infrastructure crumbled, with unrepaired roads seemingly an endemic condition.

The notable exceptions to this state of affairs were India, where democracy performed well, even if the economy did not; and the "four little dragons" (also called the "gang of four") of Singapore, Hong Kong, Taiwan, and Korea, where the economies functioned superbly even though the political systems were not particularly commendable, Hong Kong perhaps excepted.

Elsewhere, "instability" became the generic term to describe this set of unfavorable conditions so widespread throughout the former colonial world. The new states seemed to have both inherited the wind and been bequeathed the imperial debris. They were ill prepared for the onrush of problems from without and constrained by the colonial structures and institutions found within. Unlike the first decolonized country of the late eighteenth century, the United States, those decolonized countries of the late twentieth century were not and could not pretend to be part of a "new world."

Nkrumah's metaphor of the ship of state was significant because it was anachronistic: there was no horizon toward which to sail; there was no lonely sea to cross. The world was, quite simply, filled up. The postcolonial responsibility was essentially to undo the clutter: crowded cities, unemployment, trade imbalance, inefficient bureaucracies, insufficient educational establishments. And yet all such needful activities were largely constrained or twisted by a global economic system itself undergoing major change.

The growth period of the international economy took place in the two decades in which decolonization occurred and ended abruptly with the oil crisis of 1973 when the international cartel OPEC (Organization of Petroleum Exporting Countries) both raised prices and curtailed production, thus creating an energy shortage which most adversely affected the new postcolonial countries that had based the forward movement of their own economic engines on that fuel. The condition was further aggravated by the fall in prices for other raw materials and for agricultural products, the mainstay of so many of the economies of these countries, economies that were in effect still colonial in nature. Perhaps more significant was the emergence of a global agricultural economy. Developed nations, the United States in particular, were exporting grain in large quantities to the former colonial regions, which demanded wheat, for instance, because of changes in diet and nutrition.

Such a generalization was not true, however, for Sub-Saharan Africa where chronic food shortage was a major concern. The montage of causes there produced a gloomy picture. With soils often too poor to allow any appreciable increase in agricultural output, with population growth resulting from improved medical conditions and better hygiene, with population shifts to urban areas reducing the rural labor supply, with such urban development requiring more food, and with governmental policy directed to export cash crops (bananas and cocoa, among the most obvious), Sub-Saharan Africa was grey with despair.

Given the range of economic disparity existing among nations in the postcolonial era, Western analysts considered the need to redivide the world into horizontal components of economic success—or lack thereof. Designations of "rich" and "poor" nations or "industrial" and "non-industrial" no longer sufficed. There were now four categories: "developed nations," "newly developing nations," "less developed nations," and "least developed nations"—this last category implying a state of economic hopelessness.

Such divisions were only delineated in the last twenty years when global experts began to realize that international relations were no longer dominantly political but were heavily influenced by economic issues. The old eighteenth-century term "political economy" was reinvented to describe the new importance of international trade and commercial arrangements, the new role of the state in fostering research and the creation of new industries, the new significance of multinational corporations as "actors" on the world stage.

This brief assessment of a very complicated and unstable world condition is meant to stand as a preface to the developments required of and desired by the former colonial territories, now standing as independent states.

What is now obvious, if it was not then seen in the afterglow of the setting imperial sun, is that most of the first generation of political leaders were not up to the new global tasks thrust upon them. These people and their governmental cohorts were not formally trained nor disposed by experience to be managers or technocrats. They were trained in what are called the "liberal professions"—law, education, and journalism—with some schooled in medicine as well. Their supporters also ranged along a narrow occupational spectrum, not for the most part professional. This group included the petty bourgeoisie (the famous "market women" of Ghana, for instance) and guerrilla fighters. Few if any in high government office were schooled or experienced in the field of international finance or commerce. There were no local equivalents of the Eurocrats, that new breed of technocrats who viewed industry beyond national boundaries, and of whom Jean Monnet, instrumental in forming the European Coal and Steel Community in 1951, is always selected as exemplary.

The power elite in the newly emerging states was, for its time, unusually one-dimensional, skilled in most aspects of political behavior and tactics. Moreover, it treated national and international affairs as continuing matters of diplomacy and ideology, considered essentially as postcolonial and not post-modern. Moreover, the so-called political base upon which the new political power rested was limited in scope and unstable at best. The well-known and much described Western bourgeoisie which both motivated and controlled the economies of the "developed" nations was nearly non-existent in most of the former colonies. Its closest analogue was an administrative middle class, its revenue not generated but derived, its members salaried bureaucrats. Well-developed and organized labor forces were another exception; and the new state apparatus often sought to eliminate or subsume under state control such organizations, as indeed quickly happened in Ghana where the labor movement was both broken and alienated when a strike in 1961 was forcibly ended by the government. In Tanganyika the ruling party TANU (Tanganyika African National Union) abolished the labor union and set in place its own state-controlled apparatus.

Moreover, the lack of radical or revolutionary change in colonially predetermined institutions and structures was a major consideration. With the possible exception of Ho Chi Minh's Vietnam the state structure and the administrative form remained essentially what they had been. The national state, cynics would remark, was only the colony fitted out with a new flag. (The frequently employed expression was "flag sovereignty.") The obvious changes were lateral moves, as Asians and Africans went from the outside to the inside, as the offices once held by Europeans as colonial administrators became those held by Asians and Africans as state ministers. [The radical Algerian writer] Frantz Fanon denounced this condition in *The Wretched of the Earth:* "The native bourgeoisie that comes to power uses its class aggressiveness to corner the positions formerly kept by foreigners." Fanon's fear was that the new nationalism might be as self-serving as had been the old colonialism.

Politically alert, economically uncertain, the new leadership doubly depended on Europeans and Americans: first, for financial assistance in realizing development plans; and, second, for the technological advice to realize them. What truly confounded the issue was obvious: economic growth was preceding economic development. To generate new financial resources for the state, the increase of "colonial" produce was encouraged, not diversification of the economy or, more pressingly, the guarantee of sufficient crops to meet the needs of national consumption. (In Nigeria, for instance, in the first decade after independence, agricultural production decreased by 2 per cent from its level in the last year of colonial rule. The situation of Ghana was little better: an increase of 0.3 per cent in the first postcolonial decade was dismally followed by a 3.1 per cent decrease in the second decade.) The single-crop economy of colonial days thus continued. The bananas of the Ivory Coast, the tea of Sri Lanka (formerly Ceylon), the peanuts of Senegal increased in number of tons yielded but prices did not increase commensurately. One of the most commented on examples was of cocoa in Ghana where the tonnage increased from 350,000 in 1960 to 495,000 in 1965 with little appreciable increase in farmers' incomes. This seeming disparity of more produced and little more gained resulted from a decline in world market prices for most raw materials in the 1960s and 1970s and because of the continuing foreign control of these raw materials by profit-seeking corporations based in Europe or America.

Growth also inhibited where it did not preclude development. The lack of what has been called "technology transfer" was significant. In Ghana at the time of independence when cocoa was the major export product, there was only one Ghanaian horticulturalist. In the Belgian Congo at the time of independence, there were not even ten Africans with university degrees and fewer than 200,000 individuals who had finished high school. Technological positions were retained or assumed by Europeans and, now, by Americans as well. Urban planners, economists, and engineers carried their thoughts and their baggage to the Third World countries, while American universities established centers of research abroad to assist with the multifaceted process called "modernization."

Few of the new national leaders were prepared for or predisposed to careful consideration of the problems that independence brought. Almost all of these individuals, the "founding fathers" of their nations, fared poorly at their new-found tasks. Their experience had been principally colonial and acquired in three phases. First, these later leaders stood as young reformers or opponents of the colonial system, primarily from the position of being students within it and writers of tracts, articles, and books about or against it. Second, they assumed positions of leadership of movements or parties seeking reform or demanding independence. Those in the latter category were often deemed subversive by the colonial authorities and were therefore frequently imprisoned. This group, consisting of individuals as geographically diverse as Nehru of India, Ben Bella of Algeria, and Nkrumah of the Gold Coast (Ghana), formed a cohort described as "prison graduates." Of this number, the most unusual in sentence received and spirit maintained is Nelson Mandela, who became president of the Republic of South Africa. Mandela was imprisoned from 1962 to 1991 and yet emerged from this horrendous experience to become the most respected, effective, and conciliatory of the modern African leaders. Third, members of this political cohort were tolerated, allowed, or even encouraged as they sought national independence, working within the colonial system in order to eliminate it. There is widespread agreement, for instance, that the reason why the transition of power in Ghana went so smoothly was the cooperation and friendship established between the last British governor of the colony, Charles Arden-Clarke, and Kwame Nkrumah.

In one lifetime the cycle of political devolution occurred. Or, better, between youth and middle age, the new national leaders had participated in major historic change. As men in their forties and fifties, they assumed the authority they had long struggled to have, as in the case of Ho Chi Minh; or they were moved by the currents of the time from cooperative outsider to independent leader. One instance of this latter coincidence of biography and nationhood may serve to make the point. President Leopold Sedar Senghor of Senegal, born in 1906, was a university student in Paris in the 1920s. He there encountered African-Americans like the poet Langston Hughes who were celebrating the Harlem Renaissance, the literary movement that, it might be said, gave lyrical voice to the phrase coined by Marcus Garvey, "Black is beautiful." In the late 1930s Senghor became a literature teacher at the prestigious Lycée Louis le Grand in Paris; he then served as a soldier in the French army (and was taken as a prisoner of war) in 1939–40. Elected after the war as a representative from Senegal to the French National Assembly, he served as one of the grammarians for the Constitution of the Fourth Republic and soon acquired the title and office of minister in the [French] government of Premier Edgar Faure, 1955–6. Senghor was then president of Senegal from 1960 to 1980. His productive lifetime spanned the era of decolonization, the fifty years between the 1920s and the 1970s.

Whatever their experience and intentions, each of the leaders in Senghor's political class was confronted with the difficulty of structuring new political institutions, of finding means to create a sense of national unity, and of assuring the economic betterment of the country. The task was formidable, the results too often short of the many desires and demands voiced by diverse segments of the population. Illiteracy and venality compounded the national situation. Obi Okonkwo, the hero of [Nigerian writer] Chinua Achebe's novel *No Longer at Ease,* is a bright, well-trained idealist who sees in Nigeria a country lost in ignorance and corruption, hence unlikely to achieve democracy. And yet he concludes with some hope, "England was once like this."

The truth of his statement cannot be questioned. However, it was the striking and widely publicized contrast between the rhetoric of independence and the occurrence of corruption that made the matter so politically debilitating in the postcolonial situation. Nkrumah was not the only leader to fall over such an issue. Unlike Senghor, who voluntarily left the office of president, many of the others were overthrown or ousted, their policies and practices found to be inadequate, corrupt, or anti-democratic. In round numbers and raw figures, some 75 *coups d'état,* mostly military in nature, occurred in the former colonial world in the first three decades of independence. Ghana underwent three between 1966 and 1972; Nigeria, two in 1966 alone. Military leaders appeared in Indonesia and the Philippines, in Algeria and Zaire, these here mentioned to suggest the geographical range of the phenomenon.

Earlier analyzed as a sign of grave political instability and a gross failure of democratic institutions—most obviously, the "Westminster system," or the form of parliamentary government which the British proudly listed as their gift to the new nations—more recent research suggests that military rule resulted because the army, as one of the few well-organized, well-trained, and nationwide groups, could serve as "guardian," "broker," or "gatekeeper," could attempt to bring back on course errant civilian governments that had failed in creating a sense of unity, that had failed to achieve economic betterment.

However, the record of military leadership became one of military dictatorship, a condition that was prominent for two decades. The 1970s and 1980s were the years of rule by those called the "Big Men": authoritarian, ruthless, self-serving. Among this substantial group three stand out vividly. The first was Idi Amin who terrorized the population of Uganda as its ruler from 1971 to 1979, and who brutally forced out the Indian population of the country and exterminated his political opposition. The second was Emperor Bokassa I (formerly a military officer named Jean Bedel Bokasso) who had been president of the Central

African Republic since 1965 but who, rather in imitation of Napoleon, took the title of emperor in 1976 and indulged in an elaborate coronation ceremony in 1977 that has been estimated to have cost one-quarter of the nation's annual income. He was finally overthrown on September 21, 1979, after his regime killed some 100 schoolchildren who were protesting about the price of school uniforms that Bokassa had both designed and demanded must be worn. The third figure, the longest in power and most devastating in effect, was Mobutu Sese Seketo, who as president of the country he named Zaire from 1965 until 1997 oppressed his people, imprisoned his opposition, and drained the nation of its wealth, with his personal financial worth estimated in billions of dollars. Zaire, now the Democratic Republic of the Congo, was the richest African nation in terms of natural resources. At the end of Mobutu's reign, its population was one of the poorest.

However, it was the economic condition, more than any other factor, that has aggravated the political situation and has denied the hopes of those who saw decolonization as the opening of a new era. With the notable exceptions of the "four little dragons," those economically successful small states that have become major industrial and financial powers with a high standard of living, grouped along the Pacific Rim where geographical location has been a major advantage, the new nations did not significantly improve themselves over their previous colonial situation in the first two decades of independence. In the decade of the 1990s, however, Malaysia and India have moved dramatically forward in the field of computer technology, while part of Sub-Saharan Africa has also enjoyed improvement with increased private investment and new economic leadership.

In explanation of the lack of better economic performance after independence, the theory of "neo-colonialism" was widely posited. One of the most popular, if not original, explanations of this condition was Kwame Nkrumah's book *Neo-colonialism, The Last Stage of Imperialism* (1965). Just as Lenin "updated" Marx to explain the persistence of capitalism, so Nkrumah "updated" Lenin to explain the persistence of imperialism in a new guise. As he states: "The result of neo-colonialism is that foreign capital is used for the exploitation rather than for the development of the less developed parts of the world." Less blatant, more subtle, and therefore all the more pernicious than its predecessor colonialism, neo-colonialism, goes the argument, locks the former colonial territories into positions of client states of the major industrial-capitalist powers. Nkrumah singles out the United States as "the very citadel of neo-colonialism." The control that it maintains is assured through capital loans, domination of the world market and international aid. Nkrumah protests this condition, as his book indicates; and his turn to the political left in the last years of his administration is in part a result of his perceptions.

On a broader scale, imperialism and colonialism have been seen as functions of a "world capitalist system" that has developed and expanded until it reaches around the world and into every nation. In such an analysis the older core-periphery argument first used by the imperialists themselves to explain global expansion is now redesigned as the template of a global economic theory. In a bitter analysis of this condition cast in terms of development and underdevelopment, the Guyanese scholar Walter Rodney explained, as the title of his book states, *How Europe Underdeveloped Africa* (1972). "Imperialism" was for him nothing other than "the extended capitalist system, which for many years embraced the whole world." It was through this economic exploitation that the Western nations, mindful of their own position of economic advantage and needful of the raw materials of Africa, "underdeveloped" that continent, set it back economically by prohibiting its healthy and beneficial growth.

In all too many nation states newly emerged from their colonial status, sovereignty in principle has not allowed independence of action in fact. The geography of the situation and the current condition of the global economy seem to have prohibited this attainment, even if the condition does not result from direct conspiracy, as some of the critics would have it.

In current global economic analysis, arguments such as those proposed by Nkrumah and Rodney have only historical significance; they are otherwise irrelevant. The contemporary situation is one now described as "post neo-colonialism." Not the former colonial conditions but the current global ones configure and control the world. Most obviously, the NICs ("newly industrializing countries"), of which Singapore and Korea seem the most striking, have assumed a place in the world market vaster than their physical size would seem to allow. With high gross income products and an ever-increasing individual standard of living, these small states fall into the category that was once labeled "Western." Conversely, many areas of the world exploited by the "West" in its imperialist era are now without much interest to European or American capitalists. Much of Sub-Saharan Africa has been "marginalized," deprived both of the assistance and investment that had rushed in during the 1970s. Visiting South Africa in March 1997, the wife of the president of the United States, Hillary Clinton, acknowledged this problem when she stated that "we have to rethink that engagement [formed by the Cold War and oppressive African regimes] and determine what the United States can do to help countries like South Africa and others . . . to move toward democracy and self-sufficiency."

Whatever that thinking may be, and wherever considered, it will not follow the line of progress that was so praised as the previous century closed. Today's global pattern is seen, if seen at all, rather like a vast game of cat's cradle: the linear combinations of social and economic development, of transnational activities, are being reworked to form new and inconstant designs. The position of the United States as the world's chief debtor nation is some proof of this change, and so is the remarkable increase in the export trade from China in the last ten years. The remarkable success of the Korean automobile and electronics industries would be still another, as would be the shift in trade balance between the United States and Mexico, which now favors Mexico.

From this newly reworked pattern of global political and economic power and position, no simple conclusion is possible. Only this much is certain: imperialism and colonialism as ideologies justifying policies and institutions designed to ensure economic advantage through imposed political control are henceforth historical phenomena. In this sense, decolonization is complete.

Standing as proof of a new era and proclaimed as a sign of the advent of the shift of world power to Asia are the Petronas Towers in Kuala Lumpur, Malaysia. Completed in 1997, these twin towers stand at 1,483 feet each. They are the tallest buildings in the world and expressive of new corporate wealth, a measure of Malaysia's recent industrial success, particularly as the principal exporter of computer semiconductors. The buildings, part of a new urban complex under construction, are situated on the grounds of the old Selangor Turf Club which, as part of the British colonial legacy, raced thoroughbred horses until 1992, when the sound of hooves was replaced by that of bulldozers; when the not-so-old in this part of the world noisily gave way to the very new.

Cultural Revolution Convulses China

Jonathan D. Spence

China's revolution did not end with Mao Zedong's proclamation of the People's Republic in 1949. Mao established a Soviet-style regime with a rigid party-run dictatorship, which pursued a policy of rapid industrialization. Although great strides were made, Mao and many of the senior Communist leaders around him were not satisfied—in part, because the Soviet government feared and distrusted its giant neighbor and did much less than it could have to help. In 1958, during a widening political rift with the Soviet Union, Mao launched his "Great Leap Forward," a crash policy of speeding up industrialization through such draconian means as herding the peasants into huge "communes" and attempting to make steel in primitive rural blast furnaces. The result was widespread disruption, misery, and starvation, without making much significant progress toward a modern industrial society. By the early 1960s, Mao had to pull back, and more moderate leaders came to the fore.

But the aging revolutionary still longed to recapture the spirit of his peasant movement of the 1920s and 1930s. China's educated young people also chafed at the sight of older, cautious bureaucrats dominating the Communist Party and controlling opportunities for advancement and excitement. In the People's Liberation Army (PLA, the successor to the peasant army that had fought the Japanese and conquered Chiang Kai-shek's Nationalists), Mao's handpicked leader, Lin Biao, fanned enthusiasm for a renewed revolutionary struggle. In 1966, these forces

surged together to begin, with Mao's encouragement, a "cultural revolution" whose slogan was to purge China of everything "old" and hide-
bound. Before the Cultural Revolution ran its course about 1969 and
was reined in by more moderate elements in the PLA, China was torn
by a massive uprising of its ultraradical youth.

Yale University historian Jonathan D. Spence has written a massive
and eloquent history entitled *The Search for Modern China*. In the excerpt from this book that follows, Spence discusses the beginnings of
the Cultural Revolution—certainly the most disruptive of the great upheavals of the 1960s, dwarfing in its intensity and destructiveness anything that happened in the Western world during that tumultuous
decade. At the point where this excerpt takes up the tale, Chinese radicals are reacting to the published works of a respected Chinese intellectual, Wu Han, who used examples drawn from Chinese history to
criticize abusive rulers—implicitly, Mao himself.

So were the lines at last drawn, beyond effective mediation, for
the cataclysmic central phase of what Mao and his supporters
called the Great Proletarian Cultural Revolution. This movement defies simple classification, for embedded within it were many impulses at once feeding and impeding each other. There was Mao Zedong's view that the Chinese revolution was losing impetus because
of party conservatism and the lethargy of the huge and cumbrous bureaucracy, which had lost its ability to make speedy or innovative
decisions. Mao declared that many party bureaucrats "were taking
the capitalist road" even as they mouthed the slogans of socialism.
There were, too, Mao's sense of his advancing age—he was now
seventy-three—and his concern that his senior colleagues were seeking to shunt him aside. There were straightforward elements of factional struggle pitting Jiang Qing and the Shanghai radicals against
those in the Peking [Beijing] cultural bureaucracy who wanted to
maintain their own power bases. There were the political strategies
of those who diverged sharply with Mao over the pace and direction
of change, among whom were such veteran Communists at the apex
of the government as [President] Liu Shaoqi, Deng Xiaoping, Chen
Yun, and Peng Zhen. There were the personal political ambitions of
Lin Biao and those who supported him in his efforts to expand the
role of the army into politics, and make the PLA a centerpiece of
cultural change.

These factional fires were fueled by the anger of students frustrated
over policies that kept them off the paths of political advancement because the students had the ill fortune to be born to parents who had
had connections with the Guomindang [the Nationalist Party of Chi-

ang Kai-shek], the landlords, or the capitalist "exploiters" of the old regime and were therefore classified as "bad" elements by the CCP [Chinese Communist Party]. There were as well millions of disgruntled urban youths who had been relocated to the countryside during the party campaigns of earlier years, or in line with the plans of Chen Yun and others to save the cost to the state of providing subsidized grain supplies for such city residents. There were those, within the largest cities, who were denied access to the tiny number of elite schools that had become, in effect, "prep schools" for the children of influential party cadres. (With the shortage of colleges in China, and the thickets of complex entrance examinations that still stood in the way to them, only education in this handful of schools could assure access to higher education.) And finally there were those who felt that party positions were monopolized by the uneducated rural cadres of Mao's former peasant guerrilla days, and that these people should now be eased out to make way for newer, more educated recruits.

In the late spring and summer of 1966, events moved to a swift yet unpredictable climax. In May the report of the Group of Five, calling for caution in cultural reform, was repudiated by the Central Committee [of the Communist Party]—clearly at Mao's urging—and a purge of the cultural bureaucracy commenced. Peng Zhen was ousted, other key figures in the Ministry of Culture removed, and attacks launched against the writers of the Three-Family Village articles and against Wu Han and his family.* The protests and criticisms spread throughout China's university system after Nie Yuanzi, a radical philosophy professor at Peking University, wrote a large wall poster attacking the administration of her university. Attempts by Deng Xiaoping, Liu Shaoqi, and others to send "work teams" onto the campuses to quell the disturbances backfired as more and more radicals among faculty and students turned on party members. Turmoil spread swiftly to the Peking high schools, and squads of students were issued arm bands by the Cultural Revolution radicals declaring them to be "Red Guards"—the vanguard of the new revolutionary upheaval.

To underscore his vigor and health, Mao Zedong took a July swim in the Yangzi River near Wuhan, where the 1911 revolution had first erupted. The swim was given euphoric coverage in the party press, which presented it as an event of huge significance to the Chinese people. Back in Peking, Mao heated up the revolutionary rhetoric even further by declaring that Professor Nie's "big character poster" was "the declaration of the Paris Commune of the sixties of the twentieth century; its significance far surpasses that of the Paris commune." The Paris Commune of 1871, about which Marx had written

* Wu Han died in 1969 of illness following the brutal treatment to which he was subjected.

with great passion, had been considered a pinnacle of spontaneous socialist insurrection and organization in Western history. Now Mao was claiming that China would exceed it. Of course there would be hostile forces, he noted, just as there had been in France. "Who are against the great Cultural Revolution? American imperialism, Russian revisionism, Japanese revisionism, and the reactionaries." But China would "depend on the masses, trust the masses, and fight to the end."

In early August 1966, the Central Committee issued a directive of sixteen points on the Cultural Revolution, calling for vigilance against those who would try to subvert the revolution from within. Still there were enough cooler heads in office for a sentence to be inserted suggesting that debates "be conducted by reasoning, not by coercion or force," and that "special care" be taken of scientists and technical personnel. But as August drew on, Mao Zedong, from a stand atop the Tiananmen gate, entrance to the former Imperial Forbidden City in Peking, began to review gigantic parades of chanting Red Guards, all waving their copies of his little red book of quotations. Initially composed largely of students from the elite schools, the Red Guard ranks were now swelled by other disaffected and frustrated students, and by those from the provinces drawn by the revolutionary rhetoric and their reverence for Mao as father of the revolution. Lin Biao heightened the public euphoria with his own declarations. "Chairman Mao is the most outstanding leader of the proletariat in the present era and the greatest genius in the present era," Lin told a Red Guard rally on August 18. What Mao had done was to create "a Marxism-Leninism for remoulding the souls of the people." By the end of August, Lin had developed a formulaic description of Mao as "our great teacher, great leader, great supreme commander and great helmsman" that became standard usage in China.

In the autumn and winter of 1966, the struggles grew deeper and more bitter, the destruction and loss of life more terrible. With all schools and colleges closed for the staging of revolutionary struggle, millions of the young were encouraged by the Cultural Revolution's leaders to demolish the old buildings, temples, and art objects in their towns and villages, and to attack their teachers, school administrators, party leaders, and parents.

Under the direction of a small group of Mao's confidants, along with his wife Jiang Qing and other Shanghai radicals, the party was purged at higher and higher levels until both Liu Shaoqi and Deng Xiaoping were removed from their posts and subjected to mass criticism and humiliation, along with their families.

The leaders of the Cultural Revolution called for a comprehensive attack on the "four old" elements within Chinese society—old customs, old habits, old culture, and old thinking—but they left it to local Red Guard initiative to apply these terms. In practice what often happened was that after the simpler targets had been identified, Red Guards eager to prove their revolutionary integrity turned on anyone who tried to hold them in check, anyone who had had Western education or dealings with Western businessmen or missionaries, and all intellectuals who could be charged with "feudal" or "reactionary" modes of thinking. The techniques of public humiliation grew more and more complex and painful as the identified victims were forced to parade through the streets in dunce caps or with self-incriminatory placards around their necks, to declaim their public self-criticisms before great jeering crowds, and to stand for hours on end with backs agonizingly bent and arms outstretched in what was called "the airplane position."

With the euphoria, fear, excitement, and tension that gripped the country, violence grew apace. Thousands of intellectuals and others were beaten to death or died of their injuries. Countless others committed suicide, among them Lao She, the author of the novel *Cat Country*, which had spoken so eloquently in 1932 against the Chinese who turned on each other. Many of the suicides killed themselves only after futile attempts to avoid Red Guard harassment by destroying their own libraries and art collections. Thousands more were imprisoned, often in solitary confinement, for years. Millions were relocated to purify themselves through labor in the countryside.

The extent of this outpouring of violence, and the rage of the young Red Guards against their elders, suggest the real depths of frustration that now lay at the heart of Chinese society. The youth needed little urging from Mao to rise up against their parents, teachers, party cadres, and the elderly, and to perform countless acts of calculated sadism. For years the young had been called on to lead lives of revolutionary sacrifice, sexual restraint, and absolute obedience to the state, all under conditions of perpetual supervision. They were repressed, angry, and aware of their powerlessness. They eagerly seized on the order to throw off all restraint, and the natural targets were those who seemed responsible for their cramped lives. To them Mao stood above this fray, all-wise and all-knowing. The disasters of the Great Leap had never been widely publicized, and in any case could be attributed to inept bureaucrats or hostile Soviets and Americans. Mao spoke still for hope and freedom, and in the absence of any convincing counterclaims, the wild rhetoric about his powers was accepted as true.

Another explanation for the extent of this violence can be found in the nature of Chinese politics and personal manipulation over the past seventeen years. All Chinese were now enmeshed in a system that controlled people by assigning class labels to them, by making them totally dependent on the "bosses" of their particular units, and by habituating them to mass campaigns of terror and intimidation. Such a system bred both fear and compliance.

Embedded within this frenzied activism was a political agenda of great significance, what might be called a "purist egalitarianism" that echoed the values of the Paris Commune of 1871 so vividly evoked for China by Mao Zedong. This involved much more than the confiscation or destruction of private property: demands were heard now for the complete nationalization of all industrial enterprises, the abolition of all interest on deposits in the state banks, the eviction of all landlords from their own houses, the elimination of all private plots and a restrengthening of the commune system, and the ending of all traces of a private market economy—down to the poorest peasant selling a handful of vegetables from his wheelbarrow at the village corner.

The peak of this profoundly radical program came during the first month of 1967, in what has been termed the "January power seizure." Backed by the Cultural Revolutionary group in Peking, a variety of militant Red Guard organizations attempted to oust party incumbents and take over their organizations all over China. The campaign was triggered by New Year's Day editorials in the press that called for "worker-peasant" coalitions to "overthrow power holders factories, mines and rural areas," and urged these worker-peasant groups to ally with "revolutionary intellectuals" in the struggle. The Red Guards were told to view the Cultural Revolution as the struggle of one class to overthrow another, and to exempt no one in that struggle; unlike 1949, they were told, when the CCP had had to show some caution in taking power so as not to alienate the centrists and liberals, in 1967 "everything which does not fit the socialist system and proletarian dictatorship should be attacked."

The result was a bewildering situation in which varieties of radical groups, not coordinated by any central leadership, struggled with party leaders and with each other. The battles at the provincial level show this best. One seizure attempt, in Heilongjiang province, northern Manchuria, was led by a former opponent of the Great Leap Forward who now tried to prove his loyalty to Mao by showing his revolutionary fervor. In Shanxi, it was the vice-governor of the province who joined with Red Guards to oust the other party leaders. In Shandong, the second secretary of the Tianjin municipal committee worked with a member of the Shandong party committee to found a Provincial Revolutionary Committee. In Guizhou, it was the deputy political commissar of the province who allied with the Red Guards.

It was difficult in many such cases to tell if these were real or sham power struggles—whether "the masses" were really seizing power or whether party leaders were merely pretending to hand over power while in fact continuing to exercise all their old functions under loose Red Guard supervision. This latter was clearly the case in Guangdong province, where the first party secretary, Zhao Ziyang, handed over his seals to the "Red Flag faction," a loose federation of railway workers, demobilized soldiers, teachers, college and high-school students, and film-studio workers. Having made his gesture, Zhao and his staff continued to run the province.

The word *radical* was used in many ways at this time. In Shanghai, for instance, where the power seizure was defined as successful, it was the 500,000 strong Scarlet Red Guards, a workers' organization, who began by making the strongest demands for better wages, working conditions, and the right to leave their work and participate in "revolutionary experiences" without losing pay. Similar demands were launched by millions of other workers around China, from pedicab drivers to cooks, from street peddlers to train engineers. Workers on short-term contracts and other temporary laborers were especially vocal, often demanding permanent job status and awards of several years' back pay. But such actions, initially radical-seeming, were soon branded by leaders of the Cultural Revolution as "economism." The Scarlet Red Guards' stance was labeled "conservative" by other groups, such as the equally huge Shanghai Workers' General Headquarters, which claimed the radical label for themselves. During the last months of 1966, battling factions of both student and worker Red Guards had managed virtually to paralyze Shanghai: the shipping of goods on the wharves was completely disrupted; railway service was in chaos or, in some cases, stopped entirely when lines were cut; the city was jammed with millions of Red Guards, returnees, or fugitives from the countryside; and stores opened for shorter and shorter hours as food supplies fell to dangerously low levels. In this context, the January 1967 "radical" power seizure in Shanghai can also be seen as a successful attempt to prevent the workers from gaining truly independent power.

This stage of struggle began when one of Jiang Qing's closest allies, Zhang Chunqiao, traveled to Shanghai in early January 1967. After gaining control of the most influential newspapers and ordering the workers to return to their jobs, Zhang held a series of mass meetings and rallies to criticize and humiliate members of the Shanghai party leadership who were accused of "economism" for giving in to workers' demands for better pay. Joined by Yao Wenyuan (who had fired the first major shots against Wu Han the year before), Zhang used the PLA [People's Liberation Army] to restore order in the city and to develop the new slogan "Grasping Revolution and Promoting Production." While PLA troops guarded airfields, banks, freight terminals, and docks, student Red Guards were used in place of workers still refusing to return to their jobs.

Zhang and Yao, however, also had to fight militant student Red Guards who wished to maintain solidarity with the workers. In late January mass student groups held a struggle session against Zhang and Yao themselves, and also "arrested" the latter's main propaganda writers. Only in early February, with massive military support, was order restored to the liking of the Cultural Revolution leaders. On February 5, Zhang announced the formation of a new institution, the Shanghai People's Commune, which created a truly paradoxical situation. For under the guise of this most revolutionary sounding of titles, those who had so thoroughly purged their own party tried now to bolster their own positions as China's new leaders, and to force a return to obedience of the very students and workers who had sought to usher in a new age of freedom.

Chairman Mao Speaks

Mao Zedong

Alongside the heroes of the Cuban Revolution, Fidel Castro and Che Guevara, the most charismatic revolutionary figure of the second half of the twentieth century was China's Mao Zedong. Mao's accomplishments and (even more so) his pronouncements on revolutionary strategy and tactics were idealized all over the globe by young people dreaming of dramatic, convulsive change that would liberate themselves and raise their societies out of dull routine and social oppression. Shortly before the Cultural Revolution engulfed China, a small book with a flaming red cover was printed in Beijing that consisted of very short excerpts from Mao's writings and speeches. Called *Quotations from Chairman Mao Tsetung*, this so-called Little Red Book was brandished by millions of parading Chinese Red Guards, and in translation it was avidly read by hundreds of thousands of revolutionary enthusiasts throughout the world. It is impossible to understand either the fervor or the destructiveness of the Cultural Revolution without being acquainted with the ideas and the tone of these *Quotations*.

"Fewer and better troops and simpler administration." Talks, speeches, articles and resolutions should all be concise and to the point. Meetings also should not go on too long. . . .

Without the efforts of the Chinese Communist Party, without the Chinese Communists as the mainstay of the Chinese people, China can never achieve independence and liberation, or industrialization and the modernization of her agriculture. . . .

The Chinese Communist Party is the core of leadership of the

Excerpted from *Quotations from Chairman Mao Tsetung* (Peking: Foreign Languages Press, 1972).

whole Chinese people. Without this core, the cause of socialism cannot be victorious. . . .

A well-disciplined Party armed with the theory of Marxism-Leninism, using the method of self-criticism and linked with the masses of the people; an army under the leadership of such a Party; a united front of all revolutionary classes and all revolutionary groups under the leadership of such a Party—these are the three main weapons with which we have defeated the enemy. . . .

We must have faith in the masses and we must have faith in the Party. These are two cardinal principles. If we doubt these principles, we shall accomplish nothing. . . .

In class society everyone lives as a member of a particular class, and every kind of thinking, without exception, is stamped with the brand of a class. . . .

It is up to us to organize the people. As for the reactionaries in China, it is up to us to organize the people to overthrow them. Everything reactionary is the same; if you don't hit it, it won't fall. This is also like sweeping the floor; as a rule, where the broom does not reach, the dust will not vanish of itself. . . .

A revolution is not a dinner party, or writing an essay, or painting a picture, or doing embroidery; it cannot be so refined, so leisurely and gentle, so temperate, kind, courteous, restrained and magnanimous. A revolution is an insurrection, an act of violence by which one class overthrows another. . . .

Apart from their other characteristics, the outstanding thing about China's 600 million people is that they are "poor and blank". This may seem a bad thing, but in reality it is a good thing. Poverty gives rise to the desire for change, the desire for action and the desire for revolution. On a blank sheet of paper free from any mark, the freshest and most beautiful characters can be written, the freshest and most beautiful pictures can be painted. . . .

War is the highest form of struggle for resolving contradictions, when they have developed to a certain stage, between classes, nations, states, or political groups, and it has existed ever since the emergence of private property and of classes. . . .

History shows that wars are divided into two kinds, just and unjust. All wars that are progressive are just, and all wars that impede progress are unjust. We Communists oppose all unjust wars that impede progress, but we do not oppose progressive, just wars. Not only do we Communists not oppose just wars, we actively participate in them. As for unjust wars, World War I is an instance in which both sides fought for imperialist interests; therefore the Communists of the whole world firmly opposed that war. The way to oppose a war of this kind is to do everything possible to prevent it before it breaks out and, once it breaks out, to oppose war with war, to oppose unjust war with just war, whenever possible. . . .

Every Communist must grasp the truth, "Political power grows out of the barrel of a gun.". . .

People all over the world are now discussing whether or not a third world war will break out. On this question, too, we must be mentally prepared and do some analysis. We stand firmly for peace and against war. But if the imperialists insist on unleashing another war, we should not be afraid of it. Our attitude on this question is the same as our attitude towards any disturbance: first, we are against it; second, we are not afraid of it. The First World War was followed by the birth of the Soviet Union with a population of 200 million. The Second World War was followed by the emergence of the socialist camp with a combined population of 900 million. If the imperialists insist on launching a third world war, it is certain that several hundred million more will turn to socialism, and then there will not be much room left on earth for the imperialists; it is also likely that the whole structure of imperialism will utterly collapse. . . .

All reactionaries are paper tigers. In appearance, the reactionaries are terrifying, but in reality they are not so powerful. From a long-term point of view, it is not the reactionaries but the people who are really powerful. . . .

Weapons are an important factor in war, but not the decisive factor; it is people, not things, that are decisive. The contest of strength is not only a contest of military and economic power, but also a contest of human power and morale. Military and economic power is necessarily wielded by people. . . .

The atom bomb is a paper tiger which the U.S. reactionaries use to scare people. It looks terrible, but in fact it isn't. Of course, the atom bomb is a weapon of mass slaughter, but the outcome of a war is decided by the people, not by one or two new types of weapon.

Tet and the Vietnam War

Stanley Karnow

Tet is the Vietnamese new-year celebration, normally a time of rejoicing. In 1968, however, Vietnam was a grim land of war. The United States had almost 600,000 troops in the Republic of (South) Vietnam, trying to suppress the Communist-led Vietcong peasant insurgency movement supported by North Vietnam. As American bombers relentlessly blasted the North, U.S. generals in the South kept up a steady stream of optimistic forecasts of eventual victory over the Vietcong and their Northern backers. The U.S. public was growing tired of the war, and a vehement antiwar movement was surging through U.S. college campuses. Still, most Americans did not advocate a unilateral withdrawal from Vietnam.

In late January 1968, while the Vietnamese were celebrating Tet, the Vietcong and their North Vietnamese allies suddenly abandoned their cautious guerrilla-strategy and tried to seize South Vietnam's major cities. They hoped to spark popular uprisings in these cities, which included the capital, Saigon (today known as Ho Chi Minh City). Reported in full-color detail on American television, the Tet offensive shocked the American public, for the Pentagon had for months been claiming that the Communists were on the defensive and could hardly sustain the war much longer.

The Communists actually considered the Tet offensive a failure, for they were repulsed with heavy losses and failed to hold a single city—nor did the anti-American uprising for which they hoped materialize. Yet in a strategic sense it was a victory, for it convinced a broad section of the American public that the war could not be won by any acceptable means. It was the beginning of the shattering defeat of the United States in the Vietnam War, which culminated in a negotiated withdrawal from South Vietnam in 1973 and the fall of Saigon in 1974.

Excerpted from *Vietnam: A History*, by Stanley Karnow. Copyright © 1983 by WGBH Educational Foundation and Stanley Karnow. Reprinted with permission from Viking Penguin, a division of Penguin Putnam, Inc.

Journalist Stanley Karnow's engrossing book about the war, *Vietnam: A History*, of which an excerpt appears here, explains what happened.

On the evening of January 31, 1968, the spectacle suddenly changed. Now, Americans saw a drastically different kind of war. The night before, nearly seventy thousand Communist soldiers had launched a surprise offensive of extraordinary intensity and astonishing scope. Violating a truce that they themselves had pledged to observe during Tet, the lunar New Year, they surged into more than a hundred cities and towns, including Saigon, audaciously shifting the war for the first time from its rural setting to a new arena—South Vietnam's supposedly impregnable urban areas.

The carefully coordinated series of attacks exploded around the country like a string of firecrackers. Following an abortive foray against the coastal city of Nhatrang, the Communists struck at Hoi An, Danang, Quinhon, and other seaside enclaves presumed to have been beyond their reach, and they even rocketed the huge American complex at Camranh Bay. They stormed the highland towns of Banmethuot, Kontum, and Pleiku, and they hit Dalat, the mountain resort that by tacit accommodation had been spared the conflict. Simultaneously, they invaded thirteen of the sixteen provincial capitals of the populous Mekong delta, among them Mytho, Cantho, Bentre, and Soctrang, and they seized control of scores of district seats, disrupting the Saigon regime's fragile pacification programs. They fought stubbornly, sometimes blindly, and frequently abandoned their flexible tactics to defend untenable positions. In many places, they were swiftly crushed by overwhelming American and South Vietnamese military power, its destructive capacity brought to bear with uncommon fury—and often indiscriminately. They also displayed unprecedented brutality, slaughtering minor government functionaries and other innocuous figures as well as harmless foreign doctors, schoolteachers, and missionaries. Nowhere was the battle fiercer than in Hué, which Communist units held for twenty-five days, committing ghastly atrocities during the initial phase of their occupation.

The Communists staged their boldest stroke against the Saigon region, deploying some four thousand men, most of them in small teams. One of their key objectives was the U.S. embassy, situated in the heart of the sprawling metropolis, which was assaulted in the early morning darkness of January 31. An American officer, later assessing the operation by the standards of a conventional soldier, derided it as a "piddling platoon action." The feat stunned U.S. and world opinion.

The U.S. embassy, an ugly concrete pile shielded by thick walls, was an eyesore in the neighborhood of handsome pastel buildings of the French colonial vintage. . . .

The nineteen Vietcong commandos assigned to the job began their preparations three months earlier. As a gesture of confidence, the United States had recently transferred full responsibility for the defense of Saigon to the South Vietnamese authorities, whose notions of security were notoriously lax. Accordingly, the commandos easily moved arms, ammunition, and explosives into Saigon from their base near a rubber plantation thirty miles to the north, concealing the shipments in truckloads of rice and tomatoes. Inside the city, they stored the matériel in an automobile repair shop whose proprietor, suspected by the South Vietnamese to be an enemy agent, had somehow eluded jail. Nor was American security much better. The Vietcong squad had evidently relied for guidance on a clandestine confederate who had worked for years in the U.S. mission as a chauffeur, nicknamed Satchmo. He was to die during the attack, a Soviet machine gun beside him.

The commandos, jammed into a truck and a taxicab, pulled up in front of the embassy at nearly three o'clock in the morning. Vaulting from the vehicles, they quickly blasted a hole in the wall and rushed into the compound, automatic weapons blazing. Within five minutes, they had killed four GIs and another one shortly thereafter. Four Saigon policemen, theoretically on guard outside, fled as soon as the shooting started. Ambassador Ellsworth Bunker, asleep at his residence a few blocks away, was hustled off to safety at the home of a subordinate. The ranking American diplomat inside the chancery building, Allen Wendt, a junior economic specialist doing routine night duty, locked himself in the fortified code room. A half hour later, a shocked State Department official telephoned from Washington, where it was midafternoon of the previous day. News of the attack had just come over the Associated Press teletype, and Lyndon Johnson was frantically demanding information.

WAR HITS SAIGON, screamed the front-page headline of Washington's afternoon tabloid *The News.* But newspaper accounts paled beside the television coverage, which that evening projected the episode, in all its vivid confusion, into the living rooms of fifty million Americans. There, on color screens, dead bodies lay amid the rubble and rattle of automatic gunfire as dazed American soldiers and civilians ran back and forth trying to flush out the assailants. One man raced past the camera to a villa behind the chancery building to toss a pistol up to Colonel George Jacobson on the second floor. The senior embassy official shot the last of the enemy commandos as he crept up the stairs.

Nearly six and a half hours after the action began, the Americans declared the site secure, and General Westmoreland appeared to speak to reporters. Dressed in starched fatigues, he delivered a televised statement as stiff as his uniform. The Communists had "very deceitfully" taken advantage of the Tet truce "to create maximum consternation," he intoned, concluding optimistically that their "well-laid plans went afoul."

But as they watched Westmoreland's reassuring performance on their television screens, Americans at home could also see the carnage wrought by the offensive in the vicinity of Saigon. . . . In undertaking so widespread a drive, however, the Communists had stretched themselves thin, and inside the capital their squads continued to assault police posts, army barracks, prisons, and other installations with almost hopeless desperation. Nevertheless, the dimensions of their offensive dazzled American officers; one of them, as he tracked the assaults on a map of the Saigon region, thought it resembled a pinball machine, lighting up with each raid.

Hardly had television crews finished covering the fight for the U.S. embassy than another skirmish erupted nearby. American and South Vietnamese units, their dead lying in the street, were blasting an enemy band of thirteen men and a woman barricaded inside an apartment house after a reckless bid to break into the presidential palace, the most heavily fortified building in the capital. Not far off, cameras concentrated on the siege of Saigon's main radio station, grabbed by Vietcong commandos during the night. That evening, as they watched the battle on television, American audiences heard the staccato voice of a correspondent on the spot, doing his best to explain the chaotic images. "There are an undisclosed number of Vietcong inside," he sputtered. "They're surrounded by South Vietnamese troops, and they're pinned down inside."

Western correspondents could not, of course, report from the Communist side during the offensive. Years after the war, though, a Vietcong veteran of the operation against the Saigon radio station, Dang Xuan Teo, related his version of the episode—and his account revealed, among other things, the ability of the Communists to prepare a campaign of such magnitude without detection by either the U.S. or South Vietnamese authorities. . . .

But the most memorable image of the upheaval in Saigon—and one of the most searing spectacles of the whole war—was imprinted the next day on a street corner in the city. General Nguyen Ngoc Loan, chief of South Vietnam's national police, was the crude cop who had brutally crushed the dissident Buddhist movement in Hué two years earlier. Now his mood was even fiercer: Communist invaders had killed several of his men, including one gunned down with his wife and children in their house—and Loan was roaming the capital in an attempt to stiffen its defenses.

That morning, Eddie Adams, an Associated Press photographer, and Vo Suu, a Vietnamese cameraman employed by the National Broadcasting Company, had been cruising around the shattered town. Near the An Quang temple, they spotted a patrol of government troops with a captive in tow. He wore black shorts and a checkered sports shirt, and his hands were bound behind him. The soldiers marched him up to Loan, who drew his revolver and waved the bystanders away. Without hesitation, Loan stretched out his right arm, placed the short snout of the weapon against the prisoner's head, and squeezed the trigger. The man grimaced—then, almost in slow motion, his legs crumpled beneath him as he seemed to sit down backward, blood gushing from his head as it hit the pavement. Not a word was spoken. It all happened instantly, with hardly a sound except for the crack of Loan's gun, the click of Adams's shutter, and the whir of Vo Suu's camera.

At the "five o'clock follies," as correspondents in Saigon called the regular afternoon briefings held in the U.S. Information Service auditorium, Westmoreland exuded his usual confidence. But his report was smothered the next morning in America's newspapers, whose front pages featured the grisly photograph of Loan executing the Vietcong captive. And the next evening, NBC broadcast its exclusive film of the event—slightly edited, to spare television viewers the spurt of blood bursting from the prisoner's head.

Meanwhile, the most bitter battle of the entire war was unfolding in Hué, the lovely old town of temples and palaces, reconstructed by the emperor Gia Long in the nineteenth century to replicate the seat of his Chinese patron in Beijing. Communist forces crashed into the city from three directions in the early hours of January 31, meeting little resistance from the government division based there. They ran up the yellow-starred Vietcong flag atop the Citadel, an ancient fortress in the center of town, and then their political cadres proceeded to organize the worst bloodbath of the conflict.

Five months before, as they began to prepare for the assault, Communist planners and their intelligence agents inside the city meticulously compiled two lists. One detailed nearly two hundred targets, ranging from such installations as government bureaus and police posts to the home of the district chief's concubine. The other contained the names of "cruel tyrants and reactionary elements," a rubric covering civilian functionaries, army officers, and nearly anybody else linked to the South Vietnamese regime as well as uncooperative merchants, intellectuals, and clergymen. Instructions were also issued to arrest Americans and other foreigners except for the French—presumably because President de Gaulle had publicly criticized U.S. policy in Vietnam.

Vietcong teams, armed with these directives, conducted house-to-house searches immediately after seizing control of Hué, and they were merciless. During the months and years that followed, the remains of approximately three thousand people were exhumed in nearby riverbeds, coastal salt flats, and jungle clearings. The victims had been shot or clubbed to death, or buried alive. Paradoxically, the American public barely noticed these atrocities, preoccupied as it was by the incident at Mylai—in which American soldiers had massacred a hundred Vietnamese peasants, women and children among them. Revisiting Vietnam in 1981, I was able to elicit little credible evidence from the Communists to clarify the episode.

General Tran Do, a senior Communist architect of the Tet offensive, flatly denied that the Hué atrocities had ever occurred, contending that films and photographs of the corpses had been "fabricated." In Hué itself, a Communist official claimed that the exhumed bodies were mostly of Vietcong cadres and sympathizers slain by the South Vietnamese army after the fight for the city. He also blamed most of the civilian casualties during the battle on American bombing. But he hinted that his comrades had participated in at least a share of the killing—resorting to familiar Communist jargon to explain that the "angry" citizens of Hué had liquidated local "despots" in the same way that "they would get rid of poisonous snakes who, if allowed to live, would commit further crimes." Balanced accounts have made it clear, however, that the Communist butchery in Hué did take place—perhaps on an even larger scale than reported during the war. . . .

If the Americans and their allies were napping before the Tet upheaval, the Communists also blundered. "We have been guilty of many errors and shortcomings," their initial appraisal of the campaign confessed, deploring such deficiencies as their failure to inspire the South Vietnamese population to rebel or their inability to rally Saigon government soldiers and officials to their banners. Many North Vietnamese and Vietcong troops were plainly disenchanted by the realization that, despite their enormous sacrifices during the campaign, they still faced a long struggle ahead. Official reports expressed alarm at the erosion of morale among those who had "lost confidence" in the Communist leadership and had become "doubtful of victory, pessimistic, and display shirking attitudes.". . .

Revisiting Vietnam after the war, I was astonished by the number of Communist veterans who retained bad memories of the Tet episode—and openly recalled to me their disappointment at its outcome. Dr. Duong Quynh Hoa, at the time a secret Vietcong operative in Saigon, had joined the commandos invading the capital. In retrospect, she bluntly denounced the venture as a "grievous miscalculation" by the Hanoi hierarchy, which in her view had wantonly squandered the southern insurgent movement. Captain Tran Dinh

Thong, a North Vietnamese regular, was equally frank. He remembered feeling "depressed and worried about the future" after the abortive operation, and he blamed its planners for having "incorrectly" surveyed the situation beforehand. Even General Tran Do conceded that the attacks had not been a resounding triumph. Indeed, he explained to me, the Tet campaign went in an unexpected direction: "In all honesty, we didn't achieve our main objective, which was to spur uprisings throughout the south. Still, we inflicted heavy casualties on the Americans and their puppets, and that was a big gain for us. As for making an impact in the United States, it had not been our intention—but it turned out to be a fortunate result."

After the war, in an angry tirade against the press, General Westmoreland alleged that voluminous, lurid, and distorted newspaper and particularly television reports of the Tet attacks had transformed a devastating Communist military defeat in Vietnam into a "psychological victory" for the enemy. Peter Braestrup, who covered Vietnam for *The Washington Post,* leveled the same charge in his book *Big Story,* contending that "crisis journalism" had rarely "veered so widely from reality" than it did in describing and interpreting events during that period. But public opinion surveys conducted at the time made it plain that, whatever the quality of the reporting from Vietnam, the momentous Tet episode scarcely altered American attitudes toward the war.

American opinion toward the war was far more complicated than it appeared to be on graphs and charts. Public "support" for the war had been slipping steadily for two years prior to Tet—a trend influenced by the mounting casualties, rising taxes, and, especially, the feeling that there was no end in view. For a brief moment after the Tet offensive began, Americans rallied round the flag in a predictable display of patriotic fervor. But their mood of despair quickly returned as the fighting dragged on, and their endorsement of the conflict resumed its downward spiral.

The Crises of October 1973: Middle East Conflict, Oil, and Watergate

Daniel Yergin

A series of unexpected events rocked the West in October 1973, causing many to wonder seriously whether the global dominance of the capitalist democracies led by the United States was coming to an end.

On the holiest day of the Jewish calendar, Yom Kippur (October 6), the Egyptian and Syrian armies—well supplied by the Soviet Union—mounted a surprise attack on Israel. The Israeli armed forces sustained a serious initial defeat and began to run dangerously low in military supplies. At the same time, the cartel of major petroleum-exporting nations (OPEC), which was led by Saudi Arabia and Iran, announced a dramatic increase in the price of oil. Then, after U.S. president Richard Nixon decided that Israel must not fall to its Arab enemies, American aircraft launched a massive mission to resupply the Jewish state's reeling armies. This enabled the Israelis to regain the offensive and repel the attack. In retaliation, the Arab members of OPEC announced substantial cuts in oil shipments to every Western country that supported Israel. The Soviet Union, standing behind its Arab clients, sent ships to the Middle East car-

Excerpted from *The Prize: The Epic Quest for Oil, Money, and Power,* by Daniel Yergin. Copyright © 1991, 1992 by Daniel Yergin. Reprinted with permission from Simon & Schuster, Inc.

rying more heavy armaments for Israel's enemies—including detectable traces of what seemed to be nuclear weapons. Nixon responded by putting American armed forces on a full alert—just two steps away from going to war.

While all this was happening, on Saturday night, October 19, President Nixon ordered his attorney general to fire Archibald Cox, the special prosecutor who had been investigating the tangled Watergate scandal and had been making himself unwelcome at the White House with his demands for the president's secret tape recordings of his Oval Office conversations. When the attorney general refused, Nixon fired him—and then fired the assistant attorney general, who also refused to take the action he had demanded. Only the solicitor general, third in command at the Justice Department, finally complied with the presidential order. This famous "Saturday Night Massacre" proved, however, to be only a bump on the road toward Nixon's eventual resignation from office in disgrace—the first and so far only American president to suffer such a fate, and a severe blow to American morale.

This piling up of a string of rapid-fire, ominous crises is narrated by historian Daniel Yergin in his book *The Prize: The Epic Quest for Oil, Money, and Power*, an excerpt from which appears here.

"The Third Temple Is Going Under"

Once war broke out, America's number-one objective quickly became to arrange a truce, whereby the belligerents would pull back to their prehostilities lines, to be followed by an intensified search for a diplomatic solution. The United States wanted, as a top priority, to keep out of direct involvement; it did not want to become too obviously engaged in supplying the Israelis against the Soviet-supplied Arabs, but this was thought to be unlikely owing to the purported Israeli superiority. While U.S. policy would not countenance an Israeli defeat, it regarded the best outcome, in the words of one senior official, as one in which "Israel won, but had its nose bloodied in the process," thus making it more amenable to negotiation.

Something far worse, however, than a bloody nose suddenly appeared to be at hand, owing to the second big miscalculation on the part of Israel (the first being that there would be no war at all). Israel had assumed that it had enough supplies to last for three weeks of war. . . . Now, immediately thrown on the defensive by an Egypt and a Syria both richly equipped with Soviet weapons, the Israelis found themselves devouring materiel at an alarming pace, one far greater than anything they had anticipated. That miscalculation of requirements would prove a grave one for Israel; it would also lead directly to a staggering change in world oil.

On Monday, October 8, two days after the surprise attack, Washington told the Israelis that they could pick up some supplies in the United States in an unmarked El Al [Israel Airlines] plane. That, it was thought, would be sufficient. But Israel was still reeling from the initial attack. A distraught Moshe Dayan, Israel's Defense Minister, told Premier Golda Meir that "the Third Temple is going under," and Meir herself prepared a secret letter to Richard Nixon, warning that Israel was being overwhelmed and might soon be destroyed. On October 9, the United States realized that the Israeli forces were in deep trouble, and were becoming desperately short of supplies. On October 10, the Soviet Union began a massive resupply to Syria, whose forces had started to retreat, and then to Egypt. The Soviets also put airborne troops on alert and began encouraging other Arab states to join in the battle. The United States then started discussions about having more unmarked El Al planes come to the United States for additional supplies. At the same time, the State Department began pressing American commercial carriers to provide charters to ferry materiel to Israel. Kissinger thought such an approach could be relatively low profile and would avoid out-and-out United States identification with Israel. "We were conscious of the need to preserve Arab self-respect," Kissinger later said. But the huge scale of the Soviet resupply soon became evident. And on Thursday, October 11, the Americans realized that Israel could lose the war without resupply. In Kissinger's and even more so in Nixon's formulation, the United States could not allow an American ally to be defeated by Soviet arms. Moreover, who could know the consequences of a fight to the death?

On Friday, October 12, two private letters were sent to Nixon. One was from the chairmen of the four Aramco companies—Exxon, Mobil, Texaco, and Standard of California—hurriedly sent, via John McCloy. [Aramco is the consortium of American oil companies jointly producing oil in Saudi Arabia.] They said that the 100 percent increase in the posted price of oil that the OPEC delegation in Vienna was demanding would be "unacceptable." But some kind of price increase was warranted since "the oil industry in the Free World is now operating 'wide open,' with essentially no spare capacity." Yet they had something even more urgent they wanted to communicate. If the United States increased its military support for Israel, there could be a "snowballing effect" in terms of retaliation "that would produce a major petroleum supply crisis." There was a further warning. "The whole position of the United States in the Middle East is on the way to being seriously impaired, with Japanese, European, and perhaps Russian interests largely supplanting United States presence in the area, to the detriment of both our economy and our security."

The second letter was a desperate message from Israel's Premier, Golda Meir. Her nation's survival and the lives of its people, she wrote, now hung in the most precarious balance. Her warning was confirmed around midnight on that Friday, when Kissinger learned that Israel might well run out of critical munitions over the next several days. He also learned from Secretary of Defense James Schlesinger that all efforts to arrange commercial charters had failed. The American airlines did not dare risk either an Arab embargo or terrorist attacks, and they certainly did not care to send their planes into a war zone. In order for the United States government to draft them into service, they said, the President should declare a national emergency. "If you want supplies there," Schlesinger told Kissinger, "we are going to have to use U.S. airlift all the way. There's no alternative. There are not going to be new supplies without a U.S. airlift."

Kissinger had to agree. But he asked Schlesinger to get the Israelis' word that United States Air Force planes could land under cover of darkness, be unloaded, and be back off the ground by daybreak. If they were not seen, the resupply could be kept as inconspicuous as possible. Before daylight Saturday morning, October 13, Schlesinger had the Israeli promise, and the Military Airlift Command began to move supplies from bases in Rocky Mountain and Midwestern states to an airfield in Delaware. But the American planes would need a refueling stop on the way to Israel. On Saturday morning, the United States asked Portugal for landing rights in the Azores. It took direct and blunt pressure from President Nixon himself to get the required permission.

Still, Washington hoped to keep the low profile, but the presumption of secrecy did not take into account an unexpected act of nature. There were powerful crosswinds at Lajes airfield in the Azores, which would have put the huge C-5A transports at risk, so they were held back in Delaware, their bellies crammed full of supplies. The crosswinds did not diminish until late afternoon, which meant a half-day's delay. As a result, the C-5As did not arrive in Israel in the darkness of Saturday night. Instead, they came lumbering out of the sky on Sunday during the day, October 14, their immense white stars visible for all to see. The United States, instead of keeping to its position of honest broker, was now portrayed as an active ally of Israel. The aid had been extended to counterbalance the huge Soviet resupply to the Arabs, but that did not matter. Not knowing of the strenuous efforts to keep American aid in the background, Arab leaders assumed that it was meant to be a dramatic and highly visible sign of support.

The Israelis had succeeded in stopping the Egyptian offensive before it could break through the critical mountain passes in the Sinai, and on October 15, they launched the first of a series of successful counteroffensives against the Egyptians. Meanwhile, in Vienna on October 14, OPEC had announced the failure of its negotiations with the companies, and the Gulf OPEC countries scheduled a meeting in Kuwait City to resume the oil price issue on their own. But most of the delegates had remained in Vienna, since the breakdown of the talks with the companies, and now they found themselves stranded. They were frantically trying to book airplane seats, but because of the war, the airlines had canceled virtually all flights into the Middle East. It appeared that the delegates would not be able to leave at all, meaning that the scheduled meeting in Kuwait would not take place. Then, at last, it was discovered that one flight was still operating—an Air India jet through Geneva that made an intermediate stop at Kuwait City—and, on the evening of October 15, many delegations rushed to the airport and hastily boarded the plane.

On October 16, the delegates of the Gulf states—five Arabs and an Iranian—met in Kuwait City to pick up where the discussions had been left off a few days earlier in [Saudi oil minister] Yamani's suite in Vienna. They would not wait any longer for the companies to reply. They acted. They announced their decision to raise the posted price of oil by 70 percent, to $5.11 a barrel, which brought it into line with prices on the panicky spot market.

The significance of their action was twofold—in the price increase itself, and in the unilateral way in which it was imposed. The pretense that the exporters would negotiate with the companies was now past. They had taken complete and total charge of setting the price of oil. The transition was now complete from the days when the companies had unilaterally set the price, to the days when the exporters had at least obtained a veto, to the jointly negotiated prices, to this new assumption of sole suzerainty by the exporters. When the decision was taken, Yamani told one of the other delegates in Kuwait City, "This is a moment for which I have been waiting a long time. The moment has come. We are masters of our own commodity."

The exporters were ready for the expected anguished complaints about the size of the increase. They announced that consuming governments were taking 66 percent of the retail price of oil in taxes, while they received the equivalent of only 9 percent. The Iranian oil minister, Jamshid Amouzegar, said that the exporters were merely keying prices to the forces of the market, and they would set prices in the future on the basis of what consumers were willing to pay. It was for the momentous October 16 decision on price that Yamani had advised George Piercy of Exxon to listen to the radio. As events turned out, however, Piercy learned about it from the newspapers.

If the OPEC exporters could unilaterally raise the price of oil, what might they do next? And what would happen on the battlefield? At the White House, the next day, October 17, Richard Nixon expressed his concern to his senior advisers on national security. "No one is more keenly aware of the stakes: oil and our strategic position." Historic meaning was being given to that statement the same day, halfway around the world, again in Kuwait City. The Iranian oil minister had left the meeting, and the rest of the Arab oil ministers arrived for an exclusively Arab conclave. Their subject was the oil weapon. It was on everybody's mind. The Kuwaiti oil minister declared, "Now the atmosphere is more propitious than in 1967."

Embargo

Yet there remained the question of what exactly Saudi Arabia would do. Despite [Egyptian president Anwar] Sadat's importuning, King Faisal was reluctant to take any action against the United States without more contact with Washington. He sent a letter to Nixon, warning that if American support for Israel continued, Saudi-American relations would become only "lukewarm." That was on October 16.

On October 17, at the time that the oil ministers were meeting in Kuwait City, first Kissinger and then Kissinger and Nixon together received four Arab foreign ministers. They were led by the Saudi, Omar Saqqaf, whom Kissinger would characterize as "gentle and wise." The discussions were cordial, and there seemed to be some common ground. Nixon had pledged to strive for a cease-fire that would make it possible to "work within the framework of Resolution 242," the United Nations resolution that would return Israel to its 1967 borders. The Saudi Minister of State seemed to affirm that Israel had a right to exist, so long as it was within its 1967 borders. Kissinger explained that the American resupply should not be taken as anti-Arab, but rather was "between the U.S. and the USSR." The United States had to react to the Russian supply. He added that the status quo ante in the region was untenable, and that, after the war was over, the United States would undertake an active diplomatic role and work for a positive peace settlement.

To Saqqaf, Nixon made the ultimate promise: the services of Henry Kissinger as negotiator, which seemed to be Nixon's idea of a sure-fire guarantee of success. Nixon also assured Saqqaf and the other foreign ministers that, despite his Jewish origins, Kissinger "was not subject to domestic, that is to say Jewish, pressures." He went on to add, "I can see that you are concerned about the fact that Henry Kissinger is a Jewish-American. A Jewish-American can be a good American, and Kissinger is a good American. He will work with you." Kissinger was writhing with embarrassment and anger as the President made his gratuitous remark, but Saqqaf was nonplussed. "We are all Semites together," Saqqaf deftly replied. And then the Minister of State made his way to the White House Rose Garden, where he told reporters that the talks had been constructive and friendly, and where, according to the press, it was all smiles, graciousness, and mutual compliments. After the meetings with Saqqaf and the other Arab foreign ministers, Kissinger told his staff he was surprised that there had been no mention of oil, and that it was unlikely that the Arabs would use the oil weapon against the United States.

That, however, was exactly what the Arab oil ministers in Kuwait City were contemplating. Early in 1973, in one of his "thinking aloud" speeches about Egypt's options, Sadat had discussed the oil weapon. And around that time, at his urging, experts from Egypt and other Arab countries had begun drawing up a plan for the use of the oil weapon, taking into account the growing energy crisis in the United States. The Arab delegations in Kuwait City were familiar at least with the concept before the October 17 meeting. But at the meeting itself, radical Iraq had a different notion. The chief Iraqi delegate called on the Arab states to target their ire on the United States—to nationalize all American business in the Arab world, to withdraw all Arab funds from American banks, and to institute a total oil embargo against the United States and other countries friendly to Israel. The chairman of the meeting, the Algerian minister, dismissed such a proposal as impractical and unacceptable. Yamani, on instructions of his King, also resisted what would have been a declaration of all-out economic warfare against the United States, the consequences of which would have been, to say the least, very uncertain for all parties concerned. The angry Iraqi delegates withdrew from the meeting and from the whole embargo plan.

Instead, the Arab oil ministers agreed to an embargo, cutting production 5 percent from the September level, and to keep cutting by 5 percent in each succeeding month until their objectives were met. Oil supplies at previous levels would be maintained to "friendly states." The nine ministers present also adopted a secret resolution recommending "that the United States be subjected to the most severe cuts" with the aim that "this progressive reduction lead to the total halt of oil supplies to the United States from every individual country party to the resolution." Several of the countries immediately announced that they would start with 10 percent, rather than 5 percent, cutbacks. Whatever their size, the production cuts would be more effective than a ban on exports against a single country, because oil could always be moved around, as had been done in the 1956 and 1967 crises. The cutbacks would assure that the absolute level of available supplies went down. The overall plan was very shrewd; the prospect of monthly cutbacks, plus the differentiation among consuming countries, would maximize uncertainty, tension, and rivalry within and among the importing countries. One clear objective of the plan was to split the industrial countries right from the start. . . .

Events moved rapidly after the Kuwait City meetings. On October 18, Nixon met with his Cabinet. "When it became clear that the fighting might be prolonged and the Soviets began a massive resupply effort, we had to act to prevent the Soviets from tilting the military balance against Israel," he told the Cabinet officers. "This past weekend, therefore, we began a program of resupply to Israel." Recalling his discussions the day before with Saqqaf and the others, he continued, "In meeting with the Arab foreign ministers yesterday, I made the point that we favor a cease fire and movement towards a peace settlement based on U.N. Resolution 242. Arab reaction thus far to any resupply effort has been restrained and we hope to continue in a manner which avoids confrontation with them." He was being optimistic.

The next day, October 19, Nixon publicly proposed a $2.2 billion military aid package for Israel. It had been decided on a day or two earlier, and word of it was conveyed to several Arab countries in advance so that they would not be surprised by the announcement. The strategy was to try to assure that neither Egypt nor Israel ended up in a position of ascendancy, with the result that both would have reason to go to the negotiating table. That same day, Libya announced that it was embargoing all oil shipments to the United States.

At two o'clock Saturday morning, October 20, Kissinger departed for Moscow to try to devise a cease-fire formula. On board the plane, he learned further stunning news. In retaliation for the Israeli aid proposal, Saudi Arabia had gone beyond the rolling cutbacks; it would now cut off all shipments of oil, every last barrel, to the United States. The other Arab states had done or were doing the same. The oil weapon was now fully in battle—a weapon, in Kissinger's words, "of political blackmail." The three-decade-old postwar petroleum order had died its final death.

The embargo came as an almost complete surprise. "The possibility of an embargo didn't even enter my mind," said a senior executive of one of the Aramco companies. "I thought that if there was an outbreak of war and if the United States was on the side of Israel, there was no way that the U.S. companies in Arab countries would not be nationalized." Nor was much thought given in the United States government to the prospect of an embargo, despite the evidence at hand. . . . To be sure, whatever the nature of [Saudi King] Faisal's discussions with Sadat, and whatever promises Sadat may have heard, Faisal and the other conservative Arab leaders were reluctant to directly challenge the United States, a country on which they depended for their security. Moreover, they might have been surprised, even shocked in a way, had the United States not provided supplies to Israel. What transformed the situation and finally galvanized the production cuts and the embargo against the United States was the very public nature of the resupply—the result of the cross-winds at the Lajes airfield in the Azores—and then the $2.2 billion aid package. Not to have acted, some Arab leaders thought, could have put certain regimes at the mercy of street mobs. Yet the public show of support for Israel also provided them with a sufficient pretext to take on the United States, as others clearly wanted to do.

Even the embargo itself was not the end of stunning events on October 20. It was only in Moscow on Sunday morning that Kissinger learned what had transpired in Washington the night before. In what became known as the Saturday Night Massacre, a critical point in his Presidency, Nixon fired the special prosecutor, Archibald Cox, who had been appointed to investigate the Watergate scandal, and who had subpoenaed the President's secret office tape recordings. Access to those tapes had become the centerpiece of the struggle between the President and the Senate—to ascertain how much Nixon himself had been directly involved in a maze of illegalities. Immediately after the firing, Attorney General Elliot Richardson and his chief deputy, William Ruckelshaus, resigned in protest. "And now," White House Chief of Staff Alexander Haig told Kissinger over the telephone, "all hell has broken loose."

The Third-Rate Burglary

Throughout the clash of arms in the Middle East and the weeks of crisis over oil, one key actor was otherwise preoccupied. Richard Nixon was thoroughly entangled in the series of events that escalated from what he called a "third-rate burglary" into the unprecedented series of Watergate scandals, at the center of which was the President himself. The United States had seen nothing remotely like it since Teapot Dome [an oil-government scandal in the 1920s]. The unfolding of the Watergate saga during the October War; the country's obsession with it; its effects on the war and the embargo, on American capabilities, and on perceptions within the United States—all interacted to create a strange, surrealistic dimension to the central drama on the world stage. For instance, on October 9, the day that a desperate Golda Meir signaled that she wanted to fly to Washington to plead personally for aid, Nixon was working out the resignation of Vice-President Spiro Agnew [over charges of taking bribes], who asked Nixon to help him find work as a consultant and complained that the Internal Revenue Service was trying to find out how much he had paid for his neckties. On October 12, the day that senior American officials realized that Israel might lose the war and were grappling with how to resupply, they were summoned to the White House for what Kissinger described as an "eerie ceremony," in which Nixon introduced Gerald Ford as his choice for his new Vice President.

In the weeks that followed, though Nixon would temporarily depart his own personal crisis and weave in and then out again of the world crisis, effective control over American policy was lodged in the hands of Henry Kissinger, who, in addition to being Special Assistant for National Security, had also just been appointed Secretary of State. Kissinger's original base had been twofold—Harvard's Center for International Affairs, housed in space borrowed from the Harvard Semitic Museum, and his service to Nixon's great rival, [New York Governor] Nelson Rockefeller. This former professor, who had fled to the United States as a boy, a Jewish refugee from Nazi Germany, and whose ambition once had been no loftier than to become a certified public accountant, now came, through the strange twists of Watergate and the crumbling of Presidential authority, to be the very embodiment of the legitimacy of the American government. Kissinger's public personality expanded to oversized dimensions to fill the vacuum created by a discredited Presidency. He emerged— for Washington, for the media, for the capitals around the world—as the desperately needed figure of authority and continuity at a time when confidence in America was being severely tested.

Too much seemed to be happening. The media and the public mind were overloaded. But Watergate, and the President's predicament, had direct and major consequences for the Middle East and for oil. Sadat might, at least arguably, never have gone to war had a strong President been able, after the 1972 election, to use his influence to open a dialogue between Egypt and Israel. An undistracted President might also have been able to address the energy issue with greater focus. And once the war began, Nixon was so preoccupied, his credibility so diminished, that he could not provide the Presidential leadership required for dealing with the belligerents, the oil exporters and the explicit economic warfare against the United States—and the Russians. For their part, foreign leaders could not comprehend this strange Watergate process, part ritual, part circus, part tragedy, part thriller, that had gripped American politics and the American Presidency.

Watergate gave, as well, a lasting cast to the energy problems of the 1970s. The accident of coincidence—the embargo and the Saturday Night Massacre, Watergate and the October War—seemed to imply logical connections. Things meshed in hazy, mysterious ways, and this impression left deep and abiding suspicions that fed conspiracy theories and obstructed more rational responses to the energy problems at hand. Some argued that Kissinger had masterminded the oil crisis to improve the economic position of the United States vis-à-vis Europe and Japan. Some believed that Nixon had deliberately started the war and actually encouraged the embargo to distract attention from Watergate. The oil embargo and illegal campaign contributions by some oil companies, which were part of the illegal loot extracted from corporate America by the Committee to Reelect the President, flowed together in the public's mind, greatly expanding the traditional distrust of the oil industry and leading many to think that the October War, the embargo, and the energy crisis had all been created and masterfully manipulated by the oil companies in the name of greed. Such various perceptions were to last much longer than the October War or the Nixon Presidency itself.

Alert

In Riyadh [the capital of Saudi Arabia], on the afternoon of October 21, the day following the Saturday Night Massacre, Sheikh Yamani met with Frank Jungers, the president of Aramco. Using computer data about exports and destinations that the Saudis had requested from Aramco a few days earlier, Yamani laid out the ground rules for the cutbacks and the embargo the Saudis were about to impose. He acknowledged that the administration of the system would be very complicated. But the Saudis were "looking to Aramco to police it," he said. "Any deviations by the Aramco offtakers from the ground rules," he added, "would be harshly dealt with." At one point, Yamani departed from the operational details to ask Jungers a more philosophical question. Was he surprised by what had just happened? No, Jungers replied, "except that this cutback was greater than we had anticipated."

Yamani then pointedly asked if Jungers would be "surprised at the next move if this one didn't produce some results."

"No," said Jungers, "I would not be surprised."

Jungers's own guess, based upon his previous conversations with Yamani and other information, was that the subsequent move would be "complete nationalization of American interests if not a break in diplomatic relations." This was suggested by Yamani in his final ominous comment to Jungers: "The next step would not just be more of the same."

In Moscow, meanwhile, Kissinger and the Russians completed a cease-fire plan. But in its implementation over the next few days, it ran into serious snags. Neither the Israelis nor the Egyptians seemed to be observing the cease-fire, and there was the imminent possibility that Egypt's Third Army would be captured or annihilated. Then came a blunt and provocative letter from Leonid Brezhnev to Nixon. The Soviet Union would not allow the Third Army to be destroyed. If that happened, Soviet credibility in the Middle East would also be destroyed and Brezhnev, in Kissinger's words, would "look like an idiot." Brezhnev demanded that a joint American-Soviet force move in to separate the two sides. If the United States would not cooperate, the Soviets would intervene unilaterally. "I shall say it straight," Brezhnev menacingly wrote. His threat was taken very seriously. It was known that Soviet airborne troops were on alert, and Soviet ships in the Mediterranean seemed to be proceeding in a belligerent fashion. Most worrying, neutron emissions from what might be nuclear weapons had been detected on a Soviet freighter passing through the Dardanelles [the Turkish straits] into the Mediterranean. Was Egypt the destination?

A half dozen of the most senior American national security officials were summoned to a hurriedly called late-night emergency meeting in the White House Situation Room. Nixon himself was not awakened for the meeting on the advice of Alexander Haig, who told Kissinger that the President was "too distraught" to join them. Some of the participants were surprised to find that the President was not there. The officials grimly reviewed the Brezhnev message. Direct Soviet military intervention could not be tolerated; it could upset the entire international order. Brezhnev could not be allowed to assume that the Soviet Union could take advantage of a Watergate-weakened Presidency. There was further reason for alarm. Over the previous few hours, United States intelligence had "lost" the Soviet air transport, which it had been tracking as the planes ferried arms to Egypt and Syria. No one knew where the planes now were. Could they be on their way back to Soviet bases to pick up the airborne troops, already on alert, and carry them into the Sinai?

The officials in the White House Situation Room concluded that the risks had suddenly escalated; the United States would have to respond resolutely to Brezhnev's challenge. Force would have to be prepared to meet force. The readiness state of American forces was raised to DefCon 3 and in some cases even higher, which meant that, in the early morning of October 25, the American military went on a nuclear alert around the world. The message was clear. The United States and the Soviet Union were squaring off directly against each other, something that had not happened since the Cuban Missile Crisis. Miscalculation could lead to a nuclear confrontation. The next hours were very tense.

But the following day, the fighting in the Middle East stopped, Egypt's Third Army was resupplied, and the cease-fire went into effect. It was just in time. The superpowers pulled back from their alerts. Two days later, Egyptian and Israeli military representatives met for direct talks for the first time in a quarter of a century. Egypt and the United States, meanwhile, opened a new dialogue. Both had been objectives of Sadat when he first conceived his gamble a year earlier. The nuclear weapons were sheathed. But the Arabs continued to wield the oil weapon. The oil embargo remained in place, with consequences that would extend far beyond the October War.

Islam Against the West?

Bernard Lewis

Although it originated in the late nineteenth and early twentieth centuries, since the early 1970s the growing assertiveness of what the media call "Islamic fundamentalism" in many Muslim countries has troubled those in the West who think that their own values of rationalism, secularism, and pluralism represent the culmination of progress. In Muslim lands as diverse as Iran and Algeria, Pakistan and Egypt, or Libya and Sudan, powerful movements arose that demanded the reorganization of society along the lines of strict Islamic orthodoxy. Sometimes the "fundamentalists" (a term they reject) took power, most notably in Iran in 1979. Sometimes they have struggled unsuccessfully (so far) for power, as in Algeria and Egypt. And in every Islamic country, the Islamists are a force to be reckoned with. With varying degrees of intensity, they reject what they see as the corrosive influence of Western (that is, Christian, Jewish, and Marxist) culture. They insist that the Qur'an (Koran) and Islamic law serve as the basis for all essential relationships in their societies—an attitude that lies at the very heart of Islam, which is a faith based on the whole community's submission to the will of God.

Bernard Lewis, one of the Western world's leading historians of Islamic history and culture, in the 1990 article that follows discusses why Islamic "fundamentalists" consider the West in general and the United States in particular their greatest enemy. The Islamist movement almost certainly will be a formidable legacy from the twentieth to the twenty-first century, although it must be stressed that not all believing Muslims consider themselves "fundamentalists." Iran, for example, has recently experienced a widespread popular reaction against pushing the Islamist agenda too far.

Reprinted from "Roots of Muslim Rage," by Bernard Lewis, *Atlantic Monthly,* vol. 266, no. 3, September 1990. Reprinted with permission from the author.

In one of his letters Thomas Jefferson remarked that in matters of religion "the maxim of civil government" should be reversed and we should rather say, "Divided we stand, united, we fall." In this remark Jefferson was setting forth with classic terseness an idea that has come to be regarded as essentially American: the separation of Church and State. This idea was not entirely new; it had some precedents in the writings of Spinoza, Locke, and the philosophers of the European Enlightenment. It was in the United States, however, that the principle was first given the force of law and gradually, in the course of two centuries, became a reality.

If the idea that religion and politics should be separated is relatively new, dating back a mere three hundred years, the idea that they are distinct dates back almost to the beginnings of Christianity. Christians are enjoined in their Scriptures to "render . . . unto Caesar the things which are Caesar's and unto God the things which are God's." While opinions have differed as to the real meaning of this phrase, it has generally been interpreted as legitimizing a situation in which two institutions exist side by side, each with its own laws and chain of authority—one concerned with religion, called the Church, the other concerned with politics, called the State. And since they are two, they may be joined or separated, subordinate or independent, and conflicts may arise between them over questions of demarcation and jurisdiction.

This formulation of the problems posed by the relations between religion and politics, and the possible solutions to those problems, arise from Christian, not universal, principles and experience. There are other religious traditions in which religion and politics are differently perceived, and in which, therefore, the problems and the possible solutions are radically different from those we know in the West. Most of these traditions, despite their often very high level of sophistication and achievement, remained or became local—limited to one region or one culture or one people. There is one, however, that in its worldwide distribution, its continuing vitality, its universalist aspirations, can be compared to Christianity, and that is Islam.

Islam is one of the world's great religions. Let me be explicit about what I, as a historian of Islam who is not a Muslim, mean by that. Islam has brought comfort and peace of mind to countless millions of men and women. It has given dignity and meaning to drab and impoverished lives. It has taught people of different races to live in brotherhood and people of different creeds to live side by side in reasonable tolerance. It inspired a great civilization in which others besides Muslims lived creative and useful lives and which, by its achievement, enriched the whole world. But Islam, like other religions, has also known periods when it inspired in some of its followers a mood of hatred and violence. It is our misfortune that part, though by no means all or even most, of the Muslim world is now going through such a period, and that much, though again not all, of that hatred is directed against us.

We should not exaggerate the dimensions of the problem. The Muslim world is far from unanimous in its rejection of the West, nor have the Muslim regions of the Third World been the most passionate and the most extreme in their hostility. There are still significant numbers, in some quarters perhaps a majority, of Muslims with whom we share certain basic cultural and moral, social and political, beliefs and aspirations; there is still an imposing Western presence—cultural, economic, diplomatic—in Muslim lands, some of which are Western allies. Certainly nowhere in the Muslim world, in the Middle East or elsewhere, has American policy suffered disasters or encountered problems comparable to those in Southeast Asia or Central America. There is no Cuba, no Vietnam, in the Muslim world, and no place where American forces are involved as combatants or even as "advisers." But there is a Libya, an Iran, and a Lebanon, and a surge of hatred that distresses, alarms, and above all baffles Americans.

At times this hatred goes beyond hostility to specific interests or actions or policies or even countries and becomes a rejection of Western civilization as such, not only what it does but what it is, and the principles and values that it practices and professes. These are indeed seen as innately evil, and those who promote or accept them as the "enemies of God."

This phrase, which recurs so frequently in the language of the Iranian leadership, in both their judicial proceedings and their political pronouncements, must seem very strange to the modern outsider, whether religious or secular. The idea that God has enemies, and needs human help in order to identify and dispose of them, is a little difficult to assimilate. It is not, however, all that alien. The concept of the enemies of God is familiar in preclassical and classical antiquity, and in both the Old and New Testaments, as well as in the Koran. A particularly relevant version of the idea occurs in the dualist religions of ancient Iran, whose cosmogony assumed not one but two supreme powers. The Zoroastrian devil, unlike the Christian or Muslim or Jewish devil, is not one of God's creatures performing some of God's more mysterious tasks but an independent power, a supreme force of evil engaged in a cosmic struggle against God. This belief influenced a number of Christian, Muslim, and Jewish sects, through Manichaeism and other routes. The almost forgotten religion of the Manichees has given its name to the perception of problems as a stark and simple conflict between matching forces of pure good and pure evil.

The Koran is of course strictly monotheistic, and recognizes one God, one universal power only. There is a struggle in human hearts between good and evil, between God's commandments and the tempter, but this is seen as a struggle ordained by God, with its outcome preordained by God, serving as a test of mankind, and not, as in some of the old dualist religions, a struggle in which mankind has a crucial part to play in bringing about the victory of good over evil. Despite this monotheism, Islam, like Judaism and Christianity, was at various stages influenced, especially in Iran, by the dualist idea of a cosmic clash of good and evil, light and darkness, order and chaos, truth and falsehood, God and the Adversary, variously known as devil, Iblis, Satan, and by other names.

The Rise of the House of Unbelief

In Islam the struggle of good and evil very soon acquired political and even military dimensions. Muhammad, it will be recalled, was not only a prophet and a teacher, like the founders of other religions; he was also the head of a polity and of a community, a ruler and a soldier. Hence his struggle involved a state and its armed forces. If the fighters in the war for Islam, the holy war "in the path of God," are fighting for God, it follows that their opponents are fighting against God. And since God is in principle the sovereign, the supreme head of the Islamic state—and the Prophet and, after the Prophet, the caliphs are his vicegerents—then God as sovereign commands the army. The army is God's army and the enemy is God's enemy. The duty of God's soldiers is to dispatch God's enemies as quickly as possible to the place where God will chastise them—that is to say, the afterlife.

Clearly related to this is the basic division of mankind as perceived in Islam. Most, probably all, human societies have a way of distinguishing between themselves and others: insider and outsider, in-group and out-group, kinsman or neighbor and foreigner. These definitions not only define the outsider but also, and perhaps more particularly, help to define and illustrate our perception of ourselves.

In the classical Islamic view, to which many Muslims are beginning to return, the world and all mankind are divided into two: the House of Islam, where the Muslim law and faith prevail, and the rest, known as the House of Unbelief or the House of War, which it is the duty of Muslims ultimately to bring to Islam. But the greater part of the world is still outside Islam, and even inside the Islamic lands, according to the view of the Muslim radicals, the faith of Islam has been undermined and the law of Islam has been abrogated. The obligation of holy war therefore begins at home and continues abroad, against the same infidel enemy.

Like every other civilization known to human history, the Muslim

world in its heyday saw itself as the center of truth and enlightenment, surrounded by infidel barbarians whom it would in due course
enlighten and civilize. But between the different groups of barbarians there was a crucial difference. The barbarians to the east and
the south were polytheists and idolaters, offering no serious threat
and no competition at all to Islam. In the north and west, in contrast,
Muslims from an early date recognized a genuine rival—a competing world religion, a distinctive civilization inspired by that religion,
and an empire that, though much smaller than theirs, was no less
ambitious in its claims and aspirations. This was the entity known
to itself and others as Christendom, a term that was long almost
identical with Europe.

The struggle between these rival systems has now lasted for some
fourteen centuries. It began with the advent of Islam, in the seventh
century, and has continued virtually to the present day. It has consisted of a long series of attacks and counterattacks, jihads and Crusades, conquests and reconquests. For the first thousand years Islam
was advancing, Christendom in retreat and under threat. The new
faith conquered the old Christian lands of the Levant and North
Africa, and invaded Europe, ruling for a while in Sicily, Spain, Portugal, and even parts of France. The attempt by the Crusaders to recover the lost lands of Christendom in the east was held and thrown
back, and even the Muslims' loss of southwestern Europe to the Re-
conquista was amply compensated by the Islamic advance into
southeastern Europe, which twice reached as far as Vienna. For the
past three hundred years, since the failure of the second Turkish
siege of Vienna in 1683 and the rise of the European colonial empires in Asia and Africa, Islam has been on the defensive, and the
Christian and post-Christian civilization of Europe and her daughters has brought the whole world, including Islam, within its orbit.

For a long time now there has been a rising tide of rebellion
against this Western paramountcy, and a desire to reassert Muslim
values and restore Muslim greatness. The Muslim has suffered successive stages of defeat. The first was his loss of domination in the
world, to the advancing power of Russia and the West. The second
was the undermining of his authority in his own country, through an
invasion of foreign ideas and laws and ways of life and sometimes
even foreign rulers or settlers, and the enfranchisement of native
non-Muslim elements. The third—the last straw—was the challenge
to his mastery in his own house, from emancipated women and rebellious children. It was too much to endure, and the outbreak of
rage against these alien, infidel, and incomprehensible forces that
had subverted his dominance, disrupted his society, and finally violated the sanctuary of his home was inevitable. It was also natural
that this rage should be directed primarily against the millennial en-

emy and should draw its strength from ancient beliefs and loyalties.

Europe and her daughters? The phrase may seem odd to Americans, whose national myths, since the beginning of their nationhood and even earlier, have usually defined their very identity in opposition to Europe, as something new and radically different from the old European ways. This is not, however, the way that others have seen it; not often in Europe, and hardly ever elsewhere.

Though people of other races and cultures participated, for the most part involuntarily, in the discovery and creation of the Americas, this was, and in the eyes of the rest of the world long remained, a European enterprise, in which Europeans predominated and dominated and to which Europeans gave their languages, their religions, and much of their way of life.

For a very long time voluntary immigration to America was almost exclusively European. There were indeed some who came from the Muslim lands in the Middle East and North Africa, but few were Muslims; most were members of the Christian and to a lesser extent the Jewish minorities in those countries. Their departure for America, and their subsequent presence in America, must have strengthened rather than lessened the European image of America in Muslim eyes.

In the lands of Islam remarkably little was known about America. At first the voyages of discovery aroused some interest; the only surviving copy of Columbus's own map of America is a Turkish translation and adaptation, still preserved in the Topkapi Palace Museum, in Istanbul. A sixteenth-century Turkish geographer's account of the discovery of the New World, titled *The History of Western India,* was one of the first books printed in Turkey. But thereafter interest seems to have waned, and not much is said about America in Turkish, Arabic, or other Muslim languages until a relatively late date. A Moroccan ambassador who was in Spain at the time wrote what must surely be the first Arabic account of the American Revolution. The Sultan of Morocco signed a treaty of peace and friendship with the United States in 1787, and thereafter the new republic had a number of dealings, some friendly, some hostile, most commercial, with other Muslim states. These seem to have had little impact on either side. The American Revolution and the American republic to which it gave birth long remained unnoticed and unknown. Even the small but growing American presence in Muslim lands in the nineteenth century—merchants, consuls, missionaries, and teachers—aroused little or no curiosity, and is almost unmentioned in the Muslim literature and newspapers of the time.

The Second World War, the oil industry, and postwar developments brought many Americans to the Islamic lands; increasing numbers of Muslims also came to America, first as students, then as teachers or businessmen or other visitors, and eventually as immigrants. Cinema and later television brought the American way of life, or at any rate a certain version of it, before countless millions to whom the very name of America had previously been meaningless or unknown. A wide range of American products, particularly in the immediate postwar years, when European competition was virtually eliminated and Japanese competition had not yet arisen, reached into the remotest markets of the Muslim world, winning new customers and, perhaps more important, creating new tastes and ambitions. For some, America represented freedom and justice and opportunity. For many more, it represented wealth and power and success, at a time when these qualities were not regarded as sins or crimes.

And then came the great change, when the leaders of a widespread and widening religious revival sought out and identified their enemies as the enemies of God, and gave them "a local habitation and a name" in the Western Hemisphere. Suddenly, or so it seemed, America had become the archenemy, the incarnation of evil, the diabolic opponent of all that is good, and specifically, for Muslims, of Islam. Why?

Some Familiar Accusations

Among the components in the mood of anti-Westernism, and more especially of anti-Americanism, were certain intellectual influences coming from Europe. One of these was from Germany, where a negative view of America formed part of a school of thought by no means limited to the Nazis but including writers as diverse as Rainer Maria Rilke, Ernst Jünger, and Martin Heidegger. In this perception, America was the ultimate example of civilization without culture: rich and comfortable, materially advanced but soulless and artificial; assembled or at best constructed, not grown; mechanical, not organic; technologically complex but lacking the spirituality and vitality of the rooted, human, national cultures of the Germans and other "authentic" peoples. German philosophy, and particularly the philosophy of education, enjoyed a considerable vogue among Arab and some other Muslim intellectuals in the thirties and early forties, and this philosophic anti-Americanism was part of the message.

After the collapse of the Third Reich and the temporary ending of German influence, another philosophy, even more anti-American, took its place—the Soviet version of Marxism, with a denunciation of Western capitalism and of America as its most advanced and dangerous embodiment. And when Soviet influence began to fade, there was yet another to take its place, or at least to supplement its working—the new mystique of Third Worldism, emanating from Western Europe, particularly France, and later also from the United States, and drawing at times on both these earlier philosophies. This mystique was helped by the universal human tendency to invent a golden age in the past, and the specifically European propensity to locate it elsewhere. A new variant of the old golden-age myth placed it in the Third World, where the innocence of the non-Western Adam and Eve was ruined by the Western serpent. This view took as axiomatic the goodness and purity of the East and the wickedness of the West, expanding in an exponential curve of evil from Western Europe to the United States. These ideas, too, fell on fertile ground, and won widespread support.

But though these imported philosophies helped to provide intellectual expression for anti-Westernism and anti-Americanism, they did not cause it, and certainly they do not explain the widespread anti-Westernism that made so many in the Middle East and elsewhere in the Islamic world receptive to such ideas.

It must surely be clear that what won support for such totally diverse doctrines was not Nazi race theory, which can have had little appeal for Arabs, or Soviet atheistic communism, which can have had little appeal for Muslims, but rather their common anti-Westernism. Nazism and communism were the main forces opposed to the West, both as a way of life and as a power in the world, and as such they could count on at least the sympathy if not the support of those who saw in the West their principal enemy.

But why the hostility in the first place? If we turn from the general to the specific, there is no lack of individual policies and actions, pursued and taken by individual Western governments, that have aroused the passionate anger of Middle Eastern and other Islamic peoples. Yet all too often, when these policies are abandoned and the problems resolved, there is only a local and temporary alleviation. The French have left Algeria, the British have left Egypt, the Western oil companies have left their oil wells, the westernizing Shah has left Iran—yet the generalized resentment of the fundamentalists and other extremists against the West and its friends remains and grows and is not appeased.

The cause most frequently adduced for anti-American feeling among Muslims today is American support for Israel. This support is certainly a factor of importance, increasing with nearness and involvement. But here again there are some oddities, difficult to explain in terms of a single, simple cause. In the early days of the foundation of Israel, while the United States maintained a certain distance, the Soviet Union granted immediate *de jure* recognition and support, and arms sent from a Soviet satellite, Czechoslovakia, saved the infant state of Israel from defeat and death in its first weeks of life. Yet there seems to have been no great ill will toward the Soviets for these policies, and no corresponding good will toward the United States. In 1956 it was the United States that intervened, forcefully and decisively, to secure the withdrawal of Israeli,

British, and French forces from Egypt—yet in the late fifties and sixties it was to the Soviets, not America, that the rulers of Egypt, Syria, Iraq, and other states turned for arms; it was with the Soviet bloc that they formed bonds of solidarity at the United Nations and in the world generally. More recently, the rulers of the Islamic Republic of Iran have offered the most principled and uncompromising denunciation of Israel and Zionism. Yet even these leaders, before as well as after the death of Ayatollah Ruhollah Khomeini, when they decided for reasons of their own to enter into a dialogue of sorts, found it easier to talk to Jerusalem than to Washington. At the same time, Western hostages in Lebanon, many of them devoted to Arab causes and some of them converts to Islam, are seen and treated by their captors as limbs of the Great Satan.

Another explanation, more often heard from Muslim dissidents, attributes anti-American feeling to American support for hated regimes, seen as reactionary by radicals, as impious by conservatives, as corrupt and tyrannical by both. This accusation has some plausibility, and could help to explain why an essentially inner-directed, often anti-nationalist movement should turn against a foreign power. But it does not suffice, especially since support for such regimes has been limited both in extent and—as the Shah discovered—in effectiveness.

Clearly, something deeper is involved than these specific grievances, numerous and important as they may be—something deeper that turns every disagreement into a problem and makes every problem insoluble.

This revulsion against America, more generally against the West, is by no means limited to the Muslim world; nor have Muslims, with the exception of the Iranian mullahs and their disciples elsewhere, experienced and exhibited the more virulent forms of this feeling. The mood of disillusionment and hostility has affected many other parts of the world, and has even reached some elements in the United States. It is from these last, speaking for themselves and claiming to speak for the oppressed peoples of the Third World, that the most widely publicized explanations—and justifications—of this rejection of Western civilization and its values have of late been heard.

The accusations are familiar. We of the West are accused of sexism, racism, and imperialism, institutionalized in patriarchy and slavery, tyranny and exploitation. To these charges, and to others as heinous, we have no option but to plead guilty—not as Americans, nor yet as Westerners, but simply as human beings, as members of the human race. In none of these sins are we the only sinners, and in some of them we are very far from being the worst. The treatment of women in the Western world, and more generally in Christendom, has always been unequal and often oppressive, but even at its worst it was rather better than the rule of polygamy and concubinage that has otherwise been the almost universal lot of womankind on this planet.

Is racism, then, the main grievance? Certainly the word figures prominently in publicity addressed to Western, Eastern European, and some Third World audiences. It figures less prominently in what is written and published for home consumption, and has become a generalized and meaningless term of abuse—rather like "fascism," which is nowadays imputed to opponents even by spokesmen for one-party, nationalist dictatorships of various complexions and shirt colors.

Slavery is today universally denounced as an offense against humanity, but within living memory it has been practiced and even defended as a necessary institution, established and regulated by divine law. The peculiarity of the peculiar institution, as Americans once called it, lay not in its existence but in its abolition. Westerners were the first to break the consensus of acceptance and to outlaw slavery, first at home, then in the other territories they controlled, and finally wherever in the world they were able to exercise power or influence—in a word, by means of imperialism.

Is imperialism, then, the grievance? Some Western powers, and in a sense Western civilization as a whole, have certainly been guilty of imperialism, but are we really to believe that in the expansion of Western Europe there was a quality of moral delinquency lacking in such earlier, relatively innocent expansions as those of the Arabs or the Mongols or the Ottomans, or in more recent expansions such as that which brought the rulers of Muscovy to the Baltic, the Black Sea, the Caspian, the Hindu Kush, and the Pacific Ocean? In having practiced sexism, racism, and imperialism, the West was merely following the common practice of mankind through the millennia of recorded history. Where it is distinct from all other civilizations is in having recognized, named, and tried, not entirely without success, to remedy these historic diseases. And that is surely a matter for congratulation, not condemnation. We do not hold Western medical science in general, or Dr. Parkinson and Dr. Alzheimer in particular, responsible for the diseases they diagnosed and to which they gave their names.

Of all these offenses the one that is most widely, frequently, and vehemently denounced is undoubtedly imperialism—sometimes just Western, sometimes Eastern (that is, Soviet) and Western alike. But the way this term is used in the literature of Islamic fundamentalists often suggests that it may not carry quite the same meaning for them as for its Western critics. In many of these writings the term "imperialist" is given a distinctly religious significance, being used in association, and sometimes interchangeably, with "missionary," and denoting a form of attack that includes the Crusades as well as the modern colonial empires. One also sometimes gets the impression that the offense of imperialism is not—as for Western critics—the domination by one people over another but rather the allocation of roles in this relationship. What is truly evil and unacceptable is the domination of infidels over true believers. For true believers to rule misbelievers is proper and natural, since this provides for the maintenance of the holy law, and gives the misbelievers both the opportunity and the incentive to embrace the true faith. But for misbelievers to rule over true believers is blasphemous and unnatural, since it leads to the corruption of religion and morality in society, and to the flouting or even the abrogation of God's law. This may help us to understand the current troubles in such diverse places as Ethiopian Eritrea, Indian Kashmir, Chinese Sinkiang, and Yugoslav Kossovo, in all of which Muslim populations are ruled by non-Muslim governments. It may also explain why spokesmen for the new Muslim minorities in Western Europe demand for Islam a degree of legal protection which those countries no longer give to Christianity and have never given to Judaism. Nor, of course, did the governments of the countries of origin of these Muslim spokesmen ever accord such protection to religions other than their own. In their perception, there is no contradiction in these attitudes. The true faith, based on God's final revelation, must be protected from insult and abuse; other faiths, being either false or incomplete, have no right to any such protection.

There are other difficulties in the way of accepting imperialism as an explanation of Muslim hostility, even if we define imperialism narrowly and specifically, as the invasion and domination of Muslim countries by non-Muslims. If the hostility is directed against imperialism in that sense, why has it been so much stronger against Western Europe, which has relinquished all its Muslim possessions and dependencies, than against Russia, which still rules, with no light hand, over many millions of reluctant Muslim subjects and over ancient Muslim cities and countries? And why should it include the United States, which, apart from a brief interlude in the Muslim-minority area of the Philippines, has never ruled any Muslim population? The last surviving European empire with Muslim subjects, that of the Soviet Union, far from being the target of criticism and attack, has been almost exempt. Even the most recent repressions of Muslim revolts in the southern and central Asian republics of the USSR incurred no more than relatively mild words of expostulation, coupled with a disclaimer of any desire to interfere in what are quaintly called the "internal affairs" of the USSR and a request for the preservation of order and tranquillity on the frontier.

One reason for this somewhat surprising restraint is to be found in the nature of events in Soviet Azerbaijan. Islam is obviously an important and potentially a growing element in the Azerbaijani sense of identity, but it is not at present a dominant element, and the Azerbaijani movement has more in common with the liberal patriotism of Europe than with Islamic fundamentalism. Such a movement would not arouse the sympathy of the rulers of the Islamic Republic. It might even alarm them, since a genuinely democratic national state run by the people of Soviet Azerbaijan would exercise a powerful attraction on their kinsmen immediately to the south, in Iranian Azerbaijan.

Another reason for this relative lack of concern for the 50 million or more Muslims under Soviet rule may be a calculation of risk and advantage. The Soviet Union is near, along the northern frontiers of Turkey, Iran, and Afghanistan; America and even Western Europe are far away. More to the point, it has not hitherto been the practice of the Soviets to quell disturbances with water cannon and rubber bullets, with TV cameras in attendance, or to release arrested persons on bail and allow them access to domestic and foreign media. The Soviets do not interview their harshest critics on prime time, or tempt them with teaching, lecturing, and writing engagements. On the contrary, their ways of indicating displeasure with criticism can often be quite disagreeable.

But fear of reprisals, though no doubt important, is not the only or perhaps even the principal reason for the relatively minor place assigned to the Soviet Union, as compared with the West, in the demonology of fundamentalism. After all, the great social and intellectual and economic changes that have transformed most of the Islamic world, and given rise to such commonly denounced Western evils as consumerism and secularism, emerged from the West, not from the Soviet Union. No one could accuse the Soviets of consumerism; their materialism is philosophic—to be precise, dialectical—and has little or nothing to do in practice with providing the good things of life. Such provision represents another kind of materialism, often designated by its opponents as crass. It is associated with the capitalist West and not with the communist East, which has practiced, or at least imposed on its subjects, a degree of austerity that would impress a Sufi saint.

Nor were the Soviets, until very recently, vulnerable to charges of secularism, the other great fundamentalist accusation against the West. Though atheist, they were not godless, and had in fact created an elaborate state apparatus to impose the worship of their gods—an apparatus with its own orthodoxy, a hierarchy to define and enforce it, and an armed inquisition to detect and extirpate heresy. The separation of religion from the state does not mean the establishment of irreligion by the state, still less the forcible imposition of an anti-religious philosophy. Soviet secularism, like Soviet consumerism, holds no temptation for the Muslim masses, and is losing what appeal it had for Muslim intellectuals. More than ever before it is Western capitalism and democracy that provide an authentic and attractive alternative to traditional ways of thought and life. Fundamentalist leaders are not mistaken in seeing in Western civilization the greatest challenge to the way of life that they wish to retain or restore for their people.

A Clash of Civilizations

The origins of secularism in the West may be found in two circumstances—in early Christian teachings and, still more, experience, which created two institutions, Church and State; and in later Christian conflicts, which drove the two apart. Muslims, too, had their religious disagreements, but there was nothing remotely approaching the ferocity of the Christian struggles between Protestants and Catholics, which devastated Christian Europe in the sixteenth and seventeenth centuries and finally drove Christians in desperation to evolve a doctrine of the separation of religion from the state. Only by depriving religious institutions of coercive power, it seemed, could Christendom restrain the murderous intolerance and persecution that Christians had visited on followers of other religions and, most of all, on those who professed other forms of their own.

Muslims experienced no such need and evolved no such doctrine. There was no need for secularism in Islam, and even its pluralism was very different from that of the pagan Roman Empire, so vividly described by Edward Gibbon when he remarked that "the various modes of worship, which prevailed in the Roman world, were all considered by the people, as equally true; by the philosopher, as equally false; and by the magistrate, as equally useful." Islam was never prepared, either in theory or in practice, to accord full equality to those who held other beliefs and practiced other forms of worship. It did, however, accord to the holders of partial truth a degree of practical as well as theoretical tolerance rarely paralleled in the Christian world until the West adopted a measure of secularism in the late-seventeenth and eighteenth centuries.

At first the Muslim response to Western civilization was one of admiration and emulation—an immense respect for the achievements of the West, and a desire to imitate and adopt them. This desire arose from a keen and growing awareness of the weakness, poverty, and backwardness of the Islamic world as compared with the advancing West. The disparity first became apparent on the battlefield but soon spread to other areas of human activity. Muslim writers observed and described the wealth and power of the West, its science and technology, its manufactures, and its forms of government. For a time the secret of Western success was seen to lie in two achievements: economic advancement and especially industry; political institutions and especially freedom. Several generations of reformers and modernizers tried to adapt these and introduce them to their own countries, in the hope that they would thereby be able to achieve equality with the West and perhaps restore their lost superiority.

In our own time this mood of admiration and emulation has, among many Muslims, given way to one of hostility and rejection. In part this mood is surely due to a feeling of humiliation—a growing awareness, among the heirs of an old, proud, and long dominant civilization, of having been overtaken, overborne, and overwhelmed by those whom they regarded as their inferiors. In part this mood is due to events in the Western world itself. One factor of major importance was certainly the impact of two great suicidal wars, in which Western civilization tore itself apart, bringing untold destruction to its own and other peoples, and in which the belligerents conducted an immense propaganda effort, in the Islamic world and elsewhere, to discredit and undermine each other. The message they brought found many listeners, who were all the more ready to respond in that their own experience of Western ways was not happy. The introduction of Western commercial, financial, and industrial methods did indeed bring great wealth, but it accrued to transplanted Westerners and members of Westernized minorities, and to only a few among the mainstream Muslim population. In time these few became more numerous, but they remained isolated from the masses, differing from them even in their dress and style of life. Inevitably they were seen as agents of and collaborators with what was once again regarded as a hostile world. Even the political institutions that had come from the West were discredited, being judged not by their Western originals but by their local imitations, installed by enthusiastic Muslim reformers. These, operating in a situation beyond their control, using imported and inappropriate methods that they did not fully understand, were unable to cope with the rapidly developing crises and were one by one overthrown. For vast numbers of Middle Easterners, Western-style economic methods brought poverty, Western-style political institutions brought tyranny, even Western-style warfare brought defeat. It is hardly surprising that so many were willing to listen to voices telling them that the old Islamic ways were best and that their only salvation was to throw aside the pagan innovations of the reformers and return to the True Path that God had prescribed for his people.

Ultimately, the struggle of the fundamentalists is against two enemies, secularism and modernism. The war against secularism is conscious and explicit, and there is by now a whole literature denouncing secularism as an evil neo-pagan force in the modern world and attributing it variously to the Jews, the West, and the United States. The war against modernity is for the most part neither conscious nor explicit, and is directed against the whole process of change that has taken place in the Islamic world in the past century or more and has transformed the political, economic, social, and even cultural structures of Muslim countries. Islamic fundamentalism has given an aim and a form to the otherwise aimless and formless resentment and anger of the Muslim masses at the forces that have devalued their traditional values and loyalties and, in the final analysis, robbed them of their beliefs, their aspirations, their dignity, and to an increasing extent even their livelihood.

There is something in the religious culture of Islam which inspired, in even the humblest peasant or peddler, a dignity and a courtesy toward others never exceeded and rarely equalled in other civilizations. And yet, in moments of upheaval and disruption, when the deeper passions are stirred, this dignity and courtesy toward others can give way to an explosive mixture of rage and hatred which impels even the government of an ancient and civilized country— even the spokesman of a great spiritual and ethical religion—to espouse kidnapping and assassination, and try to find, in the life of their Prophet, approval and indeed precedent for such actions.

The instinct of the masses is not false in locating the ultimate source of these cataclysmic changes in the West and in attributing the disruption of their old way of life to the impact of Western domination, Western influence, or Western precept and example. And since the United States is the legitimate heir of European civilization and the recognized and unchallenged leader of the West, the United States has inherited the resulting grievances and become the focus for the pent-up hate and anger. Two examples may suffice. In November of 1979 an angry mob attacked and burned the U.S. Embassy in Islamabad, Pakistan. The stated cause of the crowd's anger was the seizure of the Great Mosque in Mecca by a group of Muslim dissidents—an event in which there was no American involvement whatsoever. Almost ten years later, in February of 1989, again in Islamabad, the USIS center was attacked by angry crowds, this time to protest the publication of Salman Rushdie's *Satanic Verses.* Rushdie is a British citizen of Indian birth, and his book had been published five months previously in England. But what provoked the mob's anger, and also the Ayatollah Khomeini's subsequent pronouncement of a death sentence on the author, was the publication of the book in the United States.

It should by now be clear that we are facing a mood and a movement far transcending the level of issues and policies and the governments that pursue them. This is no less than a clash of civilizations—the perhaps irrational but surely historic reaction of an ancient rival against our Judeo-Christian heritage, our secular present, and the worldwide expansion of both. It is crucially important that we on our side should not be provoked into an equally historic but also equally irrational reaction against that rival.

Not all the ideas imported from the West by Western intruders or native Westernizers have been rejected. Some have been accepted by even the most radical Islamic fundamentalists, usually without acknowledgment of source, and suffering a sea change into something rarely rich but often strange. One such was political freedom, with the associated notions and practices of representation, election, and constitutional government. Even the Islamic Republic of Iran has a written constitution and an elected assembly, as well as a kind of episcopate, for none of which is there any prescription in Islamic teaching or any precedent in the Islamic past. All these institutions are clearly adapted from Western models. Muslim states have also retained many of the cultural and social customs of the West and the symbols that express them, such as the form and style of male (and to a much lesser extent female) clothing, notably in the military. The use of Western-invented guns and tanks and planes is a military necessity, but the continued use of fitted tunics and peaked caps is a cultural choice. From constitutions to Coca-Cola, from tanks and television to T-shirts, the symbols and artifacts, and through them the ideas, of the West have retained—even strengthened—their appeal.

The movement nowadays called fundamentalism is not the only Islamic tradition. There are others, more tolerant, more open, that helped to inspire the great achievements of Islamic civilization in the past, and we may hope that these other traditions will in time prevail. But before this issue is decided there will be a hard struggle, in which we of the West can do little or nothing. Even the attempt might do harm, for these are issues that Muslims must decide among themselves. And in the meantime we must take great care on all sides to avoid the danger of a new era of religious wars, arising from the exacerbation of differences and the revival of ancient prejudices.

To this end we must strive to achieve a better appreciation of other religious and political cultures, through the study of their history, their literature, and their achievements. At the same time, we may hope that they will try to achieve a better understanding of ours, and especially that they will understand and respect, even if they do not choose to adopt for themselves, our Western perception of the proper relationship between religion and politics.

To describe this perception I shall end as I began, with a quotation from an American President, this time not the justly celebrated Thomas Jefferson but the somewhat unjustly neglected John Tyler, who, in a letter dated July 10, 1843, gave eloquent and indeed prophetic expression to the principle of religious freedom:

> The United States have adventured upon a great and noble experiment, which is believed to have been hazarded in the absence of all previous

precedent—that of total separation of Church and State. No religious establishment *by law* exists among us. The conscience is left free from all restraint and each is permitted to worship his Maker after his own judgement. The offices of the Government are open alike to all. No tithes are levied to support an established Hierarchy, nor is the fallible judgement of man set up as the sure and infallible creed of faith. The Mahommedan, if he will to come among us would have the privilege guaranteed to him by the constitution to worship according to the Koran; and the East Indian might erect a shrine to Brahma if it so pleased him. Such is the spirit of toleration inculcated by our political Institutions. . . . The Hebrew persecuted and down trodden in other regions takes up his abode among us with none to make him afraid. . . . and the Aegis of the Government is over him to defend and protect him. Such is the great experiment which we have tried, and such are the happy fruits which have resulted from it; our system of free government would be imperfect without it.

The body may be oppressed and manacled and yet survive; but if the mind of man be fettered, its energies and faculties perish, and what remains is of the earth, earthly. Mind should be free as the light or as the air.

The Century Ends, 1980–2000

PREFACE

In 1980 informed Western observers of global trends generally looked into the future and saw a gloomy picture. The West, most thought, had lost its accustomed hegemony. Inflation was rampant, and economic productivity was slowing almost to a standstill. Energy and raw materials were now in short supply. Pollution was rampant, a seemingly inevitable by-product of modern industry. The Soviet Union, although no longer particularly dynamic, had plainly come to stay, and would be making life difficult for the Western democracies far into the future. Computers might well turn the next generation's life into a regimented grind, with too much information about individuals in too few hands and with creativity stunted by soulless button-pushing. In short, the world would have to learn to live with less—that "small is beautiful."

The shortsightedness of most of these gloomy predictions was underscored by the dramatic events of the years 1980–2000. Communism, not capitalism, entered its death throes, and between 1989 and 1991 the Soviet Union collapsed. China, where the Communist Party remained in power, adopted many aspects of the capitalist market system (although not political democracy). Morale in the Western world, especially the United States, improved enormously as revolutions in information science and biotechnology sparked an immense economic resurgence. Many—although not all—environmental problems proved less intractable once technology and economic incentives entered the equation. In short, the next century seemed to hold the promise that many problems that had once seemed unmanageable would become malleable and solvable.

The Fall of Communism

Martin Malia

As late as 1985, the Cold War balance of power in the world seemed destined to endure as far into the twenty-first century as anyone could see. The Soviet Union, Western experts (including CIA analysts) insisted, had become a "mature" society, and its governing ideology of Marxism-Leninism seemed firmly entrenched as a rival to the value systems of the democracies of Europe and North America.

In 1985, "young" Mikhail Gorbachev (he was only in his fifties: extremely young among the gray old neo-Stalinists who had long dominated the Soviet elite) was chosen to head the Soviet Communist Party. Gorbachev was an idealist. He believed that Marxism-Leninism could be revived and infused with new energy. He hoped to capture the enthusiasm of a younger generation of Soviet technocrats and workers, to rid the Soviet system of abuses and inefficiencies, and regain the progressive momentum that he believed had characterized the movement that Lenin had led in 1917.

Gorbachev's reforms (called *perestroika*, or "restructuring," and *glasnost,* or "openness") were extremely popular in the West. Well-wishers in the democratic world saw "Gorbi" as one of their own: a liberal reformer. In the Soviet Union, too, Gorbachev aroused many early hopes of a more just, efficient, and prosperous society. But the problems of the Marxist-Leninist system went so deep that no reforms could salvage it. The more Gorbachev tampered with Soviet institutions, the faster they crumbled. In 1987, the near-catastrophic meltdown of the reactor in a nuclear power plant at Chernobyl, in the Soviet Ukraine, which Gorbachev's government at first attempted to cover up, probably did more than any other single

Reprinted with permission from the publisher of *Russia Under Western Eyes: From the Bronze Horseman to the Lenin Mausoleum,* by Martin Malia, Cambridge, MA: The Belknap Press of Harvard University Press, Copyright © 1999 by the President and Fellows of Harvard College.

event to discredit the whole secretive, jerry-built system. By 1989, Soviet power had decayed to such an extent that the Soviet satellite countries of Eastern Europe, beginning with Poland, reestablished democratic institutions, set about restoring capitalism, and in every other respect freed themselves of Soviet domination that dated back to the late 1940s. Meanwhile the Communist Party within the Soviet Union had to abandon its exclusive hold on power. The rapid dismantling of the system that Lenin and Stalin had built reached a symbolic climax in November 1989 when the Communist East German regime collapsed and the hated Berlin Wall was breached. These dramatic events made the year 1989 truly memorable in global history—perhaps as important as the events that exactly two hundred years earlier, in 1789, had ushered in the French Revolution.

Martin Malia is a lifelong student of Russian history who teaches at the University of California at Berkeley. His 1999 book *Russia Under Western Eyes: From the Bronze Horseman to the Lenin Mausoleum*, from which this selection is taken, surveys the history of Western attitudes toward Russia and the Soviet Union, from the eighteenth century when liberal Western writers like Voltaire admired the "enlightened" reforms of autocratic Russian rulers like Catherine the Great, through the mid–twentieth century when many Western "progressives" saw Soviet communism as the harbinger of a model of social justice for the entire globe. The most recent installment of this infatuation with Russia, Malia believes, was the enthusiasm of Western journalists, politicians, and academics for "Gorbi's" *perestroika*—an enthusiasm that took little heed of the complexities of Russian reality.

B ut soon [in the late 1970s], the West found itself on the far side of détente. With the invasion of Afghanistan, SALT II went by the board; and with [dissident scientist Andrei] Sakharov's exile to [the city of] Gorkii for protesting it, the last of the dissidents was silenced. By the turn of the 1980s Soviet Russia offered the world a bleaker visage than at any time since Stalin's death. In the first half of the decade, Western public opinion on the Right anxiously echoed Reagan's castigation of the Evil Empire, and on the Left it agonized over the dangers of a new Cold War.

As it turned out, these bleak years were the prelude to a Western romance with Russia the like of which the world had not seen since the days of Voltaire. . . . This began when Mikhail Gorbachev was elected general secretary in 1985, the first change at the top in Russia in twenty years. His election soon led to a campaign of domestic reforms known as *perestroika*, or "restructuring," and to the announcement of bold "new thinking" in international relations. Between these two initiatives, the frustrated expectations that generations of Western progressives had placed in the Soviet experiment seemed on the point of realization.

The change that touched the widest circle in the West was the one that concerned everyone directly: the attenuation and then the end of the Cold War. It soon became apparent that "new thinking" meant that the Soviet Union was withdrawing from the arms race, and doing so essentially on Western terms. Most crucially, she gave up the SS-20s [intermediate range ballistic missiles, aimed at Western Europe], an abdication sealed by the Intermediate-Range Nuclear Forces agreement of December 1987. Then, at the beginning of 1989 the Soviet government withdrew from Afghanistan, liquidating the last vestiges of the so-called second Cold War [1979–1985].

The great question, of course, was why the Soviet Union, after decades of denouncing the West for "dealing from positions of strength," suddenly became so accommodating. One answer, perhaps predominant at the time, was that the Soviet regime had undergone a genuine change of heart, abandoning class struggle for "universal human values," as Gorbachev asserted. So, one might conclude, Communism had not been entirely bad, after all. Another explanation, discretely subscribed to by Western governments, was that the Soviet economy was flagging so badly that Gorbachev had no alternative to accommodation with the far stronger West; and if the Soviet leaders accepted their capitulation so graciously, it was because they themselves had lost faith in Communism's superiority. Both explanations are undoubtedly true, though the decline was the more basic and indeed the cause of the change of heart.

In any event, with the Cold War as good as over, Western attention shifted to the internal drama of *perestroika*. It proceeded to unfold in a dizzying succession of reforms: a (modest) economic liberalization; a policy of *glasnost*, or limited freedom of expression; and then "democratization," or an effort to transfer some power from the Party to elected soviets. This process culminated in May and June of 1989, with the meeting of the First Congress of People's Deputies. Among these deputies were [dissident Soviet historian Roy] Medvedev, working to save the system through reform, and the recently liberated Sakharov, working to undo the system by abolishing "the leading role of the Party."

Here were changes, surely, that put paid to the Cold War notion that the Soviet Union was a "totalitarian" system incapable of reforming itself. It seemed clear that Soviet modernization, despite the inordinate costs of the Stalinist "aberration," had produced a developed, "pluralistic" society with which Western democracies could "do business," in conservative Prime Minister Margaret Thatcher's words. Indeed, for many observers Gorbachev's *perestroika* meant more than Soviet Russia's drawing abreast of Western democracy; it meant that, after rectifying Stalin's departures from Leninism, she was at last on the verge of "socialism with a human face." The principal proponents of the Soviet system's capacity for reform, [American] Professors Stephen Cohen and Jerry Hough, propounded this view (though with less direct terminology) on television and in the op-ed columns of the major national newspapers.

Indeed, "Gorbi," as he was now called worldwide, was a hero to all ideological camps, from Ronald Reagan to the students on Tiananmen Square to Berliners ready to assault their infamous Wall; he was the "man of the decade" for *Time* magazine, the welcome guest of the pope, and the laureate of the Nobel peace prize. No Communist leader had ever evoked such international enthusiasm, neither "Uncle Joe" [Stalin] in the darkest days of the Second World War, nor Comrade Lenin among the first generation of Cominternists. Among pre-Communist Russian leaders, not even the Agamemnon of the European coalition against [Napoleon] Bonaparte, [Tsar] Alexander I, approached the veneration accorded Gorbi. . . .

This "Gorbomania," however, presents us with something of an enigma—though, this time, a Western rather than a Russian one. Although relief at the Cold War's ending accounts for part of this enthusiasm, it is hardly enough to explain the extravagant lengths to which it was carried. Gorbachev was hailed as if he and *perestroika* had brought the answer to some great questions of human destiny, as if there was meaning in his reforms far beyond their significance for Russia herself. It was as if *perestroika* meant that Communism had at last redeemed itself in some non-Marxist way by healing the schism within modern civilization through the convergence, not of institutions and economies, but of existential values. Of course, in reality, nothing of the sort had occurred; the Soviet system had simply given up being Soviet. But this was indeed enough to produce a great international catharsis. This is perhaps what was involved in the West's lyrical Gorbachev moment, as the Spectre turned out to be something of a kitten after all.

Then, at the height of the euphoria [in early 1989], everything fell apart. The general secretary, like his predecessor in reforming Communism, Khrushchev, had clearly not read [the nineteenth-century French social philosopher Alexis de] Tocqueville on the dangers for bad governments that attempt to transform themselves; nor had he even adequately pondered his predecessor's [Khrushchev's] fate. [Khrushchev had been deposed as Soviet leader in October 1964, for what his successors called his "hare-brained scheming."] In the same month as the Congress of People's Deputies, Poland's Communist reformers held elections—which were won by a re-legalized Solidarity. When the Poles and the other East Europeans saw that

Moscow was too weak to react, the fraternal dominoes started falling one by one. By November [1989] the Berlin Wall was down, and by December the regime of Nicolae Ceausescu in Romania had perished violently. The hard-won external empire and the hitherto vital security glacis vanished into thin air without Moscow offering the slightest resistance.

At the end of this *annus mirabilis* [year of miracles] it was only a question of time before the Soviet Union itself would implode. The boomerang of *perestroika* crossed back over the frontier in January 1990, as Lithuanians took to the streets to demand "sovereignty"; by June Boris Yeltsin had prevailed on the Russian Federation's parliament to declare "sovereignty," too; soon all the other Soviet republics followed suit, thereby in effect dismantling the internal empire.

The next prop of the system to collapse was the command economy. The limited experiments of *perestroika* with cooperatives, partial autonomy from the plan for state enterprises, and joint ventures with foreign concerns quickly escalated into demands for a genuine market economy. By the fall of 1990, Gorbachev and Yeltsin together had agreed to a Five-Hundred-Day Plan for conversion to the market. And this step triggered, the following year, the collapse of the system's core institution: the Party.

The terminal crisis of 1991 began with the inevitable reaction against the escalating changes since 1989. Party diehards attempted to repress the Lithuanians with military force. They then tried to depose Yeltsin as chairman of the Russian Supreme Soviet, or parliament. So Yeltsin and the parliament replied by instituting democratic elections for a new office: president of the Russian Federation. In June Yeltsin won the election on the first round.

This outcome could only provoke the final confrontation. In August the Soviet government (quaintly referred to at the time in the West as "coup plotters") declared a state of emergency. When Gorbachev failed to endorse it, as they seem to have expected, they declared him deposed. The government failed utterly, however, to put down the resistance of Yeltsin and the democrats to what had now become an illegal coup. In consequence, though Gorbachev was nominally restored, the victorious democrats proceeded to disestablish the Soviet system. In September, the Party was dissolved and then banned. In December, the "Union" was abolished out from under Gorbachev.

In the euphoric years 1989–1991, therefore, everywhere behind the now shattered iron looking-glass the peoples undertook to invert "really-existing" socialism. One after another they set about restoring private property, profit, and the market as the basis for replacing partocracy with democracy, thereby negating that "negation of the negation" which for Marx had defined Socialism. From the Elbe to the

Urals and beyond they proclaimed their determination to transform themselves back into "normal societies" and so "return to Europe."

Thus, amid the ruins of the empire the fruits of the experiment were liquidated too. The reputedly world-historical turning of October was annulled and all its results were repealed. The Party, the Plan, the Police, and the new civilization purportedly fostered by those institutions—all wound up on the notorious "ash heap of history" to which Trotsky had consigned Bolshevism's adversaries in October [1917]. It was as if 1917 had never occurred.

History's "logic" was hence set back to the level of 1789–1793. For despite the shadow of the Terror, the universal citizenship posited by the Jacobin Republic has turned out to be the irreversible political norm of modernity—a formula implicitly containing whatever distributive justice the sovereign citizenry might legislate. And so, by 1991 it had been proved beyond a reasonable doubt that there exists no such thing as a Socialist society at the exit from capitalism; there waits only a Soviet-type regime, and such a regimen *is* reversible. All Europe was thus set right side up again, and the continental gradient returned to its normal, West-East declivity.

What had happened to produce so precipitous a fall from the heights of superpower status and of vanguard social model? And why did a regime that had made a career of armed coups and coercive revolutions from above give up without a fight?

A favorite explanation is that the return of the repressed nationalities was the primary cause of the collapse. And indeed, in the last year of *perestroika* their "parade of sovereignties" was a visible component of the system's decomposition. Nationalist disaffection, however, was less a cause than an effect of the decay: after all, for seven decades the Party had easily repressed its minority nationalities. Similarly, it was less the strength of Russia's democrats than the Party's weakness that made it possible to overthrow the regime in August 1991; for every Communist chief from Lenin to Brezhnev had made short shrift of critics and oppositionists. So what had changed to make the structure suddenly so vulnerable?

The answer really is quite simple, and the dissidents had spelled it out well before the actual day of reckoning. The cause of the Soviet collapse was the intrinsic unviability of the upside-down Leninist Party-state as a "social" system; this, in turn, derived from the intrinsic impossibility of the Marxist fantasy of human emancipation through socialism-as-noncapitalism. In consequence, after the initial success of Stalin's red-hot drive to build socialism, the system congealed into a systemic Lie concealed only by the "wooden language" of the One True Teaching. Soviet socialism had in fact been an illusion throughout its career; ideology alone had made it appear to be as real as its obverse on the capitalist side of the looking glass.

Concretely, the chain reaction of the collapse unfolded as follows: The chief legitimizing postulate of the regime had been that socialism is more productive as an economic system than capitalism. Under Stalin, and indeed as late as Khrushchev, it seemed that this might well turn out to be true. As the Cold War wore on, however, it became increasingly clear that the Soviet economy, except for its military arm, was declining relative to the West. Yet Gorbachev—to the end committed to the "socialist choice made in October"—believed he could revive the system and hence preserve its superpower status. He therefore undertook to reanimate the system with a whiff of *glasnost* by permitting the comrade fish to speak out critically and, as he hoped, constructively.

Instead, the Soviet intelligentsia transformed itself into a veritable Third Estate of dissidents. A few months of speaking the truth and—behold!—the logocratic spell that held the decrepit structure together was broken. Just as Marx had "found Hegel standing on his head and stood him on his feet again," so the dissidents did the same to the world's premier Marxist regime. Radiantly inverted Soviet pretensions were set on their real clay feet and "demystified"; and soon all Sovietdom saw that the Party-emperor had no clothes.

Forthwith the country ceased to live according to the Lie. And without the protection of the Lie, the regime lost confidence in its legitimacy, thereby depriving the once ruthless instrument of Lenin and Stalin of the will to coerce. Hitherto impotent democrats and nationalists could therefore challenge a superpower with impunity. And so, that power perished like an insubstantial phantasmagoria when its guiding ideology was confounded by "really-existing" modernity.

President Václav Havel's New Year's Day Address, 1990

Václav Havel

Among the dramatic events of 1989, the fall of the Berlin Wall was perhaps the most symbolic, but the almost instantaneous journey of Václav Havel from prison cell to Hradčany Castle, the official residence of presidents of Czechoslovakia (and earlier of kings of Bohemia) was equally stirring. Havel, a poet and playwright, had been one of the founders of the "Charter 77" movement in his homeland—a loose coalition of intellectual dissidents against communism whose purpose was neither to overthrow the Leninist system by force nor to "reform" it from within, but simply to empower people forced to live under it to detach themselves from it as much as possible. Mental independence, inner strength, and a realization that the system was hopelessly rotten and would someday fall of its own weight—these were the humanistic values that Havel and his fellow dissidents cultivated in themselves and (as best they could) encouraged their fellow-citizens to nurture. Those who were known to support the aims of Charter 77 paid a heavy price: blighted careers, constant surveillance and harassment, exile, or prison. But the dissident movement, though small, remained a force, and silently most Czechs and Slovaks honored it.

When the Communist system fell in Czechoslovakia in November 1989—the process was so peaceful that it was called the "Velvet Revolu-

Excerpted from President Václav Havel's New Year's Day address, Czechoslovakia, January 1, 1990.

tion"—a spontaneous call spread through the country: "Havel to the Hradčany." Before the year was over he had been elected to the presidency, and
on New Year's Day 1990 he broadcast this address to his nation.

Dear fellow citizens. For the past 40 years on this day you have
heard my predecessors utter different variations on the same
theme, about how our country is prospering, how many more billion
tons of steel we have produced, how happy we all are, how much we
trust our government, and what beautiful prospects lie ahead of us.
I do not think you appointed me to this office for me, of all people,
to lie to you.

Our country is not prospering. Whole sectors of industry are producing things in which no one is interested, while the things that we
need are in short supply. The state, which calls itself a state of the
working people, is humiliating and exploiting the workers. We have
laid waste and soiled the rivers and the forests that our forefathers
bequeathed to us, and we have the worst environment in the whole
of Europe today.

But not even all of that is the most important thing. The worst
thing is that we are living in a decayed moral environment. We have
become morally ill, because we have become accustomed to saying
one thing and thinking another. We have learned to not believe in
anything, not to have consideration for one another, and only to look
after ourselves. Notions such as love, friendship, compassion, hu-
mility, and forgiveness have lost their depth and dimension.

The previous regime, armed with its arrogant and intolerant ideology, denigrated man into a production force and nature into a production tool. It made talented people who were capable of managing their own affairs and making an enterprising living in their own
country into cogs in some kind of monstrous, ramshackle, smelly
machine whose purpose no one can understand.

When I talk about a decayed moral environment, I do not mean
merely [our former leaders]. I mean all of us, because all of us have
become accustomed to the totalitarian system, accepted it as an un-
alterable fact, and thereby kept it running. In other words, all of us
are responsible, each to a different degree, for keeping the totalitarian machine running. None of us is merely a victim of it, because all
of us helped to create it together.

Why do I mention this? It would be very unwise to see the sad
legacy of the past 40 years as something alien to us, handed down
to us by some distant relatives. On the contrary, we must accept this
legacy as something that we have brought upon ourselves. If we can
accept this, then we will understand that it is up to all of us to do

something about it. We cannot lay all the blame on those who ruled us before, not only because this would not be true, but also because it could detract from the responsibility each of us now faces—the responsibility to act on our own initiative, freely, sensibly, and quickly.

Let us not delude ourselves: not even the best government, the best parliament, or the best president can do much on their own. Freedom and democracy, after all, mean that we all have a part to play and bear joint responsibility. If we can realize this, hope will return to our hearts.

After Apartheid

The Economist

Apartheid, meaning "apartness," is a word in the Afrikaans language of the white South Africans who descend from seventeenth-century Dutch settlers. (They arrived at roughly the same time that other Dutch were founding what is now New York.) Shortly after World War II, the Afrikaaner National Party took control of the (white-dominated) government of South Africa and implemented the apartheid policy of total racial segregation. Blacks, Asians, and people of mixed race (called "coloureds") were denied all political rights and were confined to the bottom of the socioeconomic scale—despite the fact that they constituted more than 70 percent of the South African population.

Although it remained in place for about half a century, apartheid could not stand. Gradually Western opinion was mobilized against it, as government after government adopted sanctions that undermined South Africa's economy. Much as the apartheid system sought to prevent the emergence of nonwhite middle classes, some members of the suppressed racial groups became educated, and few nonwhites accepted the lowly roles to which they were assigned. Slowly South Africa became engulfed in a low-level civil war that occasionally flared up in spectacular violence.

With the end of the Cold War, the last real international prop for the apartheid system fell: the West's worry about Communist influence in the South African liberation movement. By the early 1990s the South African government had to make one concession after another to the African National Congress (ANC), a multiracial but predominantly black movement that aimed to turn South Africa into a democracy giving equal rights to all its citizens. Free elections were finally held in 1994, resulting in the ANC winning almost two-thirds of the vote. The ANC's leader, Nelson Mandela, who had been serving a lifetime prison sentence since 1956, had been released only a few years earlier and became South Africa's new president. He proved himself a man of great

Excerpted from "South Africa: The End of the Miracle?" *The Economist,* December 13, 1997.
Copyright © 1997 by The Economist, Ltd. Reprinted with permission from *The Economist.*

moral stature and statesmanship, insisting that justice and dignity for South Africa's nonwhite majority was compatible with ensuring the rights and property of the white minority.

Like Russia after communism, however, post-apartheid South Africa was no paradise. Years of frustration, oppression, and struggle had embittered racial relationships for many South Africans, and a wide gap in education and wealth separated formerly privileged whites from formerly downtrodden nonwhites. What had been political violence on both sides turned into some of the world's highest rates of violent crime. Mandela, now an elderly man, would soon have to yield power to a new generation of black South African politicians who might not share his magnanimity and vision. In 1997 the British newsmagazine *The Economist* published the report on South Africa's problems and prospects that appears here.

If scare stories were an export-earner, South Africa would be a rich place these days. The country, it is said, is gripped by criminal anarchy. Skilled people are packing up and emigrating. Bureaucracies are paralysed by inexperience and intransigence. The economy is bogged down in low growth. The ruling African National Congress (ANC) and apartheid-era politicians alike are haunted by their unsavoury past.

In short, it is whispered, the "miracle" of 1994, when South Africa buried its divided past and inspired awe in the outside world, is starting to unravel. It's just that no outsider dares say this aloud, the pessimists continue, for fear of appearing racist, or of spoiling an alluring myth, or of seeming to criticise Nelson Mandela, whose courage and moral stature set him above reproach.

Two contradictory, but equally logical, visions of South Africa's future have been advanced since 1994. On a continent that so reliably embarrasses optimism, some regard South Africa's current troubles as the first skid down the African slope to economic collapse, ethnic warfare, lawlessness and corruption. The opposite view, inspired by the country's repeated ability to defy the pessimists, is that the government has learned from others' mistakes: South Africa will be the African exception.

Neither version tells the whole story. As the country begins to come to terms with a less predictable post-Mandela age, what are South Africa's prospects of squaring up to its chief tasks—building a prosperous and more equitable economy; removing nagging sources of instability; and containing an explosive racial mix?

For those inclined to gloom, there are economic worries aplenty. . . . Government finances still look bad. . . . Even when the economy expands, jobs do not. . . . Part of the problem is the heavy state-imposed cost to employers of hiring and firing, which has risen under the government's new labour laws. In addition, the labour market is made sticky by an illiterate and unskilled workforce, which pushes up the cost of scarce skilled labour.

The government has failed to put education at the centre of its reforms. The minister responsible is uninspiring. Thousands of teachers have quit under a well-intentioned but badly implemented scheme to move them to poorer schools. In formerly black schools, teachers still on the payroll cannot always be bothered to turn up; when they do, they teach in bleak, ill-equipped classrooms. Examination papers often circulate in advance. It isn't even possible to know whether the performance of black students, dismal in the past, has improved: the government no longer analyses examination results by race. In 1994, the last year it did so, only 49% of blacks, who make up three-quarters of the population, passed the school-leaving examination; the equivalent figure for whites was 97%.

This is not exactly the stuff of economic miracles. Yet the gloom is by no means unrelieved. Dull though the recent growth rate of the economy may seem, it has been positive, and for five consecutive years—a feat the country had failed to achieve for more than two decades. . . . The rate of inflation is down. . . . Net foreign direct investment, though low, has at least flowed in. . . .

So far South Africa has escaped the economic turbulence afflicting much of Asia. Like other countries, it is somewhat at the mercy of flighty, short-term capital—but external resources have not been needed to finance a swollen balance-of-payments deficit. . . .

Though the benefits of economic growth are spreading only slowly to the black majority in the form of jobs, the government is trying to improve conditions for the neediest. Tin shacks and thatched mud-walled huts, where chickens peck at the ground and goats graze, are still the depressing lot of the majority. Over a quarter of adults are still illiterate. But, since 1994, 1.2m houses have been wired up with electricity, and fresh-water taps have been installed for 1.7m people, eliminating the long walks women had had to make to fetch firewood and water. For the first time many villagers have been dignified with a proper address.

At the same time, a new black middle-class is doing quite well. Today [1997], 6% of blacks are classified as "rich", meaning among the top fifth of earners, compared with only 2% in 1990. These are the enthusiastic consumers of life insurance, golf-club memberships and mobile telephones, whose children now learn to play the violin or dress up in tennis whites alongside their white classmates. Black businessmen today control no less than 9% of the stockmarket—their companies are known as "black chips"—up from nothing in 1991.

Perhaps most important, the ANC-led government is preparing the ground for greater economic stability in the future. Such is the free-market zeal of ANC ministers that it is sometimes easy to forget that only a few years ago this was a party bent on nationalising the mines, all manner of industry and the banks. Not only did the government change its mind about that, lately it has also sold an airline and radio stations, partly sold the telecommunications utility, and now plans to privatise a number of other businesses. Stricter competition laws are being drafted to stir some vigour into the oligopolistic corporate world. . . .

This shift in thinking has not been easy, nor is it complete. The ANC in government includes members of Cosatu, the main trade-union federation, and the South African Communist Party. Neither has given up faith in interventionist economics. At a recent Cosatu conference, hundreds of delegates jeered the government's conservative macroeconomic policy. When the ANC meets in Mafikeng for its national conference next week, angry voices will be urging it to alter course.

Whether it does depends on Thabo Mbeki—currently the deputy president . . . [and now Mandela's successor as president]—and his team of economic ministers. They have already taken charge of economic policy and much else, as President Mandela has gradually reduced his executive role. Mr Mbeki claims, startlingly, that he will stick to his economic policy even if, one day, it costs him his friends in the unions. This is quite a declaration. Right now, the ANC's party machine is a shambles. . . . That leaves Mr Mbeki treading a delicate line between keeping them happy and suffocating the businesses on which he knows full well economic success depends.

Stolid, though not inspiring; steady, though hardly glamorous: South Africa's economy seems likely neither to boom nor to bust. Given its alarmingly turbulent performance in the past, that may be no bad thing. True, such a prospect offers no firm guarantee—if ever there could be such a thing—of political stability. If the economy fails to grow at 6% a year or thereabouts, which it probably will, unemployment will stay high. And a great army of jobless people hardly promises a peaceful, law-abiding citizenry. Yet today, of all the threats to South Africa's stability in the coming years, the most serious is probably not joblessness. It is certainly not the once-menacing white right-wing, nor even separatist Zulus. It is violent crime.

A New Fear

Tucked inside page two of the main Johannesburg newspaper is a daily round-up of violence in the city, tales too common to merit much coverage. Here is one recent day's crop: two women raped at gun-point in a hair salon; a bank robbed by five armed men; an elderly woman robbed at gun-point in her home; an unidentified dead body found in the street; security guards robbed by armed gunmen; two more security guards robbed at gun-point; one policeman shot dead;

a man found murdered in his home; a couple robbed at gun-point in their home; a man robbed at gun-point; one dead body found; another dead body found in a park.

It is difficult to dispute the seriousness of violent crime in South Africa. Policemen point out that some crimes, including murder, have declined a fraction in the past two years. Yet the murder rate remains among the highest in the world—about seven times that in the United States. In the first nine months of 1997, an average of 65 people were murdered each day. Others emphasise that, outside Johannesburg, the country is reasonably safe. Yet that city is South Africa's commercial hub, and the biggest centre of population. So common is the experience of violent crime there that it has specialised trauma clinics for victims.

The government is plainly failing to uphold the rule of law. But, disturbing as this failure may be, can the result rightly be called a descent into anarchy—as some now say? No. For the moment, that is a gross exaggeration. Admittedly, a steady ebb of skilled people is moving abroad, partly driven out (some will tell you) by crime. Yes, some investors are unwilling to pay the costs of protecting their employees, or of otherwise enticing foreigners into the country. Yes, violent crime is traumatic and shocking. But despite the violence, most South Africans carry on with their lives, go to school, herd cattle, hawk bananas, go to the office, all more or less as normal.

That said, South African crime remains grave, not least because much of it is organised. The gaping wealth-gap doubtless tempts many into opportunistic robbery. But, since South Africa's once-authoritarian police-state opened up after 1994, organised criminals have stepped in. They have come from as far as Russia and Colombia, Nigeria and China. The police last year knew of 481 criminal syndicates involved in smuggling drugs, guns, diamonds, rhino horn or luxury cars. The armed robber who holds you up in your house may well be recruited from a local township, but he is at the bottom of a highly organised chain. He delivers the stolen goods, takes his cash and scarpers. After that, the bosses and their henchmen take over.

Worse still, some of these criminals work with ex-members of South Africa's security services, whose connections can still secure false papers and get police dockets destroyed. Mr Mbeki believes that some of them may even have a political motive: "I wouldn't rule out a more orchestrated attempt to undermine the government by organised crime," he says. This web of corruption would be difficult for even an authoritarian government to control. The government's dilemma is clear: it is torn between an understanding of the damaging effect of violent crime, and a liberal determination to protect the rights of all citizens, whether victims or accused.

Small changes are under way. South Africa has just set up its first detective academy, backed by the FBI and Interpol. In the past, detective work seemed to take second place to other, often violent, means of extracting information. Parliament has finally passed new laws that will tighten bail conditions and impose minimum sentences for serious crimes such as murder, rape and armed robbery. Meyer Kahn, a pugnacious businessman, has been appointed to try to run the police better.

But this is only a start. For now, the criminal-justice system remains a mess. Dozens of convicts escape from jail each year. Only last week another six prisoners, linked to various well-publicised armed robberies, broke out in the first six months of [1997], 40% of murders were unsolved. It will take time for the government's reforms—together, one hopes, with other improvements to the system—to make South Africa a safer place.

Though criminal violence remains the greater threat to the country's stability, South Africa still treads a delicate path in containing its residual racial tensions. Neither black nor white is about to take up arms to fight for its interests. But each group still, by and large, considers its interests to exclude those of the other. Are there signs that this may change?

The Rand Club, on Johannesburg's Loveday Street, was founded in 1887. For decades it has served as the canteen of the mining industry—a place for the Randlords, the mining bosses, to swap gossip and secure deals. It is also a fair testing-ground of South Africa's shifting ethnic snobberies. This century, it has gradually extended its membership beyond the white male Anglo-Saxon overclass: first to Jews, then to Afrikaners, then (only in 1994) to women. This year, it made another concession. It admitted its first black members, among them Cyril Ramaphosa, ex-secretary general of the ANC and now a rising star of the new black business elite.

In much the same way that Afrikaners swept upwards in the 1950s and 1960s, black South Africans today are spreading into what were once bastions of white power. "We've been moving much faster and much further than the Afrikaners did," says Mr Ramaphosa, with a hint of triumph. South Africa's task is to balance a political desire to darken the complexion of institutions such as state industries, the public broadcasting agency, the bureaucracies and the universities, against the risk of repeating the crude ethnic chauvinism of the past.

The ANC, led by cosmopolitan types suspicious of tribal tradition, is mindful of this. Since the 1950s its animating spirit has been non-racialism: South Africa not only for blacks, the party has emphasised, but for all its people. Since 1994 its leaders have rammed home the message. "South Africa belongs to all who live in it, united in our diversity," reads the preamble to the constitution of 1996. "One nation, many cultures," was the catchphrase for President Mandela's inauguration. "Simunye!" sings one television station's jingle—"We are one!"—as the viewer watches pairs of carefully colour-blended citizens.

In some ways, the government has been remarkably sensitive to whites. There has been no post-revolutionary toppling of statues and icons. Roads still bear the names of past apartheid villains: Hendrik Verwoerd Drive; D.F. Malan Drive. Even some Afrikaner public holidays have been preserved (albeit with new names, such as "Day of Reconciliation"). But the days of guaranteed state employment for whites are firmly over. What ANC leaders regard as staffing institutions in a way that reflects the racial make-up of the population, grumbling whites (without irony) call cronyism.

As in the United States, such efforts can be criticised for benefiting mostly a black middle-class. Plainly, in some ways token appointments do blacks a disservice. But the government says that hiring by race serves the longer-term interests of all South Africans. As Mr Mbeki puts it: "If, in time, the majority of the black population sees that no change has occurred, one must expect that people will rebel." The result might be the sort of blatant land-grab that Zimbabwe's president, Robert Mugabe, is currently attempting, with far worse consequences for racial tension.

It should scarcely be surprising that, so soon after the controlled collapse of political apartheid, black and white still occupy worlds that coexist but seldom coincide. This is reflected in the way they vote. The two biggest parties in Parliament, the ANC, which won 63% of votes in 1994, and the National Party, which took 20%, are still supported almost exclusively by blacks and whites, respectively. Polls suggest that just 4% of whites back the ANC; less than 3% of blacks back either of the traditionally white parties—the National Party and the Democratic Party—or the Freedom Front. Even the recently formed United Democratic movement, an effort by an Afrikaner, Roelf Meyer, and an African, Bantu Holomisa, to gather multi-racial support, is favoured by just 4% of voters. Three-fifths of voters remain, now as before, stubbornly loyal to the ANC.

South Africa has an unnerving capacity to surprise. It has already shown that miracles do happen—for the events that held the world so rapt in 1994 qualify, if any do. To follow that political miracle with an economic and social one was bound to be even more difficult, and so it has proved.

Achieving everything the new government promised looked impossible back then, and still does. But South Africa's leaders have put in place some of the measures needed to make the country a more prosperous, more stable and less divided place. South Africa's future may well be unspectacular—neither miraculous nor catastrophic, more an ungainly muddling through. When you remember the legacy that apartheid bequeathed to the ANC, and the turmoil which so many predicted, that would be no small achievement.

The Technological Revolution

Mikulás Teich

Perhaps the most significant turning point in the history of humankind's understanding of the world in which we live came in the West's Scientific Revolution of the sixteenth and seventeenth centuries. Fundamental changes in this period gradually persuaded most members of the European elite of important scientific truths. The earth was not (as everyone formerly believed) the center of the universe, but a minor planet among a multitude of stars, and laws of physics were established that explained in mathematical terms many of the phenomena observable in everyday life. In the eighteenth century chemistry was set in the direction that it still follows (that is, it cut its ties with medieval alchemy), and the application of technology to manufacturing processes was largely instrumental in harnessing steam power and launching the Industrial Revolution. In the nineteenth century biology was revolutionized by Charles Darwin's theory of evolution through natural selection and by Gregor Mendel's pioneering work in genetics—the mechanism by which altered biological characteristics are passed on.

But another huge revolution in our understanding of the universe began in the early twentieth century, with the development of quantum and relativity theory. At the same time that Einstein and Planck were undermining faith in what our senses perceive, Sigmund Freud and other psychologists were questioning how rational our mental lives really are. In 1953, the discovery by two young scientists, Francis Crick and James Watson, of the molecular structure of DNA—the substance in the cells of every living creature that carries detailed instructions for that cell's reproduction—opened the way for new understandings of how life is sustained.

Reprinted from "The 20th Century Scientific-Technical Revolution," by Mikulás Teich, *History Today*, vol. 46, November 1996. Reprinted with permission from *History Today*.

Meanwhile the first electronic computers—whose immediate origins lay in defense-related projects during World War II—became operational.

The following selection, written by the Czech historian of technology Mikulás Teich, who now teaches in Great Britain, explores some of the implications of the extraordinary worldwide acceleration of scientific knowledge and technical capabilities that have occurred during the last half-century. This has truly been an epochal period in global history, comparable to the Scientific and Industrial Revolutions of past centuries.

Just before the radical political changes of 1989/90, the renowned *Times Literary Supplement* asked fifteen historians to describe the books or project they would most like to see undertaken. In the context of my long-standing historical interest in the social relations of science (going back to the early 1940s), I found Eric Hobsbawm's contribution of particular relevance.

Briefly, Hobsbawm wished to see the history of the world written since the Second World War and, in particular, focusing on the third quarter of the twentieth century. He gave two reasons for putting forward this suggestion. First, he regarded this phase 'as the most revolutionary era in the recorded history of the globe', adding 'To the best of my knowledge there has not been another period when human society has been so profoundly transformed in a matter of decades'. His second reason was that contemporaries, including politicians, have failed to comprehend just what was happening. Thus many able observers, in his view, believe honestly but erroneously, that world peace since 1945 has been maintained only by reason of nuclear deterrence.

Underlying the questions this raises is the complex relationship between science, technology and society in history in general, and in the twentieth century in particular. Here I intend to discuss these issues briefly with respect to the Scientific Revolution in the sixteenth and seventeenth centuries, the Industrial Revolution in the eighteenth and nineteenth centuries and, more extensively, to look at the Scientific-Technical Revolution of the twentieth century. These terms have themselves come under question, not least because of recurring doubts about how we identify clear self-contained periods in the evolution of science(s), technology and the economy that people can agree with. According to this view (which I do not share) the concept 'revolution' is a historiographical construction which does not reflect historical reality. All the same, the question of wherein lies the revolutionariness of the Scientific, Industrial and Scientific-Technical Revolutions merits consideration if only to avoid the danger of over-inflating, and thus putting on a pedestal, innumerable past and contemporary scientific-technical, agricultural and industrial innovations by repeatedly calling these revolutions.

The theoretical and practical directions in which Copernicus, Galileo, Kepler and Newton developed astronomy and mechanics are denoted as *the* commonly defined Scientific Revolution. Some are perplexed that this phase of scientific history can be declared 'revolutionary' when it lasted 150 years. Others dwell on the fact that these protagonists in the revolutionary transformation of astronomy and mechanics did not fully divest themselves of traditional ancient and medieval ideas. But neither the duration of the process, nor the blurred line that separates the old and the new in Copernicus' or Newton's thought is the problem.

Is there any point, then, in speaking of a Scientific Revolution in the sixteenth and seventeenth centuries? I believe there is. Its distinctive feature has to be sought after in its methodology. It was the maturation of a consolidated system of inquiry that distinguishes the investigations into natural phenomena during the sixteenth and seventeenth centuries from those of earlier times.

Partial hallmarks, such as observation, classification, systematisation and theorising were already developed in Classical antiquity, but it was during the sixteenth and seventeenth centuries that these procedures, decisively extended by systematic experimentation and quantification, and the formulation of laws of nature, began to be institutionalised, giving rise to science as is still practised today. Its birth was intricately linked to the emergence of bourgeois society and formation of the capitalist system, defined and moulded by social, economic, political, religious and cultural forces which were pushing for change.

The social dynamics of the eighteenth and nineteenth centuries received substantial impetus from the expansion and establishment of the capitalist system of industrial production in parts of Europe and America, in the train of what is termed the Industrial Revolution. It is not particularly illuminating, as I have already said, to populate history with unlimited numbers of Industrial Revolutions on the basis of technical breakthroughs perceived to be 'revolutionary'. Such an approach relies on the view that, whereas the First Industrial Revolution centred on steam, at the heart of the Second was electric power, while the Third turns—currently—on microelectronics.

In both the most general and specific senses, the Industrial Revolution is about the changeover from economies based on agriculture to ones based upon industry. It concerns a many-sided process encompassing not only technology (techniques) but also other spheres such as social structure, demography, politics and others. Between approximately 1750 and 1850, it preceded in Britain homologous and to this day unconcluded transitions to industrial economies in other countries under not identical social conditions.

It is the historical experience of the atomic bomb, microelectronics or genetic engineering, rather than analysis, that lies behind the virtually undisputed view that, in comparison with the nineteenth century, a qualitative change in the relations between science and technology has taken place in the twentieth. This has found expression in terms such as 'science-based technology' or 'science-related technology' which, however, do not do justice to the fundamental transformation that has taken place in the complex relationships between scientific discovery, technological development, practical application and social factors. Following the lead of the physicist, J.D. Bernal (1901–71), let us refer to this twentieth-century phenomenon as the Scientific-Technical Revolution. Coining the phrase in 1957, Bernal wished to underline 'that only in our time has science come to dominate industry and agriculture'. It was the Great War, the economic crisis of the Thirties, and the advent of Fascism which impelled Bernal, a highly creative thinker in matters of scientific and social evolution, to examine critically the function of science in society in the first place, leading to the publication in 1939, on the eve of the Second World War, of his seminal and highly relevant book *The Social Function of Science.* In this work, Bernal devotes a whole chapter to assessing the application of scientific knowledge to war; explaining that the close historical links between science and warfare are due not to any mystical affinity between the two, but because the urgency of war needs are greater than that of civil needs, and that in war, novelty is at a premium.

The Great War, according to Bernal, profoundly altered the situation because, in his words, 'scientists found themselves for the first time not a luxury but a necessity to their respective Governments'. At the same time, he points out, this conflation of science and war created problems. For one, there were millions who came to blame scientific developments for the sufferings they experienced during the Great War and therefore went on to reject the idea that science was intrinsically beneficial to mankind. One consequence of this was that among the younger generation of scientists there were several who began to question an involvement in military research as something entirely alien to the spirit of science.

As a Marxist, Bernal placed history firmly at the centre of his analysis of what science is about. 'To see the function of science as a whole', he wrote, 'it is necessary to look at it against the widest possible background of history.' He went on to identify three major changes which mankind has experienced since its relatively late emergence on earth. The first and second changes, the foundation of human society and civilisation respectively, occurred before the dawn of recorded history. The third change he described as 'that scientific transformation of society which is now taking place and for which we have as yet no name'. Bernal traced its origins to the related processes of the rise of capitalism and the birth of modern science in about the middle of the fifteenth century, arguing:

Though capitalism was essential to the early development of science, giving it for the first time, a practical value, the human importance of science transcends in every way that of capitalism, and, indeed, the full development of science in the service of humanity is incompatible with the continuance of capitalism.

In effect Bernal divided world history into three stages of humanity, stressing that the third stage had still to be achieved. The following passage from the concluding chapter of the book, published more than a half-century ago, may help bring Bernal a measure of recognition for his significance as one of the twentieth-century's most creative thinkers about society, man and nature:

We must realize that we are in the middle of one of the major transition periods of human history. Our most immediate problem is to ensure that the transition is accomplished as rapidly as possible, with the minimum of material, human and cultural destruction . . . belonging to an age of transition we are primarily concerned with its tasks, and here science is but one factor in a complex of economic and political forces.

There is no way to get to grips with the important issues raised by Eric Hobsbawm without going back to the chain of scientific and technical developments set in motion since the turn of this century. Take, for example, the radical rethinking about the structure of matter and space-time (as defined by the Curies, Rutherford, Einstein and others) the origins of which stem from this period. From here events coupled with military demands, economic expectations, technological feasibilities, political interests and other interlinked factors led to developments such as radar, the atomic and hydrogen bombs, electronic computers, automation and space navigation.

The penetration into the micro- and macrocosmos has provided mankind with the means, in the context of nuclear and space warfare, to destroy itself. Alternatively, it has provided impetus for governments of the USA and USSR, irrespective of their different social systems, to look for non-military solutions to international problems. Having been made aware of the real danger of self-annihilation through the use of nuclear weapons both sides stepped back. Does this not suggest that the impact of nuclear weapons on the maintenance of peace merits a thorough historical analysis in its own right?

It is not without historical interest that the early history of electronic computing intertwines with radar and atomic bomb development during the Second World War. The first electronic computer, built for the United States army, went into operation in 1946. It became known under the acronym ENIAC (Electronic Numerical Integrator and Computer). The computer set up in connection with the construction of the hydrogen bomb received the name MANIAC reflecting, it is said, the opinion of some of the participants about the whole project. ENIAC contained 18,000 electronic valves, it weighed 30 tons and consumed 50,000 watts. Forty years later a computer containing a 25mm^2 microchip and performing similarly, was 100 times quicker and 10,000 times more reliable, but used up only 1 watt of electrical energy.

This was the consequence of the discovery of the transistor in the Bell Laboratories in the USA (1947–48). It ushered in a development regarded by many as the greatest revolution in the history of technology. Certainly, the alterations in manufacturing techniques by employing microelectronic devices go far beyond the consequences of novel production technologies, introduced and developed during the Industrial Revolution. In a penetrating article Simon Head (writing for *The New York Review,* February 29th, 1996) argued that, in comparison with the situation during the Industrial Revolution, a much broader variety of middle-income workers in manufacturing and service occupations is threatened by the application of information technology. The following extract underlines the point clearly:

> In manufacturing there has been the advent of 'lean production,' the techniques of mass production originating mostly in Japan and now diffused throughout the industrialized world. In industries such as automobiles, electronics and machine tools, lean production has three main requirements: products must be easy to assemble ('manufacturability'); workers must be less specialized in their skills ('flexibility of labour'); and stocks of inventory must be less costly to maintain (components arrive at the assembly plant 'just in time,' and so save on both warehousing and financing costs).
>
> The second big change has been in service industries such as banking, communications, and insurance, where 'reengineering' has transformed the work of many employees, costing large numbers of them their jobs. Just as Henry Ford once found a substitute for skilled craftsmen in rows of machines arranged along an assembly line, so the experts called reengineers have combined the skills of specialist clerks and middle managers into software packages that are attached to desktop computers.

As far as I know, it was in Czechoslovakia, from 1965 onwards, that the most searching endeavor to investigate the Scientific-Technical Revolution as a social and historical phenomenon was undertaken on an interdisciplinary basis by a team formally attached to the Institute of Philosophy of the Czechoslovak Academy of Sciences. Headed by the philosopher, Radovan Richta, the team eventually included sixty men and women active, not only in philosophy, but also in the fields of economics, sociology, psychology, political science, history, medicine, the theory of architecture and environment and encompassing several branches of science and technology.

By the spring of 1968 the material embodying the results of their collective labours was assembled and appeared in print in July of that year. What is impressive is that over 50,000 copies of the Czech and Slovak editions were sold out immediately, demonstrating the broad and intense degree of concern in the country for the issues explored in the book. Recognised abroad as a significant contribution to the literature on the social and human dimensions of twentieth-century scientific and technological developments, the volume of findings was translated into several foreign languages.

In order to acquaint the foreign reader with the climate in which the book came about, a short explanatory section was added to the introduction from which the following extract is taken:

> The work was conceived in an atmosphere of critical, radical searching and intensive discussion on the way forward for a society that has reached industrial maturity while passing through a phase of far-reaching socialist transformation. In the light of theoretical enquiries, we saw an image of all modern civilization. The choice advanced in our hypothesis emerged as a practical problem.

These sentences may appear rather remote, so perhaps, a brief comment is in order. To say that the team was somehow consciously participating in the preparation of the events that are known as the 'Prague Spring of 1968' would be misleading. Nevertheless, its work constitutes an integral part of the latter's history (as yet to be written), in the sense that the analysis produced regarding the social and human impact of the twentieth-century scientific and technological development also led to poignant critical questions about the Czechoslovak social environment and the perspective of building Socialism and Communism in Czechoslovakia respectively. Moreover, it especially emphasised the need to take into account the fullness of man's inner life:

> Hitherto individual socialist endeavor has tended to be put at a disadvantage ... individual initiative has been curbed by a mass of directives. ... An urgent task in this field, in which scientific and technological advance can make an especially hopeful contribution, is to bring into operation a variety of ways by which the individual can share in directing all controllable processes of contemporary civilization and to do away with some of the restricting, dehumanizing effects of the traditional industrial system.

The changed political climate, following the entry into Czechoslovakia of Soviet military units (and from Poland, Hungary, GDR, and Bulgaria) on August 20th, 1968, put paid to this promising, organised approach to the historical process in which science and technology, under capitalism as well as socialism, had become cardinal.

As to enquiries by scholars in the West into the nature of the scientific-technical progress in the twentieth century, they are valuable and much information may be gleaned from them. But the reality is that, despite the unfolding of social science policy studies since the 1960s, critical contributions to the problem of how to define and assess the Scientific-Technical Revolution failed to appear. Possibly this has something to do with Thomas Kuhn's influential *The Structure of Scientific Revolutions* (1962, 1970) which, to all intents and purposes, paid no attention to the socio-historical context.

Let us take the Internet, presently much talked about for its signally pervading impact on a variety of social, economic, political and cultural activities. To a historian it is, or should be, of interest that its origins go back to the US government's concern, following the launching of the Sputnik (1957), to safeguard its communications system revolving around a few isolated supercomputers. Writing in the *Guardian* recently, Martin Woollacott, respected writer on economic affairs, notes 'the extraordinary hope invested in the Internet which is acquiring a curiously religious connotation' and continues:

> It is new, it is all-pervasive. It is, like the Holy Ghost, insubstantial and yet present everywhere. It transports its users weightlessly and effortlessly around its virtual geography. In the beginning was the Web? Somehow, it is hinted, this new form of communication will produce the explosion of growth, the expansion of knowledge, and the means of global democracy that the world requires. Yet the promise of the Web is vague, and the reality of hardship today, and perhaps of worse tomorrow, is clear.

Then there is the Human Genome Project (HGP) which impinges on legal, commercial, ethical and a host of other matters. Here too, as in the case of the Internet, the post-1945 involvement of an American government agency—the Department of Energy—in human genetics is of historical interest. Asking questions about genetic effects of radiation in the wake of the bombing of Hiroshima and Nagasaki eventually evolved into the multi-partite and multi-stage project which is to establish, by 2005, the sequence and comprehensive analysis of an estimated 3 billion base pairs in the human DNA.

HGP's representative figures maintain grandiloquently that it will lead to 'the understanding of the essence of man' and of the 'determining force behind historical events'. They are less keen on examining what one among them, Robert A. Weinberg—a professor of biology at Massachusetts Institute of Technology and a member of the Whitehead Institute for Biomedical Research—has said. Weinberg points to the danger of misusing genetic information by insurance companies and government agencies threatening persons who are looking for employment or indeed planning to marry. He concludes gloomily:

> As a biologist I find this prospect a bitter pill. The biological revolution of the past decades has proven extraordinarily exciting and endlessly fascinating, and it will, without doubt, spawn enormous benefit. But as with most new technologies, we will pay a price unless we anticipate the Human Genome Project's dark side. We need to craft an ethic that cherishes our human ability to transcend biology, that enshrines our spontaneity,

unpredictability, and individual uniqueness. At the moment, I find myself and those around me ill-equipped to respond to the challenge.

In a similar way to the Scientific Revolution in the sixteenth and seventeenth centuries and to the Industrial Revolution in the eighteenth and nineteenth centuries, the Scientific-Technical Revolution in the twentieth century is both a factor and a product of social change. The radical difference with the latter lies in the unprecedented global influence of the chain of scientific and technical developments since the turn of the century on society worldwide. The effect on human and social conditions are further underlined by the positive as well as negative experiences following ventures into the nucleus of the atom and the cell.

At the same time and related to it has been the growth of various, private and public, forms of economic socialisation. After the collapse of the Soviet-type of societies, it shows most visibly in the commanding position in the world economy of transnational (multinational) companies. In the early 1990s, according to a United Nations study, these accounted for one third of global output. But as Martin Woollacott observes, pointing to recent behaviour of Shell in Nigeria, the multinationals are in a moral crisis:

> Multinationals are insisting not only that they take an absolutely neutral line on the politics of the countries in which they invest and trade, but they must 'work with' local standards of ethics and morality. . . . The worst suspicion is that corporations have gone beyond any supposed neutrality over political conditions to develop an attachment to a particular level of bad government: not so bad as to create chaotic conditions for business, but tough enough on its citizens to ensure a combination of public order, cheap labour, and low environmental and safety costs.

In his lecture at the Salzburg Festival in 1994 George Steiner, a critical commentator on contemporary cultural life, censured the barrenness of European culture at the end of the millennium by stressing, among others, that the landings on the Moon have not inspired the creation of a single great poem, picture or metaphor. Not known for being an advocate of radical social transformation, Steiner exclaims despairingly:

> The only manifest energies are those of money. Money has never smelt more sharply, it has never cried more loudly in our public and private concerns . . . there are at present fewer and fewer voices which articulate a philosophy, a political or social theory, an aesthetic which would be both in the European heritage and of world relevance.

The twentieth-century Scientific-Technical Revolution, in order to come into its full human and humane heritage, calls for a type of society very different from forms of social organisation known so far, and in that lies its revolutionariness.

1899–1900
Boxer Rebellion in China.

1899–1902
Boer War: British conquest of southern Africa.

1900
Max Planck publishes his first paper on quantum theory.

1904–1905
Russo-Japanese War.

1905
Albert Einstein publishes his first paper on relativity; revolution in
  Russia.

1907
Triple Entente formed (France, Great Britain, and Russia).

1908
Austria-Hungary annexes Bosnia-Herzegovina.

1910–1911
Revolution in Mexico begins.

1911–1912
Revolution in China begins with overthrow of Ch'ing dynasty.

1914
Assassination of Archduke Franz Ferdinand; Great War (World War I)
  begins.

1917
February and October Revolutions in Russia (overthrow of the czar;
  Bolshevik seizure of power); U.S. entrance into World War I.

1918
Allied victory in World War I.

1919
Paris Peace Settlement (Treaty of Versailles and other treaties).

1919–1921
Civil war in Russia, ending in Bolshevik victory.

1922
Mussolini takes power in Italy.

1927
Chiang Kai-shek attempts to destroy Chinese Communist Party; Long March begins.

1929
Stalin consolidates power in USSR and launches industrialization drive; crash on Wall Street begins the Great Depression.

1931
Japanese invasion of China begins; in India, Gandhi's march to the sea initiates large-scale campaign of nonviolent civil disobedience against British rule.

1933
Hitler takes power in Germany; Franklin D. Roosevelt inaugurated as U.S. president, beginning the New Deal in the United States.

1934
Starvation in Ukraine climaxes Stalin's drive for collectivization.

1936–1938.
Great purges in USSR.

1938
Munich crisis: Czechoslovakia forced to cede Sudetenland to Germany.

1939
German scientists discover nuclear fission; Hitler-Stalin pact concluded; Nazi Germany invades Poland September 1, beginning World War II.

1940
Hitler conquers western Europe but fails to defeat Great Britain in air war.

1941

Manhattan Project (secret research to build an atomic bomb) begins in the United States; Germany invades USSR; December 7 Japanese attack on Pearl Harbor brings United States into World War II.

1942–1943

Battle of Stalingrad: turning point of World War II.

1944

D-Day, June 6: Western allies (United States, Britain, Canada) invade Nazi-occupied France.

1945

Defeat of Nazi Germany and Fascist Italy; first nuclear device tested, followed by atomic bombing of Hiroshima and Nagasaki; Japan surrenders, ending World War II; formation of United Nations.

1946–1947

Cold War begins.

1947

British rule in India ends; amid considerable bloodshed (including assassination of Gandhi), subcontinent is partitioned between India and Pakistan; invention of transistor, a key component in modern computers.

1948

Berlin blockade; political division of Europe into Communist and non-Communist spheres hardens; Israel becomes independent state and defeats Arab invaders.

1949

USSR tests first nuclear device; Communist victory in China.

1950–1953

Korean War.

1953

Death of Stalin; Francis Crick and James Watson announce discovery of structure of DNA molecule, revolutionizing biology.

1954

France defeated by Vietnamese insurgents at Dienbienphu; de facto partition of Vietnam; U.S. Supreme Court declares school segregation unconstitutional, giving powerful impetus to U.S. civil rights movement.

1957

Ghana granted independence by Great Britain, initiating rapid end of colonial rule in Africa; Soviet Union launches first artificial earth satellite, Sputnik; Treaty of Rome establishes European Economic Community (Common Market), beginning process of West European integration.

1959

Revolutionary forces led by Fidel Castro take power in Cuba, leading to bitter confrontation with the United States and spread of revolutionary fervor throughout Latin America.

1962

Algeria wins independence from France after a bitter struggle; nuclear war narrowly averted in Cuban missile crisis.

1963

Assassination of President John F. Kennedy.

1965

United States begins buildup of military forces in Vietnam amid escalating domestic opposition to the war.

1966–1969

Cultural Revolution in China.

1967

Six-Day War between Israel and Arab neighbors ends with Israeli seizure of West Bank, Sinai, and Golan Heights.

1968

Tet offensive in Vietnam; violent disturbances in United States and France, including assassinations of Martin Luther King Jr. and Robert F. Kennedy; USSR crushes Czechoslovak reform movement.

1969

U.S. astronauts land on moon.

1973

Vietnam War ends; Yom Kippur War in Middle East; OPEC sharply raises world oil prices and Arab petroleum exporters boycott Western supporters of Israel; U.S. forces go on alert over possible Soviet shipment of nuclear weapons to Middle East.

1974

U.S. president Richard Nixon forced to resign because of Watergate scandal.

1975
Fall of South Vietnam to Communist forces; Helsinki Final Act accepts human rights and postwar European boundaries as basis for international relations.

1977
Formation of Charter 77 movement in Czechoslovakia.

1979
Overthrow of shah initiates Islamic revolution in Iran.

1980
Solidarity movement in Poland begins to challenge Communist rule.

1981
Great Britain joins European Common Market.

1985
Mikhail Gorbachev comes to power in USSR; begins process of reform.

1989
Revolutions sweep Eastern Europe; prodemocracy movement in China ends with Tiananmen Square massacre.

1991
U.S.-led coalition in Persian Gulf War drives Iraqi invaders from Kuwait but fails to overthrow Iraqi dictator Saddam Hussein; Soviet Union collapses after a coup by Communist hardliners fails; disintegration of Yugoslavia begins.

1994
Apartheid regime ends in South Africa; democratic rule by black majority leads to election of Nelson Mandela to the presidency.

1995
Dayton Accords sanction de facto partition of Bosnia-Herzegovina.

1999
India and Pakistan test nuclear weapons, deepening tension in South Asia; NATO bombing forces Serbia to relinquish control of Kosovo.

2000
Y2K arrives without predicted global chaos.

FOR FURTHER RESEARCH

Before the Great War

M. Barratt-Brown, *The Economics of Imperialism*. Harmondsworth, England: Penguin Books, 1974.

Peter Gay, *Freud, Jews, and Other Germans: Masters and Victims in Modernist Culture*. New York: Oxford University Press, 1978.

J.M. Hart, *Revolutionary Mexico: The Coming and Process of the Mexican Revolution*. Berkeley and Los Angeles: University of California Press, 1987.

Adam Hochschild, *King Leopold's Ghost: A Story of Greed, Terror, and Heroism in Central Africa*. Boston: Houghton Mifflin, 1998.

H. Stuart Hughes, *Consciousness and Society: The Reorientation of European Social Thought, 1890–1930*. New York: Random House, 1961.

James Joll, *The Origins of the First World War*. New York: Longman, 1992.

Thomas Kohut, *Wilhelm II and the Germans: A Study in Leadership*. New York: Oxford University Press, 1991.

Gabriel Kolko *The Triumph of Conservatism: A Reinterpretation of American History, 1900–1916*. Chicago: Quadrangle Books, 1963.

W. Bruce Lincoln, *In War's Dark Shadow: The Russians Before the Great War*. New York: Dial Press, 1983.

Arno J. Mayer, *Persistence of the Old Regime: Europe to the Great War*. London: Croom Helm, 1981.

William O'Neill, *The Progressive Era*. New York: Dodd, Mead, 1975.

E.R. Tannenbaum, *1900: The Generation Before the Great War*. Garden City, NY: Anchor Books, 1976.

World War I

Cyril B. Falls, *The Great War*. New York: Putnam, 1959.

Robert H. Ferrell, *Woodrow Wilson and World War I, 1817–1921*. New York: Harper & Row, 1985.

Fritz Fischer, *Germany's Aims in the First World War.* New York: W.W. Norton, 1967.

Paul Fussell, *The Great War and Modern Memory.* New York: Oxford University Press, 1975.

John Keegan, *The Face of Battle.* New York: Vintage Books, 1976.

Barbara Tuchman, *The Guns of August.* New York: Macmillan, 1962.

John Williams, *The Other Battleground: The Home Fronts—Britain, France, and Germany, 1914–1918.* Chicago: Henry Regnery, 1972.

The West and Russia Between the Wars

Martin Broszat, *The Hitler State.* New York: Longman, 1981.

F.L. Carsten, *The Rise of Fascism.* 2nd ed. Berkeley and Los Angeles: University of California Press, 1982.

Robert Conquest, *Lenin.* London: Fontana, 1972.

Joachim Fest, *Hitler.* New York: Harcourt Brace Jovanovich, 1974.

Sheila Fitzpatrick, *The Russian Revolution, 1917–1932.* 2nd ed. New York: Oxford University Press, 1994.

George Gamow, *Thirty Years That Shook Physics.* Garden City, NY: Anchor Books, 1966.

Paul Johnson, *Modern Times: The World from the Twenties to the Eighties.* New York: Harper & Row, 1983.

Ian Kershaw, *Hitler: 1889–1936: Hubris.* New York: W.W. Norton, 1999.

Charles P. Kindleberger, *The World in Depression, 1929–1939.* London: Allen Lane, 1973.

William E. Leuchtenberg, *The Perils of Prosperity, 1914–1932.* Chicago: University of Chicago Press, 1970.

Robert S. Lynd and Helen Merrell Lynd, *Middletown in Transition: A Study in Cultural Conflicts.* New York: Harcourt Brace, 1937.

Charles S. Maier, *Recasting Bourgeois Europe: Stabilization in France, Germany, and Italy in the Decade After World War I.* Princeton, NJ: Princeton University Press, 1975.

Roy Medvedev, *Let History Judge: The Origins and Consequences of Stalinism.* New York: Knopf, 1972.

Detlev Peukert, *The Weimar Republic: The Crisis of Classical Modernity.* New York: Hill and Wang, 1992.

Alan Sharp, *The Versailles Settlement: Peacemaking in Paris, 1919.* Basingstoke, England: Macmillan Education, 1991.

Denis Mack Smith, *Mussolini.* New York: Knopf, 1982.

Alexander Solzhenitsyn, *The Gulag Archipelago.* Vols. 1–3. New York: Harper & Row, 1974–1978.

Robert C. Tucker, *Stalin as Revolutionary, 1879–1929.* New York: W.W. Norton, 1973.

————, *Stalin in Power: The Revolution from Above, 1928–1941.* New York: W.W. Norton, 1990.

Asia to 1945

George Antonius, *The Arab Awakening: The Story of the Arab National Movement.* New York: Capricorn, 1965.

David Bergamini, *Japan's Imperial Conspiracy.* New York: Morrow, 1971.

Frank C. Darling, *The Westernization of Asia.* Cambridge, MA: Schenkman, 1980.

Erich Erikson, *Gandhi's Truth.* New York: W.W. Norton, 1969.

J.P. Harrison, *The Long March: A History of the Chinese Communist Party, 1921–1972.* New York: Praeger, 1972.

W.J. MacPherson, *The Economic Development of Japan, 1868–1941.* New York: Cambridge University Press, 1995.

Jonathan D. Spence, *The Gate of Heavenly Peace: The Chinese and Their Revolution, 1895–1980.* New York: Viking, 1980.

Stephen Uhally, *Mao Tse-tung: A Critical Biography.* New York: New Viewpoints, 1975.

World War II

W. Craig, *Enemy at the Gates: The Battle of Stalingrad.* New York: E.P. Dutton, 1973.

Lucy W. Dawidowicz, *The War Against the Jews, 1933–1945.* New York: Holt, Rinehart and Winston, 1979.

John Dower, *War Without Mercy.* New York: Pantheon, 1986.

John Hersey, *Hiroshima.* New York: Knopf, 1946.

John Keegan, *The Second World War.* New York: Viking, 1990.

Warren Kimball, *The Juggler: Franklin Roosevelt as Wartime States-man.* Princeton, NJ: Princeton University Press, 1991.

B.H. Liddell Hart, *History of the Second World War.* New York: Put-nam, 1970.

Gordon W. Prange, *At Dawn We Slept: The Untold Story of Pearl Harbor.* New York: McGraw-Hill, 1981.

Martin Sherwin, *A World Destroyed: The Atomic Bomb and the Grand Alliance.* New York: Knopf, 1975.

John Toland, *The Rising Sun: The Decline and Fall of the Japanese Empire.* New York: Bantam Books, 1970.

Gerhard L. Weinberg, *A World at Arms: A Global History of World War II.* New York: Cambridge University Press, 1994.

The Cold War and Postwar Society

Zbigniew Brzezinski, *The Grand Failure: Communism's Terminal Crisis.* New York: Scribner, 1989.

David Caute, *The Year of the Barricades: A Journey Through 1968.* New York: Harper & Row, 1988.

William Chafe, *The Unfinished Journey: America Since World War II.* Rev. ed. New York: Oxford University Press, 1991.

John Diggins, *The Proud Decades, 1941–1960.* New York: Free Press, 1989.

John Lewis Gaddis, *The Long Peace: Inquiries into the History of the Cold War.* New York: Oxford University Press, 1987.

David Garrow, *Bearing the Cross: Martin Luther King Jr. and the Southern Christian Leadership Conference.* New York: William Morrow, 1986.

Melvyn Leffler, *A Preponderance of Power: National Security, the Truman Administration, and the Cold War.* Stanford, CA: Stanford University Press, 1992.

Allen J. Matusow, *The Unraveling of America: A History of Liberalism in the 1960s.* New York: Harper & Row, 1984.

Walter A. McDougall, *The Heavens and the Earth: A Political His-

tory of the Space Age. Baltimore: Johns Hopkins University Press, 1985.

Adam Ulam, *Expansion and Coexistence: The History of Soviet Foreign Policy, 1917–1967.* 2nd ed. New York: Holt, Rinehart, 1974.

The Decline of Colonialism and Emergence of the Third World

Raymond F. Betts, *Uncertain Dimensions: Western Overseas Empires in the Twentieth Century.* Minneapolis: University of Minnesota Press, 1985.

Colin Cross, *The Fall of the British Empire, 1918–1968.* New York: Coward-McCann, 1969.

Basil Davidson, *The Black Man's Burden: Africa and the Curse of the Nation-State.* New York: Times Books/Random House, 1992.

Trevor N. Dupuy, *Elusive Victory: The Arab-Israeli Wars, 1947–1974.* New York: Harper & Row, 1978.

K. Fields, *Revival and Rebellion in Colonial Africa.* Princeton, NJ: Princeton University Press, 1985.

H. Giliomee and R. Elphick, eds., *The Shaping of South African Society.* Capetown: Longman, 1979.

George C. Herring, *America's Longest War: The United States and Vietnam, 1950–1975.* 3rd ed. New York: McGraw-Hill, 1996.

N.H. Keddie, *Religion and Politics in Iran: Sh'ism from Quietism to Revolution.* New Haven, CT: Yale University Press, 1983.

C. Legum et al., eds., *Africa in the 1980s: A Continent in Crisis.* New York: McGraw-Hill, 1979.

George Lenczkowski, ed., *The Political Awakening in the Middle East.* Englewood Cliffs, NJ: Prentice-Hall, 1970.

I.J. Mowoe and R. Bjornson, eds., *Africa and the West: The Legacies of Empire.* Westport, CT: Greenwood Press, 1986.

Lefton S. Stavrianos, *The Global Rift: The Third World Comes of Age.* New York: William Morrow, 1981.

Theodore Von Laue, *The World Revolution of Westernization: The Twentieth Century in Global Perspective.* New York: Oxford University Press, 1987.

Modern Science, Economic Development, and the Contemporary World

T. Ali, *Global Reach.* New York: Simon and Schuster, 1974.

Timothy Garton Ash, *The Magic Lantern: The Revolution of '89 Witnessed in Warsaw, Budapest, Berlin, and Prague.* New York: Random House, 1990.

————, *We the People: The Revolution of '89.* Cambridge, England: Granta, 1990.

Francis Fukuyama, *The End of History and the Last Man.* New York: Free Press, 1992.

Misha Glenny, *The Fall of Yugoslavia.* 3rd ed. New York: Penguin, 1996.

Robert G. Kaiser, *Why Gorbachev Happened: His Triumphs and His Failure.* New York: Simon & Schuster, 1991.

David S. Landes, *The Unbound Prometheus: Technological Change and Industrial Development in Western Europe from 1750 to the Present.* New York: Cambridge University Press, 1969.

Mancur Olson, *The Rise and Decline of Nations: Economic Growth, Stagflation, and Social Rigidities.* New Haven, CT: Yale University Press, 1982.

R. Robertson, *Globalization: Social Theory and Global Culture.* London: Sage, 1992.

John L. Seitz, *The Politics of Development: An Introduction to Global Issues.* New York: Blackwell, 1988.

M. Tobias, *World War III: Population and the Biosphere at the End of the Millennium.* Santa Fe, NM: Bear, 1994.

Karel Williams, John Williams, and Dennis Thomas. *Why Are the British Bad at Manufacturing?* Boston: Routledge and Kegan Paul, 1983.